WMD

Angels, Devils & the Media
(The Extraterrestrial Control of Radio, Television, Film, and the Internet)

Gary Flanigan
© 2018 by Gary Flanigan

WMD: *Angels, Devils & the Media*
(The Extraterrestrial Control of Radio, Television, Film and the Internet)

Copyright 2018 © by Gary Flanigan. All rights reserved.

No part of this publication may be reproduced, stored in a retrieval system or transmitted in any way by any means, electronic, mechanical, photocopy, recording or otherwise without the prior permission of the author except as provided by USA copyright law.

All scripture quotations are taken from the *Holy Bible, King James Version.* Cambridge, 1769. Used by permission. All rights reserved.

Several dictionaries and publications are quoted within the text:
Dictionary.com, copyright © 2018 by Lexico Publishing Group, LLC
Merriam-Webster's Collegiate Dictionary, Tenth Edition, copyright © 2018 by Merriam-Webster, Incorporated
Bible Statistical Data, Matt Keller, Deaf Missions © 2003
Black's Law Dictionary, Seventh Edition, copyright © 1999 by West Group
Wikipedia, copyright © 2018
Theomatics II: God's Best Kept Secret Revealed, copyright © 1994 by Del Washburn
IMDb.com Movie Plot Summaries

ISBN 9780999650714

ACKNOWLEDGEMENTS

Marion and Dash

CONTENTS

Foreword 9
Introduction: Star Wars 11
1   AVP 18
2   Michael 35
3   Interstellar 50
4   Minority Report 66
5   Eve of Destruction 79
6   The Omen 96
7   Seven 114
8   Armageddon 141
9   The Black Hole 166
10   White Noise 178
11   Out of Africa 202
12   Jungle Fever 218
13   Hidden Figures 239
14   Friday 258
15   Babylon 5 278
16   The Watch 299
17   Third Watch 312
18   The Temple of Doom 330
19   Out of Time 339
20   The Matrix Reloaded 348
Addendum 360
About the Author 365

> "The media's the most powerful entity on earth.
> They have the power to make the innocent guilty and to make the guilty innocent,
> and that's power. Because they control the minds of the masses."
>
> — *MALCOLM X*

FOREWORD

I grew up hearing my parents, pastor, and old folks quoting scriptures from the Bible. I heard them well enough to become a successful husband, father, police officer, military veteran, and currently California licensed private investigator. And, being around during a time of war, and moving into law enforcement and then investigations as a professional, you see a lot of troubling things. The kinds of things that make you question the existence of God. How could a loving and merciful God allow very bad and emotionally disturbing things to happen to the human beings that he died on an old rugged cross to save?

A former career in protective services makes you read your Bible. My Bible had given me the answers. WMD helped me apply the questions. I call it the paperback edition of the Bible category in the television show Jeopardy. Answer first and question second.

Priding myself as being a TV and film critic, WMD opened my eyes to just how the Bible and media are unexpectedly connected. It's like looking at something you've seen all of your life, then suddenly seeing it like you never had before. The Bible has always put things into perspective. But, in the context of God versus Satan where the X's and O's can clearly be seen is arresting even for an ex-lawman.

"Why did the devil pick on Adam and Eve?" As slick as I always hear the preacher say the devil is, didn't he have something better to do with his time? From a Biblical perspective, has this planet really been visited by aliens? What did happen to all of those dinosaurs? Having a bachelor's degree from California State University, as well as having been all over the world courtesy of the U.S. Navy, I thought I knew a few things. But when it came to those things that I thought had obvious answers, through the reading of the author's words, I gradually grasped what it means to not see the forest for the trees.

WMD, even though theory in a few respects, it gives me something to think about from a Bible-based vantage that is consistent with the knowledge and understanding that I already have. Today's world is technological. Satellite radio, television, the internet, my cell phone; WMD bridges the digital divide between the Bible and what's happening now. It's New Testament meets New Media. And, as far as extraterrestrial beings, it's God v. Devil over who's going to use radio, TV, film, and the internet in an attempt to control our individual mind and the collective conscience. And, when you seriously think about it, the media is a "weapon of mass destruction." Its ability to influence can be used for either destroying good or deconstructing evil.

The Bible has always put a face on the powers that be. The author, through the pages of WMD, points a flashlight at that face so it can be seen just a little clearer and better.

-- Herbert J. Tillman, PI

INTRODUCTION: STAR WARS

"In the beginning God created the heaven and the earth."
—*GENESIS 1:1*

When the beginning began probably places finger to forehead every time a starry sky is looked upon. Is the earth only 4.5 billion years old or should we add another 8.5 making a 13-billion-year guesstimate? According to many who unconditionally accept the Genesis account, earth is only 6,000-years-old, plus or minus. If you buy the 6K, archeological ruins such as Gobekli Tepe in Southeastern Turkey, Tiwanaku (Puma Punku) in Bolivia, Dwarka, in the Gulf of Cambay (India), and the Sphinx of Giza (Egypt) all remain unsolved mysteries. And, if you are mindset on a traditional Sunday school interpretation, dinosaur bones and Earth Science 101 have to be kicked to the curb.

If earth has made only 6,000 trips around the sun, how do you explain the Indiana Jones types who stumble upon stuff that pre-dates 4000 BC by hundreds of millions of years? Is carbon-14 dating a hoax or "alternative fact" concocted by some men in black who want to keep the entire world in the shade? Is it possible to be scientific and Christian when it comes to Creation, or is philosophical separation so far apart that never the two shall meet?

This book is more about questions than answers. As a matter of fact, if you run it through some kinda editorial line edit, you'd find over 800 questions, most being rhetorical.

What the problem is? Too many people think they have answers to questions that can only be answered by personal faith. And, what is faith? Well, that's something only the individual questioner can answer, not the author of any book. Faith comes in all sizes, shapes, flavors, and colors. And, yes, "faith" can even be a person, literally and figuratively. Therefore, when you find it, her, or him, faith has a way of turning question marks into periods that doubts can't erase.

Regardless of philosophical position, once upon a time there were dinosaurs. And, dinosaurs as an earth dominating species were not contemporaneous with man. In spite of archeological finds where the paw prints of T-Rex and the footprints of Adam seem to appear in the same concrete, Jurassic Park and the Garden of Eden were separated by eons. What is the realistically sensible possibility that Eden was actually Jurassic Park? When Genesis 1:1 indicates "in the beginning," no data determining "when" is provided. Deuteronomy 29:29 says there are "secret things." Since Genesis is hush-hush regarding the beginning of time, pinpointing earth's exact birth date is a secret. But just because something is secret, it doesn't mean being clueless. The same Bible that opens with a secret closes with a revelation.

Revelation 12:7-9:

> "And there was war in heaven; Michael and his angels fought against the dragon, and the dragon fought and his angels, and prevailed not, neither was their place found anymore in heaven. And the dragon was cast out, that old serpent, called the devil and Satan."

WMD: Angels, Devils, and the Media (The Extraterrestrial Control of Radio, Television, Film and the Internet) has two subtitles for a reason. This "war" begins in heaven and not on earth. That makes the combatants extraterrestrials. Angels and devils are extraterrestrial entities. Unfortunately, science fiction has twisted science fact into a Hollywood depiction. It is the portrait of extraterrestrials as alien and predator opposed to angel and devil that causes disconnect.

Because it's war, it should not be surprising that war strategies will be used. Disinformation is a war strategy. Its use is exemplified by WMD. However, rather than Weapons of Mass Destruction in the conventional sense, the "mass" is short for mass communications. The capability of communicating a message to a mass audience has the ability to control minds. That means the "M" in WMD is acronymically broad. I'm talking mind control, mind manipulation, mental alteration – *Manchurian Candidate* (1962/2004) kind of stuff.

It's not any international government at work as far as the controlling, manipulating, and/or altering. The governmental agencies in play here are interstellar – the kingdom of God and the princedom of Satan. It's the "war" brought to view by Revelation. This is the war of all wars that the world has been mentally manipulated to ignore in spite of spiritual profession that transcends denominational and religious affiliations.

Is Revelation to be taken literally or figuratively? If you say both, then what part is literal, and which is figurative? Since it is the revelation of Jesus, not the apostle John, why would Christ offer figurative information that doesn't have literal interpretation?

First, who is Michael? This author has a theory. But before going there, let's say Michael represents the "good force" and the dragon the "dark side." Revelation 12:12 says the dragon, also called the devil and Satan, got punted to planet earth. He lost and took refuge on the third rock from the sun in our own Milky Way galaxy's solar system.

If you consider yourself to be a Christian, and by faith you believe the Bible to be fact, then you accept what went down just like "it is written." If you are a Christian who also happens to be a seeker of knowledge, the spiritually intellectual challenge is reconciling faith with fact. When Hebrews 11:1 asserts faith being the "evidence of things not seen," that doesn't suggest faith is blind. The concept of "blind faith" is a Biblical contradiction when faced with the fact that throughout the Bible it was the mission of Jesus Christ to "give sight to the blind" (Luke 4:18). Being blind is being in the dark even when you're blinded by light. Having biblical faith doesn't mean being stupid to physical facts.

Example: by faith we may believe according to Genesis 2:7 that God breathed into man's nostrils the "breath of life." By physical fact we know the "breath of life" is oxygen. Don't believe it? Well, have someone forcefully place a pillow over your face and push down. Without a breath of fresh air, there is no life when it comes to a "living soul." Even though we may not understand all that goes into the living soul process of man's creation as presented in Genesis, we're not stupid that minus air or oxygen you become nothing other than dead.

When faced with faith confronted by facts, if you believe the Bible to be the immutable and unerring word of God, there should be no contradictions on the pages of its 66 books even though written by mere mortals. If you really believe it to be a fact that the entity called God really does exist and he is a Supreme Being, shouldn't God be supreme enough to "fact check" before allowing a book to be released in his name and with his approval of the message (Revelation 22:16)?

If the Bible has one contradiction, that's confusing. And, just because 1 Corinthians 14:33 says, "God is not the author of confusion," then "Houston, we have a serious problem." The problem is attempting to fit a square peg into a round hole. In an effort to be defenders of the faith, facts cannot be ignored. Doing so is an offense to God as well as yourself.

Daniel 12:4 is a wakeup call. When the prophet says, "Knowledge shall be increased," he ain't talkin' 'bout a smarter smart phone. The Biblical denotation of knowledge is all about wisdom as such applies to spiritual discernment and understanding. Consider Hosea 4:6:

> "My people are destroyed for lack of knowledge: because thou hast rejected knowledge, I will also reject thee, that thou shalt be no priest to me: seeing thou hast forgotten the law of thy God, I will also forget thy children."

The "my people" referred to are believers in God. If you are a believer, do you think God is going to reject you because you didn't pick up the latest model this or that? Are you and your children doomed because you didn't upgrade? The "law of thy God" is not only the moral law found in the Ten Commandments. The law of God that most people have forgotten deals with the laws of science. Those laws are forgotten because we take them for granted. Science is knowledge that transcends both Sunday and Sabbath schools.

Consider the fact that the average person generally speaking knows right from wrong. Even when you get up on the wrong side of your bed or someone else's, the average person is going to think about it. Whether your thoughts are pre- or post your actions, thinking about what you've done cancels out forgetting about what you've done. And that's why premeditation raises both eyebrows instead of just one.

The average person is going to think about the moral law of God before saying "F" it (the "F" word being "forget"). But the average person typically doesn't think about the laws of science. Gravity is a law of science spelled physics. The law of physics in essence is a "law of God." We may apply the word "gravity" to various situations figuratively, but we usually don't think about it in an everyday scientific literal sense. When someone or something physically falls, most folks forget gravity is the culprit.

Consider Luke 4:9-12:

> "And he brought him to Jerusalem, and set him on a pinnacle of the temple, and said unto him, If thou be the Son of God, cast thyself down from hence: For it is written, He shall give his angels charge over thee, to keep thee: And in their hands they shall bear thee up, lest at any time thou dash thy foot against a stone. And Jesus answering said unto him, It is said, Thou shalt not tempt the Lord thy God."

What was the temptation? Well, Satan was attempting to get Jesus to employ supernatural powers (angels) to defy the law of gravity. The law in this situation had physical implications as well as moral. Because Jesus was operating in a physical world as a physical human being, mankind is governed by physical laws. If Jesus had forgotten that fact, he would have jumped, thus tempting God to save him from physical injury.

Consider the fact that if the "law of thy God" as found in science didn't exist, there could be no such thing as miracles. A miracle is the contravention of physical laws. That's why miracles and other events that contradict natural laws (physics) are called supernatural.

If a plane falls to ground from 40,000 feet, it's a miracle if a human occupant survives. The human body is not designed to sustain sudden impact acceleration caused by a g-force over 75. Thus, it's not the fall that kills you; it's the sudden stop from that height. In fact, if you fell from any height that allows you to fall at a similar g-force speed and your sudden impact was nothing but thin air, you'd still be DOA. Parachutes don't put a hold on gravity. They're designed to neutralize g-force acceleration by decelerating the speed of the fall.

The human body is governed by certain gas laws of physics. Again, oxygen is one of those gasses. The human body is designed to breathe oxygen, not carbon monoxide. If you smoke cigarettes, you have "forgotten" the law of God. If you're a smoker, every day you wake up is a miracle because you are tempting the law of God. Here the temptation is premeditative since the cigarette pack has a warning label.

The human body is governed by certain chemical laws of physics. H_2O is one of those chemicals. The human body is designed to drink water, not any liquid that contains a substantial amount of the psychoactive drug ethanol (informally called alcohol). If you are a drinker in the "drunkard" sense of the word, you are tempting the law of God.

In the face of clear and present danger, when people ignore the "law of God" that includes the laws of science, it's either the lack of knowledge or forgetfulness that prompts physical destruction and rejection. Rolling the dice when it comes to God's laws, morally or physically, sooner or later you're gonna lose. When you roll the dice when it comes to any law, you're gambling with house money – the house being your own. The house of God doesn't pay for your speeding ticket; you do.

If Luke 4:9-12 is a bet Jesus Christ wouldn't take, intelligently ask yourself, how smart would it be for you? The problem is the human incapacity to accept the fact that a Supreme Being is not constrained by the human inability to comprehend what appears incomprehensible. It appears incomprehensible that six-stories tall, 100-ton dinosaurs roamed the earth. But rather than accepting the fact that Daniel says, "knowledge shall be increased," the knowledge that sheds light on dinosaurs and other mysteries sits unexamined and not seriously researched, investigated, and expounded from the pulpit. Being closed-minded to knowledge severely restricts revelation. Subsequently, those things which might be viewed either discreetly or overtly as seeming Biblical contradictions are either blindly accepted or altogether written off.

Just consider how ridiculous political surrogates and Congressional officials appear when their response to serious questions is both evasive and deflective to the point of being ignorantly silly. Do you think the kingdom of God would want spokespersons and representatives that reflect the dimwitted mindless manor of ilk who defend what's indefensible? Would you want an individual representing you whose arguments are peppered with asinine statements that side-step a straight answer to a yes or no question? Calling yourself a Christian while selling your soul whenever the price is professionally right or partisan right is straight outta Jerusalem (Luke 4:7-9).

But is pointing the finger at the messenger of madness the real issue when it comes to any war be it waged on earth or in heaven? How often we forget that "whiz of a wiz" that was, was in cinematic reality something else. Standing behind the curtain was someone totally unanticipated by Dorothy and friends.

Even a yellow-brick road can be paved with disinformation and painted to camouflage its true color – deception.

1 AVP

"But sanctify the Lord God in your hearts and be ready always to give an answer to every man that asketh you a reason of the hope that is in you with meekness and fear."
– 1Peter 3:15

Drawn from the above, the word "answer" is connected with "reason." If you can't give a reasonable answer to how on earth did Adam and T-Rex coexist? Or, to whom on earth did Cain marry up with in the land of Nod, then as a Christian you are lunchmeat for all who question the validity of God and the veracity of the Bible. Beyond Jewish history, prophecies, motivational and inspirational teachings, is there more between Genesis and Revelation that meets the eye by touching the heart?

If you ask yourself or anyone to tell you what they get out of reading the Bible, a typical answer is inspiration. An atypical answer that's still typical is object lessons. Even though the Bible contains 31,240 texts, rare is the soul who sees the Bible as a textbook.

Isaiah 1:18 says, "Come now, and let us reason together, saith the LORD." Here's that "reason" word again.

Once more, Hosea writes in 4:6: "My people are destroyed for lack of knowledge." What's noteworthy is the fact that at issue is knowledge, not emotion. God knows folks will wave their hands in the air like they just don't care, do somersaults and back flips, even slap the hell out of the person pew'd next to them when it come to lovin' the Lord or Jesus. But both Isaiah and Hosea take the position right along with Peter that if your emotion is not based on reason that's grounded in knowledge, your destruction is waiting at the door. It's the inability to make the Bible an intellectual experience as much as an emotionally-charged spiritual one that enables the powers that be to manipulate and/or control the human mind.

When the human mind does little more than nothing in attempt to know the mind of God as revealed in his word as presented in the Bible, your knowledge increases/decreases commensurately. If it's always about getting that emotional, inspirational, and spiritual high, what happens when your love comes down – all the way down?

In the beginning, it says God created the heaven and the earth. Since earth is in the heavens and there's "war in heaven," earth is in a war zone. It's the challenge many have in merging the inspirational Biblical high with the intellectual Biblical high that keeps many Biblically half asleep.

If "religion is the opium of the people" as Karl Marx said, then "the devil made me do it," as Flip Wilson said, only registers in support of the assertion. What Marx said, many will consider profound. What Flip said, many others will find profane – a mockery or joke. Christendom can't have it both ways. Trying to switch-hit won't get you to first base when it comes to the kingdom of God.

Intellectual assent with regards to the Bible is a decision made in the head that lacks commitment in the heart. If mental belief is not accentuated by physical action, mountains cannot be literally and figuratively moved. Disney deals in wishes, Jesus Christ in prayer. Wishing upon a star to get a job done is a whole lot different from praying to God for strength to make it happen. That's why it's "faith the size of a mustard seed" and not "close your eyes and blow out a candle."

Satan is a fallen angel. In the Bible, there is the frequent identification of angels as stars (Revelation 1:20). When you do that Rose Royce number and "wish upon a star," you have absolutely no idea who you're calling on for help. That means, if you flip the script on Flip, and write him off with a "he so crazy," you're also flipping the script on the Scriptures. If Satan is not to be taken seriously, then you better come up with a non-Biblical alternative that philosophically explains evil's inexplicability.

The white guy who blows away nine innocent folks in a South Carolina church because he hates Black people is in the same spiritual boat with the Black guy who blows away five innocent Texas cops because he hates white people. Likewise, the yellow guy who slaughters 50 because he hates LBGTQ's is spiritually no diff. Who or what really made them do it? Bad parenting? Bad company? ISIS?

Neither murderous incident was straight outta Hollywood. It was reality TV after the fact. If horrific incidents are terroristically inspired, who ultimately inspires the terrorist? Where on earth does the spirit to commit crime and dastardly deeds originate?

"The thief cometh not, but for to steal, and to kill, and to destroy."
— John 5:4

The Jesus many profess to love makes it plain that the criminal mind is a supernatural thing. It's "interplanetary" and "extraordinary" just like Ben E. King sings. However, if Jesus is only your "quick fix" in times of trial and tribulation, then what went down in Charleston and Dallas and Orlando is strictly restricted to flesh and blood origins. And, from Las Vegas to *NextPlace*, you follow Alice down the rabbit-hole right behind all the media reporters and cameramen looking for the next killer's motive. Does knowing motive squeeze the paste back into the tube? Blood back into the vein? Life back into the lifeless?

What was Cain's motive? Jealousy? Envy? When it's the brother from another mother who has the issue, Jesus points the finger at the "sins of the father."

> "Ye are of your father the devil, and the lusts of your father ye will do. He was a murderer from the beginning, and abode not in the truth, because there is no truth in him. When he speaketh a lie, he speaketh of his own: for he is a liar, and the father of it." — John 8:44

Being a liar has become accepted as a new normalcy for many who call themselves Christian and Evangelical. With regards to liars and their lovers, however, the "old normalcy" is Revelation 22:15. And this explains exactly why there was a need for a virgin birth – an immaculate conception. The original "fall guy" is identified; Revelation 12:9.

If there is a story behind the story, there is a motive behind the motive. From a biblically spiritual perspective, the motive behind evil has been and always will be Satan. But if you ain't buying "the devil made me do it," you really ain't buying the Bible beyond its poetry and prose. Finding answers to double jeopardy questions will continue to remain repetitively elusive.

When it comes to being in real world jeopardy, it's the failure to frame answers in the form of spiritual questions that causes cluelessness.

Unquestionably, there is a "dark force" with those who do devilish things. But calling such things devilish is a misnomer if one believes there's a God, but no devil. Inherent in such a belief is the domino effect.

Example: If there's no devil, there's no God. Since God calls out Satan, if Satan doesn't exist, God is a liar. When the word of God is marginalized by a failure to believe the seemingly unbelievable, God is unwittingly relegated to a size no bigger than our individual ability to comprehend the incomprehensible.

> "God is not a man, that he should lie; neither the son of man, that he should repent: hath he said, and shall he not do it? or hath he spoken, and shall he not make it good?"
> — Numbers 23:19

God cannot be God if what he says is false. The refusal by mainstream media to seriously deal with the spiritual cause and effect of worldwide mayhem is the aftermath of a war game strategy employed by Satan. The earthy powers that be in the forms of network and station owners, CEOs, directors, editors, and bureau chiefs (even though they bring their own individual persuasions to the conference table) are unwitting pawns in a cosmic battle pitting good versus evil.

Whenever a lyrical "chain of fools" are governmentally empowered to run a country, the blame rests more on that country's media than it does on the foolhardy and those pushing a fool's gold agenda. When disinformation is given a soapbox, you can't honestly finger-point the messengers of foolishness. To the contrary, it's the fool who provided the soapbox.

An undergirding premise of WMD is mind manipulation operates on the perception of reality and not reality itself. If you can convince an individual that this is that or what is, isn't, then truth, in reality, becomes twisted. What's termed disinformation is straight-up deception.

WMD is not willing to concede mankind being smart enough to systematically mastermind and orchestrate deception on a worldwide scale over a period of centuries and counting. When billions of people are involved and the politics are spiritual (good v. evil), you've just crossed over into the *Twilight Zone*.

The fact that Revelation 12:9 asserts Satan's ability to "deceive the whole world" establishes him as a master manipulator of human perceptions.

You wanna talk about fake news, false flags, and conspiracy theories? Then serious talk has to begin where these modern day terms first begun – Revelation 12:9. Sane people don't habitually lie and support habitual liars minus spiritual deception just as sane people don't randomly commit murder for reasons that are morally illogical based on their own self-professed moral principles. Realized or not, there's an 800-pound elephant in the room that's being spiritually ignored.

Subsequently, applicable to the question regarding who ultimately inspires the terrorist – who ultimately inspires a government? The Bible has a whole lot to say about governments; code word "kingdoms." The story behind the story, therefore, is not governmental interference internationally (Russia), but extraterrestrially.

Whenever an extraterrestrial connection is dismissed with a cynical "Yeah right," a brick wall is psychologically constructed separating natural and supernatural – man and God. If you consider yourself to be Christian, the result of such should be your unequivocal conclusion God is real. This belief in turn should necessitate that your reality of God is rooted in something other than smoke and mirrors. Unless you've had a "burning bush" moment, the Bible is the only basis for the word you've heard separating the reality of God from smoke and mirrors – Romans 10:17.

Consider the following:

> "I am become a stranger unto my brethren, and an alien unto my mother's children." — PSALMS 69:8

If you read it for what it says, Jesus Christ as God incarnate is being characterized as an alien. By dictionary definition, if you are "not of this world," you are in fact, an extraterrestrial.

Can the Bible make who and/or what God is any plainer than through the following?

> "And he said unto them, Ye are from beneath; I am from above: ye are of this world; I am not of this world." – John 8:23

And:

> "Jesus answered, My kingdom is not of this world: if my kingdom were of this world, then would my servants fight, that I should not be delivered to the Jews: but now is my kingdom not from hence." – John 18:36

The Revelation 12:7-9 "war" is a fight between sentient beings that are in fact (not fiction) aliens that aren't ancient. If you take the Bible seriously, God and angels along with Satan and demons have always been on this planet. They've been hanging around here since Hector was a pup. But when reading Revelation, rather than employing the word devil, or Satan in a vacuum constrained by traditional religious interpretation, what happens when these beings or entities are viewed as extraterrestrials? Science fiction takes on the plausibility of science fact.

Consider games of chance such as the lottery. When the jackpot hits a half-billion or more, the odds of winning are 1 in 300-million plus. The higher the prize, the more hopeless the odds become. But, Bingo! Sooner or later that 1 in 300-million shows up and collects. Even though the odds may be astronomical, they are not impossible.

Now reverse the thinking; see it in terms of the universe. There are astrophysicist estimates that there are 10 trillion galaxies in the cosmos. Our Milky Way galaxy has an estimated 100 billion stars minimum. That being the case there's a 1 with 24 zeros after it number of stars above and beyond our scope framed by Hubble.

Now are the odds astronomically great or small that extraterrestrials have visited this planet? With all that outer space, do you really think that life only exists on earth? And, human beings, who continue to discriminate against each other because of skin color, are the most intelligent creatures to be found amongst all those 1,000,000,000,000,000,000,000,000 stars? When a little less than half the populous of one of the greatest nations on earth is willing to elect an admitted racist as their national leader that's indicative that a little less than half the residents of that nation aren't ready for "prime time" where and when time is measured in terms of eternity.

When 1 Corinthians 15:50 maintains, "Flesh and blood cannot inherit the kingdom of God; neither doth corruption inherit incorruption," and Jesus Christ says, "Except a man be born again, he cannot see the kingdom of God" (John 3:5), the bottom line is if you can't get your mind right, don't even think about star trekking. Your final destination eternally speaking is the neighborhood cemetery. Your grave is your "homegoing."

So, when it comes to the question, "Are we alone," Matthew 28:20 has already provided the answer. But, when it comes to reality, a Christian Bible based reality check indicative of celestial beings is not one most choose to embrace even when they embrace a Christian ministerial officiated wedding and a Christian ministerial officiated funeral. Go figure.

The only reason UFO's are unidentified is because they are supernaturally blocked from being identified. The odds of earth's extraterrestrial visitation are not 1 in 1,000,000,000,000,000,000,000,000, but rather 1,000,000,000,000,000,000,000,000 in 1. Don't believe it? Well, intelligently ask yourself what are the odds of moving into a house that hasn't been visited by a pest control service and not find an ant, roach, or spider? The sheer number of bugs on this planet means no matter the house or neighborhood, if the *Orkin* man hasn't paid a visit, you will see an "uninvited guest." The odds you won't are astronomically against all odds you will. The same applies to the universe.

The modus operandi of Satan is showmanship. Certainly, based on the m.o. of the devil and his angels, they would have showed up in a spacecraft and landed on the White House lawn during the Truman Administration if they could have. Since there is "war in heaven," the Roswell incident could/should be seen as a devilish running of a heavenly blockade. With regards to Revelation 12:7-9, Michael is the "Orkin Man."

Since we can wrap our individual heads around the concept of aliens as media depictions, why not take the leap with respect to their portrayals as angels versus devils and demons? The acceptance should be a physical reality for all who believe in the existence of God.

The Bible does not treat the devil as a figment or concept. If you believe in God, Satan is God's antithetical nemesis. Just as God is a Spirit through which the concept of love is physically manifested in the physical form of Jesus Christ, Satan is a physical entity through which the concept of hate is physically manifested as the devil. That means the foolishness of a Flip Wilson in a metaphysical analysis is more profound than most will ever come close to imagining.

Consider John 1:18, "No man hath seen God at any time; the only begotten Son, which is in the bosom of the Father, he hath declared him."

Can you see intelligence? You can see manifestations of intelligence (or lack thereof). But intelligence is in actuality a conceptual noun. An instruction manual is a manifestation of the knowledge or intelligence required to do something. Minus that knowledge being put into words and fixated in tangibly written form, that knowledge and intelligence is just out there somewhere in space – outer and/or cyber. So if knowledge exists, God exists; the two are inseparable.

Exodus 33:20 reads, "no man can see the face of God and live." Perhaps, one reason is the human brain is like a computer. When a computer is interfaced with too much information a download-overload either freezes or crashes the system. Imagine what would happen if a human being interfaced with a universal mind.

When Exodus 33:20 is viewed in the context of God being all knowledge (as in omniscient), can a man or woman "see the face of God and live" in terms of such a close encounter? When understood beyond the poetry and prose, Exodus 33:20 makes all the sense in the world.

Example: consider $a^2 + b^2 = c^2$. Even though it's an equation as popular as $E=mc^2$, for most it's a "hidden figure" that still finds many clueless. If by chance you are one of that many, it's the Pythagorean Theorem that the Scarecrow in the *Wizard of Oz* tried to recite, but bungled. Correctly put, with regards to the three sides of a right triangle, the square of the hypotenuse (the side opposite the right angle) is equal to the sum of the squares of the other two sides.

Now, if the Scarecrow's newfound brain couldn't even get his A-B-C's right, think about an equation dealing at the end of the alphabet:

$(x+yi) + (x'+y'i) = (x'+y'i) + (x+yi)$,
$\{(x+yi) + (x'+y'i)\} + (x''+y''i) = (x+yi) + \{(x'+y'i) + (x''+y''i)\}$,
$(x+yi) + (x'+y'i) = (x'+y'i) + (x+yi)$,

$$(x+yi)\{(x'+y'i) + (x''+y''i)\} = (x+yi)(x'+y'i) + (x+yi)(x''+y''i)$$
$$\{(x+yi) + (x'+y'i)\}(x''+y''i) = (x+yi)(x''+y''i) + (x'+y'i)(x''+y''i)$$
$$(x+yi)\{(x'+y'i) + (x''+y''i)\} = \{(x+yi)(x'+y'i)\}(x''+y''i)$$

Further, imagine the "theory of everything." There's a thing called the Akashic Records. Analogously, it's likened to an immense photographic film, registering all the desires and earth experiences of our planet. Those who perceive this astral projection will see pictured on that film strip all the life experiences of every human being since time began along with the reactions to the experiences of the entire animal kingdom.

What if the Akashic along with all of the information on the internet were downloaded directly into your brain? Could you handle the truth?!

It's impossible for us to physically wrap our finite minds around what God in physical reality is. It's a mystery. But an unwillingness to contemplate Biblical mysteries is what fuels the perception and acceptance of those mysteries being misinterpreted as contradictions. For the atheist who says there is no God, it's simply a failure on the atheist's part to understand what or who God is in the context of a physical universe on a cosmic consciousness level.

Does Swahili or any language you can't speak exist? Isn't the language still there regardless of individual ability to comprehend? God is all knowledge, thus making God in name an all-knowing entity, that knowledge in and of itself has no beginning and it has no end. It exists beyond discovery and human understanding. Because the cure for cancer hasn't been revealed doesn't mean the chemistry for the cure doesn't exist. Where it gets deep, however, if the knowledge for everything exists, there is the knowledge for knowledge itself to transform itself into any form it chooses. This then is the science behind Matthew 19:26:

> "But Jesus beheld *them*, and said unto them, With men this is impossible; but with God all things are possible."

Because God is omniscient, the knowledge embodied in the entity called God knows how to do all things. Consequently, if you know how to do "all things," all things are possible. If not, there's a scriptural paradox of epic proportions.

If you are a science-fiction buff, you've watched enough Star Trek to be familiar with the terms matter and antimatter. And if you watch enough History and Learning Channel, you've probably heard the word Strangelet. Strangelets are quarks that could easily be spelled quirks. They're neither antimatter nor nuclear matter; they're "strange matter," hence the name. The moral of the story: there's stuff out there that the brightest minds on this planet can't even begin to fully understand or explain. When you are a sho'nuff for real scientist and the best you can do is call whatever it is strange, that's telling you something about John 1:3: "All things were made by him; and without him was not anything made that was made."

Just as there are "secret things," there's also "strange things." Only the knowledge embodied in "God" is answers to secretly strange questions provided.

Jesus Christ is the materialization of God – God incarnate. When John 1:1, 2, and 14 read, "In the beginning was the Word, and the Word was with God, and the Word was God; the same was in the beginning with God; and the Word was made flesh;" substitute the word "Word" with the word "knowledge."

When Jesus healed the sick, do you think it was magic? When you get sick and the doctor writes a prescription, is that magic? When you have all knowledge, you know how to manipulate the molecular structure of water in order to instantaneously turn it into *Arbor Mist* or vintage *Dom Perignon*. And replicating the DNA structure of two fish in order to feed 5,000 people is child's play when you have the know-how.

But knowing the science behind turning water into wine and feeding 5,000 out of a lunchbox doesn't diminish the majesty of a Supreme Being, it magnifies it. Your ability to use a calculator to add, subtract, multiply, and divide doesn't marginalize your mental ability to do the math, it facilitates it. You still have to know what buttons to press. The universe is governed by laws of physics. The fact that those laws exist doesn't preclude the creator of those laws from using them.

Consider John 10:34-35:

> "Jesus answered them, Is it not written in your law, I said, Ye are gods? If he called them gods, unto whom the word of God came, and the scripture cannot be broken."

Even though "gods" is spelled with a lower case "g" the operative word is "Word" when understood that "the word of God" is knowledge. It's the knowledge of God that makes human beings "gods" whether you're a believer in God or not. And that's the inherent contradiction of atheism. Just as your name doesn't define all that you are, the name "God" doesn't define all that God is. The name "God" that hangs some folks up is a term of reference just like your name. If you suddenly decide you no longer want to be called by your name, Shakespeare got it right, "A rose by any other name would smell as sweet," just as dog poop by any other name stinks.

Infinite knowledge and infinite intelligence has to be called something in a physical universe that to human beings is an unknown reality. The Bible's call is the term God.

HAL 9000, *2001: A Space Odyssey* (1968) was a "sentient computer." Its intelligence was artificial, but it had the capacity to feel, perceive, and reason (think). Now, this isn't an implied suggestion that God is some kind of inanimate super computer. The only relevance is in the theory that knowledge (intelligence) can become so advanced that its existence cannot be defined in terms of known reality. HAL 9000 had transcended existence as a mere computer. In this 1968 feature, for all intents and purposes, HAL had sentience. It even posed the question, "Will I dream?"

'Dream' is an abstract noun, which makes it a concept. When a computer, which is a machine, begins to formulate, process, and then apply intuitive abstract concepts in a one-on-one communication that borders on being conversational, that machine has just crossed over into *The Twilight Zone*.

How far is IBM's *Watson* away from sentience? Have you ever asked Apple's *Siri* how she's feeling today?

Then there's *Her* (2013). That's the flick about a guy who gets sprung for a female voiced computer operating system (OS) with artificial intelligence. Keeping it unreal, you've got to admit a pleasant sounding IVR beats the clerk in the flesh with a nasty attitude. Nevertheless, or more, if IBM and Apple can take baby steps when it comes to knowledge and intelligence, what makes you think knowledge and intelligence within a cosmic realm has either boundaries or limitations?

Because Christendom as a whole doesn't advocate venturing very far off the pages of the Bible when it comes to spiritual enlightenment, when it comes to elementary school science and world history not many are smarter than a fifth grader. Astonishingly, there are pyramids in Mexico and Peru that are just as awe inspiring as those in Egypt. And, the trip about these Mexican and Peruvian ancient structures is their similarity in design to the big three sitting on the Giza plateau.

When considering the Washington Monument-looking structures standing tall throughout ancient Egypt, common sense suggests these obelisks weren't being built for landscape beautification only. They had a practical purpose. And, given that many of these cone capped monoliths were discovered as having crystalline granite properties, there is strong speculation that each could have been employed for use in some kind of a wireless transmitter array. These ancient obelisks were comparable to power rods that could harness and transmit electromagnetic signals.

Radio, as well as your cell phone, requires very tall towers in order to send and receive signals. Since Hebrews 9:23 talks about "patterns of things in the heavens," should we be so narrow in view and scope to think that "heavenly patterns" can only have applicability when it comes to redemption. Egypt and Mexico are pretty much on opposite sides of the world. Intelligently ask yourself just how do people living 7,000 miles apart, not to mention a couple thousand years before Columbus, come up with basically the same blueprints for a building?

Ephesians 2:2 doesn't find Paul referring to Satan as "the prince of the power of the air" in a figurative vacuum. Satellite and wireless communications are propagated through the literal vacuum of space – the electromagnetic spectrum. Electromagnetic waves are waves that can travel through the vacuum of inner and interstellar space. Mechanical waves, unlike electromagnetic waves, require the presence of a material medium in order to transport their energy from one location to another. Sound waves are examples of mechanical waves, while light waves are examples of electromagnetic waves.

If you're old school or have a young school kid, you know something about crystal radios. It's the simplest form of radio receiver. It needs no power source other than that received from the power of the radio waves being transmitted. WMD offers the theory that extraterrestrial intelligences are using the media to manipulate and control the thinking of human beings. Mankind is merely a proxy – a folder in an *X-Files* cabinet. It's therefore important to understand that when it comes to media, the technology associated with its use as a mass communications mechanism, vehicle, and tool didn't first come into play with Samuel Morse's 1830's invention of the telegraph.

Why were Pharaoh and his boyz mixing galena and pyrite crystalline minerals into the construction of these obelisks? If they were receiving radio signals, who do you think was on the other end sending messages, Guglielmo Marconi (1874-1937)?

The Pre-Columbian Tello Obelisk discovered in Peru is a monument to the Inca Civilization.

Consider 1 John 1:5:

> "This then is the message which we have heard of him, and declare unto you, that God is light, and in him is no darkness at all."

Being all-knowledge and infinite intelligence, by virtue of embracing light in terms that are self-descriptive, God accords himself all of the attributes pertaining to "light." Because the scripture quoted says God is light, that means God is also radiant energy, scientifically speaking. That being the case, God spans the entire electromagnetic spectrum, which starts with the radiant energy that enables the usage of radio, and progresses through television, radar, satellite communications, microwave relays, photography, human vision, sterilization, x-ray examinations, cancer therapy, research physics, and research astronomy.

Because the word of God often has a double meaning, the duality of 1 John 1:5 and the Christian belief that Jesus is God in the flesh, that one text establishes Jesus Christ as the synthesis of all energy imaginable.

Google "the Shroud of Turin." Research focuses on the determination of how the image could have formed on the linen and what type of radiation could have produced it. In the midst of all the theories, natural and supernatural, the scientific consensus is the image scorched on the Shroud is biophysical in its nature. Knowledge of such "biophysical radiation" is currently beyond our scientific understanding. So, herein, the "perception" of reality becomes a reality of physics. The belief in the Shroud's perceived sacred authenticity is rendered, "Hmmmm." The fact of the matter is something made that image!

When connecting the dots, and 1 John 1:5 is a big one, the fact that "God is light" perfectly explains how the Shroud image was formed if it is authentic.

Jesus, as a resurrected cosmic being, is the only complete and perfect light source. That translates into God not only being "the light of the world" in accordance with John 8:12, he is also the "light of the world" as a dynamic function of your dentist's x-ray machine, as well as your cell phone. Both emit forms of electromagnetic radiation. But whether ionizing or non-ionizing, the operative word is radiation. Provided the Shroud of Turin is *the real deal Holyfield*, the burial cloth the body of Jesus was wrapped in indisputably evidences the miraculous resurrection of Christ.

The fact that John 20:7 points out the "linen clothes" were lying separate from the "napkin" is very significant. Two messages are being sent.

First, since Biblical attention is given the linen clothes, they are both physically and perhaps even prophetically distinct. Because the Shroud of Turin exists, its biophysical radiation connection further illustrates "God is light." Subsequently, the glory of God in the form of a resurrected Jesus Christ is illuminated for all to see and consider scientifically.

Second, the "wrapped together" or folded napkin suggests that the Resurrection was not the end, but the beginning. When rising from the dinner table, folding a napkin isn't the same as balling it up and throwing it on the plate. Essentially, John is saying Jesus didn't "drop the mic."

Wrapping the napkin and placing it separate from the linen says, "I'm coming back."

Since our inability to see the "light" doesn't interfere with the functional reality of wireless devices that emit radiant energy, should our visual limitations impede our ability to see the light when it comes to a more comprehensive understanding of the Bible?

The Bible's use of the term 'light' is not restricted to the metaphysical. Light is a physical phenomenon. Because you are reading the words of this book you are physically seeing visible light as a property of the electromagnetic spectrum.

Go online when there's time and look at a chart of the Electromagnetic Spectrum. It extends from below the low frequencies used for modern radio communication to gamma radiation at the short-wavelength (high-frequency) end, thereby covering wavelengths from thousands of kilometers down to a fraction of the size of an atom. Visible light lies toward the shorter end. The limit for long wavelengths is the size of the universe itself. The short wavelength limit is in the vicinity of the Planck length.

Just in case you're curious, a Planck length is as small as the universe is big. The significance of bringing any and all of this up only serves to exemplify the all-encompassing knowledge that is God, and the minute glimpse mankind is given in attempt to basically understand the cosmic depth and universal scope respecting exactly what John 1:3 means.

With all of that in mind, consider 2 Corinthians 11:14:

"And no marvel; for Satan himself is transformed into an angel of light."

Given the fact the "light" concept applies with God, the same also can be applied to Satan. Analyzed within the context of electrical terminology because of the words 'transformed' and 'light,' a transformer is an electrical device that transfers electrical energy between two or more circuits through electromagnetic induction. Fundamentally, transformers are used to increase or decrease the alternating voltages in electric power applications. When a transformer in your neighborhood crashes either by a lightning strike, or a driver knocking down a pole, the electricity to your place of business goes out. When Paul says, "don't marvel," he's not only talking about Satan as a source of "spiritual light," he's talking physics since an electrical application may also be applied.

Consider Luke 10:18:

"And he said unto them, I beheld Satan as lightning fall
from heaven."

Lightning is an electric current! Again, given the duality of Biblical scripture, is the metaphorical reference to Satan as an "electrical current" made in mere vacuum? That's either figurative or literal?

With specific regard to your television as well as your PC, at each point where there is a critical transfer of energy from one medium to another, a transducer or transformer mechanism is required. For example, a microphone transducer transforms sound patterns into electrical patterns. A television camera transforms light patterns into electrical patterns. And a transmitter transforms electrical frequency patterns into the higher frequency domain of radio frequency energy, which is part of the electromagnetic spectrum. So, given the appellation "prince of the power of the air," a more apropos conceptualization of the devil being "transformed into an angel of light" couldn't be offered. Again, we're talking both physical and spiritual. If folks could see the physical or tangible in the same "light" that they do the spiritual and what's mistaken to be only figurative, just think of how much more "living" the Bible becomes.

The TV series and the movie *The Transformers*, strictly from a sci-fi point-of-view, has "serpent" in the Garden of Eden implications. Wasn't the serpent or snake actually the devil or Satan in disguise? That means Satan can transform (shapeshift) into a serpent just as comfortably as he can into a minister preaching the Gospel of Jesus Christ. Or, he can just as comfortably shapeshift into a form of radiant energy that can navigate the frequencies that are being technologically decoded by any electronic device having a transformer mechanism.

Because television and the internet are used to foster and promote iniquity (however limited or expansive), the technological nature of both, along with electromagnetism's basic natural force, together provide a chemistry whereby the spirit of Satan is actually transformed into an electrical pattern that is radiant or "light" energy. Again, not symbolically transformed, but literally transformed.

The devil is an extraterrestrial creature. Sure, he's an angel Biblically speaking, but scientifically he is a predator. This predator, as Biblically revealed, has supernatural powers; i.e., "juice" that's electrical just as much as it is socio-political and economic. Satan can take what a chameleon does to a whole 'nother level. But if you can't wrap your noggin around the Bible as being anything other than Bible stories with emphasis on the stories, then it's a big challenge to see the techno-spiritual connection.

A shapeshifter can look like anything or anybody. That means it can take "identity theft" to a whole 'nother level. Therefore, when considering all of the above with regards to Satan's real world intrinsic capabilities, add on the fact that the devil is also a spirit. If the airwaves are inundated with evil and wickedness in the forms of killings, murders, rapes, thefts, sex, lies, and videotapes, the airwaves are conveying the spirit of the devil. Subsequently, since Satan is the devil and the devil is Satan, because both television and internet protocols transform light patterns into electrical patterns that are reconverted into light patterns for reception by the human eye, Satan is in fact technologically "transformed," just as Scripture prophesizes. And this transformation is physical in nature just as much as it is spiritual.

Individuals who use radio, television, film, and the internet to communicate messages that glorify evil have aligned themselves with Satan in regards to Revelation 12:7. All who traffic in hatred, racism, bigotry, sexism, xenophobia, and all other forms of socially divisive speech are physical and spiritual operatives in the devil's camp. Whether they realize it or not, their ignorance will lead to their eternal damnation.

When it comes to whose side you're on with respect to "war in heaven" and alien versus predator (AVP), the airwaves are unquestionably a *mind field*.

2 MICHAEL

"Yet Michael the archangel, when contending with the devil he disputed about the body of Moses, durst not bring against him a railing accusation, but said, The Lord rebuke thee." —JUDE 1:9

We can't begin to mentally process there being an extraterrestrial war without totally understanding the identity of Michael and his angels (Revelation 12:7).

Let's examine this in the context of everyday people. Smokey Robinson and the Miracles; Diana Ross and the Supremes; Harold Melvin and the Blue Notes; Kool and the Gang; Gladys Knight and the Pips; Martha and the Vandellas. Is there the least bit of confusion with respect to who's calling the shots? Even though folks may have thought Teddy was the man, Harold's name was out front of the Blue Notes in spite of his voice.

Who in the heaven is Michael? His identity hangs more than a few Christians up.

Daniel 12:1 reads in part:

"And at that time shall Michael stand up, the great prince which standeth for the children of thy people."

If somebody stands up for you, they've got your back. Jude 1:9 shows what it means to stand up. Michael went to bat for Moses. Since this dispute was about the body of Moses, it's obvious that Satan was making a case that Moses needed to stay dead and stinking. If the devil was to have his way, there would be no resurrection to eternal life for Moses. But given the fact that this entity named Michael is a "stand up" guy, we find Michael saying to Satan, *"Rebuke you!"* And even though rebuke isn't a four-letter word, it still has a "K" in it. Standing up for Moses is representative of doing so for all human beings.

1 Thessalonians 4:16 reads:

"For the Lord himself shall descend from heaven with a shout, with the voice of the archangel, and with the trump of God: and the dead in Christ shall rise first."

Rewind; Jude says Michael is the archangel. So, if "the Lord" has the voice of Michael, let's back into who's who.

Philippians 2:11: "And *that* every tongue should confess that Jesus Christ *is* Lord, to the glory of God the Father."

In John 10:27-28, Jesus Christ says:

> "My sheep hear my voice, and I know them, and they follow me: And I give unto them eternal life; and they shall never perish, neither shall any man pluck them out of my hand?"

1 Thessalonians 4:16 and John 10:27-28 are linking the ability to resurrect the dead to the capability of both Michael and Jesus. So, intelligently ask yourself are the "dead in Christ" going to hear two voices or just one. Are they going to hear an angel's voice or the voice of Jesus Christ?

Back in the day, there was no confusion when you heard the voice of Smokey. That's why his name was out front. It was Smokey and "his" Miracles. The same applied to Diana, Gladys, and Martha. But when it came to Harold and Kool, some folks got confused. Some folks thought Teddy Pendergrass was Harold Melvin, and James "J.T." Taylor was Robert "Kool" Bell. The problem wasn't a mix-up regarding the voices heard; the head scratching was due to the titles. All folks knew the voices (if not the names), and they followed what they heard all the way to the record shop.

Because God "is not the author of confusion," do you think he's going to make Jesus lead vocalist and then put Michael out front on all the album and CD covers? Buying the right message under the wrong name is misleading. If it's your voice that's being heard, shouldn't it be your voice that's being followed?

John 11:25-26 can't make "Oh yeah" any more resounding:

> "Jesus said unto her, I am the resurrection, and the life: he that believeth in me, though he were dead, yet shall he live: And whosoever liveth and believeth in me shall never die."

Jesus is the resurrection because he is the archangel! Wasn't it the voice of Jesus that said, "Lazarus, come forth" (John 11:43)? The roles of

Jesus and Michael are identical when it comes to mankind's salvation and resurrection unto eternal life. Both are inseparable when it comes to both title and entitlement. They are one in the same.

But, if you're still questioning, there's Joshua 5:13-15:

> "And it came to pass, when Joshua was by Jericho, that he lifted up his eyes and looked, and behold, there stood a man over against him with his sword drawn in his hand: and Joshua went unto him, and said unto him, Art thou for us, or for our adversaries? And he said, Nay; but as captain of the host of the LORD am I now come. And Joshua fell on his face to the earth, and did worship, and said unto him, What saith my lord unto his servant? And the captain of the LORD'S host said unto Joshua, Loose thy shoe from off thy foot; for the place whereon thou standest is holy. And Joshua did so."

This swordsman identifies himself as "captain of the host of the Lord." Being captain means being in charge as in being out front, Smokey and Diana style. When considering that Luke 2:13 establishes the connection between angels and a multitude of heavenly hosts, making the connection that the swordsman that Joshua is speaking with is the same Michael whose host of angels is fighting against the devil and his angels is obvious. Again, the being Joshua sees has "his sword drawn." The captain of the host of the Lord isn't fighting with Joshua. If a policeman has his gun drawn, it tells you something is going down. Since evidence points to this man being an "angel" and this angel doesn't have his sword drawn against Joshua, just who do you think this angel is prepared to deal with using an instrument of war? Instruments of war are used in a war.

There is no identity crisis with respect to Michael. The "captain of the host of the Lord" is the Michael of Revelation 12. And because Michael is also identified as the archangel with all the rights, privileges and honors thereunto appertaining Jesus Christ, that fact firmly establishes that Michael is none other than Jesus Christ himself.

It's important to understand with respect to God incarnate that the name Jesus is given as an earthly name whereas Michael is the Godly name that's probably always and forever been known throughout the hallowed halls of heaven. If you believe Jesus is God in the flesh, prior to Jesus being in the flesh what do you think he'd have written on his business card? God? Lord?

How did Jesus introduce himself on earth? Matthew 21:11 reads he was known simply as "Jesus of Nazareth." If earthly humility and simplicity is any indication of heavenly style and profile, a business card with either GOD or LORD doesn't match the Christ like pattern of behavior.

Throughout the Bible, Jesus is shown to be about names and not so much titles. Perhaps that's why we see the name Michael being representative of the being who would be born Jesus. The name Michael as a designation serves as "the example and shadow of heavenly things" comparable to Jesus as that example and shadow's reflection (Hebrews 8:5).

Consider Matthew 1:21:
> "And she shall bring forth a son, and thou shalt call his name JESUS: for he shall save his people from their sins."

Acts 4:12:
> "Neither is there salvation in any other: for there is none other name under heaven given among men, whereby we must be saved."

Matthew 6:9:
> "After this manner therefore pray ye: Our Father which art in heaven, Hallowed be thy name."

Acts reads, "under heaven," and Matthew says, "in heaven." The name Michael, drawing from Revelation 12, is "in heaven" while the name Jesus, indicative of Matthew 1:21 is "under heaven." Should there be any confusion in understanding what time it is when it comes to Michael and Jesus being one and the same individual?

Luke 2, and the "multitude of the heavenly host praising God" with reference to the birth of Jesus are undeniably "Michael's angels." Certainly, Isaiah 9:6 can't make that fact any more apparent. The coming Messiah (Jesus Christ) is called the "Prince of Peace." Doesn't that scriptural calling make the already existent Michael "the great prince" just as Daniel indicates?

When the dots are connected, your favorite blind man can see who's who!

Also, consider the red-lettered fact that Revelation 22:16 reads, "I Jesus have sent my angel to testify unto you these things in the churches. I am the root and the offspring of David, and the bright and morning star."

When Jesus says he is the "root and offspring of David," he is reaffirming his humanity. And when he says, "bright and morning star," he is confirming his continual position as "Commander-In-Chief" of all angels under the heavenly identity belonging to the celestial being called Michael. By using the coordinating conjunction "and," Jesus is saying he is both.

But if there are still lingering doubts about Jesus being Michael, there's Revelation 19:10. John is so overwhelmed he drops to his knees to worship the angel showing what he saw: "And I fell at his feet to worship him. And he said unto me, See thou do it not: I am thy fellow servant, and of thy brethren that have the testimony of Jesus: worship God: for the testimony of Jesus is the spirit of prophecy."

Provided the stance taken regarding John worshiping an angel being prohibited, intelligently ask yourself why Joshua was allowed to worship the angel identified as the captain of the host of the Lord? Why there and not here? With Joshua, it was cool; but with John a no-no.

There's no double standard because there is no contradiction. Michael the archangel is not an angel in terms of a created being. If Michael were an angel in the conventional sense, there would be a big contradiction. Joshua would not have been permitted to fall on his face and worship a conventional angel. Archangel is a title. It is a rank of hierarchy, no different than captain. This is why Joshua was permitted to worship the captain of the Lord's host because in this instance, the captain was the being who would be born 14 centuries later into the world as Jesus Christ.

Neither Bill Clinton nor Barack Obama were soldiers. Yet by virtue of being President, they're also accorded the title Commander-In-Chief of the United States armed forces. Commander-In-Chief is to the title of President what archangel is to the title of God. Both positions are part of the job description.

An unobstructed view of Jesus Christ as the archangel Michael, who is also captain of the host of the Lord, amplifies what Jesus meant when he told Peter:

> "Thinkest thou that I cannot now pray to my Father, and he shall presently give me more than twelve legions of angels?"
> — MATTHEW 26:53

At that time, a Roman legion was comprised of between 3,000-6,000 men. Do the math. Because Jesus Christ is cosmic Commander-In-Chief as Michael, he could have had anywhere between 36,000 and 72,000 angels dispatched to his immediate service.

But let's back up and play with semantics. The verse just cited says, "He shall presently give me." Now, that's real significant wording. If you are in a hostage situation and you manage to get a call off to the police, does the police dispatcher "give" you the police?

By definition, the word give implies the transfer of possession. The police dispatcher is called a dispatcher for a reason. By definition, a dispatcher sends. The only thing a dispatcher gives is an address with pertinent information. And that's given to the police being dispatched, not the person initiating the call.

Jesus could have said, "Thinkest thou that I cannot now pray to my Father, and he shall presently SEND me more than twelve legions of angels?" But the fact that the word "give" was used instead of "send" speaks volumes. Using the word "give" suggests Jesus had the résumé to be given possession of twelve legions of angels. Do you seriously think Jesus would employ the word "give" presumptuously? Sending help and being given possession or authority over the help sent are two different things.

Now, even though the "that's a leap" counter-argument may be proffered that this interpretation only applies to a KJV English translation of the Bible, the fact is you are reading this book in English, not Swahili. Since it is what it is in English, the relevance for discussion can't be written off as inconsequential. It supports the point that when it comes to the Word of God, God foreseeing that you read/speak English, Jesus chose his words very precisely.

How many soldiers can the Commander-In-Chief of the USA pray to Congress or by executive order have deployed anywhere in the world? When you break it down, isn't it further compelling what Jesus was saying when he said:

"Father, forgive them; for they know not what they do." — LUKE 23:34

"They" did not know who they were dealing with as Jesus on earth, aka Michael in heaven. And today there are those who still don't know who they are dealing with as Jesus on earth and Michael in heaven.

Consider one more thing concerning Joshua's encounter with the "captain of the Lord's host." Joshua is told, "Loose thy shoe from off thy foot; for the place whereon thou standest is holy."

Doesn't that sound familiar?

> "And the angel of the LORD appeared unto him in a flame of fire out of the midst of a bush: and he looked, and, behold, the bush burned with fire, and the bush was not consumed. And Moses said, I will now turn aside, and see this great sight, why the bush is not burnt. And when the LORD saw that he turned aside to see, God called unto him out of the midst of the bush, and said, Moses, Moses. And he said, Here am I. And he said, Draw not nigh hither: put off thy shoes from off thy feet, for the place whereon thou standest is holy ground." — EXODUS 3:2-5

It was the "angel of the Lord" who appeared to Moses out of "a flame of fire out of the midst of a bush." And, this scripture says when "the Lord saw" Moses stop to check it out, that "God called unto him out of the midst of the bush."

Here we find the "angel of the Lord" and "God" himself linked together in name and title as one. In the New Testament, the Bible refers to Jesus as "Lord," and in the Old Testament, here we find Exodus referring to "the Lord" as "God." So what does that say to those who have problems believing that Jesus is God in the flesh? Or ask where in the Bible does Jesus say he is God?

What Jesus does say in John 5:39 is, "Search the Scriptures; for in them ye think ye have eternal life; and they are they which testify of me."

The entire Bible from Genesis to Revelation is a testament that reveals who on earth and in heaven Jesus Christ is. It's compelling that John 5:39 reads, "ye think" rather than "ye know." There's a big difference between reading the Bible and "searching" it. Isaiah 28:9-10 breaks "it" down:

> "Whom shall he teach knowledge? and whom shall he make to understand doctrine? them that are weaned from the milk, and drawn from the breasts. For precept must be upon precept, precept upon precept; line upon line, line upon line; here a little, and there a little."

Because many only read, many only "think" they know. There's a big difference between thinking somebody's done you wrong and knowing they did.

The movie *Michael* (1996) was a denigrating portrayal of Jesus Christ. Because many are clueless when it comes to Michael, the pulpit was as quiet as that proverbial church mouse. The Hollywood presentation of Mother Teresa as a Hoochie Mama would have gotten more play in terms of outrage. But when you don't know what time it is, you miss the train, the plane, and the boat.

Yes, the "captain of the Lord's host" of angels has to be Michael because according to Revelation 12:7-9, it's Michael's angels who are fighting Satan and his angels. If you are the captain of the ship you are in charge of the ship. And, if you are "captain," all of the sailors on the ship are under your command because of your title.

The argument simply doesn't fly that Michael is an ordinary angel for the simple fact that the "angel of the Lord" appeared to Moses in the burning bush and it was God's voice Moses heard speaking to him out of the bush.

Do you seriously think there were two beings in that bush? Why would God need an angel as a sidekick to have a conversation with Moses? Since the word 'angel' is employed in direct identification connection with God, there's neither heavenly nor earthly reason to believe archangel wouldn't have the same applicability when associated with Michael as Jesus Christ, and as the Lord thy God as an identifier as well.

Accept it, both Joshua and Moses are told by Michael to do the exact same thing—take them Jordans off!

Subsequently, with Michael being identified, the question that begs answering is what jumped this war in heaven off?

Ezekiel 28:12-15 offers the first clue:

"Thou wast perfect in thy ways from the day thou wast created, til iniquity was found in thee."

Two things are gleaned from that statement. One, angels are created beings. God created Lucifer as a perfect angel. And this perfect angel made a perfect devil out of himself. Go figure.

Paul, in 2 Thessalonians 2:7 references "the mystery of iniquity." Because God is perfectly good, the fact that his perfectly good creation turned out perfectly bad or iniquitous is a mystery. So, it can't be figured out. Lucifer, now Satan the devil, is a paradox.

Two, there's the question of finding. "Iniquity" was "found" in this angelic being so what exactly was the cause of this finding.

Isaiah 14:11-15 slam dunks. When reading these five verses in their entirety, the word "pomp" sums it up from the beginning. Ezekiel keys in on "perfect in beauty" and Isaiah drops the mic. Lucifer got the big head. He started to see himself as all that and a bag of chips. Pomp is short for pompous. In essence, Lucifer became "too sexy for himself."

Isaiah finds Lucifer giving his own self a "high five."

1. "I will ascend into heaven"
2. "I will exalt my throne above the stars of God."
3. "I will sit also upon the mount of the congregation, in the sides of the north."
4. "I will ascend above the heights of the clouds."
5. "I will be like the most High."

Five times we find this angel saying, "I will." It's all about what he will do. And, it's all about "Ascension."

Consider the Gospel according to Maxwell:
> *So shouldn't I realize;*
> *You're the highest of the high*
> *If you don't know then I'll say it;*
> *So don't ever wonder."*

If you're wondering *YouTube* Maxwell's hit song. "You're the highest of the high" is a helluva lyric to apply to a mortal soul.

However, for those who won't buy the Gospel according to Maxwell, *YouTube* the one according to John, as in Coltrane. It's also titled *Ascension*.

Oh yeah, the kingdom of God speaks to folks on many levels. Coltrane's *Ascension* album raised a whole lot of music eyebrows. Even some of the purists had to WTF this work in the privacy of their own minds. But as one commentator so eloquently put it: "*This music can only be understood in the context of John Coltrane's belief in music as a method for pursuing an ecstatic mystical experience. The musicians are indeed listening to each other, but there is no score, no agreed upon time signature, chord progression, or key.*"

In other words, what you hear on this track is organized egotistically driven "confusion" and "chaos."

Now, some folks say Lucifer was an angel of music and he could sing several eight note octaves simultaneously. Whether or not Satan has or had this polyphonic overtone singing ability the Bible doesn't say. Ezekiel 28:13, along with passages in the books of Job, Isaiah, and Psalms only hint there being a music connection. Whatever the "ecstatic mystical experience" behind Coltrane's *Ascension*, for sure it parabolizes the fact that "ascending" to heights or positions where you don't belong creates nothing but sheer confusion and utter chaos.

Perhaps unwittingly allegorical, Maxwell and Coltrane prove a point; in addition to pompous, this creature is bombastic. Straight from the word of God, bombast and narcissism are traits of Satan. Any time you find a narcissistic individual ranting and raving about what he or she will do, as well as who they are and what they are about, the spirit of Satan is written all over them. They are devils waiting to bust hell wide open.

And they'll take all willing to follow along in that proverbial handbag or basket for the ride.

The "war in heaven" was an attempted coup. Obviously, Lucifer being the devil he is believed he could run the kingdom of God better than God.

Carefully consider Genesis 1:2: "And the earth was without form, and void; and darkness was upon the face of the deep." When pondering that passage there's either a reasonable explanation or a glaring contradiction.

Carefully consider the one and only preceding verse along with Isaiah 45:18:

> "For thus saith the LORD that created the heavens; God himself that formed the earth and made it; he hath established it, he created it not in vain, he formed it to be inhabited."

When connecting the Genesis 1:1 dot with Isaiah 45:18 dot, what happened in Genesis 1:2? Again, Isaiah plainly states, "he created it not in vain." Yet, in Genesis 1:2, "the earth was without form, and void."

The dictionary definition of "vain" is: baseless or worthless; ineffectual or unsuccessful; futile or foolish; good-for-nothing. And the dictionary definition of "void" is: useless, ineffectual, empty, and vain.

Since Genesis maintains God created the earth, and Isaiah sustains that creation was "not in vain," how did the planet get all torn up by the very next verse? The entire second verse of Genesis meets the dictionary definition of vain. As a matter of fact, definition-wise, void and vain are interchangeable.

If God, in the beginning, didn't create earth in a form that fits the dictionary definition of void and vain, how did it wind up looking that way one text later? Is there a discrepancy in the Genesis and Isaiah accounts? Just as God is not the author of confusion, he's not the author of chaos. Again, anytime you see confusion and anywhere you find chaos, the spirit of Satan is being represented whether it's realized or not. Genesis 1:2 is a confusing and chaotic description of earth at its creation if "The Creation" jumped off at Genesis 1:3. Unless it's to be seriously believed that "in the beginning God created" a whacked earth, then all subscribing to only a 6,000-year planetary lifespan better get a second opinion.

For the many that don't have understanding when it comes to discussions of earth science, it's the imbalance involving theology and science that disadvantages many church congregations. This is why Lucifer is able to boast, "I will sit also upon the mount of the congregation, in the sides of the north."

When you are sitting in a church pew, you are seated amongst a "congregation." In essence, you are facing the pulpit cartographically looking "north" in terms of a flat map perspective. If your pastor lacks understanding with regards to whom and what Satan scientifically is, that "lack of knowledge" cloaks all references to Satan from the pulpit in a garment of technical obscurity. The failure to call Satan out for the devil he is vicariously places him at the "mount" or in front of the congregation by making him a proverbial fly on the wall. If you're a member of that church congregation, you hear his name, but you don't really see who or what he is even though in name he's right in front of your eyes. In words that are Lucifer's, that's essentially being seated "upon" the "mount" as in up front of the "congregation."

Drawing from Hollywood, it's significant to note that not calling Satan out for the devil he is makes exorcising his presence from the body ineffectual. The "body" in this case is the church. The fact that there are flesh and blood devils in a church from pastor to parishioner is the result of comfortability. Human nature doesn't permit people to stay in an environment for long when they are uncomfortable. Individuals who have the "devil in them" don't hang around where there's preaching that disturbs a devilish spirit. The power of the Holy Spirit is one of conviction. Satan cannot sit "upon the mount of the congregation" unless that congregation as a whole makes him feel comfortable. When the sheets are pulled off and an individual is revealed for whom they really are, they gots-to-go without being told by flesh and blood.

Unfortunately, Satan's comfortability stems from church folks not really knowing who or what the devil is beyond cursory spiritual application. For example, when you are personally comfortable with an individual who is clearly shown to have a lying spirit, you have personally placed Lucifer "upon the mount of your congregation" be ye a church member or not. The "congregation" therein can be actual as well as vicariously distant. It can be those you personally hang with, as well as those you have no personal relationship with at all. Again, there's Revelation 22:15 – all liars and all lovers of liars are held in the same regard because the personal affinity for a devilish spirit is the tie that binds.

Consider Isaiah 14:16: "They that see thee shall narrowly look upon thee, and consider thee, saying, 'Is this the man that made the earth to tremble, that did shake kingdoms.'"

That one lone verse implies that there is a physical identity disconnect when it comes to Lucifer, now Satan, the great red dragon, that old serpent called the devil. In street terms, if you look upon someone like that, and then say something like that there, you're calling them out for who they physically are as opposed to who they've been spiritually reputationed to be.

Lucifer got his ass kicked by God Almighty, and getting slapped on the blackhand side to earth resulted in a temper tantrum. Genesis 1:2 is a snapshot. Revelation 12:12 portends this snapshot. Geology and paleontology tell us that in the past 540 million years there have been five major extinction events when over 50% of earth's animal species died. Although there are 10–14 million species of life currently on the earth, more than 99 percent of all species that ever lived on the planet are estimated to be gone. The most recent extinction event is said to have occurred about 65 million years ago. That extinction involved dinosaurs.

When Genesis 1:2 says, "And darkness was upon the face of the deep," that's Satan's Instagram. Darkness is a metaphor for "the dragon" and "his angels." Drawing from Ezekiel 28:13, irrefutably, Satan was on earth as Lucifer, an unfallen angel, long before Genesis 1:2 and not afterward. His creation as a sentient being is assigned to the dateless past right along with the creation of heaven and earth. Lucifer, a.k.a. the anointed cherub who became Satan the devil, is part of the creation that took place in Genesis 1:1. Even though Eden was "re-planted" on the "third day" and referenced in retrospect in Genesis 2:8, neither the names Satan nor anointed cherub appear in the narrative.

Evidently, drawn from Revelation 12:9, the devil was *persona non grata* Genesis 1:3-31. And, if such were the case, isn't it understandable why this fallen angel either shape-shifted into a serpent or demonically possessed one for his post-Ezekiel 28 Eden re-entrance? The "anointed cherub" (Satan) snuck into the Garden as a snake!

Satan is identified by exact name in 15 Old Testament verses with 11 of those found in the first two chapters of Job. This confirms this entity's existence and knowledgeability to the Old Testament writers dating back as early as pre-Mosaic (2000 BC). Such knowledgeableness means Satan could have been called out by exact name as being in Eden. Since he wasn't, the implication strongly suggests that Genesis 1:3-31 is the RE-CREATION as opposed to THE CREATION.

Satan's existence as Lucifer and Lucifer's absence as Satan cannot be Biblically explained minus a pre-Genesis 1:2 and a post-Genesis 1:2 creative/re-creative act respectively. The Bible's avoidance in using the name Lucifer and anointed cherub in a context that post-dates the planet's pristine appearance is therefore telling. There was the commission of a crime so terrible by Lucifer that the kingdom of God is both literally and figuratively done with this entity. God would not even bring himself to say his name. It's essentially, "Speak to the hand!"

A six literal day creation of the earth that many think is represented in Genesis 1:3-31 contradicts what's represented in Genesis 1:1 and Isaiah 45:18. The first verse of Genesis reads the heaven and the earth were created in the beginning. Do verses 3-31 say anything about "heaven" being created in six literal days?

But if you believe the heavens were initially created on Day 4 (Genesis 1:14-19), why did it take six days to create earth and only 24 hours to create everything else we see in the nighttime sky?

Until Copernicus had the 'aha' experience that earth revolved around the sun instead of vice versa, folks embraced beliefs that just didn't add up. Likewise, it just doesn't add up that it took God longer to create one planet than it took him to create hundreds of billions of planets, moons, stars, and galaxies.

As a matter of logistical fact, the heavens and the earth had to have been already created by the time we get to Genesis 1:3. If not what is the light source for days 1, 2, and 3? The sun had to have already been in the sky for "the evening and the morning" to be the yardstick for determining days 1-3.

Isaiah 9:5-7 reads:
> "For every battle of the warrior is with confused noise, and garments rolled in blood; but this shall be with burning and fuel of fire. For unto us a child is born, unto us a son is given: and the government shall be upon his shoulder: and his name shall be called Wonderful, Counsellor, The mighty God, The everlasting Father, The Prince of Peace. Of the increase of his government and peace there shall be no end, upon the throne of David, and upon his kingdom, to order it, and to establish it with judgment and with justice from henceforth even for ever. The zeal of the LORD of hosts will perform this."

Reading between the lines, words such as battle, warrior, blood, child, born, son, government, Counsellor, God, Father, Prince of Peace, kingdom, judgment, and justice are all uniquely associated with Michael and Jesus inseparably linking the two together.

Undeniably, Michael is the "Born Identity" Jesus Christ.

3 INTERSTELLAR

*"I knew a man in Christ above fourteen years ago,
(whether in the body, I cannot tell; or whether out of the body, I cannot tell:
God knoweth;) such an one caught up to the third heaven."*
—2 CORINTHIANS 12:2

The above passage finds the apostle Paul writing that he knew a man "caught up." In one way or another, maybe we all do. But without getting too deep into either Paul's or our own individual religious cosmology, it's safest to say that there are divisions of heaven similar in context to the ordinal classifications given grade school matriculation. If Paul, speaking of himself, was caught up to the third heaven, he was outside of earth's atmosphere. Earth's atmosphere is where birds and planes navigate. Such a place in inner space can be considered the "first heaven."

In terms of the "second heaven," is there any plausible deniability in the possibility that such could be thought of as outer space? Take the horizontal distance across the state of New Jersey and turn it vertically. That's about how many miles it is between ground zero and interplanetary space. Once you hit the 70 mile straight up marker, you've reached the outer limits of earth's atmosphere.

But since Revelation 12:8 makes it plain that the Devil and his angels were kicked completely out of heaven, guess where the "war in heaven" is now being fought? Newsflash; guns ain't blazin' in the "third heaven." It's all happening down here on the ground. Earth is now the "war in heaven" battle zone. The fight isn't staged on moon or Mars because mankind can't get there as a populous. So, the "war in heaven" brought to our attention in Revelation is here on earth. And, of course, this is exactly why Revelation 12:12 gives the "inhabiters" of earth a shout out.

If Paul and Jesus have any credibility, heaven (*the third heaven*) is more than pie-in-the-sky-in-the-sweet-by-and-by. It's neither a figment of the imagination nor is it some hallucinogenic cloud-nine. Heaven is a real place in a physical universe where extraterrestrials that have maintained their loyalty to the kingdom of God are. The only extraterrestrials presently working this planet, if you buy the Bible, are either Michael and his angels, or Satan and his. There are no friendly ET's laying over here on earth to say "hey" on their way to somewhere else. According to Revelation 12, definitely earth and probably this entire solar system is a "no fly zone."

But, in following the path of further discussion started previously, we have to venture down Alice's rabbit hole to find just what Dorothy was looking for somewhere over that rainbow. When it comes to Satan and angels being viewed as extraterrestrials, questions of this magnitude find most folks not wanting to get all that deep.

There's nothing wrong with taking the blanket position that Jesus is God, and Savior; end of discussion. However, because John 5:39 finds Jesus saying, "Search the scriptures…in them ye think," that's suggesting a wise person better start taking a closer look at whatever it is they're thinking. Just maybe what's required is a better understanding than we think?

Television and film have ruined the image of an alien. But, then and again, some factions of the U.S. Congress haven't helped much either. Searching the scriptures from an "angels as aliens" perspective takes the Bible outside the realm of *Wonderland* when it comes to the stark probability that earth has been around longer than six millennia. Such an understanding demonstrates without demonizing science's role in complimenting the Bible, not conflicting with it.

If evangelists, preachers, teachers, and theologians were as versed in astronomy, archaeology, and biology as they are in hermeneutics and the principles of Biblical exegesis that one would have to attend a seminary to master, how much more of the Ephesians 6:11 "whole armour" would Sly Stone's everyday people be better prepared to strap on? Can you take a stroll through your mind and envision Satan as the non-cinematic being he is?

Instead of being made-up to look like a vagina with teeth, the motion picture optics ala the *Predator* (1987) are as far from Biblical depiction as east is from west. Ezekiel 28:17 calls Satan out as a creature of beauty. However, when it comes to the "art of war," in all likelihood Satan wrote the cosmic book upon which all terrestrial dealing with the subject matter is based. Again, disinformation is a tactic. It serves the princedom of Satan well to paint a devil red with horns, tail, and pitchfork than as a being you'd like to introduce to mama or pops. Being portrayed as grotesque camouflages true colors as a Biblical "angel of light."

When searching the Scriptures, there is no implication whatsoever that angels as extraterrestrials are byproducts of sexual intercourse. Drawing directly from the scriptures, sex is a planet earth thing. The artistic designers of the *Alien* movie's facehugger in their fanciful attempt to send a subliminal message otherwise are Biblically billions of miles and scores of scriptural verses off base. If you are a believer in a Supreme Being (God), in order to seriously think that an alien as in *Alien* as in an extraterrestrial as in an angel came into existence through a vaginal canal is to deny Ezekiel 28:15 and the validity of Psalms 8:5 and Genesis 1:27.

Previously pointed out, angels are created beings. And drawn from the latter two texts, neither Adam nor angels got here as the result of two other angels copulating. Modeling a belief cinematically contrary to Biblical influence or persuasion suggests that binomial reproduction permeates the universe meaning nothing is exceptional regarding God's creation of mankind as male and female. Geocentric-Aristotelian type physics based on beliefs that we are the center of the universe is just as backward thinking today as it was back when. Hollywood's fixation on cinematically incorporating images of male and female private parts as representative of extraterrestrial close encounters has Sigmund Freud written all over it. But, rather than penis envy or vagina obsession on the parts of writers, producers, and directors, is it possible that the creative impulse to introduce phallic and uterine symbols is of extraterrestrial origin?

Are fallen angels psycho-sexually envious of mankind's genitalia and ability to employ such in a procreative manner? When remembering where Freud had his head in Psych 101, the answer is hell-to-the-yes!

People obsess over what they don't have and can't get. Subsequently, compulsive-obsessive disorders are rooted in envy and jealousy. When reading Isaiah 14:13-14, it doesn't take a Freud to go figure. Lucifer is clinically off the chain. He is textbook neurotic in wanting to "be like Mike." The devil has a God complex. And given the fact that mankind is made in the image of God, guess what!

Astronomers estimate that the visible universe contains around a hundred billion galaxies. Each one of those galaxies is estimated to contain around a hundred billion stars. That means the known universe has 10 followed by 21 zeroes worth of stars in it; or 10 sextillion suns like our own. Now what if each one of those stars had an inhabitable planet like our own?

> "In my Father's house are many mansions: if it were not so, I would have told you. I go to prepare a place for you."
> — JOHN 14:2

When looking at the heavens on a starry night, "many" is an understatement. Sextillion anything is a whole lot of sex. Subsequently, the princedom of Satan is not only sexually obsessed, it's also materially obsessed. When it's that number of "mansions" and you've been kicked out of the neighborhood it shouldn't be a mystery why evil "does what it do."

When people go postal after receiving a pink slip, imagine the kingdom of God sending out a number of pink slips sufficient to cover a third of all the angels in the universe.

> "And his tail drew the third part of the stars of heaven, and did cast them to the earth" — REVELATION 12:4

> "And I beheld, and I heard the voice of many angels round about the throne and the beasts and the elders: and the number of them was ten thousand times ten thousand, and thousands of thousands." — REVELATION 5:11

When metaphysically doing the math; 10,000 x 10,000 = 100,000,000 divided by 3 = 33,333,333. In other words, if we just take the cardinal number of angels we know are out there factoring out the ordinal number Satan pulled indicative of Revelation 12:4, that's a whole lot of predatory aliens hitting earth at one time! Just imagine a confederation of thirty-three million devils descending on a life sustaining habitable planet; pissed with an ax to grind.

Once again, faced with cosmic questions like, "*Are we alone?*" if you buy the Bible, what do you think? The sheer size of interstellar space suggests that the universe is teeming with intelligent life. And that's life that probably doesn't altogether look like us. So again, for all who have problems with diversity based on skin color, what if green was added to the mix?

If you are a racist, supremacist or closet bigot, when it comes to a Christian afterlife, don't even think about it. If you can't deal with differences in skin as such involves your own species, God in heaven knows you can't deal with skin color as it involves totally different species.

On earth, it's called racism; in heaven, it might be called speciesism. Just contemplate the mindset and heart that takes pride in killing animals for sport. The spirit behind the motivation is no different than the spirit behind the devastation capsulized by Genesis 1:2. Just in case mansions are code word for planets, are those John 14:2 dwelling spots only being prepared for the human species to live in isolation from all other species? There are guesstimates that all of the people that have ever lived on planet earth from the creation of Adam and Eve totals somewhere between 100 and 110 billion. The population on earth today is estimated to be a little over 7 billion. That means if human beings were "all alone" in the universe, each person who ever lived could have their very only galaxy. Of course, that's not what John 14:2 had in mind. The numbers do add up and they're into trillions. And once numbers get beyond T-street, they have no numerical relevance in our day-to-day lives.

If you had a trillion dollars, you could spend all of it in fifty years by spending only $50-million a day. However, if you only had a billion bucks you could go through that pretty quick. All you'd have to do is blow around a quarter million a day for the next ten years.

One of the all-time best perspectives on large numbers comes in the form of a quip involving the dude who asks God, "How long is a million years to you?" God replies, "A million years to me is like a second." Then the guy says, "Wow, how much is a million dollars to you then Lord?" And, God replies, "A million dollars to me is like a penny." The guy thinks, and then says to God, "Could I have a penny?" God answers, "Sure, give me a second?"

When it comes to the universe and distances that defy comprehension, the kingdom of heaven has to employ eternity as the only yardstick to get from here to there. And, of course, this is exactly why 2 Peter 3:8 says what it does: "One day is with the Lord as a thousand years, and a thousand years as one day." The being we call God is not constrained by time or the inability to process large numbers.

Indicative of Revelation 1:20 and 12:4, consider the Biblical fact that "stars" frequently represent angels. A universe with 10-sextillion stars can accommodate 100,000,000 angels plus thousands of thousands more. Astronomy 101 should be a required course for anyone seeking ministerial ordination, or interest in storefront preachin'. As a matter of fact, a nighttime fieldtrip to the neighborhood observatory on a clear night should be mandatory for all church congregations. Seeing Saturn's rings, the Pleiades star cluster, and Jupiter's red-spot with the naked eye is a spiritual experience that rivals any weekday Bible study session.

Such a visit reaffirms Psalms 19:1: "The heavens declare the glory of God; and the firmament sheweth his handywork." And, should you take the time to read the remaining verses and key on the words and phrases: speech, sheweth knowledge, language, line is gone out through all the earth, end of the world, tabernacle for the sun, end of the heaven, circuit, and heat, such prose is metaphorically associated with earth science.

Who doesn't know that "lines" with regards to earth are latitude and longitude references? Or "circuit" with respect to the "end of the heaven" is alluding to the universe, planetary and galactic orbits, and the space-time continuum?

These mathematical models may be algebraically expressed as formulas. And formulas are a "speech" and "language" that "shows knowledge."

When the Bible is read with more than history in mind, a-whole-nother panoramic perspective suddenly comes into play. When "the heaven" is seen as meaning the universe, all of the interstellar knowledge NASA knows becomes relevant to Bible study and interpretation. It is therefore puzzling why so many have such a time and technology constrained understanding of Jesus Christ, angels, Satan, and devils. Neither the kingdom of God nor the princedom of Satan is checked by either time or technology.

Ecclesiastes 1:9-10:
> "The thing that hath been, it is that which shall be; and that which is done is that which shall be done: and there is no new thing under the sun. Is there any thing whereof it may be said, See, this is new? it hath been already of old time, which was before us."

Do you realize the water that you drink is the same water that's been here on this planet for the past billion plus years? It just keeps getting recycled. And Solomon, who authored the above passage, is telling us that the technology behind our electronic gear was here when he was. We're just now catching up with the technology that's always been.

If you can think out of the box, illustrative is Luke 4:5-7:
> "And the devil, taking him up into an high mountain, shewed unto him all the kingdoms of the world in a moment of time. And the devil said unto him, all this power will I give thee, and the glory of them: for that is delivered unto me; and to whomsoever I will I give it. If thou therefore wilt worship me, all shall be thine."

Matthew 4:8 gives an account of the same temptation only referring to the mountain as "exceeding high." Reflecting specifically on what Mathew and Luke are both saying about this mountain experience is extremely interesting. Unlike the temptation experience of Jesus being taken "into" a city and set "on a pinnacle" (Matthew 4:5/Luke 4:9), here we find Christ being taken by the devil into a mountain.

When examining these temptation texts all together isn't it apparent that both Matthew and Luke know the difference between "into" and "on" since both men use the two words separately in the same chapters and within 3-5 verses of each other?

Now, note "mountain" is singular not plural. Going "into" a mountain is different than going "into" the mountains. If you go "into" a mountain, you are going inside of a cave. Drawn from the way it's written, Satan took Jesus into a cave.

Caves are dark. Just what was there to see inside this particular dark cave? We don't have to speculate because both Matthew and Luke say what's happening whether it's believed or not. God and those sentient beings we call angels are not constrained by space, time, and technology. Because we live in a technological world doesn't mean that technology we have today only came into existence when we first discovered it. The Bible plainly states Satan showed Jesus "all the kingdoms of the world in a moment of time." Aren't we shown exactly the same thing when we're in front of a television that's connected to satellite or cable?

What about when we're online? Just how many "kingdoms" can we visit with a Wi-Fi'd cell phone or laptop. And, if we just happen to be seated on a rug while we're surfing channels or the internet, there's our magic carpet ride. Our magic wand is a handheld remote control or index finger on a keypad.

Note what Satan says next. What do you think is meant by "all this power?" What power is being referenced? Is it all about the political "power" of the kingdoms shown? Or, is it possible that the technology the devil employed to show those kingdoms is the power being referred to.

Satan had already tempted Jesus to defy the law of gravity by putting him "on" a tall building. That means the devil didn't take Christ up "into" a mountain for the purpose of jumping off. You have to be on a mountain to jump off of it; you don't jump "into" it. If height wasn't a jumping off factor, why was this mountain's selection "exceeding high?" Why not just go with a hill or something Galilee Sea level?

Of course, we're speculating and there could be any number of reasons why this-is-this and that-is-that. But when circling back to Isaiah 1:18 and "Come now, and let us reason together," that's pretty strong encouragement when it comes to "analyze this/analyze that." For those who want to know, the info is there. For those who don't, it's still there regardless.

Technologically speaking, being on an "exceeding high" mountain is having a very tall transmitter tower. Communications towers are put in "exceeding high" places for a technological reason that a search of the internet will explain in detail. The bottom line, however, if your First Century cave is built-out like a 21st Century television station with satellite uplink and downlink capabilities, that's something you'd want to hide in a very remote location. What's more remote than a cave hidden beneath a mountaintop?

Communication antennas and masts are on the summits of the Rock of Gibraltar in Europe, Mount Lee in California, and Stone Mountain in Georgia. However, rather than being hidden in a cavern beneath the summits, the transmitter housing and associated installations are above ground in plain sight. Since Ecclesiastes 1:9 makes it plain that, "There's nothing new under the sun," that means the wireless technology we have today is not universally unique? The silicon found inside of whatever was at hand from the creation of earth. If George Washington Carver could have gotten hold of some silicon instead of peanuts, the man had "*A Beautiful Mind*." He probably could have done in 1910 what it took Jack Kilby and Robert Noyce nearly a century to do later.

The temptation of Christ that went down inside of that cave involved predatory alien technology. Since we're talking media, where was Superman's hideout?

Well, *The Fortress of Solitude* appearing in comic books is in a cave. And, even though it is fictional, the giant crystal cave located in the Naica Mine in Chihuahua, Mexico isn't. For Superman, the fortress or quartz crystal cave was an information technological storage house. In fact, quartz crystals are piezoelectric, meaning their mechanical characteristics can affect electronic circuits. Crystal filters are commonly used in communications devices such as radio receivers. Subsequently, herein we find fictional art imitating factual life.

The theory that the third temptation of Christ involved Satan as extraterrestrial technologist is not farfetched when you start connecting the dots. Only when we open our minds and fast-forward what Matthew and Luke are saying to a modern day interpretive analysis and understanding do we realize that the "power" Satan used in his attempt to impress Jesus Christ was no different in concept than the technological power used today to change a television channel by remote control. The technology behind wireless and satellite telecommunications is the "all this power" Satan is boasting. The power to sit in a chair or on a sofa and change TV channels without getting up is powerful. You can literally see "all the kingdoms of the world in a moment of time" depending on what's being shown on each channel as you surf.

Now, for all of those who were on the scene prior to television remotes and the only way to change a channel was to get on up; a handheld device that could keep you sitting down would have been very impressive. If somebody had such a device circa the 1950s and 60s and said, "*All this power*" will I give you, you'd know full well what power they'd be talking about handing you. The only power in play in that scenario is the ability to switch television channels.

The remote control device used doesn't have any power over the television programming content that's being shown on the set. Hence, the same would be analogous to the mountain cave temptation of Christ. The power Satan is employing in Matthew and Luke is technological. In order to believe that Satan was "delivered" power over all the kingdoms of the world is to believe that God handed the devil his *MasterCard*. That being the case, Satan's power would have been absolute. And absolute power on earth would have made Satan a king, not a prince.

How do we Biblically know this to be so? Well, consider King of Kings (1961). That movie title was taken from Revelation 19:16. And, it was rubber stamped by Jesus himself in John 18:37 when Pilate said, "Art thou a king then?"

Well "then" consider Matthew 28:18. It preludes what's called "The Great Commission." It reads, "All power is given unto me in heaven and in earth." So, if "all this power" of Luke 4:6 was "all that," then all that power of Matthew 28:18 wasn't "all that!"

Who "then" are you going to believe? The words of Satan? Or, "the Word" of Jesus Christ?

Search the scriptures from Genesis to Revelation and you'll never find the devil being referred to as the king of this world. But, given the fact that Satan says in Luke 4:6, "and the glory of them," that suggests a separation between the ability to show (the technology) and what was shown (the kingdoms). The devil's power play involved the remote control device (the power) separate from the programming content (the glory).

Satan then as today only has the ability to influence. The "kingdoms" known as television networks today can operate either under the influence of God or the influence of Lucifer. Network programming can either glorify God, or it can glorify Satan. This is "the glory" Satan was pitching to Jesus. And that is the combination of power and glory Christ rejected.

How high would you jump if the devil, or a devil, offered you control of a major television network? Let's say Fox News. Or, a telecommunications company such as Sinclair Broadcast Group (with emphasis on sin)? Would you compromise your personal integrity by reading a propagandistically prepared script in order to keep a job? Whose ass would you kiss (or maybe even take it to the next level) to have that kind of power and glory? When the word "sin" appears in the name of a broadcast company that uses its power to control and manipulate in the Luke 4:5-7 manner demonstrated by Satan, do you think it merely coincidental? Or, is somebody other than this author telling you something!

The Biblical fact that we find Satan saying, "all this power will I give… for that is delivered unto me…and to whomsoever I will I give it" is a helluva statement if the power being referenced is the radio wave component of the electromagnetic spectrum. What most fail to realize is the power of radio and television stations along with radio and television networks is their ability to control airwave frequency space and/or channel position. Minus one or the other or both, that station and/or network is powerless. Its mass communications and mass audience outreach is limited. And, of course, that's the issue when it comes to low power stations versus high power ones. Consistent with Matthew and Luke, the operative word is still and always will be power.

Back in the day as well as here in the now, Black owned local radio and television stations are a rare commodity. Because of overt and institutional racism, discrimination, and bigotry, the power to acquire a spectrum frequency is the issue above and beyond anything else. Having real estate and equipment is nothing without commercial access to the broadcast airwaves as physically defined by the electromagnetic spectrum.

Even presently, when traveling across country or stopping in any city, you can typically find a radio station programming R&B, Gospel, or Blues at the end of the dial. The 1300Hz to 1600Hz position on AM is the technically least desirable respecting signal strength and quality. The far right end of the AM receiver is to radio ownership what chitlins are to a fine dining restaurant.

When we find Satan asserting that "to whomsoever I will I give it," discrimination in all of its sundry forms that either restrict or prevent equal opportunities in the commercial acquisition of radio and television frequencies, or radio and television network channel position on cable, satellite, and subscription systems validates that statement. Racism with regards to the electronic media is cosmic. The princedom of Satan has a problem with people socio-politically categorized as colored. The "powers that be" that systematically keeps Blacks, Hispanics, and others off the mainstream airwaves have a Biblical and metaphysical connection that's just as formidable as any flesh and blood driven force. Therefore, with regards to "war in heaven," earth's airwaves enable Satan as "prince of the power of the air" to hold that title uncontested (Ephesians 2:2).

A point repeated, mind manipulation operates on the perception of reality and not reality itself. If you can convince an individual something is real, it becomes their individual reality in spite of truth. This is the art of deception making it an "art of war." Thus, it was Satan who wrote the book, not Sun Tzu!

Be that as it may, however, from a metaphysical interstellar perspective, some things are spiritually predictable given their status of seeming unpredictability. Those powers that derive their power from satanic intervention are not all powerful. Whether a presidential election or a Super Bowl outcome, more often than not what is thought to be the working of Satan in actuality may be the "unsearchable judgments" of God. History has always given witness to God using a crooked stick to beat a straight path.

While it may be disconcerting that your favorite team didn't come away with the gold, those Roman 11:33 "ways past finding out" are a testament that God's "Will" will ultimately be done. The reason the "power" of the electronic media was given the devil, again, we can only speculate. Since the angelic name Lucifer etymologically means "day star" and earth's day star is the sun, perhaps everything geophysically tied to earth falls under Satan's jurisdiction by virtue of his namesake. The sheer fact that the name Sun Tzu has geophysical implications is noteworthy. Revelation 12:1-9 finds sun, war, deception, and Satan all inextricably linked. Go figure.

Maybe it was an interstellar birthright thing? Ezekiel 28:13 does maintain that Satan had this planet "covered" with "every precious stone." Interestingly, if you check out each of those rocks or gems, they're all birthstones. Subsequently, as the "anointed cherub," this "covering" suggests a type of caretaker relationship. The name Lucifer (day star) couldn't make his employment in that capacity any more apparent. The sun celestially takes care of the earth. Without the sun, the earth could not exist as the habitat for life as we know it. Lucifer, unquestionably, was positioned as earth's caretaker.

Seriously, just who do you think the "Parable of the Wicked Tenants" involving the "husbandmen" of Luke 20:9, Mark 12:1, and Matthew 21:33 is ultimately talking about? These tenants or husbandmen enjoyed a caretaker relationship only. They had no power beyond that which they were temporarily given. But, they got the employment capacity of their relationship to the "vineyard" (earth) twisted.

Also compelling, in addition to "prince of the power of the air," Jesus calls the devil out as "prince of this world" (John 14:30). Being called a prince in both instances denotes entitlement in both instances. That's entitlement to take care of and not to rule over. Again, being called prince and not king means the devil was not handed unchecked authority on earth. The king is "the man." The prince only takes care of what the king tells him to take care of or do. Lucifer, just like the tenants or husbandmen, is on assignment only. He, just like the tenants or husbandmen, doesn't have a legally conclusive deed to the land that's issued by the kingdom of heaven.

Consider Exodus 20:11: "For in six days the LORD made heaven and earth, the sea and all that in them is." In addition to that statement being an integral component of the Fourth Commandment which is an integral component of the *Ten Commandments*; it's a notice of copyright ownership. By using the word "made," ownership of earth is established as being the creative work of God. Therefore, in the absence of the Bible indicating any transfer of ownership or assignment of copyright to either Satan or his corporation, the caretaker relationship Satan enjoys is maintained. Satan has no legal entitlement or authority beyond that given him as prince. That means when it comes to Luke 4:6, the "all" in "*All this power*" ain't all that.

Conversely, Satan would like all to believe it is. But all who know the Bible know that the devil is a liar. And liars are not going to tell the truth when it's detrimental to what they want falsely believed. This explains why the word "world" is Biblically used and not the word earth. In case you didn't realize it, there's a big difference between earth and world. "Prince of this world" and "prince of this earth" are not inseparable terms.

Would the lover in you say, "I'm gonna rock your earth?" For the lover that ain't in you, it's easy to understand how we're all collectively on earth and at the same time individually living in our own little world. Who doesn't know what it means to be off into your world with or without headphones and earbuds?

Take the question, "*What's happening in your world?*" The individual living in Possumneck, Mississippi, is probably gonna have a different response from the one living in Beverly Hills, California. With these thoughts in mind, Satan's world princedom is Biblically well defined and limited.

Who rules your world? Is your world being rocked by a king, or a prince? Since Jesus uses the pronoun "this," reference to world is further qualified.

The media is termed both the Fourth Estate and Fifth Estate. Being termed an estate along with use of the electromagnetic spectrum, the media is a geophysical part of "this world" as applied to our own individual worlds. Unless you live in a wilderness far removed from technological society, you're going to be exposed to some form of electronic communications. When "prince of the power of the air" and "prince of this world" are viewed together, Satan's princedom is a "new world order." It's new because the world God created in the beginning according to Genesis 1:1 and Isaiah 45:18 is ordered. Satan's intro into the mix (Genesis 1:2) caused disorder. It's "this world's" disorder that differentiates the new from the old.

Consider John 17:14-16:

> "I have given them thy word; and the world hath hated them, because they are not of the world, even as I am not of the world. I pray not that thou shouldest take them out of the world, but that thou shouldest keep them from the evil. They are not of the world, even as I am not of the world."

This prayer prayed by Jesus is for all disciples of Christ and not just the contemporaneous twelve. It addresses the age old "how to" be in the world and not of the world.

By virtue of you reading this book, you do not live in a wilderness far removed from technological society. You are exposed to some form of electronic communications. Consequently, you are in "the new world order." You are in the "matrix." However, whereas the movie *Matrix* exists on two planes which are the physical and the cyber, the matrix alluded by John 17 is deeper. It's all inclusive. It's not only physical (earth) and cyber (radio, TV, film, internet), it's spiritual, metaphysical, and quantum mechanical.

Movies like *The Matrix* (1999) are not written in a vacuum. The messages inherent go way beyond "for entertainment purposes only." Unfortunately, very few realize that the Bible goes way beyond "for inspirational purposes only." The messages inherent in those 66 books are way beyond deep. It's the deepness of the Bible that compels the princedom of Satan to use the airwaves to counter with spiritually competing and conflicting messages.

When Adam and Eve fell, the script was flipped on the original world order. The matrix of God was replaced by that of Satan. The paradigm shifted. This new world matrix opened the door to the occult beliefs that Satan is operating in the best interests of mankind. Doctrines such as Luciferianism rose. Such "isms" subscribe that it was Lucifer who wanted man to "see the light" and be like God. And, it was God who wanted to keep mankind in darkness. In essence, the satanic argument pitted knowledge versus ignorance posturing the devil as plaintiff and God as defendant. And basically, that's the name of the game today. Believers in God and Jesus Christ as God are typically "defenders of the faith." And typically, those who don't believe are pontificating based on personal opinion minus evidence either substantive or circumstantial.

The story of Prometheus that school kids applaud and adults name products and projects after is, in reality, the saga of Satan. The fire that Prometheus mythologically stole and gave to man symbolizes "illumination" with regards to mankind having access to forbidden knowledge. Subsequently, when casual conversations turn to discussions about the Cabal, Illuminati, Freemasonry, Light Alliance, and others viewed as having socio-political-economic power and enlightenment, conspiracy theories cease to be theoretical when the context is simply righteousness versus unrighteousness. A tree being known by its fruit is what it is.

The ability, therefore, to be in the world and not of the world requires capability to avoid influences that are of the matrix established in the Garden of Eden by the princedom of Satan. The "matrix reloaded" by the devil is the new world order that "this world" operates under. It's a world that's both media predicated and premeditated. And only through that predication and premeditation does the power exist to control mankind's spirit for evil and subsequent criminal intent furthering the significance of Luke 4:5-7 as a temptation of Christ.

When Huey P. Newton said, "*The spirit of the people is greater than man's technology,*" he was connecting the dots that link Luke 4:5-7 with John 17:14-16, and both with John 6:63:

> "It is the spirit that quickeneth; the flesh profiteth nothing: the words that I speak unto you, *they* are spirit, and *they* are life."

In a relatively very small space amongst all those billions of galaxies and stars, earth is the only place where Satan is called prince. By having an interstellar perspective and spiritual connection via "the words" of Jesus Christ can the technology of "this world" be greatly overcome. Not "one day," but this day.

4 MINORITY REPORT

"Then Herod, when he saw that he was mocked of the wise men, was exceeding wroth, and sent forth, and slew all the children that were in Bethlehem, and in all the coasts thereof, from two years old and under, according to the time which he had diligently inquired of the wise men." — MATTHEW 2:16

Some things are so right in front of your face that their obviousness sometimes causes you not to see them. They're overlooked like the forest you can't see because of all the trees being in the way. Thus far there's been a lot of focus on the book of Revelation. Here comes a lot more. Revelation 12:13-17, with a specific look at verses 13 and 17 leaves little doubt that Satan wants to takeout mankind. The "takeout" here is not dinner and a movie. Verse 13's employment of the word "persecute" and verse 17's "war" tells all where Satan's coming from.

The devil lost the "war in heaven," so his last stand is here on earth.

Now, the something most don't pick up on is human nature. Just like folks who think they can't see the nose on their face without a mirror, maybe their thinking would change if they just looked down and tried. Because your nose has been there all your life, it's just something you've gotten used to seeing without paying any eye-dropping focused attention.

Human nature not tempered by turn the other cheek and/or love thy neighbor is going to be hell on wheels. Somebody does you wrong, there's serious consequences and repercussions that may or may not involve 911. That's just how most humans think outside what's considered a Christian approach to dispute resolution.

Consider 1 Corinthians 2:14-16:

> "But the natural man receiveth not the things of the Spirit of God: for they are foolishness unto him: neither can he know them, because they are spiritually discerned. But he that is spiritual judgeth all things, yet he himself is judged of no man. For who hath known the mind of the Lord, that he may instruct him? But we have the mind of Christ."

It's just a "natural man" and woman thing to slap the "s" as in "smack" out of someone who slaps you first.

Does Satan have the mind of Christ? Subsequently, Revelation 12:13-17 doesn't make any logical sense in the absence of human nature.

If you relocate to another city, do you go there looking to raise hell on the new job? Start a fight with the new neighbors? Kick the neighborhood dog or poison the alley cat? With the exception of being a sociopathic warrior looking for a battlefield, it's not even a natural man thing to go off the chain that quick. Even when it comes to human nature, acting out usually requires being provoked.

On the other hand, if you have an ax to grind with your boss or neighbor, a confrontational mindset from jump is to be expected. Human nature dictates to the point of outright demands attitude if nothing else if you've been crossed.

Immediately wrong from jump, Satan, a.k.a. the dragon and his angels, are about the business of violently turning and tearing it up here on planet earth. And again, according to Revelation 12, verses 13 and 17 the target is the "woman" and the "man child."

Melodically put, *Who's That Lady*? Revelation 12:1 mentions her first:

"And there appeared a great wonder in heaven; a woman
clothed with the sun, and the moon under her feet, and
upon her head a crown of twelve stars."

Haven't we all watched enough TV to know that the best way to unscramble any mystery is to start with what you think you know first in order to lay a foundation? Once you have a foundation, you've got something to build on. Since prophecy is metaphorical, just what would a "woman clothed with the sun, and the moon under her feet, and upon her head a crown of twelve stars" be in a real world context?

Well, look up. The only context where you have both the sun and the moon is right above your head. So, who's that "woman?" Well, look down. You're standing on her. She's called Mother Earth. Isn't the earth metaphorically "clothed with the sun?" Don't the sun's rays blanket the earth?

Metaphorically put, isn't the moon under the earth's feet? Yes, earth's gravity keeps the moon where it is. General Science 101: without earth's gravitational pull, the moon would go flying off into space. That means the earth has the moon on lockdown.

What about this "crown of twelve stars?" Well, the month you were born is one of them. The twelve stars are the 12 constellations of the Zodiac, which represent the 12 months of a calendar year. Twelve is a very spiritual number in the Bible. There are the 12 Patriarchs as well as the 12 Disciples. Unquestionably, as far as "crown" goes, twelve is a royal number.

Now, there are folks who will tell you this number means this and that number symbolizes that. Well, whoopty-doo. They've probably made a fortune playing the lottery and other games of chance. If not, *what the problem is?*

The numbers either referenced or brought to view in this book are straight out of the Book – the *Holy Bible*. When numbers show up in the Bible, they don't appear there by chance. That means in the event numbers such as 1, 3, 6, 7, 12, or even 13 are cited in *WMD*, their reference is not based on *Aunt Esther's Dream Book*. They are tied to the Bible, and the Bible is employed in the interpretation.

Who's the "man child" Mother Earth brings forth? Verse 5 says this man child will be caught up to God and will rule all nations.

The only man that was born a child is Adam. Adam was made from the "dust of the ground," which is earth. So metaphorically, the woman (earth) brought forth a man child (Adam).

Was Adam caught up to God, and to a throne to rule all nations? When you read Luke 3:23 all the way through to 3:38 you end with the following: "Adam, who was the son of God."

When Revelation speaks of the woman bringing forth a man child to rule all nations, it has to start with Adam. If Adam had not been created, there would be no earthborn Jesus as the son of God. Both Adam and Jesus were the "sons of God." That means, literally speaking, even though it's Jesus who sits on the throne to "rule all nations," Adam is the figurative representation because it was through the lineage of Adam that the Christ child Jesus came into the world.

Jesus Christ's roots are traced directly to Adam. Subsequently, "she being with child cried" and "pained to be delivered" makes it clear that

Satan tried to destroy the earth to prevent Adam from being created. This fact, of course, answers the question what on earth happened between Genesis 1:1 and Genesis 1:2. There was a method to Satan's madness you typically don't find being taught in Sunday school.

Consider Revelation 12:6. When it comes to the 1,260 days, Bible scholars offer many theories. Be those as they may, the only theory relevant to this theory is one that correlates with what was happening on earth at the time. If we apply the one day as a thousand years computation illustrative of 2 Peter 3:8, then 1,260 days become 1,260,000 years. And, 1.2 million years ago earth was exactly in the middle of the Pleistocene Epoch.

What's interesting about this as far as Biblical prophecy and relevance, the Pleistocene marked earth's last glacial period, or what's incorrectly yet commonly referred to as the end of the Ice Age. And here's where evolution and the Bible cross paths in somewhat agreement. Evolutionists maintain human beings or Homo sapiens evolved into their present form during the Pleistocene. But rather, what Biblical prophecy reveals the Pleistocene to be is a creation event.

If you believe the word of God that says man was created, that creation had to occur at some point in time. That some point in time had to occur at a time that is in sequential harmony with all of the other earth species that man could not coexist with. Mankind would not and could not have dominion over a Jurassic Park teeming with dinosaurs. During the Pleistocene Epoch, there was flourishing animal and sea life as well as major extinction events brought on by major climatic shifts in the temperature. So, herein is what's intriguing to consider. If Satan in fact began his assault on the earth right after the Jurassic period, which would have been at the end of the Cretaceous Period, the 1,260,000 reprieve would have occurred during the Pleistocene Epoch. And based on what geological science confirms independent of any religious persuasion, the geologic time scale is consistent with the Bible.

Incorporated into that geologic time scale, we know that the "great red dragon" is Satan. Revelation 12 tells us that Genesis 1:2 is that point in time where the devil tried to destroy this planet (65 million years ago).

When Revelation 12:6 reads, "and the woman fled into the wilderness where she had a place prepared by God," on that time scale we're looking at 1.2 million years ago. Now, is it just a coincidence that Revelation 12:12, Isaiah 14:12, along with 1.2 million years ago, and Genesis 1:2 altogether reference Satan's fall and the consequences and repercussions it caused. That's some kind of one-two punch to be dismissed as just some kinda numerical quirk!

In accordance with Revelation 12:6, the "place that God prepared" to give the earth a breather from Satan's great wrath was the Ice Age. The Ice Age was a breath of fresh air for the planet. The Pleistocene Ice Age "chilled" everyone and everything out including Satan. There were glaciers all over the world, including the highland plateaus and mountains of Ethiopia and Kenya in East Africa.

In this regard, Job 1:6-12 provides a significant sidebar:

> "Now there was a day when the sons of God came to present themselves before the LORD, and Satan came also among them. And the LORD said unto Satan, Whence comest thou? Then Satan answered the LORD, and said, From going to and fro in the earth, and from walking up and down in it. And the LORD said unto Satan, Hast thou considered my servant Job, that there is none like him in the earth, a perfect and an upright man, one that feareth God, and escheweth evil? Then Satan answered the LORD, and said, Doth Job fear God for nought? Hast not thou made an hedge about him, and about his house, and about all that he hath on every side? thou hast blessed the work of his hands, and his substance is increased in the land. But put forth thine hand now, and touch all that he hath, and he will curse thee to thy face. And the LORD said unto Satan, Behold, all that he hath is in thy power; only upon himself put not forth thine hand. So Satan went forth from the presence of the LORD."

First, we find God being in communication with Satan. And since Job's name is brought up, we know that the point in time is after the fall of Adam and Eve. Now, even though Lucifer is no longer "anointed" and has become the devil by doing all that he's done, God has still welcomed him with open arms into the mix. If there ever was a "smh" (shaking my head) moment, this is it. Here is an example of the "peace of God, which passeth all understanding" (Philippians 4:7). Here is the "mind of Christ." Even though Lucifer has started a universal war, there in Job we find God being cordial.

"Come on in; have a sit down."

Even though Lucifer, now Satan, had tore the roof off this mother we call earth, we find God saying, "*Wassup?*" That's amazing grace! Human nature does not allow you to invite anyone to the party who has tried to turn all of your friends against you, destroyed your belongings, and is still trying to kill you. When it comes to a foe: a cup of coffee, having a beer, tea and crumpets? Don't even think about it.

Second, ponder the thought that this meeting was neither in heaven nor on earth. In accordance with Revelation 12:8, Satan was expelled from Heaven. The scripture plainly says, "Neither was their place found anymore in heaven." If this meeting was in heaven, it would be a Biblical contradiction.

Certainly, this meeting wasn't taking place on earth. When Satan was asked where he'd come from, the reply was earth. If this meeting was on earth, and Satan was confined to earth, God wouldn't have asked the obvious and the rhetorical wouldn't have made any sense. When a prisoner shows up on the Governor's doorstep, the gubernatorial first question is not "*whence comest thou?*" The logically more appropriate is "*What's your butt doing here?*"

Third, even more telling is Satan's reply all by itself. There's no ambiguity in the response. Such exactness suggests earth's proximity to the meeting's location. If Satan was roaming the universe or "the second heaven's" hundreds of billions of galaxies and planets don't you think he would have included a zip code?

Earth's position in the Milky Way is obscure to put it mildly. When beholding the magnitude of the optics, the mere mention of earth relative its place in this galaxy alone is infinitesimal in the absence of propinquity. If you were asked where you'd been, it would be analogous to you responding with the name of a street as opposed to naming city, state, or country if the place was hundreds to thousands of miles away. If you go to a meeting in Atlanta and you're asked where you came in from, and your answer is *Uhuru*; unless you are somewhere near the United Republic of Tanzania, the City of Dar es Salaam, the person asking the question wouldn't know *Uhuru* is a street. They'd probably think you'd been at the house of the Star Trek Communications Officer, Lieutenant Uhura.

Granted, God is God and fully capable of knowing exactly where that needle is in a haystack; still, there's a logic factor that goes along with God given insight, intelligence, wisdom, and plain ole common sense. All things considered, the cosmic Q & A suggests earth is close by relatively speaking and relative to this conversation.

A phrase that's elucidating: "*If the mountain will not come to Muhammad, then Muhammad must go to the mountain.*" *The Phrase Finder* meaning: "If one's will does not prevail, one must submit to an alternative."

Referencing the "dragon and his angels," Revelation 12:8 reads, "*And prevailed not.*" Indisputably, Satan's will did not "prevail." This "sons of God" meeting was staged at a location that permitted Satan's attendance should he wish to "submit."

One more time again, isn't this consistent with the personality and presence of God? Even when it comes to not only being a devil, but the devil, the kingdom of God is gracious.

Back to the sidebar; in reading Job 1:6-12, LORD is referred to seven (7) times. Revisiting Philippians 2:11: "And that every tongue should confess that Jesus Christ is Lord, to the glory of God the Father." Indisputably again, Satan was having this conversation with Jesus Christ. And, since we are reading about it in the book of Job, it was happening prior to the birth of Jesus Christ. This means Satan was dialoguing with Michael. And, Michael/Jesus has permitted Lucifer/Satan to show-up. The "*mountain,*" as it were, in this one case, came near to "*Muhammad.*" Satan was given a chance to come correct. But instead of seizing *"an alternative"* opportunity, the devil wanted to show off. Here is that 1 Timothy 3:16 "mystery of Godliness" that yin-yangs that 2 Thessalonians 2:7 "mystery of iniquity."

Now, since we see Satan being at a Godly meeting as a devil, we know once-upon-a time he was at Godly meetings as an unfallen angel. Subsequently, as the unfallen angel Lucifer, Satan was obviously privy to the business plans of God. Pointing to Genesis 1:26, the question is often pondered regarding to whom exactly is "us" and "our" referring? Many scholars hold it as a reference to Father, Son, and Holy Ghost or Spirit – that which is called the trinity. Again, since the word of God often has dual application, if you see God as three entities or three personalities in accordance with traditional hermeneutic and exegesis interpretations, so be it. However, Job 1 and 2 make a strong case that the plurality indicative of the words "us" and "our" may best be interpreted as an editorial "we."

The Preamble to the Constitution reads, *"We the People."* Even though it was written by committee of principally two or three, we know "we" principally represents more than two or three. Genesis 1:27 makes it clear that God created man. And, John 1:1-14 makes it crystal exactly who God is so there's really no real reason to trip on an object pronoun and possessive adjective.

The bottom line, as Lucifer, Satan knew that at some point in time a new species would be created in the image of God and placed on planet earth. The devil knew that new creature would be called "man" and named "Adam." And the fact that Adam sounds a whole lot like atom presupposes angel or extraterrestrial knowledgeability of a biogenetic connection.

Lucifer was no dumb angel. He didn't have to read any fig leaves or make any educated guesses when it came to planet earth and what was in store. Drawing from Ezekiel 28:13, he'd been there before. When it came to the secrets of God, he probably knew just enough to fill in the blanks. And based on how things played in the Garden, Lucifer hitting earth as Satan didn't cause him any brain damage. The devil showed up with a plan to counter God's *Master* plan.

This begs several questions.

Number one: does the "us" and "our" of Genesis 1:27 include the same "sons of God" brought to view in Job 1 and 2? Since Adam is termed a "son of God," these sons could include all sentient beings created in the image of God. Genesis 1:26-27 neither asserts nor implies that mankind's creation in the image and likeness of God is universally exclusive. It is possible and highly probable that there are other life forms in the universe that are not called man that are created in the "image and after the likeness."

Faced with the fact that man, as in Adam, as in being composed of atoms that are carbon (a key component of life on earth), what about non-earth life wherein the atomic structure isn't carbon-based? Are non-carbon creatures barred from being Godly? Are the certain unalienable rights endowed by the Creator only extended to those aliens that have a certain molecular makeup? Call it discrimination based on the number of protons, neutrons, and electrons respecting individual body chemistry. Seriously, the mere fact that there are aliens/extraterrestrials called Grays speaks volumes. Even when it comes to entities that aren't of this world, there's still a plantation mentality and pathological obsession to use skin color as a method of classification. Why is there this need on the part of some people to go there?

Number two: does Genesis 1:27 read angels only?

Number three: is it all about the Trinity? Is God talking to himself as Father, Son, and Holy Spirit? A whole lot of folks accord Genesis 1:27 such a meaning. It's strictly *Me*, *Myself*, and *I* as *One*.

When considering all of the above, consider Job 15:8 when God poses the question, "Hast thou heard the secret of God." It's not only rhetorical; it suggests that there are secrets of God that may have been heard. "Let us make man in our image, after our likeness" is obviously one such not-so-secret secret. A secret is simply not an isolated one single human being secret if it's "our" secret or a secret presented for the possible hearing of others, be they human or not.

Being party to those not-so-secret secrets as an "anointed cherub," what does the devil do? Just as Revelation 12:4 alludes, he takes a

Minority Report (2002) approach. He attempts to destroy earth before mankind's "man child" Adam can become the progenitor of a savior in the ultimate form of Jesus Christ. Through foreknowledge, precognition, whatever prescience you choose to apply, Satan knew that man would be required to show loyalty to either the kingdom of God or the princedom of Satan.

Satan's idea to test Job was probably a carryover from the Garden. Drawing directly from Job and the manner in which Satan's challenge was posed, God had to take that bet. This means even though the serpent was subtle, and Satan may have snuck into the Garden of Eden as a snake, the kingdom of God had already peeped the game. The "sons of God" meeting and the saga of Job is there to tell all that Adam and Eve's fall didn't catch God sleeping, off guard or by surprise. It had to go down just the way it did. The omniscience of God knew it.

But do you think Satan had any doubt regarding Adam and Eve's failure? He knew they didn't have a snowball's chance in hell of success. How did the devil know? Well, believe it or not, God showed his hand and thereby tipped Satan from jump. Properly understood, Genesis 1:3-4 undeniably establishes the declaration made in John 3:16: "For God so loved the world, that he gave his only begotten son, that whosoever believeth in him should not perish, but have everlasting life."

Genesis 1:3, not Genesis 3:15, is the first revelation and foreshadowing of a coming savior.

Have difficulty accepting that as a fact? Well, there's Matthew 4:16:

"The people which sat in darkness saw great light; and to them which sat in the region and shadow of death light is sprung up."

No doubt about it, seeing the end from the beginning, God knew Adam and Eve were going to fail even before they were created. But in order to give us a chance to get it right, he had to give them a chance to get it wrong.

Indeed, "in the beginning was the Word." When God said in Genesis 1:3, "Let there be light," that was both the incarnation and introduction that Michael the archangel would have to become Jesus Christ the Savior. That's why we're told in Matthew 4:16, the people who sat in darkness saw "great light."

That GREAT LIGHT was at the very beginning. It wasn't a reference to some kind of pinpoint flash going super nova. It was a spiritual light that promised the possibility of mankind's eternal life. And, in direct accord with John 1:14, it was also a portent of "the word made flesh." That's what made this light great.

The fact that Satan was tipped to the plan of salvation is furthered by Genesis 1:9-13. With the earth totally covered by water, on the "third day" the planet brings forth life. However, before doing so, earth rises up out of the water. Essentially, this is a type of baptism. It's a rebirth. And, because it occurs on the third day, it also symbolizes the resurrection of Jesus Christ.

Think about it; light shines, it doesn't spring up. The terminology is incongruous with physical reality. Just as hearing a rainbow is inconsonant, the same applies. When Matthew 4:16 says "region," it's talking about earth. The "shadow of death" is pointing to Genesis 1:2 with direct reference to "darkness upon the face of the deep." Undeniably, shadow and darkness are metaphors for Satan.

Light springing up prophesizes mankind's salvation. When "dry land appears" (Genesis 1:9) rising up out of the water the symbolism is compelling when viewed alongside Isaiah 53:2:

"For he shall grow up before him as a tender plant, and as a root out of dry ground."

The great light springing up is a metaphor of salvation that is rooted in Scripture from the very start.

Consider the following in brevity: 1 Peter 1:20; "Who verily was foreordained before the foundation of the world." Ephesians 1:14; "According as he hath chosen us in him before the foundation of the world." John 17:24; "Father, I will that they also, whom thou hast given me, be with me where I am; that they may behold my glory, which thou hast given me: for thou lovedst me before the foundation of the world." Revelation 13:8; "Father, I will that they also, whom thou hast given me, be with me where I am; that they may behold my glory, which thou hast given me:

for thou lovedst me before the foundation of the world." Matthew 25:34; "Then shall the King say unto them on his right hand, Come, ye blessed of my Father, inherit the kingdom prepared for you from the foundation of the world." Revelation 17:8: "The beast that thou sawest was, and is not; and shall ascend out of the bottomless pit, and go into perdition: and they that dwell on the earth shall wonder, whose names were not written in the book of life from the foundation of the world." Matthew 13:35; "That it might be fulfilled which was spoken by the prophet, saying, I will open my mouth in parables; I will utter things which have been kept secret from the foundation of the world."

Now, it's significant to note that all of these passages read "foundation of the world" and not "foundation of the earth." The reason is obvious. Genesis 1:1 references the "foundation of the earth." All hell didn't bust loose until Genesis 1:2. Mankind's salvation was not an issue until Satan's fall. Subsequently, Jesus Christ did not suffer from the foundation of the earth, but rather from the foundation of the world. And as brought to view in the previous chapter, the "world" being referenced by all of these scriptural passages is the "new world order" established by the princedom of Satan. This is why Jesus refers to the devil as the "prince of this world." Satan is prince of the "world" he has established on planet earth. Subsequently, if talk about a "new world order" is not talked about in an "old world" context, do those talking really know what they are talking about?

This fact is driven home by the words of Jesus Christ:

"Hereafter I will not talk much with you: for the prince of this world cometh, and hath nothing in me."
— JOHN 14:30

The bottom line; Jesus ain't talkin' much cause it ain't much more to be said. It's "speak to the hand." Whenever you tell somebody, *"Hey, it's your world,"* you know what time it is and they do to. Therefore, if we as human beings can connect the prophetic dots, it's reasonable to presume that angelic beings as extraterrestrials can do so and did do so as well. The handwriting was all over the wall from Day 3. It wasn't a question of Adam's and Eve's foul-up. It was just a question of how foul it was gonna be.

Interestingly, Jeremiah wrote about a voice being heard in Ramah; "Rachel weeping for her children (Jeremiah 31:15). Why the tears? It was the same old song with the same meaning; Satan trying to thwart the will of God by imposing his. The prophecy of Jeremiah foretold Herod's attempt to murder Jesus as a child.

And where did Herod get that idea? Satan's first attempted murder of Jesus targeted Adam as "man child." Trying to change the course of history by prior restraint isn't new. And it's naïve to believe targeting either individual or ancestry has stopped. Again, movies and TV shows that present such plot lines aren't created in a vacuum. Again, the question to be contemplated: *Is art imitating life or life art?*

The Bible is a "book of life." Because it's spiritual, there isn't a story or plot imaginable that can't be enveloped within its artistry. Even though it remains one of the bestselling books of all times, it also remains one of the least accepted intellectually. If you place your left hand on the Bible and don't honestly believe the book underneath is *the truth, the whole truth, and nothing but the truth* you might as well have that hand on a magazine. Your affirmation will fly in court, or as an oath of office. But in the sight of God, your vow is vain.

Isaiah 53:1 asks: "Who hath believed our report? The Bible is that report for the minority who can honestly raise their hand.

5 EVE OF DESTRUCTION

"And the serpent said unto the woman, Ye shall not surely die."
—GENESIS 3:4

When Satan as serpent created the most infamous love triangle of all time, angels called Cherubim brandishing a flaming sword were posted at the entrance to the Garden of Eden.

Why? Do you think Adam was going to try to get back inside the park?

Adam was a scary kind of fellow. Genesis 3:10 says after he got caught with his pants up, he hid. Then, the very next words out of his mouth put the blame on his woman.

"And the man said, The woman whom thou gavest to be with me, she gave me of the tree, and I did eat." — GENESIS 3:12

In other words, "The woman made me do it." Dude couldn't even say, "My wife" or even call her by name. But maybe that's because he didn't even give her one until Genesis 3:20. In Genesis 2:20, we find Adam giving names to everything but the being he's sleeping with; she's just a woman. Imagine having a dog you just refer to as 'dog.'

Don't think for one second Satan didn't pick up on the fact that Adam was a bit on the lame side as far as street smarts. So when you stop to really think about it, is it all that surprising that things went down the way they did? The devil can't read minds, but he's a master at reading actions.

Adam and Eve got played. While homeboy is watching the bears, lions, falcons, cardinals, hawks, eagles, orioles, blue jays, tigers, cubs, marlins, dolphins, and seahawks, Eve is wandering around the Garden all by herself. The woman didn't have any friends – not a single soul to talk to other than her man. So here comes Satan as serpent singing, "*Hey There Lonely Girl.*"

Seriously, you don't have to be a *Sigmund* or a *Sigma* to figure this thing out. When there's no one around to kick it with and you're just there, you're an easy target for the first thing that comes along. Genesis 3:1 identifies the first thing that came along as a "beast of the field."

When you've got a lone-jones you start hearing things; listening and talking back to things that don't make sense in the real world. Eve knew snakes don't talk and carry on a sequential conversation. But thanks to her boo, as in "bone of my bones," she became emotionally vulnerable. Girlfriend was a train wreck waiting to happen. And Satan was right there to play Casey Jones.

Consider the subtext of the line Satan uses:

> "For God doth know that in the day ye eat thereof, then your eyes shall be opened, and ye shall be as gods, knowing good and evil." — GENESIS 3:5

Open to what?

Eve and Satan in the form of a serpent had time for a very long conversation that didn't find Adam saying, *"Pardon my interruption."* Also obvious is the fact that after that conversation, Eve felt that she was lacking and needed some smarts.

Let's examine Satan as serpent. There are some who theorize that the serpent was actually a Reptilian alien. There are cave murals that depict these supposed creatures. Some indigenous cultures where these rock drawings are found refer to these things as *Lizard People*. Since we're talking aliens and extraterrestrials, could that which the Bible calls serpent actually be a reptilian humanoid?

Don't think so. The Bible says "serpent" and deems it a "beast of the field." A reptilian humanoid that stands upright like a man is not serpentine. Mother-wit suggests that a serpent is something like a snake; nothing like *Swamp Thing* (1982).

Did this serpent have legs? Probably is a reasonable presumption since Genesis 3:14 exclaims, "upon thy belly shalt thou go." If this serpent didn't have legs it was already on its belly. Subsequently, it wouldn't be "cursed above all cattle, and above every beast of the field" if it didn't already have something in contemporaneous commonality. Since cattle and field animals neither talk in a human language nor look like what's called snakes, the only characteristic both species could have most likely shared is legs. And, since no snake has ever been found with legs, the curse since the Garden remains in effect.

But, if in fact this serpent had legs, is there any way to surmise its realistic appearance? Again, if you buy the Bible, the Bible is its own interpreter. Isn't it interesting that Revelation 12 refers to the devil and Satan as a "dragon?"

Google a picture of the Komodo dragon. Even though it's a species of lizard, lizards are about the closest thing to a snake that can be found in the animal kingdom. Certainly, when it comes to the fantasy image of a dragon, snakes and lizards have a combination of similarities. The obvious being both are indisputably serpentine. Therefore, employment of the word serpent etymologically encompasses a creature that could reasonably have the appearance of a snake and a lizard making dragon a crossbreed term for both. Consequently, this suggests the conclusion that the Garden of Eden serpent is Satan isn't reached in a metaphorical vacuum. It's literarily confirmed by the Revelation 12:9 references to dragon, serpent, devil, and Satan all in the same breath thus giving Eve's "Dr. Dolittle" abilities physical reality as well.

Now, the Dr. Doolittle concept is very interesting when it comes to language and the Garden of Eden. Was the serpent speaking Eve's language, or was Eve speaking serpent? Since both were communicating with each other and were simultaneously being understood, there's more going on here than meets eye or ear. And, what's happening ain't farfetched when technological considerations are introduced in lieu of supernatural alien abilities?

If you are into sci-fi beyond Star Trek and the like, Stephen Hawking is a name you might know. If not, Google him. For those in the know, how was Hawking able to talk?

Well, he used a speech-generating device (SGD) coupled with a speech synthesizer. But, Hawking's thing is old school compared to here and now. Right off Star Trek, a Universal Translator (UT) featuring forty languages has been introduced. All you need are earbuds and a smartphone, and the starship Enterprise has nothing on you!

Bottom line, if human beings can boldly go where no man has gone before as far as speech, where do you think an extraterrestrial entity called Satan can go? But, failure to see the devil as an ET and fallen angels as aliens makes the Bible a book of stories that are difficult to grasp as having real world reality basis.

God asked Adam in Genesis 3:11, "Who told thee that thou wast naked," a similar question can be asked Eve: "*Who told thee that thou wast dumb?*"

Let's put holier-than-thou aside and keep it proverbially real. We have no sure bet what information Satan "opened" Eve up to. But we can reasonably speculate.

Genesis 3:6 reads in part:

> "And when the woman saw that the tree was good for food, and that it was pleasant to the eyes, and a tree to be desired to make one wise."

Wise to what?

For argument's sake, let's just say Satan didn't step to this woman in the form of a snake for casual conversation only. Intelligently ask yourself WWSD (What Would Satan Do)? The devil has already put the idea in Eve's head that there's a lot she doesn't know. And along with that line, his follow up was probably, "*And your man is a square.*"

Eve's response, "*What you mean?*"

Satan's reply, "*What you say!*"

And then it was on; show time at the hands of *Apollo*.

So, here's Eve sitting buck naked under "the tree of knowledge of good and evil" with her legs wide open talking to the devil who has shape-shifted into the form of a snake.

Do you need a road map?

The devil first got Eve to disobey the words of God by grabbing some fruit off the tree and eating it. Strike one.

In all probability, Satan then showed Eve underneath the same tree what she'd been missing in her relationship with Adam. According to the Bible, at this particular time there were only two people on the planet. What on earth was there a pressing need to be open and wise to? Better homes and gardening? Just what do you think Eve didn't know that she needed to know given the reality that her world was so limited and her lifestyle so simple?

Additionally, we can go with the tree being good for food and pleasant to the eyes, but where is this "desire" word coming from to describe a tree? The text doesn't read a fruit to be desired, but a tree. When's the last time you desired a tree; Christmas?

There's something missing in this narrative. Again, strictly for argument's sake, let's call what's missing a stronger motive. The behaviors of Eve, Satan, Adam, and God are interesting to put it mildly if Adam and Eve's disobedience was Satan's lone wolf motivation.

But before going there, for all those who can't get past the intimation that a sex act was performed on Eve by the serpent, let's deal with that first. Let's look at sex being a wile of the devil from a contemporaneous approach.

If you have a daughter (age is irrelevant), and daddy's little girl tells you that she met this man in the park. And this man is interested in her mind? How far are you gonna go with the "man in the park" story before your mind says, "*Whoa!*" If you read between the lines with just a little bit of father-wit, game doesn't have to know game to see suspect written all over that man-in-the-park's face. Rather than daddy's little girl, same applies if it's mommy's dearest.

Since Adam and Eve were the only human beings on earth, Eve had no concept of desire. She already had everything that she knew anything about. There was nothing for her to desire.

If you don't speak Yoruba, the word "owo" means nothing to you. You can't even begin to wrap your head around "owo" unless someone tells you it means money in the African language Yoruba. Only after making the etymological connection with something you can physically relate to does desire as a concept have meaning. You can only desire you some owo if you know what owo is. Otherwise, being offered some owo draws a "*Huh?*"

The devil speaking through the serpent convinced Eve that if she ate fruit from the tree that her "desires" would be awakened.

Again, desires for what?

Time to cut to the chase; contemporaneously applied, does masturbation happen without the sensation being aroused first? Rubbing the tip of your own nose does nothing other than scratch an itch if you're a typical type person. Usually, once that itch is scratched that's as far as you're willing to take it. Your "desire" to do anything else, as far as your nose goes (if you're a normal type person) is satisfied. There's no neurological wiring connecting the tip of your nose with the tip of any other appendage on your body. There's no biological hook up. There's no physiological reason for compulsive behavioral nose rubbing addiction.

For all we know, God probably hadn't connected Adam and Eve's sexual sensors. Eve's sexual appetite may have been purposely blocked and Adam's penis on lockdown in terms of blood flow.

Even though these two individuals were adults, they had childhood innocence. Just as a child has to physiologically grow into puberty and then psychologically deal with it, the same held true for earth's first couple. Even though Genesis 1:28 places sexual intercourse squarely on the table, God was not ready for Adam or Eve to come out of the sandbox swinging from the chandeliers. Drawing from Genesis 4:1, Adam and Eve didn't "know" each other like that until after their fall.

Analogous to the date who can't wait, Eve was slicked, tricked, and rushed into a situation that could contemporaneously be viewed as statutory rape. If Adam was a "man child," Eve was in essence a "grown ass" little girl. And, since Satan specializes in half-truths, in all likelihood Eve was told by the serpent that the tree bore passion fruit. That made it "a tree to be desired to make one wise" to sexual intercourse.

Even when faced with undeniable plausibility, few want to deal with the possibility that sex had anything to do with the Eden story. But, because there's "war in heaven" that's now being waged on earth, do you really think an extraterrestrial called the devil is going to take anything off the table? That saying, "all is fair in love and war" probably originated with Satan.

Eve loved Adam and that made her a war game!

When Eve was deceived to bite, chew, and "swallow," both her eyes and her body were opened to a close encounter of the sexual kind. When entertaining this theory, how elucidating Satan's words in Genesis 3:5 become and bear repeating:

> "For God doth know, that in the day ye eat thereof, then your eyes shall be opened, and ye shall be as gods, knowing good and evil."

In the Bible, the one word that connotes sexual intercourse is "knew?" In the Bible, the one word that connotes evil is "Satan?" When the devil tells Eve that she will "know evil," what's he literally saying Biblically?

The only evil in the universe for Eve to know was Satan himself. Through an illicit sex act, Satan seized the opportunity for Eve to know him intimately.

Further, there's the devil's assertion, "ye shall be as gods?"

Well, the only way for human beings to be as gods is to do what God does. And, the only thing God does that human beings can now do is create sentient life forms that can grasp the concept of God.

Once Adam and Eve became acquainted with sexual intercourse, they immediately became "as gods." The ability to create or reproduce beings that have a "living soul" makes you a god (Genesis 2:7). Human beings are the only animals having the mental capacity to accept God's plan for salvation. Salvation is immortality. Immortality is "living." A "living soul" is an immortal soul.

Let's pause for a moment and ponder. First, what is a soul? Does your dog, cat, parakeet have a soul? Does an ant, spider, bedbug, cockroach have a soul? All animal classes have something in them that causes sentience. Sentience, by definition, is the capacity to feel, perceive, or experience subjectively. A cockroach runs when a light comes on because it has sentience. Birds fly away when startled because they have sentience. A dog barks whenever it's provoked because it has sentience. Fish are caught on a baited hook, not a dry one, because of sentience. The fact that a butterfly can float and a bee can sting tells you that there's something immaterial or spiritual in all creatures that endows them with sentient capability. All animal or animated life in and of itself has sentient capability.

Scientifically we really, really, really don't know where life comes from or where it goes when it leaves the body. By faith, we accept the word of God that it is an endowment or gift from God.

Now, for those who argue that the ants or roaches they've squashed, and the deer they've killed for sport didn't have souls, intelligently ponder just why Genesis 2:7 qualifies the word soul with the word "living?" What differentiates a living soul from a soul?

Newsflash! It's immortality.

When a plane crashes and there are no survivors, the news report typically refers to the number of people on board as "souls." The report does not use "living" as a prefix. The reason is twofold obvious. One-fold, pertinent the point, the eternal destiny of those deceased passengers cannot be reported with any earthly certainty. This is why Romans 10:6 reads, "But the righteousness which is of faith speaketh on this wise, Say not in thine heart, Who shall ascend into heaven? (that is, to bring Christ down from above.)" Subsequently, "souls" is as far as that report can go.

Consider the following:

> "Jesus said unto her, I am the resurrection, and the life: he that believeth in me, though he were dead, yet shall he live: And whosoever liveth and believeth in me shall never die. Believest thou this?" — JOHN 11:25-26

Does your dog, cat, or parakeet believe in Jesus? How about that ant, spider, bedbug, cockroach, butterfly, or deer? Does any terrestrial creature native to this planet other than human beings have the sentient capability to either believe or reject a belief in Jesus Christ? Of course, the simple answer is no. The ability to believe in God and accept is what makes a "living soul." The ability to believe in Jesus as the plan of salvation provides the only opportunity for a soul's immortality. That's if you buy the Bible. If you don't, then buy your own or someone else's theory and bet your life on it.

Do you love your pet? Well, since your pet doesn't or didn't have the mindset to accept Jesus Christ, you are the only opportunity for that pet to gain immortality and become a "living soul."

Where in the Bible does it say that? That dogs and cats go to heaven? Well, try reading between the lines:

> "Jesus said unto him, If thou canst believe, all things are possible to him that believeth." — MARK 9:23

Jesus doesn't say your pet has to believe; he says you do!

Where folks get it all twisted (Genesis 2:7) is their failure to understand that "became" is a linking verb. It requires either an adjective or noun complement. By definition, "became" means to start to be something different than what already happens to be.

How many men who "became" fathers turned into deadbeat dads? Just because you "became" engaged doesn't mean you got married! Starting out as a "living soul" doesn't mean you stay a living soul. Adam started out as a "living soul." But, Genesis 5:5 tells the world what happened. Adam believed serpent/Satan instead of God/Jesus and "he died." Satan pushed the idea that "living" meant *"here and now"* – not *"always and forever."* The devil sold the concept of soul and "living soul" being one in the same and unfortunately Adam bought it.

The stark reality of John 11:25-26 is the Christian Biblical fact that if you don't believe in Jesus you are a "dead man or woman walking." And, like it or not, this explains exactly where Jesus was coming from when he said: "Let the dead bury their dead." — LUKE 9:60. Jesus was referring to "souls" who had rejected the "living soul" aspect of their physical and spiritual creation. In other words, they were zombies!

So, do non-human animals have a soul as distinguished from a "living soul?" For sure, they have something. For simplicity's sake, the answer is a resounding yes.

Once Adam and Eve got slicked and tricked, they were no longer living souls. They were *"The Walking Dead"* (series premier). Contrary to Genesis 2:17, Satan convinced the couple that they would continue being "living souls," but again, Genesis 5:5 is a testament that Satan was wrong.

Were Adam and Eve given the plan of salvation wherein they could repent and once again become "living souls?" Yes, drawn from Genesis 5:2 they were "blessed." However, the ramifications of Satan being first to turn Eve on and out still has to be considered. By implication, this means

Adam in his primordial state as a living soul was a virgin. And, if Adam was a virgin, who do you think opened his eyes by rocking his world?

> "She took of the fruit thereof, and did eat, and gave also unto her husband with her; and he did eat. And the eyes of them both were opened, and they knew that they were naked; and they sewed fig leaves together, and made themselves aprons." — GENESIS 3:6

Strike two.

Whether you want to accept it or not, it is what it is. The giveaway that sex was involved as an eye-opening experience is the words, "and they knew they were naked." In order to know nakedness, they had to be shown in a manner that enabled them to embrace the concept of nakedness.

Does your dog or cat know it is naked? Even if you dress your pet in clothing made for dogs and cats neither animal has the mental capacity to grasp the concept. The only way for your pet to know it's naked is for you to tell it. And since you can't speak dog or cat, that's impossible to do. This is why God in Genesis 3:11 asked Adam, "Who told thee thou wast naked?" Only by having capability to communicate via a mutually understood language can abstract concepts be grasped and understood. That's a fact that separates sentient beings from dogs, cats, frogs, birds, and grasshoppers. Sentient life forms have the mental capacity to grasp abstract concepts through reasoning.

Your ability to figure shit out is the "God Particle" that was genetically placed in the human brain.

Did you just pass the test?

You did if you immediately knew that "shit" as used in the above sentence was not a reference to physical manure, feces, or bodily waste. Your mental capacity to grasp the concept of "shit" being complex situations or negative circumstances is a prime feature of being a "living soul." You have to have "soul" in order to keep your "cool" when it comes to dealing with some serious "manure!"

Get the point? In other words, your instantaneous ability to know that the word "manure" was verbally inappropriate given the context of that sentence, again, is the "God Particle" in action. This is why it was necessary for the serpent to speak in the same language as Eve. This is why the serpent talked.

But here is where it gets deeper. Even though the serpent could talk, the fruit on the *tree of knowledge of good and evil* was a language barrier. As long as Adam and Eve obeyed God by leaving that fruit alone, they would have never been able to understand the language of Satan even though the serpent as Satan could speak the same language as them. Again, just like the word *owo*. Even though you can say *owo* and thereby speak Yoruba, that's as far as it goes. You have a one-word Yoruba vocabulary. However, not until your mind is "opened" to form concepts will you "know" exactly what it is your saying.

The inability to understand what you're saying in any language is always a language barrier. You may be able to speak it, but if you don't "know" it you're intellectually blocked.

With regards to the Garden of Eden, the language barrier wasn't intellectual, it was spiritual. Adam and Eve had a God connection. They both knew the will of God. Disobedience to the will of God turned a pipeline to God into a party line by spiritually exposing them to Satan.

God's selection of fruit as a test of obedience couldn't be more appropriate given the symbolism inherent when it comes to speech. Before eating anything, it first has to cross the threshold of lips and mouth. In that regard, it's significant to note that Genesis 3:3 reveals touching this fruit was just as bad as eating it. Most of the time emphasis is on eating. Folks tend to forget about the God directive with respect to touching.

Unless you're dealing with a cavewoman or man, when it comes to sex it usually begins with "touching." And of course, once the touching begins, language barriers both intellectually and spiritually come down; *all the way down*.

As soon as Eve touched, she was touched. Disobedience allowed Eve and Satan to speak the same language. That language, of course, is sex.

Now think about it; do you need an international translator in the room to have sex? Once you cross a certain threshold with a touch (mouth and lips), a Russian and homeboy or girl *straight outta Compton* can speak the same language. Inter-species communication, as well as intra-species, always has to be in a language that the receiver of the message can fully understand. In the Garden of Eden, disobedience instantly obliterated mankind's spiritual language barrier regarding extraterrestrial intelligence as such involves alien communications. The exact same conceptually applies today.

The directive of God is to steer clear of occult practices that involve spiritism (Isaiah 8:19). But, rather than obeying Divine instructions, dipping and dabbing in psychic phenomena is more popular now than it was in 17th Century Europe. What are you willing to bet that the majority of the calls to a "psychic hotline" are about a lost dog or cat? No, it's high unlikely folks are trying to find out what happened to *Spot*. Bet the Ponderosa it's more about *Tom* or *Kat*! "Seeking unto them that have familiar spirits" for a hookup in order to get advice regarding a hookup. The language is still sex.

The motion picture *Arrival* (2016) is brilliantly illustrative in driving a communications point. If you can't wrap your head around varying abstract communicative applications your ability to understand and be understood is going to disadvantaged.

But the slam dunk respecting the Eden sex theory is revealed in Genesis 3:22: "The man is become as one of us, to know good and evil." The operative word in the statement is Shakespearean: "to be or not to be." Instead of emphasis on "became" as a past tense linking verb requiring a noun complement, here we find emphasis on "become" a present tense verb that doesn't require an object, but is simply a state of existence. The verb "to be" in Genesis 3:5 is about consequence. In Genesis 3:22; repercussion.

So, specifically, what knowledge does man have to have to be as gods? It's carnal knowledge!

Once more; once man and woman discovered the act of copulation by penis-vaginal penetration, they immediately became as gods because the climactic end result of sex can and invariably does lead to the fertilization of an egg and the birth of a human being. Carnal knowledge, which is how to create life, is the only knowledge that makes man as gods. And it was the only "knowledge" that was missing from Adam and Eve's repertoire of experiences and God-given endowments.

A computer is ten thousand times smarter than the intellectually below-average man or woman, but artificial intelligence minus human embodiment can never make a baby whereas any man or woman can. Consequently, the kind of tree knowledge being Biblically referred to has nothing to do with IQ. Both Adam and Eve became "wise" to sex. Only when you are naked can you determine sex. The fact that God asked Adam who told him he was naked tells us that neither Adam nor Eve knew anything about sex. For all they knew prior to the serpent's intrusion was probably that the male and female genitalia served a urinary and waste disposal function. But when the Garden couple disobeyed God's command, their eyes became wide open to information Satan provided that God didn't want them having prior his instruction.

Who can deny that the knowledge of sex is both good and bad? Unfortunate, however, is the fact that the world's first man and woman learned about the "birds and the bees" from the devil as opposed to God. So, if that indeed was the case, is it really any surprise that Adam "hearkened unto the voice of his wife" and ate what she gave him? Obviously, if the devil showed Eve a "thing or two," Adam was had at, "Hello baby, how was your day?"

Once Satan "snaked" his way into the first woman, Adam saw his wife like he'd never seen her before. And because Genesis 3:6 plainly shows Adam didn't debate, but just ate, that tells us whatever Eve laid on her man, the brotha was whupped without much if any fight.

When you put the real in it, in order for a man who really knows God to kick God to the roadside for a piece of fruit, there's got to be more to the pieces than fruit!

Satan has neither reason nor motivation to comply with the moral standards, social sensitivities, and Victorian delicacies of human beings. The subtext here, because the Bible has plainly told us there is a "war in heaven," the devil can wreak all the havoc he wants during his pursuit of uncompromising hatred. This includes sabotaging a "Faithful and True" relationship by using deceit and trickery to either woo or distort any object of God's affection.

The same spirit that drove Satan to undermine, sabotage, and attempt to destroy the work of God, is the same spirit that drives human beings today to undermine, sabotage, and attempt to destroy the work of others they envy, covet, and thereby despise. It is the very same Garden of Eden satanic hatred that makes those of far lesser physical, mental, and moral stature to be hell-bent on destruction as opposed to construction. But, just as the devil was thwarted by God in his craftiness, history repeatedly shows the ilk of human beings who have the same nihilistic spirit are ultimately thwarted by an Almighty God in theirs. Just as "stupid is as stupid does," the same applies to evil.

All God wanted in the Garden of Eden was Adam and Eve's 50/50 love (not 70/30 or 60/40). Drawing directly from Isaiah 14:14, in addition to all other motives, Satan coveted the relationship God had with Adam and Eve. This is probably why adultery and coveting made the Top-10 (Exodus 20:14, 17).

Being jealous, Satan maneuvered Eve into committing an act of infidelity. Genesis 3:6 says, "She took of the fruit thereof, and did eat." There's really no polite way of putting it; Eve became Satan's ho. And since Genesis 3:6 ends with, "and gave also unto her husband with her; and he did eat," the devil then became Eve's pimp. Subsequently, Adam's God-given name became John, as in a prostitute's paying client. For that reason, 1 Timothy 2:14 reads, "Adam was not deceived." Adam was not tricked; even though he became one. God knew then as he knows now, a patron is not deceived into the act. The act is a transaction. Adam was sold on the idea Eve was selling and he bought it under the influence of sexual healing. He was ignorant of the fact that he was already blessed. When you can't appreciate what you're getting for thinking about what you haven't had, you might end up with nothing. The "healing" Adam thought he needed in reality was a sickness leading to his death.

Strike three.

Adam and Eve were out along with all of their progeny; the entire human race. Consider God's immediate response to what just happened. Genesis 3:14-15 reads:

"And the LORD God said unto the serpent, Because thou hast done this, thou art cursed above all cattle, and above every beast of the field; upon thy belly shalt thou go, and dust shalt thou eat all the days of thy life."

God is literally pissed. If the snake was just a mouthpiece for Satan, was it really the snake's fault? When Peter became a mouthpiece for the devil (Matthew 16:23), Jesus said, "Get thee behind me Satan," and kept it moving. Here, the serpent is physically cursed by God. "Because thou hast done this" suggests "this" had to be way, way, way more than just being Satan's linguist.

So, the question: "Done what?" Just what did the serpent do above and beyond the call of duty? Only when we stop toying with the idea that the devil is something to play with when there's need for a convenient or comfortable excuse do we realize that Satan does not play.

There's very strong circumstantial evidence that the devil used the serpent as a tool in order to penetrate Eve awakening in her the desire for sex. The serpent was not just a linguist; it was also a "cunnilinguist." The serpent became Satan's sexual surrogate. Even though Genesis 3:1 paints the serpent as subtle, was subtly the only physical requirement in Operation Garden of Eden?

Why "beast of the field" and not bird of the air; as in parrot? Parrots have skills. In addition to talking, some researchers think these birds have cognitive conceptualizations. Now, other than being human, you can't get any more subtle than that. A talking bird can do what it does and then fly away. But if sex is in play, it's obvious why a snake in the hand is way mo' better than a beak in the bush. In furthering the plausibility of the sex theory consider the following:

"(For the weapons of our warfare are not carnal, but mighty through God to the pulling down of strong holds.) — 2 Corinthians 10:4

Let's back into what Paul is saying. If the weapons of our warfare are not "carnal," then whose weapons of warfare are? Since the "war" word is being used, and the war is between God and Satan, the implication of Paul's statement is God's not using carnality in this fight, but Satan is.

The mere fact that it's God who inspires Paul to bring up carnal knowledge means it's tied to something tangible. Carnal is not popping up in a vacuum. Since carnal is scripturally employed as a weapon of warfare, we have to look at the genesis of its use as such a weapon. Obviously, the genesis is Genesis. The sexual revolution started the moment Eve came under attack.

Eve's physical assault in the Garden by Satan alias "the dragon" is the "woe" pronounced in Revelation 12:12. And it's no quirk that the first target of that woe is "woe-man."

Naturally there are those who outright reject the theory that serpentine sex was anywhere near Eden. But, strongly supporting the suspicion is Genesis 3:15:

> "And I will put enmity between thee and the woman, and between thy seed and her seed; it shall bruise thy head, and thou shalt bruise his heel."

A literal "head" up to sex being a motive in Satan's *Operation Eden* is revealed in God's 3:15 counter offensive. The operative word in 3:15 is "seed." Herein God is not addressing the serpent, but rather Satan as a sentient being. And here is where the Bible and science face off again. Unless you have a functional knowledge of biology, you'll totally miss what's being said, and why it was said so quickly.

God was disappointed that Adam and Eve chose to follow after Satan, but he was furious at what may be termed the devil's criminal intent. The fact that seed was brought up immediately by God suggests that Satan's strategic game plan was bigger than chocolate-covered strawberries and whipped cream under a fruit tree. Seed spells genetics; and once genetics is introduced into the equation, sex is an essential element in the procreative process.

Circumstantially with highly probable evidence, the fall of Adam and Eve was the first step in Satan's biological attempt to infiltrate the human race with a predatory alien life form. If Satan's overall motive was to introduce a hybrid species on this planet that would intermix extraterrestrial and human genomes, the only way to viably do that would be to bring earth's first man and woman under satanic control.

A genome is an organism's complete set of DNA, including all of its genes. Each genome contains all of the information needed to build and maintain that organism. Thus, Genesis 3:15, in addition to everything else Biblical hermeneutics and exegesis suggests, here is the missing "stronger motive." This one passage brings clarity to Revelation 12:12:

"The devil is come down to you having great wrath,
because he knoweth that he hath but a short time."

The operative two words aren't "great wrath" but rather, "short time." Satan's end game was then and still is now prolonging his existence. By hearing from the *Great Physician* that his days are numbered, the only way for Satan to prolong his existence is by seeding his spiritual genes. Setting Eve up was the first step in setting the entire human race up as surrogate breeders for an extraterrestrial sperm bank that would be both spiritual and biological.

6 THE OMEN

"Being born again, not of corruptible seed, but of incorruptible, by the word of God, which liveth and abideth for ever."
—1PETER 1:23

The Genesis 3:15 passage "enmity between thy seed and her seed" is intriguing. Some analyze this in a literal context. Since enmity connotes "enemy" as in hostility; and the Garden of Eden serpent was a snake, a lot of folks attribute a lot of folks' aversion to snakes courtesy 3:15. If you see a snake either large or small and a chill does a number up and down your spine, credit is given Divine design.

But if the sex-in-the-garden theory holds water, the snake-in-the-grass wasn't serpent it was Satan. That means the "seed" wasn't reptilian, but extraterrestrial. We know human beings have seeds, but here indication is directly given that predatory aliens do also.

The word enmity connotes a feeling or condition of hatred; ill will; animosity; antagonism. If you bristle at the thought of snakes, where's your head regarding *Rosemary's Baby* (1968)?

It might be safe to say most polls show that most people aren't freaky enough to get turned on at the thought of hooking up with Beelzebub. So, your aversion to having any kind of close encounter of a sexual kind with devil or demon is the "enmity" God has put in your spirit just as he said he would do. But in the event you personally think the very idea of that kind of love/hate relationship would be repulsive anyway, perhaps the "enmity" God is talking about is a lot less obvious.

In addition to enmity, there's "bruising" as in Satan's head and mankind's heel. Therefore, in the context of enmity and bruising combined exactly what does 3:15 mean prophetically and physically?

God, speaking to the serpent, but directly at Satan indicates man will "bruise" the devil's head. That's bruise in the context of a verb not noun. Bruise in the form of a noun is caused by a blow in the form of a verb. Prophetically speaking, what kind of physical "blow" does mankind make to Satan's head?

Believe it or not, every time you willingly reject what is Biblically representative of a spirit contrary to the Spirit of God (Galatians 5:19-21) that is a bruise to Satan's head. Your conscience that gives you the power to "*do the right thing*" is the "enmity" Genesis 3:15 is pinpointing. Just as Satan's "head" was wrapped around influencing Adam and Eve to reject the Spirit of God's influence on their life way back then, same is his game now.

Because Adam and Eve voluntarily submitted themselves to the power of Satan's influence, if God didn't put that "enmity" between mankind and Satan at the precise point of mankind's conception in the womb (the seed), then human beings would be powerless regarding anything that pops into either the devil or a devil's brain (head). Just imagine how vulnerable your mind would be without any "malware" or antivirus protection! Satan could download his thoughts directly into the human brain without check or balance. The Genesis 3:15 "enmity" is spiritual virus protection. It's a defense mechanism given by the grace of God.

But whether that protection or "enmity" is accepted as a firewall or spiritual force field is an altogether 'nother story. Even though God instills a conscience as a balance in all human beings, we know that some individuals are imbalanced. They have rejected the Spirit of God to such a degree that the mind of Satan has merged with their own. By refusing to "uninstall program," these individuals are so far gone they can't help themselves even if they wanted to.

The guy who rents a truck and speeds down a sidewalk killing and maiming dozens is a lost soul. What's the motive? How about demon possession? The god they serve is not the God of Abraham, Martin, and John or Muhammad.

Drawing from 2 Thessalonians 2:10-12, God Almighty knows these individuals are so far out that they're even beyond his reach. God realizes when you've tugged and pulled on the chain for so long and hard, there comes a time and point when the link finally breaks. Consequently, when you're off the chain to the extent you're not only out of the yard, but somewhere over into the next county, you've made enmity's enemy your friend. Bottom line, you're in a very dangerous place.

The only thing you can do for a person willing to blow themselves up in order to kill other persons is to blow them up first. Therein is the flipside of the Genesis 3:15 coin. It's the "blow" Satan makes to mankind's heel.

Psalms 49:5 reads:

> "Wherefore should I fear in the days of evil, when the iniquity of my heels shall compass me about?"

Jeremiah 13:22 reads:

> "And if thou say in thine heart, Wherefore come these things upon me? For the greatness of thine iniquity are thy skirts discovered, and thy heels made bare."

If you've ever had a bruise to your heel, or an Achilles tendon injury, you know exactly why Genesis 3:15 finds God saying "heel" and not any other part of the anatomy. If there's one spot on your body that will slow your roll without doing damage to head and heart it's your heel. Bruise your heel and the pause button is immediately hit regardless of self-will or mind over matter. It's called Achilles for a reason. As far as Greek mythology, Achilles was the man. But when shot in the heel by a Parisian arrow, he became a footnote anecdote.

Psalms and Jeremiah are raising awareness that the road to hell begins with the placement of heel to toe. When the "head" of Satan isn't bruised by man's rejection, the "heel" of mankind is bruised by Satan's acceptance.

The word incubus is defined as an imaginary demon or evil spirit that can supposedly descend upon women while they are sleeping in order to have sex. A succubus is the counterpart for men. A key word in that dictionary definition is imaginary. If the Bible is imaginary, then the incubus/succubus possibility isn't worth a second thought. But if there is a remote measure of merit to what appears to be a bigger motive to the devil's Garden of Eden scheme, then why not pick up on the words spoken by the apostle Paul in 2Corinthians 2:11:

> "Lest Satan should get an advantage of us: for we are not ignorant of his devices."

Once again, does it make any sense to think Satan wouldn't use sex as a device? There is no reason to be ignorant of anything in this day and age unless you just want to be. If the greatest trick Satan has pulled is the belief that he doesn't exist, running a very close second is the belief that his existence is in a form other than what it actually is. Few to none think of the devil as an extraterrestrial creature with his entire crew of fallen angels as predatory aliens that have infiltrated this planet (Revelation 12).

We see this "space invaders" theme time and time again played out on television and in the movies as science fiction never giving credence to the science fact that the basic premise and plotlines being cinematically presented are directly out of the Bible. If anything, the incubus-succubus approach to "*close encounters of the fifth kind*" is now old school. Today, why go after a woman or man while they are sleeping when they can be had wide awake. While it may be common knowledge that the porno industry is a multibillion dollar business generating more annual revenue than the NFL, NBA, and MLB combined, even more staggering are the numbers reflecting the millions of women and men who participate in putting the X in the X.

Comparably, because there is a hierarchal structure of extraterrestrials that gauntlet from fallen angels to demons, are the individuals employed to have sex on camera fully aware that the person they're having sex with might not even be human? How soon we forget that based on Genesis 1:26, "they" don't look like us, we look like them. These extraterrestrials weren't made in our image; we were made in theirs (Psalms 8:5).

It's important to be reminded that when the two angels came knocking in Genesis 19, they didn't have wings on their backs. These angels encountered a homosexual crew in the city of Sodom that wanted to party like it was 1999 B.C. These Sodomites didn't see these two visitors as angels; they saw them as men; fresh meat (Genesis 19:5).

Likewise, there's Hebrews 13:2:
> "Be not forgetful to entertain strangers: for thereby some have entertained angels unawares."

With angels being extraterrestrials, unawares means the chick or dude you pick up and "entertain" might not even be human. But that possibility is only personally relevant if you really believe what's written in the Bible. If you don't believe (what's written in the Bible), it's just a matter of your being unaware of the personal relevance; and the possibility of sleeping with the "enmity."

Accept it or not, mankind has been interacting with extraterrestrial intelligences from Biblical Day 6. Refusal to see such is a case of eyes-wide-shut. The adult film industry could be a breeding ground for seeding the human population with predatory alien sperm and society at large would be totally "unawares."

Genesis 6:4 reads:
> "There were giants in the earth in those days; and also after that, when the sons of God came in unto the daughters of men, and they bare children to them, the same became mighty men which were of old, men of renown."

When recalling Job defining "sons of God" as extraterrestrials, it's readily apparent that the same categorization is applied to the "giants in the earth" that were having sex with women.

Was the sex recreational or re-creational? Interestingly, these "sons of God" are neither called nor referred to as angels. But, neither were the ones in Job. Subsequently, some deductive reasoning has to be employed. Since the word angel appears in the Scriptures more than 290 times, the Bible knows angels. This lack of name calling suggests that angels and "sons of God" are being Biblically differentiated.

Why? When recalling Luke defining Adam as the "son of God," even though established as such, Adam was no angel. Man was made "a little lower than the angels" (Psalms 8:5). Because of this differentiation, we have to look for commonality to diminish any perceived mystery.

What do angels and man have in common? What's the comparison and contrast?

Well, first and obvious, in order to be termed a "son of God" one has to have a God consciousness. Again, referencing *Spot*, your dog is not a "son of God" because dogs do not have the mental capacity to grasp awareness of God as a concept. Even though Pharaoh asked, "Who is the Lord" (Exodus 5:2), Pharaoh still understood the concept. Being made in the image and after the likeness of God automatically categorizes one as a son of God.

But, don't get it twisted; being a "son" doesn't automatically make you an heir. A whole lot of sons who share the bloodline don't show up in the Will. The "Last Will and Testament" of God is referenced in both Revelation 13:8 and Revelation 21:27!

Additionally, don't get twisted over the vocabulary. "Son" is used as an all encompassing term meaning mankind. Even though Genesis 1:26 reads, "Let us make man in our image, after our likeness," Genesis 1:27 says, God created he him, male and female created he them." Subsequently, "sons of God" includes the female gender.

So, once again, drawn directly from Ezekiel 28:13/15, angels are created beings just like mankind (Genesis 1:27). Again, given the fact that the Job "sons of God" meeting wasn't on earth, it was an extraterrestrial meeting. Man being "a little lower than the angels" coupled with being in a fallen state of existence didn't have the physical capability to leave planet earth to attend that meeting. But, obviously, drawing from the conversation ensuing between God and Satan, the devil did.

Just why was Satan at that meeting? First, the extraterrestrials attending were there to "present themselves before the LORD." Again, since Philippians 2:11 establishes the Lord as Jesus Christ, contemporaneously put, this was a church meeting. Just as you go to church for the purpose of presenting yourself before the Lord, why should implication and interpretation be any different here?

So, why was Satan there?

Why does any devil go to church now? Maybe to see who's there? Scope women? Scope men? Maybe just to be seen? But, again, because we're talking church, the Spirit of God that governs truly Christian churches doesn't turn anybody away; even if they are devils. This is why that church in Charleston didn't turn that devil away. And, that's also the reason why certain preachers invite certain politicians to "present themselves" before their church congregations. You can be a well-known devil, but the Spirit of Jesus is a welcoming Spirit in spite of an evil spirit.

> "Behold, I stand at the door, and knock: if any man hear my voice, and open the door, I will come in to him, and will sup with him, and he with me. To him that overcom-

eth will I grant to sit with me in my throne, even as I also overcame, and am set down with my Father in his throne. He that hath an ear, let him hear what the Spirit saith unto the churches." — Revelation 3:20-22

This meeting of extraterrestrials in all likelihood included unfallen angels as well as beings that were not and could not be exclusively categorized as angels. These were undoubtedly God-conscious beings that had not fallen prey to Satan's influence. If Adam and Eve had not been swayed they probably would have been at that meeting as well. Because there was a "mixed multitude" of beings, they were all together classified as "sons of God." Their creation in the "image" and after the "likeness" of God, just like Adam, made them "sons."

Therefore, by definition, the "son" status also included Satan. Consider Isaiah 14:12: "How art thou fallen from heaven, O Lucifer, son of the morning!"

Inclusiveness being the case, "sons of God" can be viewed generically. However, the Genesis 6:4 "sons of God" also by definition includes fallen angels whereas the Job "sons of God" by necessity didn't. Angels in their fallen state of existence have no reason to *"present themselves before the Lord."* Angels "which kept not their first estate" have made Lucifer their lord.

What do these fallen angels have in common with man? Well, their fallen status has also made them "a little lower than the angels" of God. Consequently, because of their expulsion from heaven there's an angelic class differentiation. The term angel could no longer be used as an all-encompassing term to consistently identify them as a group.

Haven't you ever wondered why Jesus never referred to Satan as Lucifer? Rarely is the word angel even used when Biblically referencing Satan's crew. When folks stop using your name and start calling you out of it by way of metaphors, you have made that community's "*S-List.*" With respect to the Bible, the "S" stands for "sons." With regards to Satan, that's about as good as it's ever gonna get.

Yes, it's difficult sometimes to accept something that is staring you right in the face. Bible classes and commentaries typically maintain that angels are sexless creatures. More than a few biblical scholars cite Matthew 22:30, Mark 12:25 and Luke 20:35 in support of the theory that angels are neuter, and the thought that Genesis 6:4 is suggesting angels are having sexual intercourse with women is BS; to put it mildly. Matthew 22:30, however, says absolutely nothing about angels having sex. Quoting Matthew, the three passages collectively read, "For in the resurrection they neither marry, nor or given in marriage, but are as the angels of God in heaven."

Theologians embracing those Scriptures in support of all angels being asexual, however, are missing a key scriptural point. Once again, the devil and Company were kicked out of heaven. Revelation 12:8 reads, "Neither was their place found anymore in heaven." Consequently, fallen angels are no longer "as the angels of God in heaven" for the simple reason that they are no longer in heaven. Again, they are now members of a different class because they "kept not their first estate." Estate is not only defined in terms of property; it also includes social standing, rank, sociopolitical condition.

Indisputably, Genesis 6:4 indicates angels were sexually active with women. The children born from these unions, the Bible refers to as "giants." The Hebrew translation of giants is Nephilim. Goliath of Gath was a Nephilim. Prefacing 6:4, consider Genesis 6:2: "The sons of God saw the daughters of men that they were fair; and they took them wives of all which they chose."

Because these angels "left their own habitation" (Jude 1:6) and "their place" (Revelation 12:8), they were now off the chain. The expression "took them wives" implies a whole lot more than having the type of consensual sex that typically accompanies a marital relationship. "All they chose" suggests the choosing was one-sided. Did the women they chose have a choice?

Wanna talk about the "sexual harassment of women" by powerful men? Well, if you wanna put the real in it, it jumped off in Genesis 6:2!

In street vernacular, when it comes to sexual relationships, if one of the parties says, "I took it," the taking could mean to the taker that "no" means maybe or yes. Shouldn't the Bible's employment of "took" make the meaning obvious?

But indulging those who still say, "No way," the operative word when it comes to "fallen angels" isn't angels, it's fallen. Can you put anything pass the "fallen" be they human or extraterrestrial? If you've "fallen" sometimes you don't want to get up!

When indulging the idea that fallen angels are the Genesis 6:4 "sons of God," if the angels of God in heaven don't marry, why are the angels of Satan on earth marrying; i.e., taking wives?

After billions of years of being angels of God in heaven; why the sudden urge? Had they somehow caught the movie, *Earth Girls Are Easy* (1988)? If it wasn't about the magnetistic-tingle of an itch needing to be scratched, why set up housekeeping? Even though the scripture says these daughters were fine, wouldn't you think even as a "fallen angel" there would be other options than rape? Yes, "took" in the Biblical context presented should be taken as rape. And yes, a husband can rape his wife.

Once more, repeatedly, throughout Genesis when two individuals got together, a term for consensual sex is "knew." Plainly, Genesis 4:1 reads "Adam knew Eve his wife." In 6:2, these women were *Taken* (2008).

If the Bible is suggesting rape, why wouldn't the theory that the rape precedent was first established by Satan himself as rapist in the Garden of Eden? So now, is it really, really, really that farfetched to surmise that the devil "took" Eve's virginity or innocence even though she had the choice to "Just say no?"

When Mark 12:25 and Luke 20:35 are interjected, if you should be fortunate to rise from the dead, you "neither marry, nor are given in marriage," because human regeneration is no longer necessary. Only between Genesis 4 and Revelation 20 is the physical act of sex between a man and a woman a biologically regenerative necessity as opposed to a Genesis 1:28 procreative one. If the fall hadn't occurred, the pre-Genesis 4:1 directive, "Be fruitful, and multiply," would have stayed procreative. The need of a resurrection from the dead as a regenerative measure would have been preempted.

The red-lettered words of Jesus maintain the resurrected righteous will be "as the angels of God in heaven" due to the fact that angels are eternal. Angels do not require self-regeneration. Human beings on the other side of midnight won't either. Adam and Eve in the Garden of Eden were actually the physical representation and embodiment of the post-resurrected human beings Jesus is talking about in Mark 12:25 and Luke 20:35.

The tree of "carnal knowledge" was irrelevant to humanity's eternal life; the tree of life was. But, in the case of Satan and Company, the tree that sat in the midst of the garden was the bomb. Their prolonged existence in effort to counter Revelation 12:12's "short time" depended on mankind having carnal knowledge immediately. The dragon and his angels didn't know how short a time they had. But relatively speaking, isn't any time short of immortality a short time?

The life expectancy of a housefly is 28 days. What if "the fly" could live 70 years? That would be great as far as that fly is concerned until it got to its 69th year.

Revelation's reference to Satan being on the clock sends the not so subtle message that fallen angels are doomed. They no longer enjoy immortality. In order to preserve their corrupted angelic species as "sons of God" which is biologically all male, another species that was biologically compatible in terms of procreativity had to come into play. So, when God said, "Let us make man in our image, after our likeness," the "our" included the basic DNA structure of all angels. Again, all angels include fallen angels.

How do we know this genetic theory has merit? Once again, Psalms 8:4-5 juxtaposed Genesis 6:4, means angels could physically copulate with human beings and biologically procreate a hybrid species once a female species of the human race was created. Biologically Adam had the same basic genetic structure of all angels (just a little lower). The operative word here, however, is not lower but "little."

Since the Bible tells and shows angels appearing as men, the "little" doesn't suggest appearance; rather ability.

Apes are a lot lower than man in appearance and ability. If not, men and apes would be capable of mating. The fact that a "missing link" between apes and man has not been found is due to there being none to find. There is no Hominidae and Homo sapiens capability of a hookup whereby a hybrid life form can be brought to term. Apes were not made in the image of God. Since the Bible doesn't read that "the sons of God came in unto the daughters of apes," the possibility of ever finding an ape that could say, "*You damn dirty human*" is impossible. There again, a species speech/language barrier. But, included here, a sexual roadblock accompanies.

Think about it; what sex was Adam really prior to the creation of Eve? Beyond the Genesis 1:26 labeling, Adam, in the abstract, was the same sex as your computer. Dismissing any factory-imposed gender specific operating system, is your computer male or female?

Minus the existence of a biological counterpart (Eve), there is nothing by which gender can be determined. Just as Exodus 3:14 finds God saying, "I AM THAT I AM," in essence we find similarity in Genesis 2:18, "the man" IS WHO HE IS. The term "man" was merely a word employed to name the new creature God created.

Once again, with reference to the English language and its ability to be employed either "homonymically" or metonymically, the fact that God called man ADAM wherein mankind is composed of ATOMS is head scratching to say the least. Likewise, therein, the second new creature "made" being called woman. Woman, of course, is a derivative of man etymologically and physically. In *Essence* (pun intended) it took Eve's existence to define what a man actually was beyond name.

Fast-forward; is there any applicability today? Does being a woman define what it is to be a man? Or is gender identity strictly in the eye of the beholdee? Do clothes make the man or woman? Or should it continue to be what's underneath those clothes? But then, how deep does underneath go? If you are a man or boy who thinks he's a woman or girl, or a woman who feels in her heart she is a man or boy, do restroom door signs answer that question?

What about Proverbs 23:7: "For as he thinketh in his heart, so is he?"

Newsflash! There's no Biblical contradiction because Solomon didn't endorse "think like a man and act like a woman," or "think like a woman and act like a man." Solomon, the man believed to be the wisest who ever lived, is simply saying you are what you think in your heart. The caveat, of course, God didn't give you a heart to think with; he gave you a brain.

Thinking with your heart can get you in a whole lot of trouble. How many hearts had folks thinkin' they *'was so in luv'?* In love enough to have their ex's name tattooed on their behind!

It's important to understand that once Eve was created, the biological Pandora's Box was not only opened for Adam to enter, it was also there for Satan and all of his boys as well. The creation of a woman was universally unique. If this was not the case, the "church" meeting found in Job would have referenced the "sons and daughters of God." Eve undeniably had to be the first woman-kind in the universe. And, only because of her fallen state as a member of mankind, both she and her husband as the progenitor of all human beings were confined to earth. There was neither universal physical nor social reason to incorporate "daughter" into the Job "sons of God" equation. The term "daughter" was not relevant given the universal reality of a beyond earth situation.

With that in mind, and in regard to all angels as a group, it's also important to take note that Revelation 12:7 reads Michael and not Michelle. And Genesis 1:26 reads image and likeness. Not one without the other. Even though God is referred to in masculine form, there is a difference between image and likeness. The "image" of God is masculine as revealed in the name Michael and the physical appearance of both Adam and Jesus Christ. But, the "likeness" of God is sexless. If not, contrary to Genesis 1:1 and John 1:1, the stage would have been set "from the beginning" for God to be a biologically created entity. This is why we find creation in both the image and the likeness. Creation in the image minus the likeness, or the likeness minus the image would not permit God to "put all things under him" in a manner that would allow God to be "all in all" as 1 Corinthians 15:28 maintains.

The concept of sex/gender with regards to classification is defined by either of the two main categories (male and female) into which humans and many other living things are divided on the basis of their reproductive functions. In reality, for God or a Supreme Being to have a functional biological gender classification would require pre-and-post submission to real world laws governing reproductive functions no different from the ones availed by Jesus Christ.

Now, even though Jesus Christ's birth didn't involve a penis, immaculate conception did involve a process scientifically called parthenogenesis which required a host that could only be female or woman. Subsequently, for God in actuality to be gender specific in assignment, such a submission would be impossible in a physical universe where God is sexless even though called Father. God cannot be the Father if the internal "wiring" is there for a father to theoretically father, or sire, or procreate Himself. Wherein a woman or female species can be impregnated naturally, supernaturally, or artificially; a man or male species of higher order cannot. Of course, that's cannot in a physical world and universe as we know it based on how God has revealed such to us as human beings.

When it comes to universal truths, determinate terms are used for the convenience of giving us a handle to grab; to wrap our heads around to keep from getting dizzy. I AM THAT I AM is not I'm him or I'm her. It just is what it is. And, perhaps that's exactly why Exodus 3:14 says what it does.

Nevertheless, once the devil heard the words, "Be fruitful and multiply" (Genesis 1:28), Satan as serpent strategically targeted Eve because her physiology was a stratagem for countering Revelation 12:12. This meant in order for Satan to carry out a plan to further his biological and spiritual existence by infesting earth's human population with his demon seed, Adam and Eve had to fall. If they didn't there is no way on God's green earth that Satan and his angels could produce a hybrid species of aliens indicative of Genesis 6:4. If Satan hadn't awakened the sexual desire in Eve before a divinely appointed time, the devil's goal of regenerating himself and his angels on earth would not have happened.

In biology regeneration is the process of renewal, restoration, and growth that makes genomes, cells, organisms, and ecosystems resilient to events that cause disturbance or damage. In accordance with Revelation 12, "war in heaven" caused a major disturbance for Lucifer. And Lucifer, now Satan, knew some serious damage control was necessary.

When Satan and his angels were banished to earth, they were all one species labeled with a masculine determinate that in reality had yet to be defined and understood from an earthborn perspective. Being anatomically male, Eve being created as a female was the only life form anywhere that had the right stuff in order to be impregnated by a masculine species of extraterrestrials that the Bible calls angels.

Undeniably, at first, God appears cool with Adam being all by himself species-wise. If not, Adam and Eve would have been created simultaneously. When you think about it, drawing strictly from the Bible without speculation, angels had been around for billions of years as a single species. Presumptively speaking, analogously, their genitalia possibly had the sex appeal of a thumb. Just as all healthy human beings are born with a thumb; it's considered matter of fact. A thumb doesn't even have the sexual status of a middle finger. A thumb, even though it's an important part of the body, it's still just there to do a job without fanfare or hype. While the thumb is capable of multi-tasking, if you are a "healthy" human being, you don't think about sticking your thumb anywhere or any place that might be deemed as having any kind of sexual significance.

The gross misapprehension of what Matthew, Mark, and Luke are actually saying with regards to angels and marriage leads to a total disregard of what's really being said in Genesis 6:4 with respect to angels and sex.

Again, the question: Were angels sexually active before 6:4 with any other species in the universe? Based on there being no Biblical reference to "daughters of God," the answer is no. So, back to the question earlier posed. Why the sudden urge to get busy?

We can only speculate. When angels cease to be "angels of God in heaven" their nature changes. Likewise, when a human being falls out of touch with God their nature changes as well. Losing love for God as found in Jesus Christ destabilizes a "living soul." This destabilization is a spiritual law of nature that "*stem-cells*" from being created in the *image* and after the *likeness* of God. Backsliding is termed sliding for a reason. Sliding puts sliders on a slippery slope that sooner or later leads to a fall.

> "And every one that heareth these sayings of mine, and doeth them not, shall be likened unto a foolish man, which built his house upon the sand: And the rain descended, and the floods came, and the winds blew, and beat upon that house; and it fell: and great was the fall of it."
> — MATTHEW 7:26-27

Be it angel or human, slip slidin' away from a once-held belief in God as found in Jesus Christ is going to both arouse and stir affections that were previously being held in check.

> "When the unclean spirit is gone out of a man, he walketh through dry places, seeking rest; and finding none, he saith, I will return unto my house whence I came out. And when he cometh, he findeth *it* swept and garnished. Then goeth he, and taketh *to him* seven other spirits more wicked than himself; and they enter in, and dwell there: and the last *state* of that man is worse than the first."
> — LUKE 11:24-26

The moral of both sayings is once you've heard and been convicted by the Spirit of God; Satan ain't interested in being a blast from the past. Singing, *I'm On The Outside (Looking In)* is not where he wants to be. If you open the door and let him back inside you will be inclined to do things you didn't even know there were such things to do.

With regards to those "seven other spirits more wicked," there is a hierarchal structure. First, there are Cherubim. These are those that remained loyal to God. Second, there are the "fallen angels." These are the ones Jude 1:6 references. It was the fallen angels (Lucifer & Company) who engaged in sexual intercourse with women that produced Nephilim as a hybrid species. Nephilim aren't angels; they're offspring. Third, there are demons. Demons are spirits. They require a physical body to inhabit.

Subsequently, putting it all into perspective, the only conceivable purpose for these extraterrestrial and human sexual encounters (Genesis 6:4) is genetic manipulation for the purpose of engineering a *New World Order* new species. Accepting the reality of angels being extraterrestrials, it's easier to see how easy it would be for the entire earth population to become overrun with a half-human/half-predatory alien life form.

Speculatively, these aliens were not engaging themselves in recreational sex; but rather re-creational sex. If you think they were, just what do you think they had been sexually doing between their fall to earth in the dateless past and the creation of a terrestrial female species?

Masturbation? Unisexuality? Having the ability to have sex doesn't necessitate the desire to engage in the act. Satan's A-Game was the intended seeding of earth's human population with his. And, this is why God being God was hip to his game plan as early as Genesis 3:15. God is not going to allow "corruptible seed" to mix it up with "incorruptible" without check. The Flood was a serious check.

> "And God looked upon the earth, and, behold, it was corrupt; for all flesh had corrupted his way upon the earth."
> – GENESIS 6:12

The Flood wasn't about checking sin. Sin is a corruption of the spirit first that prompts performance second. If The Flood was about washing away sin, what a big waste of water. Noah wasn't off the boat a minute before he was discovered drunk and laid up butt naked in his tent. Of course, any excuse will do, but regardless of whatever that was all about, drunkenness is a sin (Galatians 5:21). So, obviously, The Flood was all about washing away something else.

The fact that Genesis 6:12 links corruption with the flesh only eight verses removed from Genesis 6:4, it's crystal what the Flood was really about. The deluge was designed to physically rid earth of a human population that had been contaminated by predatory alien life.

While the Flood of waters was successful in washing away hybrid infestation, how successful is water when it comes to germs – the kind that are sexually transmitted?

Despite decades of research leading to vast improvements in medical knowledge, there is still no cure for HIV/AIDS, genital herpes, oral herpes, chronic hepatitis B and C, HPV. Do medical science and the Bible intersect at Nephilim junction? Is it possible that these viral strains have extraterrestrial origins?

Consider the depth of 2 Peter 3:6-7:

> "Whereby the world that then was, being overflowed with water, perished: But the heavens and the earth, which are now, by the same word are kept in store, reserved unto fire against the day of judgment and perdition of ungodly men."

Why fire next time? Unlike water, fire is the only element out of the five that can destroy and completely eradicate the bacterial and viral infections found on this planet. This is why 2 Peter 3:10 follows with:

> "But the day of the Lord will come as a thief in the night; in the which the heavens shall pass away with a great noise, and the elements shall melt with fervent heat, the earth also and the works that are therein shall be burned up."

Doesn't "melt with fervent heat" get the point across? Why the need to pile on with "burn up?" Catch *Outbreak* (1995).

Second time around isn't a house cleaning, it's a nuking! It's the baptism by fire because that's the only thing that "works" when it comes to a four-letter "work" spelled germ.

> "I indeed baptize you with water unto repentance: but he that cometh after me is mightier than I, whose shoes I am not worthy to bear: he shall baptize you with the Holy Ghost, and with fire: Whose fan is in his hand, and he will thoroughly purge his floor, and gather his wheat into the garner; but he will burn up the chaff with unquenchable fire." – MATTHEW 3:11-12

Jesus isn't talking 'bout dippin' people in fire. He's talking about fumigating the place where the people who inherit eternal life are going to live. Purging a floor doesn't point to people, it's a reference to that upon which people stand. Earth is "his floor." And, "fan in his hand" is his broom.

Just as "the Spirit of God moved upon the face of the waters" (Genesis 1:2), the same Spirit will move upon the face of a melted down burned up earth in order to "sweep up" the ashes.

The literary and metaphorical consistency of the Bible is utterly amazing. How could mankind ever be new creatures in Christ if the bloodline through which Jesus Christ will be born has been infected with Satan's DNA?

Unquestionably, once you start connecting the dots, the Garden of Eden plot devised by the princedom of Satan was an omen way more complex than most think. It was and still remains a war game strategy of the devil that's basically misunderstood.

Why did Lucifer think he could win both the battle and the war? Again, that's the "mystery of iniquity." Satan and those he inspires never know their limitations. Isaiah 14:14 finds Satan saying, "I will be like the Most High." When it's all about being like instead of being, why wouldn't the devil and all narcissists like him having morally reprehensible and deplorable followers overreach when it comes to ambitions? Ambitions that ultimately lead to their own despise, demise, and surprise.

7 SEVEN

"Remember the sabbath day, to keep it holy. Six days shalt thou labour, and do all thy work: But the seventh day is the sabbath of the LORD thy God: in it thou shalt not do any work, thou, nor thy son, nor thy daughter, thy manservant, nor thy maidservant, nor thy cattle, nor thy stranger that is within thy gates: For in six days the LORD made heaven and earth, the sea, and all that in them is, and rested the seventh day: wherefore the LORD blessed the sabbath day, and hallowed it."
— EXODUS 20:8-11

"The war in heaven" that's been raging since day one is a celestial civil war. Even though the Bible has made it plain, Satan's egomania is an over-simplification if viewed in an historical vacuum. Evidenced by the death of prehistoric creatures to the demise of mankind, the undergirding theme has always been about control. That's one party having a vision not shared by the other and who will have final cut.

In a democracy, the concept of a republic will fly. When there's a kingdom, the operative word is king. This is why Matthew 6:24 holds, "No man can serve two masters."

From the throne room in heaven to a garden spot on earth, Lucifer, now Satan has lusted to be *Charles in Charge*. Rightfully, however, Michael took the position that there would be no *Charlie's Angels*. Thus, here is where we all are on the "right" side of Eden.

Genesis 3:24 tells us that Cherubim were placed at the east of Eden. That placement is symbolically significant. Man exited Paradise at the east gate. When facing north, east is always to the right. So, even though what went down in the garden was wrong, thanks to God Almighty, in the name of Jesus, mankind came out "right."

This brings us to the gist of this particular chapter. With the angelic name Lucifer meaning day star, or sun, the world's first empire (Egypt) worshipped this extraterrestrial/angel under the name Ra. Ra is the name of the Egyptian sun god.

Now, there's looking at something, and then there's looking at something. If you've really looked at some of the Egyptian Pharaohs as contemporaneously sculptured, you don't have to be a conspiracy theorist to scratch your head. At least one of these individuals doesn't really look like he's from the neighborhood called earth. That one is the Pharaoh Akhenaten. Google him in living color and draw your own conclusions.

Whether you buy looks being deceiving or not, there's strong circumstantial evidence that extraterrestrial hybridization had penetrated the Pharaonic dynasties. If this theory of alien infiltration is correct, some of the Pharaohs were Nephilim. Indeed, if such is true, this explains why Pharaoh was talking so much smack in his diatribes with Moses. He was literally getting his juice from Satan in the form of genetic chemistry.

Akhenaten was a Pharaoh of the Eighteenth dynasty. Drawn from his sculpted image, Akhenaten's elongated head, slender face, almond eyes, and just overall odd physical appearance, many believe he was an extraterrestrial hybrid. Akhenaten ruled Egypt for 17 years, and was the father of Tutankhamen; King Tut. Akhenaten is especially noted for abandoning traditional Egyptian polytheism and introducing worship centered on the Egyptian god Aten. Aten was called the sun-disk.

Now, this is a very interesting historical fact. The 18th dynasty Egyptians had more gods to worship than Bayer has aspirins to bottle, yet, during Akhenaten's reign, he managed to get all of Egypt to drop worshiping their multitude of gods and focus totally on one. From a 20th Century perspective, this would have been comparable to JFK getting the entire United States of America to become Roman Catholic.

In case you hadn't surmised, sun-disk is another name for the sun. Aten is said to have become a god as the result of first being a deceased Egyptian king. This Egyptian king dies, then rises into the heavens and unites with the sun, or Ra. Ancient Egyptians believed that Ra was their maker because to them all life came from the sun.

Connecting the dots, compared to human beings, Akhenaten looks imaginably alien. Satan is an alien. Satan's angelic name is Lucifer. The name Lucifer means day star. Earth's daytime star is the sun. Akhenaten gets all of Egypt to convert to sun worship. Now, how far do you really have to go to figure? You don't have to be a *TV Land* detective to bust this case wide open. Just consider the development of Aten as an Egyptian deity. He's a king on earth; he dies; is resurrected; and then ascends into heaven becoming one with Ra who's hailed as creator.

Sound similar in scenario with a few modifications to *The Greatest Story Ever Told* (1965) or *The Passion of the Christ* (2004) or maybe *Jesus of Nazareth* (1977).

Do you think the Egyptians thought the Aten story up all by themselves? Or do you think they had coaching? In case you didn't know, there are many stories in the Bible that have remarkable similarities with stories from other religions, legends, and myths. The Creation, the Fall, the Flood, the Virgin Birth, the Resurrection all make a show way before the birth of Jesus Christ. But is that surprising? Wasn't Satan around before the birth of Jesus Christ?

Look online; there is a worldwide market for products that are patterned after the real deal. The Louis Vuitton label has been around since 1854. Its brand and distinctive LV monogram is one of the world's most recognized product lines. The brand is estimated to be worth over $20 billion.

What makes Louis relevant to this discussion is the fact that the Vuitton brand is one of the most counterfeited brands in the fashion world due to its image as a status symbol. It's even been reported that Louis Vuitton fake merchandise accounts for close to 20% of all counterfeit fashion accessories seized in Europe.

Go online and check out real versus fake Louis Vuitton bags. Minus the touch test, can you tell the real deal, Holyfield? Whether you can or not, that's not the story behind the story. The point being made is how many really care?

Consider Isaiah 4:1:

> "And in that day seven women shall take hold of one man, saying, We will eat our own bread, and wear our own apparel: only let us be called by thy name, to take away our reproach."

Belief or not, "that day" is today. Exceptional is the individual that refuses to accept or settle for anything or anyone less than the real thing.

The lyrics to the song that Marvin and Tammi made famous have been changed to "*Ain't nothing like a good deal.*" A $70 LV handbag that looks just like the real thing baby is a bargain for all who subscribe to "fake it until you make it." Unfortunately, that's a fashion statement that fashions an individual's life beyond outward appearance.

Isaiah's seven women are all about the show. As long as they can do their own thing and be called Christian, it's all good. These seven are brought to view in the context of Christianity. But in the context of life in general, the message is perpetration. These *Maleficent Seven* are consciously willing to perpetrate a fraud. And, the trip part, they are praying to God to aid and abet in their perpetration.

Subsequently, the theme is universal. Those who have a problem with the Bible for whatever the reason, if that reasoning is not totally based on personal experience and research, but something someone told them, i.e., the "they said" sin-drome, the basis for the reasoning is flawed. Realized or not, "they" always have an agenda. And agendas can either be hidden or in your face.

The "seven women" are upfront with theirs because when it comes to spirituality, the decisions have always been presented as life and death. Biblically, "woman" symbolizes the church (Revelation 21:2). These seven represent those men and women who want to be Christians without Christ. They are willing to buy the moral philosophy, but all of the accessories that go along; no.

What the problem is? Number one, when it's only being Christian in name it's being Satan in practice. You either take the bet by betting on one or the other. There's no hedging when it comes to what is and isn't. It's either real or fake.

But in order to make an informed decision, first, an individual has got to care. If it's all about faking until making, you're willing to eat anybody's bread and wear anybody's apparel and call it a day until what you think is better comes along.

Second, in order to make an informed decision, the "touch test" has got to be taken. You can't stand back and look at what "they said." If they say the bag on the right is the one and you don't reach out and touch, they could be as wrong as the proverbial two left shoes you bought without looking in the box to see for yourself what's really there.

Third, in order to make an informed decision, you've got to taste it. It's not the best analogy, but since we're talking television and film, have you ever seen a drug deal go down where a bag of cocaine is purchased based on sight only?

"Yeah, looks like a bag of coke to me. Here's my money!"

"Okay Bobo, here's the Arm & Hammer!"

That kinda shopping don't fly in the movies; you know it won't on the street where you live. Satan is the biggest pusher that's ever lived, and he's overwhelmingly successful at getting folks to buy what he pushes solely/souly based on sight and touch only. If it looks good and it feels good, *"Deal me in!"*

Since the women represent the Christian church, why seven?

Well, that's why "that day" is now. We are living in the seventh millennium. The number 7 is a number that symbolizes perfection. If you buy the Bible, there are 4,000 years before Christ (BC) and there are 2,000 complete years after. Faced with the fact that Jesus was crucified at age 33, in the year A.D. 30, the actual birth of Christ was circa 3 B.C.

In actuality, the seventh millennial threshold was crossed in 1997. And, of course, this is why the return of Jesus Christ (if you buy the Bible) will be like "a thief in the night" (1 Thessalonians 5:2). It will be totally unexpected.

Satan as a counterfeit artist is unsuspected. The fact that there are parallel stories from the halls of Montezuma to the shores of Tripoli that are practically identical in theme and concept to those in the Christian Bible is an extraterrestrial stratagem the princedom of Satan employs. It's an *"if you can't beat them join them"* tactic to throw shade on Christianity in preference of anything but.

When a couple of Jesus' home boyz wanted to throw a heck of a lot more than shade on a few others because of their beliefs, what did Christ say?

> "And when his disciples James and John saw *this*, they said, Lord, wilt thou that we command fire to come down from heaven, and consume them, even as Elias did? But

he turned, and rebuked them, and said, Ye know not what manner of spirit ye are of. For the Son of man is not come to destroy men's lives, but to save *them*. And they went to another village." — LUKE 9:54-56

They kept it moving. Even when righteous indignation may be right, it compromises the mission, goals, and objectives set forth by the kingdom of God. "Shade," just like the serpent, is subtle. Its intent is to publicly denounce and disrespect. Satan throws shade by casting a cloud of doubt that puts the burden of proof on the victim. That means you're guilty until proven innocent. Again, the gist of WMD is exemplified, and why the media is integral to the "war in heaven" now being waged on earth.

If you know someone's spouse is in the land of the living and you ask them in the presence of others, *is your wife/husband still with you;* you just threw shade on that individual's integrity by casting a cloud of suspicion. You've made that individual a suspect without saying anything that could be considered material or substantive evidence regarding why that particular spouse wouldn't "still" be with them. You've subtly insinuated (emphasis on sin) that all ain't cozy-comfy. It ain't what it appears. When it comes to the kingdom of God, the devil does the same.

The spiritual powers that be know the earthly powers that be can be manipulated into reporting insinuation in a journalistic manner that gives suggestion substance. One more time again, the "New World Order" doesn't operate on reality; it operates on the perception of reality. Mind manipulation begins with germination – planting the seed.

While the uses of social media platforms to plant "fake news" have socio-political ramifications, the spiritual implications are marginalized by a failure to frame these activities in a moral context.

Consider Matthew 26:59:

"Now the chief priests, and elders, and all the council, sought false witness against Jesus, to put him to death."

And, Mark 14:58:

"We heard him say, I will destroy this temple that is made with hands, and within three days I will build another made without hands."

And, Luke 23:2:
> "And they began to accuse him, saying, We found this fellow perverting the nation, and forbidding to give tribute to Caesar, saying that he himself is Christ a King."

All of the above is "fake news." It was false reporting spread by First Century "social media" as an instrument to orchestrate the crucifixion of Jesus Christ. These three passages erase all doubt why God has a serious problem with liars (Revelation 22:15). Bearing "false witness" made the Top-10 for a reason. Planting false news was aggressively employed in the murder of Jesus Christ.

Needless, but necessary to say, those who traffic in lies and deceit are standing on shaky ground. If you are a media "power that be," and you report lies, spiritual "powers that be" are fully aware that the proverbial bell cannot be unrung. Reporting accusations are just as convincing and convicting as reporting facts.

If "war in heaven" was a civil proceeding, the Bible is a pleading set forth by the kingdom of God in answer to the princedom of Satan's complaint. With regards to the princedom's pleading, even though there's a world of devil's advocates, what's the beef? What's the basis for the complaint? Is it breach of contract for Lucifer being fired as the "anointed cherub?" Or is it a class action suit covering all of the dragon's angels under a retaliation/wrongful termination theory?

Given such a Biblical hypothetical, Plaintiff's strategy is based entirely on attacking defendant kingdom of God's credibility. There's no material evidence that's ever been presented by any devil's advocate that either God or Jesus is unfair, unreasonable or wrong. If a legal argument is presented in such a cosmic matter it would be based on the defendant's refusal to conclusively prove existence.

When any devil's advocate argues that God doesn't exist, the legal question with regards to the matter is standing. Satan wants mankind to believe that an invisible God who refuses to show himself in a manner that erases all doubts does not have any "standing" on planet earth. Subsequently, Satan attacks the Christian believer's faith. And that's precisely why Hebrews 11:6 reads the way it does:

"But without faith *it is* impossible to please *him*: for he that cometh to God must believe that he is, and *that* he is a rewarder of them that diligently seek him."

Back in the day, rather than faith, Satan attacked Eve's belief. Consider the fact that in the Garden of Eden the concept of faith in an invisible God was unnecessary. Adam and Eve could freely speak directly with God. Contrary to 2 Corinthians 5:7, Adam and Eve *walked by sight; not by faith*. But the script got flipped. Because the Edenic couple couldn't appreciate what they were getting for thinking about what they didn't have, they introduced the concept of having faith in the unseen.

Eve didn't see the fallen angel Lucifer. She saw what Genesis 3:1 calls a "beast of the field." If Lucifer had appeared to her as some majestic glittering and glowing creature, maybe there could be a circumstantial argument that home girl was dazzled or *bling-bling'd* into her fall. Uh-uh; she kicked God to the curb for something in beast mode. That's comparable to leaving a "good husband" for a "good ho." Or how about a "good wife" for the woman you hooked up with in an alley?

Faced with those facts, forget the possibility of sex in the Garden and focus on the "morning after" spiritual implications. Eve positioned Satan to sing "*The Girl Is Mine*." In turn, God was put in the position that a Michael Jackson/Paul McCartney type debate was completely off the table. The only card left to play was Adam, who turned up as the "Big Joker" in Eve's hand.

Oh yeah, the script got flipped immediately. Having sight unseen faith in Satan then automatically necessitates having sight unseen faith in God now. If you're the wife or husband who's suddenly put in a number two position, actions have consequences across the board particularly when those actions are thrown in your face with a smile.

So, *straight outta the Garden*, Satan makes proof of existence an issue. Matthew 4:3-6: "If thou be the son of God" *prove it*. The scribes and the Pharisees, in accordance with Matthew 12:38: *show me a sign*. Luke 23:39; that other thief on the cross: "*What you workin' with?*"

When the only signs given are on the kingdom of God's terms accompanied by the need to have faith, the princedom of Satan fills in the blanks with lies and half-truths presently termed "alternative facts."

Pure unadulterated evil camouflages lying in a form of inverse reasoning that hides positives behind negatives making statements so-called alternative facts. When the serpent told Eve, "Ye shall not surely die," hiding behind the word 'not' is 'surely.' The operative word in this instance isn't *not* as a negative; rather, it's *surely* as a positive. The placement of surely after not makes the value of surely contextually greater. In other words, Satan added a positive to a negative making the statement positive. "Not surely die" means you will die, but death will have qualifications. The statement is deceptive.

On the other hand, if the serpent had said, "Ye shall surely not die," the operative word would have been *not*. The placement of not after surely makes the value of not contextually greater. In other words, Satan added a negative of greater value to a positive making the statement negative or an outright factual lie based on what God had adamantly said.

People who deal in half-truths and "alternative facts" are worse than liars because just like Satan they employ deception in their lying as a tactical strategy. This practice is *mo'* satanic.

Back to Akhenaten, it was necessary to get away for a minute to address the arguments made by so many concerning the Bible having parallel stories from other religions, legends, and myths. Again, it's a stratagem. Only a fool tries to float counterfeit currency that doesn't resemble the real thing.

Similarities in design don't equate with authenticity. Placing your face on a hundred dollar bill doesn't mean you can take it to the bank even if you have proper identification in your wallet.

Many place their face in the front of church congregations weekly using currency called a divinity degree or Biblical Studies Certificate. While degrees and certificates are a great show of commitment and perseverance in accomplishing a calling and goal, and should be applauded, those documents can never get their holder around 1 John 4:1-2:

> "Beloved, believe not every spirit, but try the spirits whether they are of God: because many false prophets are gone out into the world."

Now, since spirits is plural, that suggests the trying isn't restricted to church matters. It also applies to classrooms, boardrooms, locker rooms, even bedrooms. The spirit of God is pervasive. It doesn't just show up on a Sunday morning, Wednesday night, or Saturday Sabbath. If the person you meet at the club or in a bar is a liar and cheat, that spirit is not of God.

When Bernie Mac, as Dollar Bill, in *The Players Club* (1998) would say, *"Trouble-Trouble,"* trouble comes from a failure to spiritually screen and vet individuals that are dealt with on a personal level.

Whatever the reason, the people of ancient Egypt didn't thoroughly try the spirits that were in their Pharaohs. Consequently, they had big trouble!

Because God is not a respecter of persons in accordance with Romans 2:11, there had to be somewhere in time over the course of Egypt's pre-Moses history that all the Pharaohs were divinely told to get their headdresses together. But, rather than taking heed to the spirit of an unseen God, they bought into the spirit of a counterfeit. If faith in an unseen Almighty is going to be strategically interrupted, it has to be strategically replaced with a counterfeit. The only thing on earth that can be both seen and perceived as almighty enough to replace God is the sun. Again, given the angelic name Lucifer meaning "day star," the sun is the one image the princedom of Satan uses to establish both name and domain.

In ancient Babylon (modern day Iraq), the principal god is Bel. Bel is the name of the Babylonian sun god. Those "Washington Monument looking structures" throughout Egypt and the world, again, they're called obelisks. That's o-BEL-isks.

In Greek mythology, one of the principal deities worshiped and adored is Helios. Helios is the name of the Greek sun god.

In ancient Rome, one of the main gods worshiped is Apollo. Apollo is the Roman sun god. That which makes Apollo Biblically relevant is his mythological roots. Connecting the dots, Apollo is said to be the son of the supreme Greek god Zeus and Leto – a nymph. If that be the case, Zeus was a fallen angel and Leto was an earth woman. Once again, Genesis 6:4 makes it plain that the "sons of god" and the "daughters of men" hooked up. Unquestionably, Apollo was a Nephilim.

Of course, when it comes to Greek and Roman mythology, your fifth-grade teacher isn't going to tell you that the Twelve Olympians of the Greek pantheon along with the Twelve Titans were all fallen angels; i.e., devils. Just imagine the affect if it was widely known that movies like *Clash of the Titans* (1981/2010), *Percy Jackson & the Olympians* (2010), *Ulysses* (1954), *300* (2006/2014), and *Immortals* (2011) were all centrally focused on the exploits of Lucifer and Company when viewed from a Christian Biblical perspective.

But maybe there wouldn't be any effect at all considering the popular appeal of movies like *The Devil's Advocate* (1997) and TV shows like *Lucifer* (2015).

Consider the gist of Isaiah 5:20:

"Woe unto them that call evil good, and good evil; that put darkness for light, and light for darkness; that put bitter for sweet, and sweet for bitter!"

When movies and television shows whitewash, sanitize and thereby normalize the devil to the extent that audiences view him as a sympathetic character, then the "medium is the message" indeed. And, radio, television, film, and the internet (media) are in fact weapons of mass and mind destruction that Satan skillfully uses.

Further, with regard to Satan in image and name, there's Mexico's Mayans. The famed Teotihuacán *Pyramid of the Sun* speaks for itself. Even though half-world-away from Egypt, we not only find solar power, there's pyramid power. The Mayan Pyramid of the Sun and the Egyptian Great Pyramid are almost equal to one another in base perimeter. The Pyramid of the Sun is nearly half the height of the Great Pyramid. The slight difference is the Great Pyramid is only 1.03 times larger than the base of the Pyramid of the Sun.

Seven thousand miles between Mexico City and Cairo yet Teotihuacán's Avenue of the Dead and Giza's pyramid plateau look like their individual layouts were based on the same surveyor's general plan diagram. But of course, looks here aren't deceiving if the architect is in fact that great deceiver the devil, called Satan.

Regardless of what, which, or if any theory one chooses to buy, the advanced mathematics, astronomical alignments, and precision tools (which have never been found) employed to build these pyramidal structures required just as much brain as brawn. That's not to say God Almighty couldn't or didn't give the men and women of Egypt and Teotihuacán the smarts to do what a lot of folks think they did without extraterrestrial help, it's just if it looks like a snake, talks like a snake, and slithers, don't say it waddles.

There are Sanskrit texts proclaimed to be thousands of years old that evidence Twentieth Century technology. Where did that knowledge come from? If the oral histories of those ancient civilizations say it came from "the gods," just who on earth were those gods who imparted the information?

The same question asked Adam has to be asked again, "Who told thee thou wast naked?"

If ancient India possessed aerodynamic technology and actually did have flying machines called *Vimanas* that were in flight thousands of years before the Wright Brothers, how did *Aircraft Construction for Dummies* reach planet earth!

Back to the Garden; didn't Satan as serpent say, "ye shall know good and evil?" Who can deny that air travel as opposed to stagecoach isn't good? Sex when there's love as opposed to sex in the absence of emotion isn't better?

The mission of Satan's princedom hasn't changed. It's always been about improving the livelihood of mankind at the cost of mankind's eternal life. Propounding either ancient or contemporary knowledge comes from the gods doesn't mean that the knowledge is all bad. Quite the contrary, it can be all good. It's just the failure to realize that there is a Genesis 3:5 this-for-that/tit-for-tat relationship that makes for a spiritual dilemma.

Back to the future, just as Satan, as Lucifer, as "day star" is shown to be "caretaker" of earth, he has also set himself up to be the benefactor of earth's principal inhabiter; human beings. Again, *Prometheus Revisited*. And, just as Prometheus liked to play with fire, when it comes to the sun as a fire ball, just how much more in your face can Satan get? Well, how about Sunday?

In view of Exodus 20:8-11, how did Sunday become the preferred day to worship God throughout the Christian world? Let's dispense with church family politics, existential ecclesiastics, denominational dogma, and doin' what you've done all your life defense mechanisms for just a minute and subjectively look at what the devil has very shrewdly and convincingly done. Absolutely nowhere in the Christian Bible does it say Sunday is cool as either a substitute or outright replacement for the seventh day Sabbath that's listed as one of the *Ten Commandments*. Find where God, Jesus Christ, Matthew, Mark, Luke, John, Peter, Paul, or Mary specifically say Saturday's out and Sunday's in.

Since such is nowhere to be found, arguing Sunday is the seventh day of the week is pretty much like trying to make a case that the earth is flat because the bubble in a carpentry balance is in the middle of the tool when it's set on your kitchen table. And arguing Saturday is the seventh day of the week is pretty much like trying to make a case that the earth is round because you have NASA photos from the Hubble Telescope.

Whether it's the bubble or the Hubble, people are going to believe what they want to see regardless of proof con or pro. The bottom line; Sunday is what it is and that's the first day of the week. It's not the seventh.

The devil is well aware that he can show you a picture of an actor caught in the act, and if the actor says, "that's not me," some will echo the actor. And God knows he can show you a picture of himself, and if the devil says, "that's not him," some will agree in spite of what they can see clearly with their very own eyes.

Just how Christendom at-large adopted Sunday, the first day of the week, in preference of Saturday, the seventh, is all over the internet. It wasn't done in secret. Roman Catholicism under the authority of the Pope proudly claims responsibility for the switcheroo. So, there's no need to belabor what you can hear straight from the pontiff's mouth.

Accept it or not, if you are into going to church on Sunday as a routine, you are doing so out of tradition. It is a tradition that's been handed down over the centuries, and you've picked up on it like so many others before. With that as basis, soberly reflect on what the Egyptian Pharaoh Akhenaten was able to do. He somehow managed to get all of Egypt during his reign to kick all of the other gods to the side for the sake of worshiping the sun god Aten. How amazing is the parallel to this day and age? All of the other days have been kicked aside for the sake of worshiping on a "sun" day.

The Egyptians were a highly intelligent people. But even though they were an advanced civilization, they embraced Akhenaten, a leader that was totally controlled by the devil. This particular Pharaoh had no power in and of himself to change the religious persuasions of the Egyptians. In order to get sane people to follow an insane course of action requires supernatural alliances. Obviously, we don't know how deep the Egyptians were off into their religion, but we do know how deep most Christians take theirs.

Be it Christians or Egyptians, to get millions on a world scale to summarily alter their personal belief systems; a mass communications methodology employing mass deception would have to be initiated. People would have to buy the notion that established patterns of socio-political religious behavior had been kicked. And "the kick" was made by someone having a pipeline to God.

It's apparent that the Egyptians believed Akhenaten had the hook up. Who had the "hook up" respecting Christians and the seventh day Sabbath commandment's exit?

Consider 2 Thessalonians 2:3-4:

"Let no man deceive you by any means: for that day shall not come, except there come a falling away first, and that man of sin be revealed, the son of perdition; Who opposeth and exalteth himself above all that is called God, or that is worshipped; so that he as God sitteth in the temple of God, shewing himself that he is God."

Just who is this "man of sin?" The giveaway is the fact that it's a man – a flesh and blood human being. It's not a machine, as in a computer. Throughout history people have vigorously pointed at anyone who can be either directly or remotely linked to Revelation 13:18's 666. Given the fact that the 40th U.S. President's is Ronald Wilson Reagan, six letters in each of his names prompted accusations that he was the culprit, "the beast." Contrary to accusation bordering on wild speculation, however, individuals constrained by their own mortality are disqualified. Since this "man of sin" was on the scene during the Apostle Paul's time, in order to fit the Biblical bill, dude has to be someone representative of an organization or estate as in being an heir. If not, Revelation 13:18 would have said "the man" as oppose to "a man."

The word "the" is a definite article. As a matter of fact, it's the only definite article in the English language. When "the" is succeeded by a noun (man) there's the presumption that the reader knows who's being referred to. Saying here comes "the man" has a different connotation than saying here comes "a man!"

Because the Apostle John, writing through the inspiration of the Holy Spirit, knows "the" points to a specific man, the indefinite article "a" is used. "A" man can be any man just like "a" corporation is not the same as "the" corporation with regards to reference.

Accept it, the only "man" that's been around since the two epistles to the Thessalonians (A.D. 51) and the Revelation of Jesus Christ as penned by John (A.D. 95) corporately operates under the title pope. From A.D. 67's Pope Linus to 2017's Pope Francis, there have been 265 popes. All of them have been "a man" because in order to be a pope an individual has to be "a man."

A Catechism for Adults authored by Fr. William J. Cogan asserts as a Q&A under its Lesson 18 titled *The Pope, the Vicar of Christ* the following:

1. What did Jesus do to make sure his Church would always be united?
    He put one man in complete charge of His Church.
2. Who has complete charge of the Church?
    The Pope, who is the bishop of Rome and The Vicar (agent) of Christ on earth.
3. Do all Catholics have to obey the Pope?
    Yes, because he speaks with the authority of Christ.
4. Can the Pope make an error when teaching religion?
    No, not when he speaks as head of the whole Church.

Cited directly from a few Catholic publications that are found on the internet, there's more:

Does the Bible support the change to Sunday?
"Most Christians assume that Sunday is the biblically approved day of worship. The Catholic Church protests that it transferred Christian worship from the biblical Sabbath (Saturday) to Sunday, and that to try to argue that the change was made in the Bible is both dishonest and a denial of Catholic authority. If Protestantism wants to base its teachings only on the Bible, it should worship on Saturday." **Rome's Challenge www.immaculateheart.com/maryonline Dec 2003.**

"The Protestant is not obliged to sanctify Sunday and to abstain on that day from unnecessary servile work? Is not the observance of the Sabbath law among the most prominent of our sacred duties? But you every Christian may read the Bible from Genesis to Revelation, and you will not find a single line authorizing the sanctification of Sunday. The Scriptures enforce the religious observance of Saturday, a day which we never sanctify." **James Car-**

dinal Gibbons, The Faith of Our Fathers (1917 Ed.), p. 72-73 (16th Edition, p 111; 88th Edition, p. 89)

"For example, nowhere in the Bible do we find that Christ or the Apostles ordered that the Sabbath be changed from Saturday to Sunday. We have the commandment of God given to Moses to keep holy the Sabbath day, that is the 7th day of the week, Saturday. Today most Christians keep Sunday because it has been revealed to us by the [Roman Catholic] church outside the Bible." **Catholic Virginian, October 3, 1947, p. 9, article "To Tell You the Truth."**

Who Made Sunday Holy?
"Perhaps the boldest thing, the most revolutionary change the Church ever did, happened in the first century. The holy day, the Sabbath, was changed from Saturday to Sunday. 'The day of the Lord' was chosen, not from any direction noted in the Scriptures, but from the (Catholic) Church's sense of its own power...People who think that the Scriptures should be the sole authority, should logically become 7th Day Adventists, and keep Saturday holy." **St. Catherine Church Sentinel, Algonac, Michigan, May 21, 1995.**

"Question: Which is the Sabbath day?
Answer: Saturday is the Sabbath day.
Question: Why do we observe Sunday instead of Saturday?
Answer: We observe Sunday instead of Saturday because the Catholic Church, in the Council of Laodicea (A.D. 364), transferred the solemnity from Saturday to Sunday."
Peter Geiermann, C.S.S.R., The Convert's Catechism of Catholic Doctrine, p. 50, 3rd edition, 1957.

Gary Frederick Flanigan

Who Do We Reverence by Keeping Sunday Holy?

"It was the Catholic church which...has transferred this rest to Sunday in remembrance of the resurrection of our Lord. Therefore the observance of Sunday by the Protestants is an homage they pay, in spite of themselves, to the authority of the (Catholic) church." **Monsignor Louis Segur, Plain Talk About the Protestantism of Today, p. 213.**

"I have repeatedly offered $1,000 to anyone who can prove to me from the Bible alone that I am bound to keep Sunday holy. There is no such law in the Bible. It is a law of the holy Catholic Church alone. The Bible says, 'Remember the Sabbath day to keep it holy.' The Catholic Church says: 'No. By my divine power I abolish the Sabbath day and command you to keep holy the first day of the week.' And lo! The entire civilized world bows down in a reverent obedience to the command of the holy Catholic Church." **father T. Enright, C.S.S.R. of the Redemptoral College, Kansas City, in a lecture at Hartford, Kansas, February 18, 1884, printed in History of the Sabbath, p. 802.**

Whose Day of Worship is Sunday?

"They [the Protestants] deem it their duty to keep the Sunday holy. Why? Because the Catholic Church tells them to do so. They have no other reason...The observance of Sunday thus comes to be an ecclesiastical law entirely distinct from the divine law of Sabbath observance...The author of the Sunday law...is the Catholic Church." **Ecclesiastical Review, February 1914.**

"Nowhere in the Bible is it stated that worship should be changed from Saturday to Sunday...Now the Church...

instituted, by God's authority, Sunday as the day of worship. This same Church, by the same divine authority, taught the doctrine of Purgatory long before the Bible was made. We have, therefore, the same authority for Purgatory as we have for Sunday." **Martin J. Scott, Things Catholics Are Asked About, 1927 edition, p. 136.**

"It is well to remind the Presbyterians, Baptists, Methodists, and all other Christians, that the Bible does not support them anywhere in their observance of Sunday. Sunday is an institution of the Roman Catholic Church, and those who observe the day observe a commandment of the Catholic Church." **Priest Brady, in an address reported in The News, Elizabeth, New Jersey, March 18, 1903.**

Now, the noteworthy significance inherent is not intended to bash Catholics or Sunday worshipers. Just as some of your best friends may cross racial, ethnic, and sexual orientation lines, the same applies to religious persuasion. What warrants print time in terms of discussion is illustration of just how easy it is to think one thing and then find out the thing you've been thinking is another thing all together.

Many people are just simply unaware of the Sunday contradiction when standing or sitting face-to-face with the Christian Bible. On the other hand, perhaps many simply just don't want to know. Be that as it may, that's not the thesis of this book, WMD. Non-information is just as much a weapon of mass or mind destruction as misinformation. If there's a bomb in a building, only a fool in that building wouldn't want to know in time to get out and warn others on the way.

When you don't know what you don't know, sometimes you get a pass. However, when it's "hear no evil, see no evil, speak no evil," that's a personal choice to remain deliberately ignorant of that which is perceived as wrong.

When you hear someone you love is cheating on you and choose to remain in the relationship silently saying nada, that's one thing. But when you see with your "lying eyes" you're being cheated on and you choose to remain in the relationship silently saying nothing, that's not something else; you're something else. Ask a friend what that "something" is!

Consider the following assessment:

> "Thus have ye made the commandment of God of none effect by your tradition. Ye hypocrites, well did Esaias prophesy of you, saying, This people draweth nigh unto me with their mouth, and honoureth me with their lips; but their heart is far from me. But in vain they do worship me, teaching for doctrines the commandments of men."
> — MATTHEW 15:6-9

Sunday considered "The Lord's Day" is the "commandment of men." How often folks say how dumb and dumber Adam and Eve was respectively. But it's not about stupid; it's about deception. The power of Satan to deceive has nothing to do with intellect. Having a degree in whatever subject it may be does not prevent you from being fooled. This is why the Bible continually refers to Satan as a deceiver "who deceiveth the whole world" (Revelation 12:9). Be it religion, politics, economics or personal relationship investments; deception has no boundaries when it comes to cause and effect. If you are passionate about a cause to the extent that you are willing to ignore truth, deception is the effect.

Even though Sunday is what it is, and if you're a Sunday goer who (after exposure to all-of-the-above) now knows what you know, how easy will it be for you to break tradition? Even if you say you love Jesus, and he's clearly telling you (not the writer of this book) that Sunday observance in honor of him is vain? Chances of you obeying the Fourth Commandment just as diligently as you obey the other nine are probably just slightly better than that earlier mentioned snowball's. Buyer's remorse is a condition most resign themselves to live with.

The Biblical seventh day Sabbath begins at sunset on Friday and runs to sunset Saturday. How easy will it be for you to give up "Friday Night Lights" if you're into high school football or basketball? And when Sade sings, "Sweet as cherry pie; wild as Friday night" she isn't talking about Bible study.

But the same question posed regarding the Garden of Eden "tree" is the same applied to the Ten Commandments' fourth; what on earth is the devilish motive? Why would Satan focus his earthly efforts on such a seemingly obscure commandment? Do most Christians even think the seventh day Sabbath commandment is that big a deal, not to even mention it being number four on the list and not top-three?

As long as you go to church one day out of seven, if you're still honoring God with your presence, WTF (what's the fuss)? Just like a belated birthday greeting, as long as you remember, it's the principal that counts, right? If you accept a birthday wish a day late and maybe a dollar short what's the problem with worshiping God a day late, particularly when you're putting that dollar in the basket on time and every time? Can you even imagine living in a world where it's, *"Easy like Saturday Morning?"* You've already made a personal investment in Sunday. When it's Sunday and you have a personal relationship, "it's complicated."

Well, newsflash! The personal relationship between Jesus as Michael and Satan as Lucifer is a lot more complicated. While for sure, the kingdom of God is certainly well aware that all of your personal relationship questions come into play when Biblical truth is met; good and bad is a helluva thing when the wrong choice is made.

Satan was able to convince a third of heaven's angels to turn against their Creator and engage in an all-out conflict/war (Revelation 12:4). Subsequently, for an extraterrestrial intelligence, getting human beings to turn against a directive of God is mere child's play. This is why deception is faster than a speeding bullet, more powerful than a locomotive, and able to leap tall buildings in a single bound. When you are deceived, you're willing to take that bullet; stand in front of that train, and take leaps that have nothing to do with faith in God much less common sense.

When it comes to the seventh day, let's apply a little modern day analogous logic. Let's say you write a song or book. And, somebody says to you, "Cool, but I don't want your name on it." I want mine. Your work; my name. What would you think? Even if this somebody paid you; would you go for it?

If you are a serious artist, and you put serious time and serious effort into your work, chances are it's not about money. It's something deep down inside your heart and soul that makes you want credit for your intellectual property. What's the price tag on your very own personal integrity? Can you be bought?

Let's rewind and say it's all about the Benjamins with you and your work. It's a work for hire. But instead of a song or book, it's a baby you bring into the world. You were paid to have or make a child. If there's a *"heart in the house tonight,"* how easy is it to take the money and run?

Your baby is your "baby" regardless of it being in print or in person. If you love your work, anyone who has a heart has an emotional attachment to a labor of love. God is no different; "for God so loved the world." You know the rest and where it's found.

God is a serious artist:

> "The heavens declare the glory of God; and the firmament sheweth his handywork."— PSALMS 19:1

The heavens and the earth are the artistic creation of Jesus Christ. God signs his name to his work by instituting the seventh day Sabbath, and along comes Satan and replaces it with his name and image. Again, the angelic name for Satan is Lucifer. The name Lucifer means "day star." Lucifer's made the sun his image. Legally speaking, it's textbook misappropriation.

Even though Lucifer was cast out of heaven, and no place other than Isaiah 14:12 do you find his angelic name mentioned, the original meaning of the name and its import remains. In all likelihood, this is another reason why Jesus referred to Satan as the "prince of this world." Representative of the name day star, once again, perhaps everything in this solar system that the sun's rays touch and have gravitational power over is under the governance of Lucifer, now Satan the devil. Whether it's Venus or Mars, day on those planets and orbital trajectory is determined by the star that we call "the sun." Technically, by name definition, Satan is not only the "prince of this world," but prince of this solar system.

By misappropriating the glory of the sun as Satan the devil, the image of the sun has been bastardized. Throughout history, our "day star" has been used by Satan to glorify himself. Because of that corruption, we find Revelation 21:23 saying what it says: "And the city had no need of the sun." The same is repeated in Revelation 22:5.

Now, it doesn't say the sun won't still be in the sky, it's merely saying that earth doesn't need its light. And the same applies to the moon.

Why? Doesn't the moon reflect the sun's light? Moonlight is the image of the sun. The chapter and verse consistency Biblically supporting all of the above is not coincidental. All anyone has to do is just take the time to prayerfully connect the dots.

Bottom line, anything Satan has employed, inclusive people, will come to an end. They won't be needed. The kingdom of God is saying, *"Done with you."*

> "What do ye imagine against the LORD? he will make an utter end: affliction shall not rise up the second time."
> — NAHUM 1:9

Blood Sport, the Slave Trade, Trail of Tears, Schindler's List, Jim Crow, and all neo-philosophies and opinions that are devilish will not come into play the second time around.

Nevertheless, this time around, when it comes to "war in heaven," Sunday is celestial plagiarism, identity theft, and appropriation of name and likeness. The aggrieved party in this cause of action is Jesus Christ. From a cosmic perspective this is what it is.

Because the seventh day Sabbath points to God, it denies the devil what he considers his due as representative of his angelic name. Mankind's willingness to honor the seventh day Sabbath according to God's command is a sign of loyalty to the kingdom of heaven. Honoring any other day, especially one that has been co-opted by Satan, acknowledges the devil's power to usurp God's authority.

Because there is "war in heaven," the Fourth Commandment sits in the "midst" of the *Ten Commandments* just as the Tree of the Knowledge of Good and Evil sat in the midst of the Garden. The "fourth" (just like the one that comes in July) is a symbol of celestial patriotism. In terms of war, it's a cosmic flag flown here on earth. It's a metaphysical banner that quickly and unapologetically identifies loyalty.

Intelligently ask yourself why Revelation 12:17 reads:

"Went to make war with the remnant of her seed, which keep the commandments of God and the testimony of Jesus Christ."

Note the phrase "*keep the commandments of God.*" Given the fact that commandment is plural, that means the Ten Commandments are a complete set. There's no one commandment in the set that's more important than the other nine. If you break the Sixth (Exodus 20:13) by killing, it carries the same weight as breaking the Ninth (Exodus 20:16) by lying. In fact, according to James 2:10, if you're a liar, you might as well keep it moving and add adultery to the mix. But inversely speaking, if you are an adulterer, you are a liar. The two go hand-in-handcuffed-hand.

Also, note "the testimony of Jesus Christ." By definition, a testimony is a declaration. The only declaration in the *Ten Commandments* is embedded in the Fourth. There's no "Thou shalt" prefacing it. And even though there's no "thou shalt" introducing the Fifth, "Honour the father and thy mother" isn't accompanied by a declaratory statement. Exodus 20:10-11 is a declaration of independence because it tells the reader that God independently "made" heaven and earth. He didn't have any help.

Now, it's very significant that Exodus 20:11 says "made" and not create with reference to "six days." As a matter of Biblical fact, the word "created" is only used three times in the entire first chapter of Genesis. Genesis 1:1 references the creation of the heaven and earth. Genesis 1:21 references the creation of sea life and birds. And Genesis 1:27 references the creation of man. With the exception of these three verses, either the word "let" or "made" is used to describe God's actions.

When God says, "Let there be light," he's saying let be what already is. When you say "let" doesn't what you're letting already exist? Try "letting" the dog out that you don't have.

Genesis 1:25 indicates God "made." That's not the same as being told God created. For example, do you "create" breakfast or do you make it? Aren't the main ingredients already there?

What about when it comes to love? Can you "make love" if love's not already there? If it ain't already there, it's better to call it exactly what it is.

Regarding Genesis 1:25, God only needed to take what was already there as far as the DNA structures of land based beasts to remake a population of land animals that could coexist with mankind. The implication is given that the creation of a new species of animal life was unnecessary. When it came to mammals, reptiles, and insects, the DNA from those land based mammals only had to be genetically modified to enable coexistence with human beings. Evidently, such wasn't the case with sea and air life.

Whales and birds required "creation." The implication is the ecosystems upon which these particular creatures were dependent for survival was shot to hell and back. Since we are well aware of how delicately balanced nature has to be when it comes to fish and fowl, something ecologically devastating had happened. All sea and air species had to be re-created. Is it possible that the dragon and his angels' banishment from heaven to earth involved a vast armada of extraterrestrial spacecraft which polluted the skies and oceans of the planet?

Once again, it's important to keep in mind that there's often a duality in what's Biblically stated. With darkness symbolizing the devil, and darkness being upon the "face of the deep" (Genesis 1:2), is it really a leap to accept "the deep" as being a symbolic reference to earth's oceans and seas? If Satan and his multitude of fallen angels were submerged in earth's waters, doesn't it make plenty sense that all of the sea life on this planet would be destroyed? Wouldn't that be consistent with all sea life on earth having to undergo a re-creation or regeneration?

In spite of contemporarily customary angel depictions, Satan and his crew didn't come here as beings with wings attached to their backs. That portrayal as previously pointed out is Biblically inconsistent. They came as beings more scientifically and appropriately termed extraterrestrials. This requires dealing with the fact that UFO phenomena are not fiction, but Biblically supported and endorsed.

Indisputably, the fish population was wiped out along with all "winged fowl." Some angelic numbers crunching supports this theory. Revisiting Revelation 5:11:

> "And I beheld, and I heard the voice of many angels round about the throne and the beasts and the elders: and the number of them was ten thousand times ten thousand, and thousands of thousands."

Since it's a geographically scientific fact that 71% of earth's surface is covered by water, with that many extraterrestrials landing there were both unidentified flying objects (UFO) in the skies and unidentified submerged objects (USO) in the oceans and seas.

When Genesis 1:2 tells us the Spirit of God moved upon the face of the waters, the face was physically that of Satan and his multitude of predatory aliens. Just look at the consistency of that thought as reflected in the terminology found in Jude 1:13:

> "Raging waves of the sea, foaming out their own shame; wandering stars, to whom is reserved the blackness of darkness forever."

Revelation 12:4-9 revisited, there's the metaphorical symbolism establishing stars symbolically synonymous with angels. Jude's "wandering stars" are undeniably alluding to fallen angels.

Then there's Jude's reference to "sea waves." While sea waves may be adjectively personified as raging, they can't be ascribed feelings. "Shame" is a feeling. Only sentient beings have feelings. Water can't even feel wet. Unmistakably, with Jude's employment of shame, wandering stars and darkness, the fact that Satan and his angels were physically in the oceans and seas of earth should be without debate.

Where did all of these extraterrestrials go? Are they still here? That discussion, "reserved" for a later chapter!

That brings us to man. God, in the presence of other celestial beings decided not to recreate any dinosaurs or apes. Instead, a new species called man was created. But, even when it comes to the creation of mankind, Genesis 1:27 indicates God created "male and female" as a new species, but Genesis 2:22 acknowledges that God "made a woman." And of course, it had to be spelled out as "made" because Eve was formed from a DNA repository that was already there; Adam's rib.

Subsequently, when we find Exodus 20:11 saying, "For in six days the LORD made heaven and earth," the passage is in harmony with Genesis 1:1 because the heaven and earth were "created" in the dateless past and not in "six" literal days.

The Fourth Commandment is a living memorial to earth's "re-creation" or restoration. The seventh day Sabbath is a reminder that Satan destroyed earth's original beauty and in "six days" God made the planet new again. It's for this reason Exodus 20:8 reads, "remember." Remember signifies remembrance.

Each and every September 11th is special? It's not just about the time and date and what went down. It's also about remembrance. Similarly applied, there's Genesis 1:2. With Satan being the OT (original terrorist), each and every Saturday, *Day 7* is also about remembrance.

8 ARMAGEDDON

"And he gathered them together into a place called in the Hebrew tongue Armageddon." — REVELATION 16:16

It's said that all truth passes through three stages: denial, opposition, and acceptance. People will fall into one of these three categories. Deniers take the position, "No way, Jose." They've been conditioned to see things one way. If that way isn't theirs – game, set, match.

Peter was a denier, but Peter's denial was out of fear. Peter knew Jesus had out-of-this-world skills because he had seen and even confessed that Jesus was the "Christ, the son of the living God." Peter denied Christ because he was scared.

The disciple Thomas was a borderline denier. He had seen Jesus do all that he did, and heard Jesus say all that he said, but this disciple's doubt was a denial of material evidence. For the Thomas type seeing isn't believing if what you see isn't enough to dispel all doubt. When it comes to God and having faith, there's always going to be a hook to hang a doubt. If not, faith wouldn't be the substance of things hoped for and the evidence of things unseen.

The second group makes up the opposition. These are the ones who make it their mission to discredit the messenger as opposed to dealing with the message. Biblically, these are the Pharisees and Sadducees types. The trip part about the opposition mentality is it will try to deny. Whereas the real deniers deny because they don't want to accept the possibility that the message could be true, the opposition opposes because they know the message is probably true.

The third category is folks who say, "*Oh yeah.*" They look at the information and allow the chips to fall where they may. They follow the bread crumbs in order to see where it all leads. Biblically, these are the folks who do what Moses did when he saw the "burning bush." They "turn aside and see why the bush is not burnt."

Up to this point, this author has made it a point to use the word theory. The reason being enough literary liberty has to be given to doubt without danger of making wildly speculative unsubstantiated assumptions. Now, however, we're at the fulcrum of reader judgment.

Also, up to this point, the author has avoided linking conspiracy with theory. A conspiracy theory alleges an event or events to be secretly influenced by a premeditated group or groups of powerful people or organizations working together. And conspiracy theories often produce hypotheses that contradict the prevailing understanding of history or what's accepted as facts. Subsequently, with the help of Hollywood and various factions of the media, "conspiracy theory" is a derogatory term that provokes a knee-jerk reaction.

A quote attributed to political scientist Michael Barkun:

"Conspiracy theories rely on the view that the universe is governed by design, and embody three principles: nothing happens by accident, nothing is as it seems, and everything is connected. They are a matter of faith rather than proof."

In theory, if you purchase a lottery ticket you could win a prize. As long as you don't purchase that lotto ticket, your win stays theoretical. But once you purchase a ticket, your win is no longer theoretical, it becomes an immediate possibility. The more tickets you purchase, the more possible and eventually more probable your chances of winning become.

Such is the case with a "conspiracy theory." As long as there is no evidence, it is a conspiracy theory. But once you have a piece of evidence, no matter how flimsy or circumstantial that evidence is, the theory becomes a possibility. The more evidence the more possible and eventually more probable that conspiracy becomes. And at some point, you no longer have a theory at all. What you have is an actual conspiracy.

Isaiah 14:12-16 is Biblical testimony constituting material evidence that Satan attempted a heavenly coup. What made the devil think he could pull off a kingdom of heaven coup d'état is totally incongruous with what we understand as reality. Definitely that's a "contradiction of our prevailing understanding of history or what's accepted as facts." Sane individuals don't take on missions they know are impossible. Mr. Phelps and the IMF are for entertainment purposes only!

What makes an angel that is a created being think that it can take on its creator, who is almighty, and prevail? But again, this is the mystery of iniquity. And, again, alongside is the mystery of Godliness giving Satan the opportunity to try. God allowed the devil to go for what he knows; give it his best shot in the most horrendous possible way.

The vandalism of planet earth as described in Genesis 1:2, the fall of Adam and Eve in the Garden of Eden, the corruption of the human race through extraterrestrial miscegenation resulting in The Flood, not to mention Pharaoh flexing his muscles, are all together sufficient evidence to term the war in heaven a conspiracy devised by Satan that simply isn't theoretical. It is an interplanetary, intergalactic, universal plan initiated by Lucifer, the fallen angel, to control heaven and the earth.

In this day and age, it is a fact that the electronic media is a principal instrument or tool in the controlling process of Satan's quest.

At the writing of this book, it is estimated that around 47% of the world population (7.5 billion) has an internet connection. In 1995, it was less than 1%.

It is therefore naïve to believe that the "power" (Luke 4:6) to reach that number of people with a determined message wouldn't be incorporated into any game plan wherein spiritual control is the agenda and primary objective. The Bible is the play book detailing the war strategies for both sides of the conflict. By searching the scriptures, we can intelligently decide whose team we want to play for, or militarily speaking, whose army we want to join. Matthew 28:18-20 is the position of "power" the kingdom of God takes with respect to agenda and objective.

The ancient aliens' theory that many theologians dismiss as non-Biblical is actually Biblically on point in many respects. The only disconnect is in terms of semantics. What ancient aliens' theorists are interchangeably calling aliens and extraterrestrials, in reality is what the Bible calls fallen angels and demons.

Drawing strictly from the Bible, since the birth of Adam only traces back six thousand years; civilizations datelined thousands of years earlier cannot possibly be human from a Biblical perspective. Does this mean that a Bible based perspective is scientifically at odds or in error?

No. It means that the archaeological discoveries of ancient civilizations determined to pre-date Adam by thousands of years have to be alien or extraterrestrial. Remember, God said, "Let us make man in our image." If the "our" includes angels, and angels include fallen angels, given the Biblical fact that "man was made "a little lower than the angels," again, we look like them more so than them morphing into the image of us. That's the only way Hebrews 13:2 makes any biological sense. Subsequently, bridging the semantics gap between celestial terminologies is an endeavor of this book.

Yes, accept it or not, the Bible is one of the most revealing and descriptive books documenting UFO and extraterrestrial phenomena ever written. Certainly, it's the most authoritative and widely read. The problem is, Satan has deceived pretty much the entire globe into believing UFOs and USOs are of the Roswell variety when in reality they are spiritually rooted celestial entities that the Bible has identified from the beginning as being here all of the time. Borrowing from *The Matrix*, the answer isn't out there; it's in the pages of the Scriptures. *"Are we alone"* is a question that doesn't dignify an answer from anyone calling themselves a Christian.

"I am with you alway, even unto the end of the world."
— MATTHEW 28:20

Genesis 32:22-30, Jacob's very close encounter, has many interpretations. Just who on earth was he wrestling? Some say no one that the incident was merely a "vision of prophecy." Others hold that Jacob's opponent was metaphorical in that the verse 30 assertion, "I have seen God face to face," would be a contradiction in the face of Exodus 33:20 and John 1:18. Bottom line, the account has been rationalized, romanticized, and mythologicalized.

But, putting a pin in commentary versus commentary for a minute, how about reading what is originally said just how it's originally written. Genesis 32:24 reads, "And Jacob was left alone; and there wrestled a man with him until the breaking of day."

Again, the Sodomites of Genesis 19 saw the "two angels" as men. Since the angels that visited Sodom were seen as men and exhibited supernatural power, and the "man" that wrestled Jacob exhibited supernatural power, a little bit of inductive reasoning suggests that supernatural powers exhibited by beings that look like men are in fact angels/extraterrestrials.

Now, if you really want to believe Jacob's "man" just happened to have martial arts skills or was adept in some kinda modified Vulcan Death Grip, there will always be a Doubting Thomas Club. Such a conclusion is no less valid than any other opinion that refuses to take the Bible at word. The fact of the matter that matters; supernatural abilities are alien to this planet. And, anybody exhibiting supernatural abilities is alien to this planet. Causing mass blindness and/or physical paralysis with a look or touch is in the same league with hitting a 700-foot home run or throwing a football end zone to end zone, 100-yards on the fly, for a touchdown. Mere mortals don't roll like that. And, that's why serious questions have to be raised respecting how the great pyramids of Giza were actually made, as well as who actually built them.

Ancient aliens' theorists are correct in part. It's just a matter of the missing part in their research being a factual discernment of who and what those ancient aliens in reality are. Just consider how clever it would it be on the part of Satan to cloak himself in the garb of either science fiction; or space aliens "on a five-year mission to explore strange new worlds, to seek out new life and new civilizations, to boldly go where no ET has gone before!"

When intelligently considering the Roswell incident, do you really think an extraterrestrial spacecraft is just going to have some kind of "wardrobe malfunction" and crash land on a farm in New Mexico? Satan and his angels threw mankind a bone labeled Roswell because they knew the media would run with it. So, the story behind the story is why?

Once more, Satan is a deceiver. He is a master at dodge and deflect. He is *The Specialist* in sending man down the rabbit hole instead of anywhere over the rainbow.

Matthew 24:26:

> "Wherefore if they shall say unto you, Behold, he is in the desert; go not forth: behold, he is in the secret chambers, believe it not."

Isn't Roswell, New Mexico, "in the desert?" Couldn't Roswell's Area 51, Hangar 84 where the alien bodies and spacecraft debris were supposedly stored be considered a "secret chamber?" If we are deceived to believe that the *"aliens are coming,"* be certain that in the devil's doing there is a hidden agenda.

Consider the fact that Satan realizes that with regards to UFO phenomena, the majority of human beings fall into either one of two camps – believers or non-believers. Since Satan probably figures that the movers and shakers in Christendom are dumb because most preach and teach that UFOs aren't scriptural, Roswell targets the secular community. But prior to addressing that bulls-eye, let's examine how scriptural UFOs really are.

Acts 1:9-11 reads:

> "And when he had spoken these things, while they beheld, he was taken up; and a cloud received him out of their sight. And while they looked steadfastly toward heaven as he went up, behold, two men stood by them in white apparel; Which also said, Ye men of Galilee, why stand ye gazing up into heaven? this same Jesus, which is taken up from you into heaven, shall so come in like manner as ye have seen him go into heaven."

What was behind the cloud? Was the cloud concealing something the men of Galilee weren't supposed to see? Who were the two men who stood by in white apparel? Are these the same two men in shining garments that Luke 24:4 says "stood by" at the sepulcher? What's up with the "shining garments?"

Well, obviously, those "two men" are angels. And, because angels are extraterrestrials, whether you want to accept it or not, these beings looked human. They didn't look like the Roswell grays; or the Predator. Again, doesn't Hebrews 13:2 make that clear?

> "Be not forgetful to entertain strangers: for thereby some have entertained angels unawares."

By not understanding what Genesis 1:26 is saying, some have managed to get the whole thing twisted. Again, angels don't look like us, we look like them!

Additionally, didn't the two men observing Jesus Christ's ascension say, "shall so come in like manner." And didn't Jesus in Matthew 24:27 confirm what his two angels said?

> "For as the lightning cometh out of the east, and shineth even unto the west; so shall also the coming of the Son of man be."

When comparing notes, do you really think the return of Jesus Christ to planet earth is going to be in the form of angels with wings like you see embedded in stained glass church windows? Or, do you think the "Second Coming" is going to be something similar to what both the two angels and Jesus said? In order to reflect what was said requires a space vehicle.

But let's go back to the "shining garments." What do you think these two angels were wearing? Once again, customarily angels are depicted with wings and halos. But absolutely nowhere in the Bible is an angel having wings encountered by a human being; yet this is the picture that's always being painted and sold. The same goes with halos.

We're not told that these two angels had wings, halos, or faces aglow like Moses when he came down off the mountain. Rather, it was what the men were wearing that caught the attention. Doesn't wearing something like a silver or chrome metallic space suit kind of squash the notion of the angel surreal? Unquestionably, these two men were extraterrestrials. And they were wearing the type of garments we've already probably seen costumed in a sci-fi flick. The reality check here, however, we're seeing similar garb in the Bible and not some sci-fi flick. Since these two men in the space suits wouldn't tell us what was behind the clouds that received Jesus out of human sight, for argument's sake, let's speculate it was some type of spacecraft. Now why does God need a spacecraft? Well, two reasons for sure.

Number one, allowing the Bible to be its own interpreter, Matthew 24:27 can't make the answer any simpler. It's so you can see him!

Certainly, we've all stood on the ground and looked upward at a 747 flying high. We're all well aware of how big a 747 is on the ground. But how big is that jet at 35,000 feet? If it wasn't for the aircraft's contrails, your eyes might not even see it at all.

But even more elucidating, how big is a cloud? Only when standing on the ground and peering skyward at a 747 flying high do we get a perspective on just how huge clouds are. When that 747 disappears into a single cloud and takes more than a few seconds to zoom out, it's readily apparent that a cloud is ideal cover for aircraft concealment. Particularly an aircraft that could very well be the size of New Orleans' Mercedes-Benz Superdome!

Revelation 1:7 provides its take on Jesus' Second Advent: "Behold, he cometh with clouds; and every eye shall see him." Every eye means those that can't pick up a jet's contrail, but sure in the heaven could see something the size and mass of a football stadium coming at them from 35,000 feet!

Of course, we don't know what was behind the cloud that Jesus disappeared into when he left earth over 2,000 years ago. And when considering Exodus 13:21-22, we don't know what was behind "the pillar of cloud by day" and "the pillar of fire by night." But in utilizing a little God given reasoning, we can intelligently speculate (for argument's sake) there was some kind of physical phenomenon concealed by both the cloud and the fire. If not, God being God could have downsized and simply used a Genesis 8:11 dove or a 1 Kings 17:6 raven.

Whichever, the fact is the scriptures have already described the manner in which Jesus Christ will return. Certainly, an armada of UFOs the size of sports stadiums appearing in the skies all over the earth would not be inconsistent with revelation. This means movies like *Arrival* portend the advent of Christ just as much as they do the surreal appearance of anything else Hollywood can extraterrestrially imagine. But, the media portrait of out-of-this-world visitors finds the Second Coming of Christ to be the last thing in mind.

Reference was previously given James and John wanting to "command fire to come down from heaven" (Luke 9:54-56).

Now isn't that an interesting way of saying what they said. Obviously, these two disciples had been around Jesus long enough to pick up on the fact that Christ was a man of prayer. If you are a Christian, when's the last time you commanded God to do something for you?

James and John were making reference to 2 Kings 1:9-14. Elijah's actions were in a military context. Therefore, militarily speaking, where did the "fire" come from when it came down from heaven?

Again, when we don't ask these questions, we adopt a totally surreal view and understanding of the Bible that leaves us intellectually hanging in a physically real universe. God would not have said in Isaiah 1:18, "Come now, and let us reason together" if he didn't want us to use our brains in understanding the Scriptures he asks us to search (John 5:39).

Unless there was an unseen spacecraft/vehicle/chariot of fire orbiting the planet comparable to the *Starship Enterprise*, the fire associated with 2 Kings 1:9 originated through spontaneous combustion.

Can fire originate without an apparent external source of ignition? Certainly, with God all things are possible. But when Biblical surrealism is always the first choice for explanation, then God is relegated to being basically a magician in a universe governed by laws of physics that he created. What's the purpose of writing a script if you can snap your fingers and make the movie? Presto, Chango, Alakazam!

James and John said "command" because their reference was to Elijah and his military conquest. They also knew that Elijah had been swooped up by a "chariot of fire." The two disciples were thinking in a military context. Note the fact that they said, "Lord," which meant their prayer was to Jesus, who was standing right beside them. Their would-be "command" was that the "command ship" somewhere there in heaven use a *Phaser*, *Photon Torpedo*, some kind of weapon to target the individuals they found offensive. James and John knew there was something in the sky that had the power to do some serious damage on earth. If not, and since they referred to Jesus as Lord, they could have simply petitioned Jesus to take care of business.

Motion picture features and television series acquaint worldwide audiences with spacecraft and their exotic weaponry as science fiction. Isn't it strange folks can buy it on screen but not on the pages of their Bible. Presenting science fact as science fiction is a stratagem of the devil. It hides the truth in plain sight causing those too busy looking up to stumble over. Where the inverse is a reverse spiritual progression is backward not forward.

Satan knows reverse psychology. He's well aware that the best way to deal with truth is to co-opt it. Manage it by making it the story you want to tell.

In Eden, Satan used science fiction to disguise science fact. Today, he takes science fact and disguises it as science fiction. By seeding the landscape with visual images of extraterrestrials as predominantly monstrous, the "war in heaven" becomes germ warfare on earth. The germ is false ideas begin microscopic and gradually grow cancerous to the body, mind, and soul. The concept of angels as aliens either good or bad is a virus that a media-programmed mind can't compute when planted deep in the subconscious.

Once again, Ezekiel 28:17 says nothing about Satan having the physical appearance of a monster. And given the fact that birds of a feather flock around together, it's probably safe to bet the ranch that his posse of fallen angels superficially don't look monstrous either. Therefore, when it comes to extraterrestrial subject matter in television and film, the thin line between reality and fantasy is often smudged.

Are sci-fi writers and producers to blame for the smudging? No more than the preachers and teachers, who fail to point out the fallacies that infect a God-conscious state-of-mind. When the book says, "pray without ceasing," and "quench not the spirit," and "prove all things" it's talking about being *en garde* when it comes to bull-crap.

Accept it or not, prayer is a tauro-scatology detector. When you "pray without ceasing" and are willing to "prove all things," you are continually open to being led by the Holy Spirit. God knows when he has an open door to your mind and heart even when you don't. This is why Revelation 3:20 says, "I stand at the door and knock." Jesus is taking the bet if he knocks long enough or loud enough, sooner or later you'll open the door even if it takes a lifetime of pounding.

Only when the spirit is quenched does the knocking stop. But it's the individual that never answers the door who does the quenching, not God. And that's exactly why 2 Thessalonians 2:10-11 reads the way it does:

> "And with all deceivableness of unrighteousness in them that perish; because they received not the love of the truth, that they might be saved. And for this cause God shall send them strong delusion, that they should believe a lie."

Keeping it real, drawn from the above, there comes a time when Jesus has to say "F" it; the "F" standing for "Forget," of course.

Media people, many of whom are journalists, are trained to be detectors of bull. Our training days are our school daze. We are constantly *en garde* against crap no matter how attractive the packaging. Media schools wire media folk to be that way even though some are just innately gifted and astute when it comes to the con. So when it comes to media professionals being slicked and tricked by the "art of the deal," there's usually something totally unsuspected in play. The unsuspected is Satan – the wiles of the devil and his minions.

It bears repeating; the greatest trick the devil has ever pulled is getting people to believe he doesn't exist, particularly journalists and media people. Matthew, Mark, Luke, and John were not only disciples and apostles, they were journalists. They were and still are "the media." If not for their investigative reporting and documentary skills, Christianity would be as popular in this day and age as Mazdaism.

Are you acquainted with Mazdaism?

Get the point!

This means the kingdom of God has a very high regard for media professionals who are willing to tell it like it is. Reporters and journalists have a seat at the big table right along with the preachers and teachers. But as such is the case with any profession, the skill sets can be employed for either good or bad.

Given the fact that the nose for news and the film director's eye rarely smells out or focuses respectively on "war in heaven" having a reality based connection with earthly events is peculiar. It defies logic that a culture willing to slap "IN GOD WE TRUST" on the back of a dollar is so hell-bent on ignoring God and pushing themes associated with Satan at every opportunity.

Of course, collegiate classrooms push journalistic objectivity that's code for *First Amendment* "separation of church and state." Matters of doctrine and dogma are never touched until there's a Waco or poison in the Kool-Aid moment. This reticence on the part of journalists to deal with Satan in the pulpit in the same manner he's dealt with in Congress and the Oval Office is a professionally disparate practice. Life and death issues that kill the soul are more debilitating than those which kill the body. Christian acceptance of the seven deadly sins as entertainment is incongruous Christian preaching their rejection.

What's 1 John 4:8 got to do with movies, television shows, video games, and "news" that exploit murder, death, and destruction in order to get ratings? Isn't it obvious, that the "god" being trusted is the god of green paper as opposed to green pastures (Psalms 23:2)?

When the media as a profession turns to profits instead of prophets, spiritual discernment is compromised. Media moguls, filmmakers, producers, directors, reporters, correspondents, and executives become the unwitting accomplices of a satanic agenda in preference to God's.

When media news organizations boast "Speaking Truth to Power," their promos are more bark than "news bite" when Ephesians 6:12 "principalities and powers" are not targeted in their speech. There is a reticence on the part of television news journalists to associate acts of evil with Satan. Intelligently ponder the journalistic willingness to publicly term any natural disaster an "Act of God."

Once again, Luke 9:56: "For the Son of man is not come to destroy men's lives, but to save *them*." Spiritually speaking, the unwillingness to say "Act of Satan" is not "speaking truth to power." It's kowtowing to a pseudo-Christian culture that's willing to embrace the existence of God to a certain extent, and not the devil to any. "Speaking Truth to Power" implies standing up to chicanery, wrongdoing, deception, and evil by calling a spade a spade.

Now, if you can't call out the age-old spiritual architect of chicanery, wrongdoing, deception, and evil, the truth being spoken is spiritually shortsighted. Your news mantra is more about politically correct perception than spiritually correct solution. Right and wrong has to be examined in the societal context of good versus evil. The Revelation 12:7 war game is chess, not checkers.

Drawn directly from the Bible (Luke 12:47-48), the kingdom of God cuts the unwitting pawn a little slack. But the premise of this book is truth versus falsehood as the focus, not saint or sinner. Radio, television, film, and the internet are the vehicles that will carry all subscribers either into spiritual light or spiritual darkness. Coupled with the internet data previously referenced, there's also an estimated 4.2 billion on this planet having access to TV. It's therefore understandable why Satan's media interests and efforts are so worldwide pervasive and UFO concentrated.

Thus far all being considered, it is reasonable to presume that the proliferation of UFO sightings around the globe is the works of the devil and his angels. There's no reason that angels in the camp of God would be engaged in these superfluous flybys and displays of aerial posturing for the benefit of mankind's curiosity and wonderment. Because the Bible plainly says God is not the author of confusion, and people are being confused by what they're seeing, then we know from strange lights in the sky to strange crop circles on the ground that the work isn't that of Michael's heavenly host. Luke 17:20 makes it crystal: "The kingdom of God cometh not with observation." It's not how Michael rolls pre-Armageddon.

Subsequently, Christendom's failure to see the Biblical connection and significance, Roswell is neither mentioned from the pulpit nor much less given a footnote in any sermon. If you went outside right now and saw the skies filled with so-called flying saucers, chances are you wouldn't know what to think. Luke 21:25-26 paints a picture of how many will respond to seeing something totally unexpected in the sky:

> "And there shall be signs in the sun, and in the moon, and in the stars; and upon the earth distress of nations, with

perplexity; the sea and the waves roaring; Men's hearts failing them for fear, and for looking after those things which are coming on the earth: for the powers of heaven shall be shaken. And then shall they see the Son of man coming in a cloud with power and great glory."

You're certainly welcome to think "coming in a cloud with power and great glory" is a fleet of weather balloons if you want. But the devil knows that won't be the case, and the "very elect" know it too.

Matthew 24:24 talks about the skills associated with the "very elect." The implication, being "elect" is not quite good enough. A fleet of space ships in reality will deceive the elect.

Returning to the idea that the Roswell incident was part of a satanic conspiracy aimed at a secular audience, Satan has always used the media to spread propaganda and disinformation. Television programs and movies pit good aliens against bad aliens. For example, take *Alien vs. Predator* (2004). The slick of the trick finds most not unwittingly or subliminally rooting for the Predator, but consciously doing so all because "the enemy of my enemy is my friend."

How soon we forget that *Predator* (1987) and *Predator 2* (1990) found this cinematic extraterrestrial eviscerating human beings without blinking a beady eye. When it comes to a devil versus a demon, the "enemy of your enemy is not your friend." Mankind doesn't have any friend other than God personified in Jesus Christ when wrestling "not against flesh and blood."

The alien bodies that crashed in Roswell, if there were any at all, was an incident orchestrated by Satan that was designed to give material credibility to the existence of intelligent life in the universe beyond our own. For the incredibly naïve it was intended to answer hint-hint on Satan's terms that mankind is not alone. Roswell was an "alternative fact." It was meant to frame the story of extraterrestrial visitation in a manner the princedom of Satan wants the true story told.

Even though the Bible has always and forever answered that question (*Are we alone?*), the devil's intent is to twist it. So, by putting Roswell on the map, movies like *E.T. the Extra-Terrestrial* (1982), and *The Day the*

Earth Stood Still (1951 and 2008) and *Contact* (1997), and *Arrival* (2016) have injected the "germ" that there are extraterrestrials who may be visiting earth with good vibrations. That is, to help mankind prosper.

Isn't prospering precisely what Satan wanted man to do when he tempted Eve? Of course, what the devil left out of his prospering help was Mr. Spock's split finger "live long and prosper."

Being the devil's advocate, how do we really know for sure that some of the UFO sightings or ancient alien theories that extraterrestrials other than devils and demons haven't been working behind the scenes helping a brotha out? Helping mankind to boldly go where we've never gone before with technology, medicine, and the like? Since this is a humongous universe, maybe there are some "good aliens" who have worm-holed their way to our planet, or star-gated from another dimension into ours? Does it have to be so black and white in terms of good and evil? Can't the so-called "Grays" be that shade of grey?

Newsflash! The Bible says there are no shades of grey. The scriptures take the position that there are only two colors in the spiritual rainbow. Those colors are light and darkness. With regards to any ancient aliens setting foot on planet earth other than Michael's angels and Satan's angels, Luke 16:26 responds:

> "And beside all this, between us and you there is a great gulf fixed: so that they which would pass from hence to you cannot; neither can they pass to us, that would come from thence."

Of course, there are those theological scholars that maintain the rich man and Lazarus is only a parable. If you agree, or ain't totally or even partly buying the Gospel according to Christianity, you don't care who shot J.R. with a "big bang theory." You're governed by another intellectual covenant. You keep it moving minus all of the above.

Never-the-more or less, however, when the Spirit of God is allowed to expand the mind beyond the boundaries of the skull allowing one to see with that pineal gland or "third eye," it becomes readily apparent that the "great gulf fixed" is undoubtedly an interstellar-interdimensional barrier reef that bars all life forms other than Michael's angels and Satan's from getting to this planet in either a peace or conquest capacity.

Astronomers continually find what's thought to be "earth-like planets" in the backyard of our galaxy. But a backyard that's only 40 light years away (235 trillion miles) traveling as fast as we can presently go (165,000 mph/gravity assisted) would take 162,585 earth years to reach.

Think about it; when there is a war, the art of war requires setting up blockades. If Cherubim were placed at the entrance to the Garden of Eden, why wouldn't such be posted to "keep the way" of planet earth!

The bottom line is just as Luke 16:26 reads, nobody gets in and nobody gets out. And this Biblically spiritual fact is scientifically confirmed by the astronomical observations of deep space massive black holes that are inexplicably spread throughout the entire known universe.

So, with such speculated as being the case, Revelation 16:14 tells us exactly who and what these UFOs that are being witnessed actually are:

> "For they are the spirits of devils, working miracles, which go forth unto the kings of the earth and of the whole world, to gather them to the battle of that great day of God Almighty."

The significance of Roswell is prophetically established in the above passage. It puts the "kings of the earth," in the forms of various world leaders, on notice that their State governments had better take the possibility and probability of an extraterrestrial world threat or alien invasion of earth very seriously. But in knowing full well that earth has already been invaded, since Satan and his angels are the celestial invaders, intelligently ask yourself what could possibly be the devil's battle plan? Is it the battle called Armageddon?

The name Armageddon is referenced only once in the entire Bible (Revelation 16:16). Consequently, subsequent chapters have to be examined for clarity.

The metaphorical symbolism employed in Revelation 16-19 involves both terrestrial and extraterrestrial forces. However, if you don't understand what Revelation 12 is saying with regards to a "war in heaven," and if you don't know who "Michael and his angels" really are, and if you don't believe UFOs have any Biblically-based material credibility, then you're just not going to have any Biblical foundation beyond *Jesus Saves* to understand what Armageddon is really all about.

This battle is not a World War I, II, Korean, Vietnam, or Gulf War type. It's the culmination of "war in heaven." What's seen here is earth's nationwide deployment of military muscle in the extraterrestrial conflict between God and Satan. To think it's a war between earthly kingdoms over Middle Eastern oil, land rights, or territorial occupation requires Biblically erasing Revelation 19:19.

> "And I saw the beast, and the kings of the earth, and their armies, gathered together to make war against him that sat on the horse, and against his army."

Because of the metaphorical symbolism, the symbolic references have to be followed all the way to a point where contextual consistency ends. That line in the sand is Chapter 20, *The First Resurrection*.

Metaphorical symbolism cannot be grasped (if grasped at all) by an exclusively linear approach rooted in a misunderstood Biblical narrative. Like bread crumbs, one has to follow where those droppings lead. There's no straight path through the forest to find home. Beginning with Armageddon's first and only mentioning, references to *kings, nations, angels, devils, making war with the Lamb*, and culminating with 19:19 are all referencing the same thing; *Apocalypse Now*.

The "him" on the horse is Jesus Christ. But if you ain't buying "him" as Michael, and his "army" as Michael's "angels" (Revelation 12:7), then by default you're going to think Armageddon jumps off as a totally terrestrial issue. This battle is an extraterrestrial engagement.

Now consider very carefully. How would world leaders and their individual governments become physically involved in celestial warfare with extraterrestrial beings? That's a fight that has world leaders instructing their armies to side with Satan.

Factually, the stage was set during Ronald Reagan's U.S. presidency with regards to his Strategic Defense Initiative (SDI) called *Star Wars*. Reagan's initiative proposed the use of ground-based and space-based systems to protect the United States from attack by ballistic strategic nuclear weapons. The initiative purportedly focused on strategic defense rather than strategic offense. But do you honestly think this technological stratagem was really all about the X's with no consideration being given to the O's?

An *Introduction to Planetary Defense: A Study of Modern Warfare Applied to Extra-Terrestrial Invasion* is a 2006 book billed as a serious look at defending the planet in the event of an extraterrestrial invasion. But, not until the 2017 revelation regarding the Pentagon's mysterious UFO program was it publicly realized that this secret initiative began in 2007; a year after the 2006 book. Bottom line, planet earth's extraterrestrial visitation was and still is being taken very seriously. Only those who are caught up in *TV Land* fantasy are "lost in space."

Whether you know it or not, both domestic and cosmic powers that be could care less if you believe. Pentagon plans were shown to have already been on the drawing board for either a real or perceived alien incursion. Hypothetically speaking, what if an emissary of the devil lands on the White House lawn with an olive branch? Or what if first contact is China's Tiananmen Square or Russia's Red Square? The Bible has forewarned that Satan will dupe world leaders to enlist on his side in order to fight against God.

It bears repeating: "And I saw the beast, and the kings of the earth, and their armies, gathered together to make war against him that sat on the horse, and against his army." The world is being prophetically hipped that Armageddon will find all of the major powers that have a nuclear arsenal fighting on the side of Satan deceived into thinking that the Second Advent of Jesus Christ is an alien invasion of planet earth!

Now, don't be confused by the allegories. Jesus Christ is not going to come riding into town on a horse. Back in the 1800's when Native Americans used the term "iron horse," it was commonly understood they were referring to a steam-bellowing train. Subsequently, when it comes to any technology that's lacks contemporaneous comparison, metaphorically describing a train as a horse is as reasonable as describing the *Starship Enterprise* as Pegasus.

The apostle John penned Revelation during first century A.D. Captain James T. Kirk and crew didn't come on the scene until 1966. In his writing, if the Apostle had been impressed to descriptively use a transportation vehicle other than a horse, do you seriously think anyone reading Revelation 19:19 prior to 1966 would have understood what John was talking about if referencing something like a Battlestar Galactica fighter craft? If you are or aren't a Trekkie, try describing a Klingon Bird of Prey. Obviously, the only frame of reference in describing this fictional spacecraft is the word 'bird.' But when you remove the bird word, you are probably very hard pressed to wrap your intellect around exactly what that thing is in a technologically framed physical universe.

If you look up in the sky and see "that thing" and are asked by a reporter to tell the world what you saw, even now you may be at a loss for words in technical terms. You will keep it simple by describing what you saw in terms that have personal acquaintanceship.

An airplane's wings are called wings because their positioning on the fuselage resembles the appendages of a bird. That small marine fish in the genus *Hippocampus* is called a Seahorse, not because it looks like a hippo, but a horse. That ocean floor multicellular parazoan animal that has a body full of pores is not referred to by biological classification – it's simply called a sponge. Real world familiarity will always frame out-of-this-world sights and sounds.

Think about it. Jesus Christ and all of his angels returning to earth in power and great glory; and the United States, Russia, China, Britain, France, India, Pakistan, Israel, Iran, and North Korea attempting to stop the Second Coming. They've been tricked by Satan into thinking that the approaching armada of spaceships is an alien invasion Hollywood style.

The United States alone has a nuclear weapons arsenal possessing enough power to destroy this planet five to 50 times over. Maybe "it ain't bragging if it's true," but when the rap is cavalier that the U.S. can totally destroy North Korea, China, and Russia in half-an-hour, does any nation need that much juice? And, by the way, what's China and Russia destroying during that same half-hour?

Since John 10:10 reads, "The thief cometh not, but for to steal, and to kill, and to destroy," isn't it obvious that the spirit behind nuclear proliferation at such an order of magnitude is supernatural? The only practical purpose behind that measure of nuclear build up is military readiness in the event of extraterrestrial invasion. The capability of throwing a knockout punch five to 50 times over only makes sense if the planet you're targeting isn't planet earth and the entities you're hitting aren't human.

If the USA knew that there was a clear and present danger of alien invasion (from a place more distant than Mexico or Syria) do you think you'd catch it on the six-o'clock news? Or do you think a unilateral decision would be discreetly made to blow that alien hangout up?

If Project Blue Book and the X-Files contain information deemed threatening to National Security, you can bet the *Ponderosa* that "*The Revelation Will Not Be Televised.*"

When considering the billions of dollars that have been and continue to be spent on the following, do you seriously think these artificial satellite probes are for exploration purposes only?

- Pioneer 10 – Launched in 1972, flew past Jupiter in 1973. Contact lost in January 2003 and is heading in the direction of Aldebaran (65 light years away) in Taurus.
- Pioneer 11 – Launched in 1973, flew past Jupiter in 1974 and Saturn in 1979. Contact lost in November 1995. The spacecraft is headed toward the constellation of Aquila (The Eagle), northwest of the constellation of Sagittarius. Barring incident, the spacecraft will pass near one of the stars in the constellation in about 4 million years.
- Voyager 2 – Launched in August 1977, flew past Jupiter in 1979, Saturn in 1981, Uranus in 1986, and Neptune in 1989.
- Voyager 1 – Launched in September 1977, flew past Jupiter in 1979 and Saturn in 1980, making a special close approach to Saturn's moon Titan. Probe entered interstellar space August 2012 and is still active.
- New Horizons – Launched in 2006, probe made flyby of Jupiter in 2007, made a flyby of Pluto in July 2015. It is currently headed

towards a flyby of the Kuiper Belt object 2014 MU69 as part of the Kuiper Belt Extended Mission (KEM). That rendezvous will occur in January 2019.

Now, intelligently ask, what's the mission objective in saying "Hey" to someone that's 100,000 earth years away? Unless there's more to the mission than what's being told, there's no reality-based logic in such a quest. When distance can no longer be measured in miles and time by human standards is an eternity, such pursuits can only be relevant to extraterrestrial agencies. Again, just as God asked Adam, "Who told thee thou wast naked," having a price tag on rockets and Pluto shots in the billions that could wipeout world hunger five to 50 times over, a similar query has to be posed NASA, "Who told you to do what you do?"

Does the possibility of a real-life *X-Files* with *Men in Black* sound preposterous? Well, when it comes to war, if governments can't be trusted to tell the truth, the whole truth, and nothing but, who can you trust?

> "And I saw heaven opened, and behold a white horse; and he that sat upon him was called Faithful and True, and in righteousness he doth judge and make war.'
> — REVELATION 19:11

Accept it, Revelation 19 reads what it reads. The devil is a liar. And it's not beyond a liar to say anything that needs to be said in order to achieve an ambition or goal. Satan was behind the crucifixion of Jesus Christ. Because Satan knows there is a real "war in heaven," do you seriously think he wouldn't inspire the use of nuclear weapons to thwart the Second Advent of Jesus Christ? Do you really believe that the Apollo moon missions became ho-hum and abruptly ceased in preference of artificial satellite missions to Mars and beyond? If your beeline destination is Mars, Pennsylvania, and the only "Rest Stop" is Moon, Virginia, does it make any sense to take Moon off the map?

When what you hear ain't matching what you see, do you believe your ears or your "lying eyes?" Of course, this is why spiritual things are spiritually discerned. Space travel is spiritual because the word of God is spiritual. 1 Thessalonians 15:50 declares, "Flesh and blood cannot inherit the kingdom of God." Given the fact that the kingdom is somewhere in outer space, it's foolish to dismiss God from the NASA equation. Here the "figures" aren't "hidden." So, if you're figuring to set up housekeeping on the moon, Mars, or anywhere other than this "mother" (earth), the book of Revelation forewarns a rude awakening is coming.

In a world where the military industrial complex has a financially motivated commercial interest in manufacturing exotic weaponry, a war against a perceived cosmic alien entity is a no-brainer to a warmongering mindset. When you are on record as a proponent of dropping bombs, launching missiles, and applauding idiots who do, you have embraced a satanic agenda.

With regards to the U.S. Constitution and the Second Amendment; just why is there need to own an AR-15 or AK-47? Well, the sho'nuff for real gorilla in the room is Exodus 20:5 and the words, "visiting the iniquity of the fathers upon the children unto the third and fourth generations." Prophetically, that text has become a fact of karma in more ways than one to the unrepentant guilty-minded that are haunted by ancestral sins.

Card carrying members of the NRA who push the right to "bear arms" that can unload hundreds of rounds a minute know payback can be something that rhymes with itch. So, the Boy Scout motto comes into their play. But, rather than a guilt-trip falsely anticipated race war for lynchings and an assortment of other racist bad deeds done, Satan fronts the NRA as fear-mongering puppets in preparation of a Biblically based star war (Revelation 16:16).

If you buy the Bible, you buy the fact that Satan, both as a contemporary and ancient alien, knows a military style assault rifle is the perfect storm for storming an extraterrestrial invasion if the invaders are Michael and his angels (Revelation 19:19).

Yes, it sounds far-fetched. But the U.S. Pentagon doesn't think so based on 2017 documents revealing the Defense Department's Advanced Aerospace Threat Identification Program.

Even in the face of children being slaughtered, maimed, and injured; and adults who have children still want to hold on to these AR and AK killing machines uncompromisingly, undeniably their madness has spiritual implications. The only spirit capable of fostering that kinda crazy has to be that of the devil that few choose to see and accept as a real-life extraterrestrial being. People, organizations, and branches of government operating under the divine influence of God in the form of a real-life Jesus Christ/Michael don't "forget their children" thereby personally giving God license to do so as well (Hosea 4:6).

The race war from a satanic perspective, however, reaches beyond domestic when U.S. officials are found in predominantly Caucasian countries such as Russia pushing NRA agendas. Chapter 12 of this book will be more poignant in addressing race as a motivating factor in a cosmic induced arms race. Until "12" just suffice it to say that Satan as an extraterrestrial has a cosmically vested interest in pitting human beings against other human beings by using fear as a tactical feature. And, tactically, the most readily identifiable feature for activating a fear that's been satanically rooted is skin-color. Believe it or not, skin-colorism historically and contemporaneously propels military and private armaments for Armageddon.

Consider the term "sand niggers." In case you didn't know, it's directed at a person of Middle Eastern or North African descent. Since the operative word isn't sand, why the need for denigration? Where is all of this derogatory, offensive, and ethnic slurring coming from beyond geographic location?

Human beings are the highest form of intelligence on this planet. The inability for humanity to be humane can only be explained by the existence of extraterrestrial entities having an agenda other than peace on earth, good will toward men. Doesn't Revelation 12:12 hit home literally?

Racism in all of its multifaceted layers and multi-faced liars is illogical. Certainly, it's incongruous for anyone claiming Christianity and "In God We Trust." Yet, it persists among the lowest of the spiritually lowdown who are found in the highest positions of a republic government.

The princedom of Satan doesn't care that the leader of North Korea is perceived as crazy. It could give a dime that Iran is perceived as a clear and present danger to whomever's national security. Satanic mileage is not got from just being crazy; it's achieved by being the crazy a Richard Pryor album calls out. That means where perception is reality, chaos and confusion past, present, and future based on race and ethnicity are the princedom's extraterrestrial end game. Satan introduced racism into the world and he is and always will be its commander and chief sponsor.

The devil as ET needs a catalyst for swaying devilish followers to be armed to the teeth. The "sins of the fathers" who continue to introduce and sponsor the racist attitudes and behaviors picked up on by their children are foundational to Revelation 19:19. If not, intelligently ask yourself just what are the "armies gathered together to make war" with? Sticks and stones?

The conspiracy orchestrated by Satan and his angels to control the heaven and the earth is ongoing. And the ability to use the media in the cosmically broad sense of the word in that effort is a critical component of that plan. Getting the public to believe that "we're not alone" psychologically paves the way for believing that our cosmic company whenever found is only interested in a hostile takeover a la *Pixels* (2015).

NASA as an acronym has all the letters of Satan with the exception of the letter "T." Perhaps since a "T" may be seen as symbolizing the cross of Christ, it explains why the agency wasn't named the National Aeronautics and Terrestrial Space Administration.

Spiritually consider NASA's obsessive quest to send a manned mission to Mars as a prerequisite for one day colonizing the planet. Do you really think it coincidental that September 28, 2015, found NASA releasing a press statement that Mars has "flowing water," and Hollywood releasing *The Martian* only four days later on October 2, 2015?

The point? From a spiritual perspective, 1 John 5:8 is the point.

"And there are three that bear witness in earth, the spirit, and the water, and the blood: and these three agree in one."

The so-called water on Mars will never be in agreement with the water on earth in accordance with 1 John 5:8. Mars is not called "the red planet" as a result of Jesus having shed any blood there. And the three that bear record in heaven that Mars will never be a habitat for mankind appear only two verses earlier (1John 5:6-7).

Simply, Mars is not a sanctified site. To sanctify something is to set it apart for special use; to sanctify a person is to make him or her holy.

Sanctification is a state of separation unto God; Mars is a state of separation from God. Respecting Matthew 5:5, the "meek" cannot "inherit" the earth if they've boldly gone. Armageddon is a planet earth thing. If you are a Christian thereby believing in the Second Coming of Christ to earth, do you think Jesus will stop at Mars in order to pick-up laundry he didn't leave?

9 THE BLACK HOLE

"But the children of the kingdom shall be cast out into outer darkness: there shall be weeping and gnashing of teeth."
—*MATTHEW 8:12*

Granted, the Bible is filled from cover to cover with imagery and figures of speech that stretch the mind to its outer limits. But remarkably, there's astonishing symmetry and consistency once one begins to see and accept what's written and read as reality-based in a physical world and universe.

Matthew 22:11-13:
> "And when the king came in to see the guests, he saw there a man which had not on a wedding garment: And he saith unto him, Friend, how camest thou in hither not having a wedding garment? And he was speechless. Then said the king to the servants, Bind him hand and foot, and take him away, and cast him into outer darkness; there shall be weeping and gnashing of teeth."

Matthew 25:29-30:
> "For unto every one that hath shall be given, and he shall have abundance: but from him that hath not shall be taken away even that which he hath. And cast ye the unprofitable servant into outer darkness: there shall be weeping and gnashing of teeth."

When recalling Luke 16:26, this "great gulf fixed" is undoubtedly referencing this "outer darkness." Our Milky Way galaxy is around 100,000 light years across. Light travels at a speed of 186,000 miles per second. This means an object traveling at the speed of light, which is the theoretical maximum speed for any object, would take a full 100,000 years to traverse the entire Milky Way.

According to NASA, the Voyager probe is traveling around 35,000 miles per hour (gravity unassisted). At this speed, the probe is capable of traversing a distance of one light year in about 20,000 years. To cross the Milky Way at this speed, Voyager would have to travel for around 2 billion years.

The "great gulf" that's fixed is both time and space. So technically, *Star Trek the Next Generation* would require 4,000 generations just to get out of the Milky Way if traveling at the universal speed limit.

When it comes to gulfs and outer darkness is all of this merely the work of Biblical writers who were hooked on allegory, metaphors, creative imagery, and figures of speech? Or, were their writings divinely inspired by a source that's been where no man or woman has physically gone before? Let's be fact of the matter, if you don't see the Bible beyond a storybook about Adam & Eve, Noah & the Ark, Moses & Pharaoh, David & Goliath, Samson & Delilah, Daniel & the Lions, and Jonah & the Whale, then it's going to be a serious challenge for you to see the Bible outside the realm of *The Lord of the Rings*.

In a physical universe, both Matthew and Luke are talking about deep space. In a metaphysical one, there are predominating popular theological interpretations: (1) the absence of God's presence, which is light, and (2) hell. Certainly, in terms of outer darkness both interpretations have merit. Definitely, because time and time and time again God is synonymously linked with light, there's absolutely no reason to think any darkness, be it outer or inner, wouldn't be applicable to both a figurative and literal interpretation of hell. However, because there is a duality to the scriptures, once a tangibly scientific interpretation is introduced to chew on, the plausibility of possibility is not remote.

In reemphasis, God, in the physical forms of Jesus Christ on earth and Michael in heaven, are extraterrestrial. Just because we don't see the big picture doesn't mean the parameters of our human vision is end of story. The main reason a little bit of knowledge can be a dangerous thing is found in the fact that a little of anything can be just enough to hang false information on when you think just a little is all you need. Strictly because most don't and won't go beyond the comfort zone of what's taught in Sunday or Sabbath School, Bible boundaries are well defined, and anything that doesn't fit neatly within is dismissed without any investigation. That's why dogma is dogmatic. When the Bible says, "prove all things." all includes the Bible.

As human beings, when we are in our right mind health-wise, we live in a real world that exists in a real universe that's governed by physical laws. Because there is the law of gravity, whether you're a fat head, big head or an air head, you're not going to float away. You're grounded unless you take a plane. Since Matthew uses the word 'outer,' he's directing attention to something outside of the inner norm. The only thing outside of the normal darkness we deal with on earth is the darkness of outer space.

Luke uses the term "great gulf fixed." Since Luke isn't talking about the body of water touching the eastern shore of Mexico, five will get you ten he's also talking about outer space. When things are obvious, it is what it is without debate. While outer darkness can certainly be open to hermeneutic and exegesis discussion amongst biblical scholars, the Bible is written for the grade school dropout. Trust your eyes and the spirit of God inside your head, when you look up and out into the sky on a starry night, that's "outer darkness." A PhD from ITC, or any other seminary, school, college, or university is not required to tell you different.

Actually, the pinpoints of light you're seeing on that starry night are light years away. Other than the sun, the closest star to earth that can be seen is Alpha Centauri which is four light years away. If you could pick Alpha Centauri out of the crowd, you're looking at a point of light that left the Alpha Centauri star system four years ago. Think back to where you were and what you were doing four years ago. Well, that's when that pinpoint of starlight we're just now seeing radiated from our closest star neighbor.

Our sun, which is also a star, is only 93 million miles away. If the sun burned out now, it would be eight minutes from now before we would even know it. That means every time we look into a nighttime sky and see stars, or a daytime sky and see the sun and moon, we are looking into the past. Stars that are hundreds of light years from earth, the light that we see with our eyes today may have left that star during the life and times of Harriet Tubman, Marcus Garvey, or Malcolm X. Some starlight just now reaching our eyes may have been radiated when Jesus lived in Nazareth. And those stars so far away that can only be seen through an observatory telescope, the light we're just now seeing may have initially left during the time of the Jurassic Park dinosaurs over 500 million years ago.

The distances are so vast that those pinpoints of light in physical reality represent stars of mindboggling size. Whereas an estimated 1,300 Earths could fit inside Jupiter; 1,000 Jupiters could fit inside the sun; 475,000 suns could fit inside Rigel (the brightest star in the Orion Constellation); and 5 billion of our suns could fit inside UY Scuti, the largest star presently known.

But all things considered, given such a "great gulf fixed," those stars would have to be such an insane size to be seen as "a thousand points of light" or anything else. With Rigel 864 light years and UY Scuti 9,500 light years from Earth, could Luke 16:26 be anymore illuminating in making its point?

Earth is only 25,000 miles in circumference. Because radio and television frequencies are part of the electromagnetic spectrum and travel at the speed of light, information sent and received is instantaneous given the 7:1 ratio between velocity and distance. This is why we are able to experience news and sports LIVE. Anything moving that fast, our physical ability to detect any delay in a broadcast signal is impossible. Making it personal, traveling at light speed means you could go from New York to LA back and forth about 75 times in one second.

In a very simplistic sense, this is what's meant by the term "space time." When the distances are so humongous that miles can't even mentally compute, how can the spatial dimensions of length, width, height be physically separated from the temporal dimension time? Perhaps all-of-the-above somewhat explains why Jesus puts such a premium on eternal life. Flesh and blood simply cannot inherit the kingdom of God for the simple reason that flesh and blood cannot go the distance.

Be that as it may, however, when it comes to flesh and blood linked to inheritance, there's an even more basic issue summed up in a three letter word; sex.

Outer space is a microgravity environment. If you basically understand how that "little blue pill" works, you understand that a penile erection requires gravity. Outer space lacks the necessary gravitational pull required to regulate a male's blood flow to his lower extremities. And, with regards to women, there would be similar challenges when it comes to "getting in the mood."

But, provided all of the above could be figured out to mutual "satisfaction," the question of pregnancy in weightlessness is even more germane. Microgravity does not permit sperm to travel at a speed conducive to getting where it needs to go beyond a snail's pace. In space, things don't shoot; they just wad. That means where there is no progeny there can be no "inheritance." Bottom line, these issues ain't talked about on the NASA Channel!

Human beings have to be physically eternal to physically deal with the reality of a physical universe called outer space. That fact alone means there is a practicality to the word of God beyond the comfort of the sweet-by-and-by.

So, what does all of that mean when it comes to the concept of *Star Trek*? Is warp speed for human beings possible outside the bounds of *TV Land*? Will mankind find a wormhole or a stargate in order to navigate the cosmos?

Newsflash! No.

If mankind in its current state of mortal existence gained access to a faster-than-light (FTL) spacecraft propulsion system, interstellar travel would be humanly manageable. Likewise, if a wormhole or stargate were found, vast distances could be traveled in minutes and hours instead of decades, centuries, and millennia. And of course, therein is the problem. FTL, wormholes, and stargates can't theoretically coexist with the Bible. If you believe the testimony of Jesus Christ, you can't run with the vision of Gene Roddenberry.

In order for *Star Trek* to fly (the Enterprise, that is), 1 Corinthians 15:50 would have to be a lie. If mankind can conquer Luke 16:26's "great gulf" by traversing distances measured in light years, man as a flesh and blood mortal being has just inherited the kingdom of God. Aren't the heavens God's kingdom? If not, then Genesis 1:1 and Psalms 19:1 are also lies.

Are you really willing to go there theoretically? Bottom line, "you can't serve two masters." It's the Bible or Hollywood? Both can't be right when it comes to flesh and blood.

The bottom line, 1Kings 18:21: "How long halt ye between two opinions?"

Again, the gist of WMD is if you are going to personally and publicly profess a belief in "GOD" or Jesus Christ then "Follow him." For most, the book commonly referred to as the Bible is the road map for following "him." If you don't buy "the book" or your heart isn't really in it, then stop perpetrating both a public and personal fraud. No more church attendance Sunday, Wednesday, Saturday, or Easter. No more solemnly swearing with hand over Bible. No more texting with use of the initials OMG. Merely standing with hat removed and hand over heart during the playing of The Star Spangled Banner will suffice when it comes to matters of the heart. The only one *"Playing Your Game, Baby"* is you.

Reflect back on what happened immediately after *The Fall*.

> "And the LORD God said, Behold, the man is become as one of us, to know good and evil: and now, lest he put forth his hand, and take also of the tree of life, and eat, and live for ever: Therefore the LORD God sent him forth from the garden of Eden, to till the ground from whence he was taken. So he drove out the man; and he placed at the east of the garden of Eden Cherubims, and a flaming sword which turned every way, to keep the way of the tree of life." — MATTHEW 3:22-24

In the abstract, employing a bit of hyperbole that's not so hyperbolical, if you were asked how long would it take to reach the Orion star system that's 800 plus light years away what would you say? Well, if you didn't have a calculator at hand, an off the cuff answer might be forever. So, think about it. If mankind had access to warp speed, wormholes, and stargates permitting a breach of the space time continuum, not only would space travel be conquered, time travel would be also. Theoretically, mankind would "live forever."

Network TV shows such as *Timeless* (2016) and *Time After Time* (2017) are straight outta the Garden of Eden when viewed theoretically. Forget going back in time in attempt to change decades and centuries old events. How about going back to the Garden and stopping either Eve or Adam from doing what they did!

Or, how about taking Golgotha Hill with an assault weapon and preventing the crucifixion of Jesus Christ! Given space and opportunity, you know somebody would try that.

Seriously, if you believe there is a God, do you honestly believe a "Supreme Being" is going to let that happen?

Newsflash! Warp speed, wormholes, and stargates make the attempt happen if mankind in a flesh and blood state has access to the technology.

If your dog had access to the technology that would allow it to open your refrigerator door, what would it do? Yes, it would eat.

In similar regard, what does Genesis 3:22 say?

> "And the LORD God said, Behold, the man is become as one of us, to know good and evil: and now, lest he put forth his hand, and take also of the tree of life, and eat…"

In terms of relative natures, dogs are to humans, what humans are to angels. If given the opportunity, we will eat – figuratively and literally speaking. The *temptation* is too great to *walk away from the love*.

So, if the "way of the tree of life" was barred from man's reach, the "way of warp drive, wormholes, and stargates" are going to be barred as well.

While all of these sci-fi shows are entertaining, drawn directly from the pages of the Bible, they are rooted in science fact. The ideas for these TV shows and movies are not just imaginations gone wild. They are based on theoretical principles inspired by extraterrestrial intelligences that know what time it is even though many folks watching these programs for "entertainment purposes only" don't.

TV and movie style vampires, werewolves, mummies, zombies, Frankenstein, time travel, and space travel are all individually interwoven into the "ye shall not surely die" tapestry. When the medium is the message and the message transmitted is Biblically conflicting, the "war in heaven" becomes a mental tug-of-war on earth. What do you believe? Who do you believe? Even though you may think the answer is obvious; easier said than done.

There is a 1979 movie entitled *The Black Hole*. Black holes are a staple for sci-fi movies because they are strange and mysterious. Billions are said to exist throughout the universe. Their mass is so great, meaning their gravitational field is so strong that even light traveling at 186,000 miles per second can't escape.

Ponder for a moment being on a dark road at night where the fog is so thick that your car's headlights won't shine beyond five feet. Second thought, that analogy isn't black enough for you. Paint your halogens with mud and then ponder being on a dark road at night in thick fog. That's a black hole. They are an astrophysical reality in a real universe. And, interestingly enough, they exist in the centers of most galaxies. And because light can't get into them, and light can't get out of them, a black hole's interior is totally invisible.

Another amazing thing about black holes is the fact that objects are not sucked into them. Black holes do not suck. Suction is caused by pulling something into a vacuum, which a massive black hole is not. Instead, objects fall into them. Again, black holes are a gravitational force. Gravity doesn't suck you. On earth, gravity only pulls you when you submit yourself to its sphere of geophysical influence. This is why we can walk, run, and do what we do without falling flat on our faces.

Only when we submit by stumbling, losing balance, and/or collapsing does gravity become involved. Gravity, therefore, doesn't pull us down; if it did we'd be down all of the time because gravity is around all of the time. If you don't play with gravity, gravity won't play with you. In the heavens, the same protocol applies because the laws of physics are universal.

There's a 1997 movie titled *Event Horizon*. And what a coincidence that the '79 *Black Hole* numerically reverses to a '97 feature where both occupy a cinematically parallel universe, astrophysically speaking.

The event horizon, when it comes to black holes, is the point of no return where the gravitational pull becomes so great as to make any escape impossible. Think of it as being comparable to standing with your feet together and falling backward with the expectation that whoever is behind will make a catch before you fall flat on your back. When it comes to a "trust fall," the event horizon is the point where a back step won't break your fall.

Now, what makes all of this Biblically relevant is Revelation 20:10:
> "And the devil that deceived them was cast into the lake of fire and brimstone, where the beast and the false prophet are, and shall be tormented day and night for ever and ever."

When the Bible talks about that place called hell, it's always a place to be either cast or thrown into. In other words, both figuratively and literally, you don't get sucked into hell. You have to get thrown there. Subsequently, in a physical universe governed by physics, is it really that far outside the scope of plausibility that a black hole could in fact be Biblical hell?

If in fact extraterrestrial sentient beings exist, and they do; and if these entities are to be disposed of just like the Bible says, and they will; what better refuse dump in the universe than an astrophysical black hole? It is an object and location that cannot be seen into, and once inside confinement is eternal. Satan and his confederates will be thrown or cast into hell. And, a black hole is about as hellacious as it gets in the known universe.

Additionally, Biblical hell is always associated with fire. Do black holes meet that requirement? Well, since Daniel says, "knowledge shall be increased," some newly discovered knowledge regarding black holes is the view that just beyond their event horizon are radiation waves. It's now maintained by more than a few astrophysicists that once the event horizon is breached, radiant energy emissions will instantaneously incinerate anything and everything prior to its reaching gravitational singularity. This means that even though radiation is not fire in the conventional sense as we might think of it, a microwave you can't see will cook a hot dog just as effectively as a campfire's flame that you can.

Better rephrase – black holes do "suck" if you are unfortunate enough to get thrown into one!

Preposterous that the location of that place the Bible calls hell is in full view of the Hubble Space Telescope? Or has the Bible always revealed it, and we are just too myopic to see the forest for all of the trees? The trees in this case are stars, and the forest is the universe.

But should it really be all that surprising? The fact that the "word was made flesh" in John 1:14 doesn't negate the fact that the same word "made all things that were made" drawing from John 1:3. "All things" happen to be everything in a physical universe.

Therefore, operating on the theory that a massive black hole is that physical place called hell, where is the "event horizon" in each individual life? Is it one event, or is it a series of events that pulls one closer, and closer, and closer to the point of no return? Certainly, we'd all like to think that life's figurative black holes are far enough away to avoid getting caught up in the capture. But the problem with that thinking is still the law of physics. No light in and none reflected out makes them invisible.

Because the title of this book both implies and asserts that the media has a major role in the war in heaven, a close look has to be given the physical characteristics of media beyond the obvious that are rather obvious when you think about it. For example, have you ever wondered why the screen on your television, laptop, tablet, or smart phone is black when it's turned off? Believe it or not, that's how close a "black hole" is to your life. Televisions, computers, and cells are terrestrial black holes. Here is where the physics of a galactic black hole and your pocket, lap, desk, table, and wall-sized ones find singularity.

Turn a TV, cell, laptop, tablet completely off. Shine a cell phone flashlight directly on it. Light from outside can't get inside the device even though light from inside can get out. Everything we see on a TV, cell, laptop, and tablet is being generated because of light emissions within by tiny pixels. Each pixel represents a color. The combination of all these pixels makes up the screen images seen. The lack of light emissions by these pixels is blackness. Therefore, the screen on a turned off electronic device is seen as black because it's neither emitting light from within nor is it reflecting or transmitting light waves from without.

The same construct applies universally. An "absolute black" object celestial and terrestrial absorbs all the colors of the visible light spectrum and reflects none of them to the eyes. Vantablack is the blackest black known to man. It was scientifically created and absorbs 99.965 percent of all visible light. This means to the human eye it is borderline invisible when seen against any background other than white.

Imagine walking into a room with ceiling, walls, and floor painted Vantablack. Those who've had the experience are quoted, "It's so dark that as you walk in you lose all sense of where you are, what you are, and especially all sense of time."

Unquestionably, Vantablack gives new meaning to: "Is that black enough for you?"

Whenever we see a basic black to Vantablack object, a range of visible light waves striking that object are being absorbed. Associated with these light waves is a continuous range of frequencies and energy (heat) conversions. Subsequently, fundamental laws of science govern physics (the universe) and chemistry (the rainbow). Whereas physics is involved with the principles of physical phenomena and the basic forces of nature giving insight into the aspects of space and time; chemistry focuses on how substances interact with each other and with energy (heat and light). This is why wearing black clothes in the summertime literally ain't cool. You burn up. Black holds (absorbs) heat. So, wearing white during the summer and not after Labor Day is more than a fashion statement. White surfaces reflect all wavelengths of light.

This suggests that within the realm of physics, chemistry, and spirituality, any environment that's governed by the principle of light emission without light penetration demands total submission to the light emanating from within.

Viewed from a scientific or "black hole" perspective, isn't it understandable why Jesus put it the way he did?

> "If any man walk in the day, he stumbleth not, because he seeth the light of this world. But if a man walk in the night, he stumbleth, because there is no light in him.
> — JOHN 11:9-10

Likewise:
> "The light of the body is the eye: therefore when thine eye is single, thy whole body also is full of light; but when *thine eye* is evil, thy body also *is* full of darkness. Take heed therefore that the light which is in thee be not darkness. If thy whole body therefore *be* full of light, having no part dark, the whole shall be full of light, as when the bright shining of a candle doth give thee light."
> — LUKE 11:34-35

The metaphorical use of the light sources being the sun and a candle is significant. The relevance of such is not just restricted to the era and there being no such thing as a light bulb or flashlight. But, when it comes to sunlight and candles, they represent the purest form of radiant light energy. Seriously, what if Maurice White would have named his group, *Earth and Wind*?

In a world bombarded with spiritual influences, radio, television, film, and the internet are a manipulative and controlling force. When it comes to the "war in heaven," why wouldn't Satan conspire to control any medium where the communication is channeled in one direction only? That direction is out since he's operating within the confines of this world. If you were the "prince of the power of the air," would you want any airway to be controlled anyway other than yours?

When Jesus Christ says, "I am the way" (John 14:6) and "I am the light" (John 8:12) the subtext is natural science just as much as it is spiritual in application. Being "the way" means even a one way closed-system communication channel is still a two-way street. Even that figurative "black hole" is still penetrable with the right competing message. And, of course, that right is "the light." The "light" found in the Word of God can penetrate the blackest of holes anybody might find themselves in. Seriously, it doesn't get any blacker than being a thief hung out to dry on a cross.

But make no mistake, one thing's for sure; if you're hanging with Jesus Christ, Luke 23:43 tells everybody, Jesus is hanging with you.

10 WHITE NOISE

"But I would not have you to be ignorant, brethren, concerning them which are asleep, that ye sorrow not, even as others which have no hope. For if we believe that Jesus died and rose again, even so them also which sleep in Jesus will God bring with him. For this we say unto you by the word of the Lord, that we which are alive and remain unto the coming of the Lord shall not prevent them which are asleep."
—*1 THESSALONIANS 4:13-15*

The human eye is able to detect only a tiny part of the electromagnetic energy we call light. This energy varies measurably according to frequency, wavelength and velocity. Previously it was indicated that light travels at a speed of 186,000 miles per second. In the portion of the electromagnetic spectrum that actually pertains to seeing light, colors range from what is termed infrared to ultraviolet. All other variants fall somewhere in between.

With regards to the physical properties of light, infrared has the longest wavelengths and ultraviolet the shortest. For example, infrared light has a wavelength of one ten-thousandth of a meter. Ultraviolet light has a wavelength of one hundred-millionth of a meter. Visible light, which is only that portion of the spectrum we can see, is sandwiched between those two extremes. This means when you see a rainbow, you are looking at a light sandwich.

Human vision can only detect light waves that are approximately one millionth of a meter in length. Subsequently, a human being's ability to see anything is a function of light's dynamic behavior.

The phenomenon of sound is not a component of the electromagnetic spectrum due to its inability to travel at light speed. But, with regard to human hearing, the same fundamental principles apply. Audible sound for human hearing is confined to a frequency range usually between 20 and 20,000 hertz. Hertz is the designation for cycles per second. It is the isolated number of wave like motions either radiant energy or a particular sound will generate during a one second unit of time.

In terms of sound, the lower an individual's voice, the longer the wavelength and slower the vibratory motion. Conversely, the higher the vocal pitch, the shorter the wavelength and faster is the frequency of motion. A James Earl Jones or a Barry White-type voice registers at a frequency around 300 hertz. And a Melvin Franklin (who sang bass with the Temptations) could hit a low note around 87 hertz. But the capability to form intelligible words at that low of a frequency is not possible for a human being. That means the human vocal chords can talk and make words only around 300 hertz. Making audible sounds and making audible words are two different and separate functions.

On the opposite end of the spectrum, a Mariah Carey or a Minnie Riperton voice could check in anywhere between 1,200-1,500 hertz. Even though the range of the human voice can go as high as 3,500 in terms of forming intelligible words, singing at that frequency is not going to get you a Grammy.

With this as a foundational basis, human beings perceive speech mainly in the frequency range 300-3,500 hertz. Even though that sound range is well within the capability range of human hearing, speech that does not fall within those parameters is typically unintelligible.

Where am I going with the Physical Science 101 class? Well, let's revisit Psalms 8:4-5:

> "What is man, that thou art mindful of him? and the son of man, that thou visitest him?" For thou hast made him a little lower than the angels, and hast crowned him with glory and honour."

Being made "a little lower than angels" means mankind can neither see nor hear as good as angels. The truth of the matter, we can't even hear as good as a dog. A dog's hearing frequency range is 50-45,000 hertz. A cat's range is 45-85,000 hertz. A bat: 2,000-120,000 hertz. A dolphin: 75-150,000 hertz. Subsequently, should your dog suddenly perk its ears; better pay attention. That could be your first alert that you aren't alone. The same holds true when it comes to your pet cat, bat, and dolphin. Human beings are sensory restricted with respect to the laws of physics as such applies to the natural world. Just as we are physically limited by what frequencies of light our eyes can perceive, we're also limited by what we can hear.

Consider Balaam's stupid ass. Numbers 22:23 indicates Balaam's donkey could see the angel "standing in the way," but Balaam couldn't. Not until God "opened the eyes of Balaam" in verse 31 could Balaam see what his supposedly dumb animal saw.

Now, what's noteworthy is the fact that the Bible says nothing about opening the eyes of the ass or donkey. The only being that needed an eye-opener was the man. Viewed and interpreted in the context of the electromagnetic spectrum, the animal's eyes were already calibrated to receive or pick up the light frequency the angel was on. Consequently, this means the next time you're walking your dog (or your ass), and you want to go one way and your dog (or your ass) wants to go another way, you'd be wise to follow your dog!

Human beings are clueless when it comes to how frequently animals see light frequencies that our eyes cannot even begin to detect. How often we ignore the fundamental fact that just because we don't see don't mean it ain't there. Every time we take a breath, we may not see what we're breathing, but nevertheless we know something called air is there.

And, of course, as it is with sight, so it is with sound. Because we don't hear doesn't mean there's surround-silence.

If a tree falls in a forest and no one is around to hear it, does it make a sound? That's the philosophical riddle we've probably all heard, but do we really understand the basis of the question. If no one is around to see, hear, touch or smell the tree, how could it be said to exist? What is it to say that it exists when such an existence is unknown?

Philosophically speaking, if a tree exists outside of human perception then there is no way for us to know that the tree exists. So then, what do we mean by existence? What is the difference between perception and reality? Those who get deep off into it say, if the tree exists outside of perception (as common sense would dictate), then it will produce sound waves. However, these sound waves will not actually sound like anything. Sound as it is mechanically understood will occur, but sound as it is understood by human sensation will not occur. So then, how is it known that sound as it's mechanically understood will occur if that sound is not perceived?

If you're scratching your head, it was necessary to go there, in order to get to what the title of this chapter is all about; that's "white noise." White noise is code name for so-called ghosts, spirits, whisperers – all the spooky stuff that goes bump in the night. And of course, it's all the scary movie stuff that's banked on all day and all night.

The tree in the forest question metaphysically grows out of the Garden of Eden right along with the tree of knowledge of good and evil. It deals with the knowledge of the unobserved world. The tree in the forest mumbo jumbo lays the philosophical foundation to intellectualize a debate over the existence of God. The atheistic argument, if you've never heard the sound of God's voice in the real world, how do you really know God exists?

But the slick of that philosophical trick isn't argued when it comes to "white noise" and the other paranormal pandering to the spiritually abnormal mind that all of these movies and television shows of the genre do.

Consider 1 Kings 19:12:
"And after the earthquake a fire; but the LORD was not
in the fire: and after the fire a still small voice."

And, consider Isaiah 30:21:
"And thine ears shall hear a word behind thee, saying,
This is the way, walk ye in it, when ye turn to the right
hand, and when ye turn to the left."

If you read between and what's written on the lines, the "sound" of God's voice is not going to be captured on an audio or video recorder so it can be exploited on a TV show or in a movie in order to be validated by a box office ticket buying and/or cable/satellite paying public.

Satan, however, wants that kind of film and television exposure. That means by necessity of a satanic agenda, you are going to see television shows that have purportedly captured images and sounds that are purportedly beyond the realm of normal existence.

Satan orchestrates and inspires philosophical discussions and debates with regards to whether or not anything that cannot be tangibly manifested in the real world exists. Since the devil knows Jesus doesn't play *"show me what you workin' wit,"* he plays it for the world to see in the form of reality TV where the reality is the paranormal.

With direct regard to manifestation, consider John 14:22:

> "Judas saith unto him, not Iscariot, Lord, how is it that thou wilt manifest thyself unto us, and not unto the world?"

What type of manifestation was this disciple looking to see? In all likelihood, it was probably a display of supernatural powers. Since the question was asked, the implication is Jesus wasn't doing enough publicly to show and convince those other than his disciples that he was in fact the Messiah. But drawn from Christ's answer, it wasn't about superfluous self-validation. The disciples had frequently seen Jesus' résumé in action as well as others on specific occasions when needed. What you saw is what you got; nothing more was Christ's position. Jesus was not into making himself a public spectacle for purposes of vainglory.

On the other hand, the public proliferation of paranormal activity throughout history and currently makes it apparent that Satan will self-promote all day and all night long. This means manifestations of paranormal phenomena are frequent and real. The Bible has not only said it; reality television shows that delve into this arena affirm it. The reality of those manifestations, however, is not what most people think. These manifestations are in actuality fallen angels, not *Poltergeist* (1982) or *Ghost* (1990).

Accept it or not, "ghost whispering" TV programs and film features are components of Satan's war game strategy. Again, there's:

> "And I saw three unclean spirits like frogs come out of the mouth of the dragon, and out of the mouth of the beast, and out of the mouth of the false prophet. For they are the spirits of devils, working miracles."
> —REVELATION 16:13-14

The "spooks" metaphysically starring in these TV shows and movies are demons. They are the same disembodied spirits that drowned the herd of swine in Mark 5. They are not dearly departed Aunt Jemima or Uncle Ben back from the grave to say, *"Hey."* The princedom of Satan knows if folks understood that these productions were all about him and his angels that would change the game. That would cut into the viewership appeal. Those who have some semblance of God consciousness and spiritual awareness as far as the Bible are not going to watch Satanism for entertainment. And yes, pure unadulterated Satanism is exactly what shows like *The Shining* (1980) and *The Shining* (TV Mini-Series 1997) happen to be.

But because of the overwhelming media popularity of these features that showcase the devil and company, we find the powers behind the powers that be becoming more embolden. If the public will embrace Satan on the down low as a ghost, why not bring him out of the closet and allow him to be seen for exactly who he actually is. Intelligently explain why you would even allow yourself to become absorbed by a TV series called *Lucifer*?

In case you didn't realize it, this FOX TV show glorifies Satan, making him a caring and likable person in human flesh. Now, just think about that for a moment from a Christian Biblical perspective. Ponder the cosmic psychology as a devilish war strategy. If you see Satan as a fictional character or caricature on screen, you don't care enough to be offended or turned off. Your moral sensibilities are not challenged in the real world. Evil that doesn't directly involve you is no big thing. The implication of the devil as an anti-hero isn't that deep; it's considered cool. You've been spiritually desensitized. The desensitization of evil gives it societal normalcy. And, subsequently, Satan and his surrogates become beings you'd like to chill with—or worse.

Is it therefore surprising that public figures without any moral compass find public acceptance? When societal standards are so low-down that Satan can get a network TV show, there's no bottom to the pit public acceptance is willing to descend.

Now, with specific regards to "white noise," the war between Michael and his angels, the devil and his, and how human beings come into play, once again, consider in part the first and only declarative sentence out of serpent/Satan's mouth – "Ye shall not surely die."

Expanding on a previous chapter wherein "surely" was surely discussed, it's important to understand why this lie was told in the deceptive form of a half-truth or "alternative fact" making it a prevarication nevertheless. With the operative word in the statement being "die," it's essential to grasp that the concept of life in death should not be confused with life after death. Through the power of Jesus Christ as the archangel Michael, there is the promise of life after death. Through Lucifer, there's the argument "life in death."

Again, the failure to give the devil his due places many in a position to be duped – played for "lack of knowledge." Risk of redundancy, the only way a human being doesn't "surely die" is if the statement is viewed in the abstract. When human beings have children and pass their unique set of genomes to their progeny, a kind of quasi-immortality is the result. Consider the fact that Genesis 3:20 calls Eve, "the mother of all living," Eve isn't "surely dead" genetically speaking. God said she would "surely die" physically, and Satan twisted God's words by putting them in the context of genetics. When the serpent makes the statement, "For God doth know that in the day ye eat thereof, then your eyes shall be opened, and ye shall be as gods, knowing good and evil" the premise is genetics. God did know full well that once Adam and Eve acquired carnal knowledge they would have the mental ability to go along with their physical capability to create life through sexual intercourse thereby allowing them to "be as gods." In accordance with Satan's argument, certainly God knew that Eve would not die biologically as long as there are flesh and blood human beings on earth.

> "God that made the world and all things therein, seeing that he is Lord of heaven and earth…And hath made of one blood all nations of men for to dwell on all the face of the earth." —ACTS 17:24; 26

Only through Adam and Eve is mankind made "one blood." If the two were making babies, and their babies were making babies ad infinitum till world's end, would they "surely die" genetically? The answer is no.

Satan told a half-truth or alternative fact. He did not tell the whole truth and nothing but the truth, so help him God. So, "under pains and penalties of perjury," the devil is facing Revelation 20:3 and 20:10!

Subsequently, herein is the "life in death" argument that's straight outta Eden. And it's the same argument that's been promoted since the planet's first couple was driven out of the Garden. It's the argument that impresses one to think that death immediately puts their beloved one in a "better place." If you think a grave or crematorium is a better place, then you have bought Satan's "life in death" argument hook, line, and sinker. Those who think their deceased friend or family member is in a "better place" are believing the same lie the devil told Eve.

The media is filled with individuals and paranormal programs claiming to have experienced near-death sensations wherein subjects have witnessed themselves floating above their bodies. Some even say they've seen deceased relatives or friends beckoning them toward or repelling them away from a bright light.

What do you believe? Who do you believe? There's no doubt these individuals are having some sort of extrasensory experience. The problem is in the interpretation of exactly who or what is behind that sort of experience. One thing for sure, if the experience is contradictory to the expressed written word of God, you can best believe that the experience is a manifestation of Satan.

According to the Bible, there is positively no life in a state of death. And anyone who says otherwise has some specific scriptural passages to refute.

Job 7:9-10 reads:
> "As the cloud is consumed and vanisheth away: so he that goeth down to the grave shall come up no more. He shall return no more to his house, neither shall his place know him any more."

Job 19:25-26 reads:
> "For I know that my redeemer liveth, and that he shall stand at the latter day upon the earth: And though after my skin worms destroy this body, yet in my flesh shall I see God."

Job does not say he will see God in any sort of spirit form. He says after worms have eaten up his body, he will be resurrected with a new body that will enable him to see God in the flesh. Doesn't Jesus say in

Luke 24:39, "Behold my hands and my feet, that it is I myself: handle me, and see; for a spirit hath not flesh and bones, as ye see me have."

The interesting thing to note here is that Jesus says "flesh and bones" and not "flesh and blood." Jesus' post-resurrection body finds there to be an absence of blood because the blood of Christ has already been shed for mankind's salvation. And of course, this is consistent with the statement that "flesh and blood cannot inherit the kingdom of God" as written in 1 Corinthians 15:50.

Psalms 115:17 reads:
> "The dead praise not the LORD, neither any that go down into silence."

Psalms 146:4 reads:
> "His breath goeth forth, he returneth to his earth; in that very day his thoughts perish."

Ecclesiastes 9:5-6 reads:
> "For the living know that they shall die: but the dead know not any thing, neither have they any more a reward; for the memory of them is forgotten. Also their love, and their hatred, and their envy, is now perished; neither have they any more a portion for ever in any thing that is done under the sun."

Let's synopsize. Job says vanish; no more going back home. The psalmist says no more praise and worship and thoughts perish. Solomon says all emotions perish. So, intelligently ask yourself what is there about any of the above that's not easily understood?

When a person dies, they don't haunt the crib. They're neither invited nor uninvited guests at anybody's house via séances, chants, divination, or associated hocus pocus. When *"thoughts perish,"* that's synonymous with brain dead. When *"memory is forgotten,"* that's not your memory of them; it's their memory of you. That means if a so-called ghost calls your name it's a lie. If their memory is gone, how is it they'd still know your name, where you live or where they once lived? A so-called ghost that knows anything about you or anything else isn't brain dead. Likewise, when brain dead, they'd no longer have any emotions like love, hate, or envy. There would be no compelling reason to holler at you period!

Intelligently ask yourself again, hypothetically speaking, if you are dead, and you know you are dead, why wouldn't you "*praise the Lord?*" If you praise God while you are alive, why stop when you're dead? If you are dead, but still alive in some kind of spirit form, does it make any sense to "dis" Jesus because in spirit form you don't need him anymore?

Job, David, and Solomon have gotten it all wrong, and the television programs presenting interviews with individuals seeing ghosts, and experiencing paranormal phenomena have got it all right?

So, if you believe in God, do you believe in God, or *The Ghost Hunters TV channel?* Or, do you believe in the filmmakers of *The Sixth Sense* (1999)?

Paul writes in Thessalonians that he "would not have us ignorant concerning them which are asleep." The Bible likens death to sleep. Consider John 11:11-14:

> "These things said he: and after that he saith unto them, Our friend Lazarus sleepeth; but I go, that I may awake him out of sleep. Then said his disciples, Lord, if he sleep, he shall do well. Howbeit Jesus spake of his death: but they thought that he had spoken of taking of rest in sleep. Then said Jesus unto them plainly, Lazarus is dead."

Jesus called Lazarus a "friend." Now, if Lazarus was in a "better place," why didn't Jesus leave him there? If Lazarus was still alive in some kind of limbo spirit form state of existence, then why was there a need for Jesus to resurrect him?

Some may say the resurrection of Jesus was the game changer. And, individuals now go from death straight to glory just like that thief on the cross who repented at the last minute.

Newsflash! When Jesus told that very fortunate man, "Verily I say unto thee, Today shalt thou be with me in paradise," his words were literally dead on point; no pun intended. The placement of the comma either in front of "today" or behind it is irrelevant when it's clearly understood what the state of the dead really is according to what the Bible actually teaches.

When the repentant man on the cross next to Christ died, just like Psalms 146:4 says, his thoughts immediately ceased. He became brain dead at the moment of death. So, when that man is resurrected, what do you think his first thoughts will be? What day do you think it will be for him? Do you think he will realize that he's been dead for more than 2,000 years?

If a person goes into a coma and stays there for however long, if they are fortunate enough to come out of it, they pick it back up where they left off. While there may be exceptions to the rule, comatose patients are typically not time conscious. They are totally unaware of the time lapse in between onset and recovery. If it was 2013 and Barack Obama was the prez when they dozed off, it'll be either "Are you kidding me?" or "WTF?" if they awakened November 09, 2016.

There is no inconsistency in the words of Jesus Christ. There is "no variableness, neither shadow of turning." When Jesus told that once so-called thief, "*today*," when dude wakes up from his 2,000 plus year nap, as far as he's concerned as well as Jesus Christ, himself, it will be "*today*." Again, remember 2 Peter 3:8: "One day is with the Lord as a thousand years, and a thousand years as one day."

Consequently, this means pointing to the resurrection of Jesus and his words to the repentant thief do not cancel out the host of scriptures that make it crystal that when you die, you are "*surely*" dead.

Therefore, drawing from all of these Bible passages, those who say they've had "near death" experiences wherein they've seen Jesus, or themselves floating away, or walking toward a bright light, or open door, chances are they are 100% accurate in terms of their testimony. It just happens to be that "near death" is exactly what it was. They were near, but they weren't dead yet. If they actually saw Jesus, then thanks be to God that he caught them prior to their walking into that bright light or through that open door.

But on the standing edge of that coin, if while experiencing a so-called near-death experience, a deceased MFSB, dear friend, or family dog is seen, then what that individual is seeing is inconsistent with the expressed written word of God.

Understandably, a point to the sky after hitting a homerun, scoring a touchdown, doing whatever you do in honor of a deceased loved one is a heartfelt in-the-moment salute. But if that index finger point or head to the sky glance is made with thought in mind that love one just saw that homerun, touchdown, whatever; whomever didn't see a thing. According to Paul, "we which are alive and remain unto the coming of the Lord shall not prevent them which are asleep." In other words, nobody is resurrected until the Second Advent of Jesus Christ. All dead stay dead "unto the coming of the Lord."

Does that mean nobody gets special treatment as far as an early resurrection like Moses evidently did (Matthew 17:3) causing Satan to have a conniption fit (Jude 1:9)? Who knows the mind of God other than God? But the rule, according to 1 Corinthians 15:51-57, and Revelation 20:5-6, in conjunction with 1 Thessalonians 4:13-17, the short answer is nobody gets special treatment.

Consider Acts 13:22:

> "And when he had removed him, he raised up unto them David to be their king; to whom also he gave testimony, and said, I have found David the son of Jesse, a man after mine own heart, which shall fulfil all my will."

Bottom line, David, who wrote a whole bunch of the Biblical Psalms, was "a man after God's own heart."

Now, consider Acts 2:29:

> "Men and brethren, let me freely speak unto you of the patriarch David, that he is both dead and buried, and his sepulchre is with us unto this day."

Bottom line, David, who wrote a whole bunch of the Biblical Psalms, who was a man after God's own heart, is still "dead and buried." In other words, he hasn't been resurrected.

Consequently, since we're plainly told that David didn't get any special early resurrection treatment, well the odds aren't all that great that a deceased loved one will fare any better. There is the first resurrection and there is a second resurrection. Revelation 20:6 says "blessed is he that hath part in the first resurrection." The Bible says nothing about a pre-first resurrection or a post second. So, why with the scriptures so crystal with respect to the state of the dead is there so much confusion and diversity of religious opinion?

First and foremost, Satan, again, is a deceiver. If he can pass himself off as *Auntie Em* or *Uncle Bud*, he knows your love for your lost will put you at his beckon call. And if the devil and his angels can impersonate any deceased human being to the extent that you are channeled a winning lottery number, horse, greyhound, or game spread, then he knows that you'll be hooked on demonics for life.

Second, the concept of life in death swings the door wide open to spiritism and the occult. Psychics, Ouija boards, tarot cards, fortune tellers, palm readers, clairvoyants, numerologists, astrologists, and all other "beyond" and back gurus and contrivances that sponsor Satan's words, "ye shall not surely die" come immediately into play. Those that tap into these sources of illumination do not realize that their sources are extraterrestrial in origin. Once you open your mind and heart to predatory alien entities that inhabit uncharted twilight zones, you are giving tacit permission for entry into the inner sanctum of your body, mind, and soul.

Given the fact that 1 Corinthians 6:19 maintains the human body is the "temple of the Holy Spirit," doesn't it make plenty sense that devils and demons would like a welcome mat invite to get in the house too?

Third, Satan uses the media to soften the public with regards to the occult by employing celebrity spokespersons and intriguing reality TV shows to make buyer beware completely unaware. Unlike the desire of Paul to have us wise to the devices of the devil, Satan would have us ignorant. If the powers behind paranormal activity can cajole people into "psychic fun" for entertainment purposes only, then a satanic extraterrestrial agenda is achieved without any serious or formidable challenge. That agenda is unwitting worldwide close encounters of the fifth kind that find human beings communicating directly with extraterrestrials masquerading as the deceased.

But, before proceeding further, let's look at this masquerade a bit further. If a baby or child dies, if there were in Biblical reality such things as ghosts, would that deceased baby or child reappear as a so-called ghost in the form of a baby or child? What about your loved one or anyone who dies of old age? Does their ghost appear aged? If you've got some years behind you, being that you are alive, would you want to stay "old" for eternity, or would you prefer to be in the prime of your life again?

Bottom line, the mere concept of so-called ghosts is illogical when considering the fact that human nature suggests that the elderly would want to be young and the young, as in babies and children who have a developing mind, would want to grow beyond puberty. Unless that ghost is a robot, it wouldn't want to appear in a physical form that's not of its own choosing.

If you were a ghost, would you really want to be stuck in the physical shape you are in now for eternity? Since *The Curious Case of Benjamin Button* (2008) is curious, age is a one way street. There are no "you" turns.

And, what about the body that's cremated or simply decomposes? Where is the physical body for that person's spirit or so-called ghost to inhabit? If your car is totaled, do you get back into that same vehicle and drive it?

Subsequently, there are too many theoretical holes when it comes to either the real or metaphysical world of what's being called ghosts. And, this is why the Bible says all that it does regarding the subject matter. The body lying in that casket is an empty shell. The spirit that once resided in that body is gone forever. That body is never inhabited by that spirit again. This is why those of a Christian persuasion should find comfort in the following:

> "*There are* also celestial bodies, and bodies terrestrial: but the glory of the celestial *is* one, and the *glory* of the terrestrial *is* another. *There is* one glory of the sun, and another glory of the moon, and another glory of the stars: for *one* star differeth from *another* star in glory. So also *is* the resurrection of the dead. It is sown in corruption; it is raised in incorruption: It is sown in dishonour; it is raised in glory: it is sown in weakness; it is raised in power: It is sown a natural body; it is raised a spiritual body. There is a natural body, and there is a spiritual body.

> And so it is written, The first man Adam was made a living soul; the last Adam *was made* a quickening spirit. Howbeit that *was* not first which is spiritual, but that which is natural; and afterward that which is spiritual."
> —1 CORINTHIANS 15:40-46

If you see a so-called ghost, you are seeing a bold face lie. If you prefer to believe your lying eyes, then the above Biblical passage is not telling the truth. Both cannot coexist as being true.

If Satan, who is an extraterrestrial, can masquerade as a serpent, isn't it plausible that his angels, who are also extraterrestrials, can masquerade as deceased people?

The hierarchal structure of angels was earlier mentioned. The Cherubim are Michael's angels. Satan's are those referred to as fallen. The Nephilim are the hybrid species resulting from fallen angels mating with human beings. Nephilim aren't angels; once again, they're hybrids. Are there Nephilim still walking the earth? Well, are Satan and his fallen angels still walking the earth?

The entities that weren't earlier mentioned in any compelling detail are demons. The 1998 movie titled *Fallen* was storylined as being about a fallen angel. Biblically speaking, however, this film characterization was actually a demon. By employing the Oscar award winning actor Denzel Washington to play the lead role, the spiritual powers behind the cinematic curtain were able to sanitize Satanism by causing the audience to identify with Denzel as opposed to the devil or a devil.

Of course, this once again is a classic example of the sophistry of Satan. Through deception and subterfuge, the face of evil is masked to the extent that the intrinsically bad appears as good.

> "Woe unto them that call evil good, and good evil; that put darkness for light, and light for darkness; that put bitter for sweet, and sweet for bitter!" — ISAIAH 5:20

Demons are the lowest of the low. They are the ultimate "body snatchers." They are disembodied spirits that need to find human or animal hosts in order to function. Once again, consider the "Legion" of Mark 5. Other than Jesus Christ exorcising this demon possessed man, what's glamorous about these devils and their satanic agenda? As soon as this "legion" of disembodied spirits was driven out of a human host, about 2,000 pigs were slaughtered as the result of demonic possession.

When revisiting and reflecting on what happened to earth's prehistoric animal, bird, and fish populations (Genesis 1:2), doesn't the above thumbnail sketch erase all doubt? "Darkness was upon the face of the deep" because the actions of those unclean spirits show that demons have an affinity for water. Unquestionably, all life in earth's oceans had to be recreated because these same unclean spirits that ran the swine into the sea in all probability possessed the bodies of all sea creatures on the planet. Demons can hide undetected from public view underwater. And, perhaps, this gives explanation why the swine ran into the water. The oceans and seas of earth were and maybe still are their hangout. The expression, "the devil and the deep blue sea" is probably reality based.

With a Bible based functional understanding of what a demon is, consider the 2010 movie release titled *Legion*. Dispensing with any comment regarding the fanciful plot and besmirching depiction of Michael the archangel, intelligently ask yourself if it makes any sense to title a movie having a storyline about God's angels, *Legion*? Doesn't Mark 5:9 plainly tell all that the name of those 2,000 demons is "Legion?"

Do you think the writers of this screenplay, along with the producers and directors are just dumb? Or do you think they had help in being Biblically naïve?

Even when you give a hallway pass for being plain ole ignorant of the time when it comes to Michael being Jesus Christ, wasn't there someone in Sunday or Sabbath school to ask if the name Legion was scripturally and theologically a good or bad fit? Entitling a movie about good angels *Legion* is like entitling a movie about fallen angels *Saints*.

Then, there's *Noah* (2014) with *Legion*, *Lucifer*, and *Fallen* cinematically all in the same boat. Respecting Noah, there's no need to slam this particular Hollywood portrayal of Genesis 6:8 through Genesis 9:29. If you're remotely acquainted with chapter and verse and caught the movie, what more can be said?

The method to Satan's madness is the ability to challenge the word of God without formidable public and sustained confutation that goes beyond denominational defense mechanisms and church pleasantries. Contrary to going high when others go low, sometimes there is a season for getting down in the weeds.

Consider the fact that atheism, agnosticism, and agnosto-atheism are all predicated upon the quest for proof as previously discussed. But exactly how do you disprove that which cannot be proved? What proof can be offered in disproof of that which can't be proved in the first place? And the proof in this place is beyond "unreasonable" doubt?

Again, those that buy-in to these God does not exist "isms" take the position that their beliefs are based on "proof." But the simple question that those who "buy-in" simply stumble over answering is where on earth did they get this so-called proof? Who on earth gave them this proof? Subsequently, who gave it to the "them" that passed it on to them? And who gave it to the "them" who gave it to the "them" that passed it on to them who are now passing it on to you?

Once more, the finite mind cannot comprehend intelligence that is infinite. Trying to disprove the existence of God by offering proof is like a dog trying to disprove the food that appears in its dog dish originally came from a grocery store. As brilliant as either *Lassie* or *Snoopy* may be, their mental ability to grasp the chain of events that had to take place prior to *Kibbles 'n Bits* making it to the dog bowl is incomprehensible. Seeing food put in the doggie dish is not proof; it's just a woof minus material evidence yay or nay.

A dog does not have the mental acuity to see beyond the knowledge to which it's exposed and the same is humanly applicable to a well-defined degree. Seeing doesn't necessarily mean believing because there's always the issue of interpretation. UFO's are seen somewhere in the world every day. It's the "U" in that acronym that hangs folks up. Say again, proof in terms of being a believer or disbeliever will never circumvent the requirement of faith when it's a matter of believing and not seeing or seeing and not believing.

Seeing and believing what your mind tells you require way more than an *Eye-Q*. But, believe it or not, people with a "high" Eye-Q typically see more than meets the mind's eye. When it comes to the jungles of *Sanpaku*, smoking the twine and being red-eyed from the wine is only half of it. Chemical and pharmaceutical induced states open the human brain to the twilight zones of the subconscious.

The Bible doesn't directly address marijuana or drug abuse not because such is a 1960s/70s phenomena. Cana (the place where Jesus turned water into wine) got its name from the same root word as cannabis indicating the plant was widely grown there. Cannabis is marijuana. To think that there weren't potheads during the time of Jesus Christ is to be naïve. The fact that Luke 7:34 finds Jesus saying that some may even call him a "winebibber" is also indicative that folks were kicking it with *Boones Farm* all over the place.

The Bible doesn't have to play DEA given the fact that there are established Biblical principles covering spiritual regulation.

> "And be not conformed to this world: but be ye transformed by the renewing of your mind, that ye may prove what *is* that good, and acceptable, and perfect, will of God." – ROMANS 12:2

Lighting up, be it in the form of a gas, a solid, or a liquid doesn't renew the mind; it deadens it by opening it up to the spiritually dead. Satan has a cloud-nine agenda. It's a conspiracy involving the legalization of any drug that facilitates paranormal communication. Not with the deceased, or so-called ghosts, but with extraterrestrial entities biblically termed fallen angels and demons.

Such contacts are an introduction to the eight banned practices of Deuteronomy 18:10-11. It is also a dark hallway leading to rooms marked reincarnation, nirvana, and karma.

The 2005 movie entitled *White Noise* is about the dead communicating with those that are alive through electronic voice phenomena (EVP). Basically, that's spirits or so-called ghosts trying to holler at you through the static of a radio or TV when no picture signal or audibly coherent and discernible sound is being transmitted.

In the 1982 movie *Poltergeist*, if you recall the little girl sitting in front of the television with palms of both hands pressed against the screen saying, "*They're here*," that was the cinematic debut of EVP or white noise. Of course, what these movies don't tell you is, "They've always been here!"

Consider the *Unsung* feature that was done on Donny Hathaway. You can YouTube it. A biographical account is given that while watching TV, Donny clicked to a channel that didn't have any transmission. The "dots" referred to as being seen on the blank/snowy television screen in technological terms, of course, is white noise. We're told that Donny "thought it was very interesting that those dots were doing what they were doing."

Just what were those dots doing?

Donny Hathaway was diagnosed as having paranoid schizophrenia. If you know the story, his death is considered a suicide. Reportedly, he jumped from the 15th floor balcony of his hotel room.

Whether the development of mental illness is a result of genetic links or chemical imbalances in the brain, the debate doesn't negate the possibility that with the onset of such, the individual affected may be more receptive than others to extrasensory perceptions. Those who claim to "see things" and/or "hear voices" may have acquired through disease an altered state of consciousness. This altered state of mind, for all we know, might even provide a reality-based explanation why Donny's dots did whatever they did.

Let's go back to *Legion*. The movie wasn't good enough, so along comes a TV series by the same name, *Legion* (2017). Now note very carefully the relatively unnoticed sophistry of Satan. "Legion" in the Bible is a pack of demons. In 2010, Legion goes from demon to rogue angel. Basically, in terms of film plot, this rogue angel has a split personality. Clinically it's called Dissociative Identity Disorder (DID). On the street it's called schizo, bipolar, whacked, and crazy-as-hell.

In 2017, *Legion*, the television series, is transformed into a Marvel Comics superhero diagnosed with guess what? Yes, schizophrenia.

The man who is the subject of Mark 5 did what he did because his mind and body had been possessed by demonic spirits. The demonic spirits here were called Legion. Legion was the cause of this man's illness.

Can you scientifically say with a hundred percent certainty that mental illnesses characterized by delusions and hallucinations are conclusively unlinked to demonic communication, interaction, possession? If the man in Mark 5 were quantum leaped to this day and age, what do you think he would be diagnosed as having? Yes, schizophrenia.

Let's go back to Donny. Didn't Satan attempt to get Jesus to jump off a building?

The brain is extraordinarily complex. The brain's nerve impulses are electrical signals that travel along an axon at about 250 mph. That's why you "drop it like it's hot!" If your nerve impulses traveled any slower, you wouldn't "feel the burn." You'd hold it until your hand was probably on fire!

A batter standing 60-feet away from a pitcher hurling a baseball at 100 mph has about four-tenths of a second to decide whether-or-not to swing. This means when a pitcher throws a slider or curve and that batter is swinging at a ball that's slid or curved into the dirt, the batter's brain has already decided that the ball looked hittable before its trajectory moved out of the strike zone. In turn, a batter's checked swing is a result of the brain picking up the ball sliding or curving far enough in advance of the plate to stop a bat swinging at 70-80 mph in about a tenth of a second.

Bottom line, when it comes to the human brain and how it processes information both physically and spiritually at the speed it does, unless you are a neurophysiologist, you're clueless!

Since the brain, therefore, is electrical, it has the physical capability to be impacted and subsequently influenced by electrical interference from external sources no differently than a radio, television, or phone is prone. Subsequently, with the brain being all that it is and more, either through disease or by way of drugs, it can be a receiver for extraterrestrial communications. It's just a question regarding whose frequency your receiver is tuned to, whose broadcast signal you're picking up.

The fact that Legion in name goes from Biblical demon to television superhero is no accidental coincidence. It's a very slick trick; a shrewd move. And, this is why Genesis 3:1 is not only referring to the serpent as "subtil," its calling Satan out also.

The devil is narcissistic. The fact that the name Legion has been around since Mark and Luke and is still associated with Satan in terms of demonic possession speaks volumes. It signals egomania and bombast being modern day signs of an individual either being sick in the head or outright demonically possessed.

An overwhelming percentage of Christendom is asleep when it comes to Satan and his utilization of white noise. Television and film sell the public the belief in ghosts rather than Biblically-identified extraterrestrial fallen angels. Certainly, these movies are more than less reality-based on the research and investigation of real life experiences with paranormal phenomena. However, the issue when it comes to media's participation in the war in heaven is not perception, but rather deception.

The perception that messages are being received from beyond the grave is no joke. It's just a deception that the messenger is someone that's been in the grave. There are EVPs (voices) that have been electronically recorded below 300 hertz and above 3,500. Some have registered as low as 80 and some as high as 22,500 hertz. Since these recording are being picked up through the white noise or static interference of electronic devices that are an operative function of the electromagnetic spectrum, these EVPs are based on frequency and not how good they sound as far as audio quality. Some of the messages are even heard as intelligible words when the recordings are played in reverse.

In reality, white noise isn't noise at all. Use of the word noise is a misnomer. More appropriate terminology would be static communication. Embedded in the static messages can be encrypted in the form of electrical patterns that only require a decryption technology to decipher.

Could some of these EVPs be faked? Certainly, just as there are UFOs that are faked. But there are those which are deemed to be unexplained, and that's why they are referred to as an "Electronic Voice Phenomenon."

Do EVPs sound like the work of deceased human beings appearing as so-called ghosts? Or does all of that sound like Satan appearing as the devil attempting to validate his existence in the form of demons?

Reflect back to an earlier chapter in this book when we talked about Satan "as an angel of light" actually having the physical capability to "transform" himself into electrical patterns which are reconverted into light patterns for reception by the human eye. Well, what do you find if Satan halts the reconversion process deciding not to return to "an angel of light" in the form of a light pattern that can be seen by the human eye?

If the devil stops the reconversion process, he becomes "an angel of sound" for reception by the human ear. The "sound of Satan," consequently, becomes embedded as an electromagnetic frequency distinguishable as a human voice in the white noise that's scientifically termed Electronic Voice Phenomenon.

Sir Arthur Conan Doyle, the author of Sherlock Holmes, wrote:

"Once you eliminate the impossible, whatever remains, no matter how improbable, must be the truth."

Is this an obvious point of logic, or is it an often-misused logical fallacy?

Breaking it down, no matter what "it" is, this statement made by Doyle is based on the assumption that truth must lie within the set of the possible, which most people define as everything that is not impossible. So, this particular point of logic is meant to be taken and applied as a practical rule of thumb.

As an investigator or a seeker of truth, you create a list of all potential explanations for a situation, and then you systematically eliminate those explanations that you can demonstrate are impossible either through logic or empirical evidence. And consequently, whatever you're left with is the solution even if it may seem extremely improbable.

But here is the problem in this statement of logic. Mark 9:23 says Jesus said, "If thou canst believe, all things are possible to him that believeth."

Repeated, there is a duality in the scriptures. When you believe in God as a supreme being and a supernatural force, you are not working within a specific framework that is governed by a materialist, rationalist, scientific view of the world. That means if you really believe in God, you really believe what God says. And, what he says is "all things are possible." And if all things are possible, consequently that means nothing is impossible. This means contrary to what Sir Arthur says, everything is on the table. No matter how wild or off the chain!

Logic breaks down in a world where one allows for the existence of that which most consider impossible. Consider, there is no such thing as the improbable when you believe "all things are possible."

Sherlock Holmes' impeccable logic operated under the assumption that magic, ghosts, aliens, ET's do not exist. When you eliminate the paranormal world of God, angels, demons, and a devil, you are not baffled when your rational explanations do not fit an irrational world you refuse to accept. You refuse to be puzzled by anything that cannot be explained by material evidence.

Consider the magic show where the magician professes to read an individual's mind. Now, if the magician appears to be accurate in doing what he or she does, logic suggests that there must be a trick. In the real world, we know for a fact that no one can get inside of someone's head and actually read their mind or thoughts word for word. That can only be done through the magic of motion pictures a'la *What Women Want* (2000.)

But in the spiritual realm where "all things are possible," comparatively speaking the list of possible explanations in the "real world" where most people live is too short. Most will never accept the possibility that the magician could actually be in cahoots or communication with supernatural forces, beings, entities, spirits, demons and a devil that are telepathically feeding or conveying personally private information based on collective observations of that individual that can be traced back to that individual's childhood. Or remotely consider that magician could in actuality be an extraterrestrial or what the Bible calls a demon?

When you really believe the word of God as written in the Bible, it is what it is when it says, "all things are possible" to him or her that believes. That which most believers fail to realize is the fact that the possibilities are not restricted to only that which God can do, but also includes that which God may allow Satan to do within the realm of the paranormal.

Let it sink in; the Bible says the devil deceives. It doesn't say he tricks. Now what a deception it would be to find that those who you think are performing tricks of magic are in actuality vessels for "the spirits of devils working miracles" in accordance with Revelation 16:14?

Because there is this cosmic conflict, the celestial forces conspiring with Satan are not going to just go away. The powers that be on the dark hand side are not going to allow folks at large to connect neither Biblical dots, nor those seen on a TV screen.

Through all the static and the noise, the Bible has made what it sees very clear in spite of anything that's heard to the contrary. This leaves us with both the logical clarification and conclusion that within the set of known phenomena, once you have eliminated all possible explanations, whatever remains, no matter how improbable, must be true simply because with God there are no impossibilities.

11 OUT OF AFRICA

"When he arose, he took the young child and his mother by night, and departed into Egypt: And was there until the death of Herod: that it might be fulfilled which was spoken of the Lord by the prophet, saying, Out of Egypt have I called my son."
—MATTHEW 2:14-15

Isn't it interesting that the pyramids of Egypt are not mentioned in the Bible? As architecturally mystifying as these structures are, absolutely nowhere are they discernibly referenced. The Bible was written over a period of roughly 2,000 years by 40 different authors from two continents writing in three different languages and not one of them takes literary notice of the big three standing alone on the Giza plateau.

Intelligently ask yourself just how do these wonders of the ancient world go so unnoticed by two score journalists over a two millennial lifespan? Is it just an oversight? Or, did God put a gag order on these triangular buildings due to what they symbolically represent?

What do they symbolically represent? Perhaps the love triangle Satan established in the Garden of Eden? But floating the idea that the pyramids of Egypt memorialize the world's first ménage trois may be a bit over the top. However, when considering the symbolism associated with God instructing the patriarch Jacob to "make an altar" and Jacob complies by setting up a "pillar of stone," do you seriously think Satan was totally oblivious to the meaning of such symbolism?

Because Lucifer, now Satan, wants to be like God, the devil has an *"altar ego."* Genesis 35 reveals that Jacob set up four pillars of stone having spiritual significance to God. The fact that Egyptian pyramids have four sides (the Great Pyramid eight) certainly has symbolic significance to something whether the world at-large realizes or not.

Just as Jesus never referenced Satan by his angelic name Lucifer, it's not stupefying to find the Egyptian pyramids dissed as well. Once again, if the pyramids either predate the existence of man, or man had extraterrestrial assistance in their construction, the kingdom of God is not going to give the princedom of Satan any honorable mention. That being the case, Egypt's pyramid staying power may not be a monument to Egypt's pharaoh's as much as it is a testament to Satan himself.

Take it to the bank, because Satan orchestrated the first illicit affair that converted God's perfect family circle into a triangle, any structure that's remotely testimonial to that Garden encounter of several kind is not going to be given props by the Word. Egypt being named in the Bible may have been considered as good as it gets. But since Egypt is in Africa and Africa by name is not mentioned, what's up with that? Is the Bible literally saying everything on the continent that's not Egypt is geographically irrelevant?

Some Biblical scholars say *au contraire* to that there. Cush, Ethiopia, and Libya are named is their take. Well, intelligently ask yourself are Alaska, USA, and Canada geographical references to North America?

Prior to Greek history, Ethiopia was known as Kush by the ancient Egyptians. Prior to American history, what was Alaska known as?

Cush, Ethiopia, and Libya represent the entire continent of Africa in name no more than Alaska, USA, and Canada represent the entirety of North America. While it's understandable there are folks who have a certain political indignation when it comes to Africa being given its props – and getting a shout out from the Bible would be a big prop – it just ain't that kind of party.

However, what the Bible refers to as Eden is the "shout out!" And, when folks know what time it is; that's enough. Carefully consider the following:

> "And the LORD God planted a garden eastward in Eden; and there he put the man whom he had formed. And out of the ground made the LORD God to grow every tree that is pleasant to the sight, and good for food; the tree of life also in the midst of the garden, and the tree of knowledge of good and evil. And a river went out of Eden to water the garden; and from thence it was parted, and became into four heads. The name of the first is Pison: that is it which compasseth the whole land of Havilah, where there is gold; And the gold of that land is good: there is bdellium and the onyx stone. And the

name of the second river is Gihon: the same is it that compasseth the whole land of Ethiopia. And the name of the third river is Hiddekel: that is it which goeth toward the east of Assyria. And the fourth river is Euphrates."
— GENESIS 2:8-14

The key to this geo-realization is the word Ethiopia taken directly from Genesis 2:13. According to these Biblical verses, a river flowed out of Eden and parted into four tributaries. Let's forget about what we don't know and deal with what we do. The first parting of the river is Pison which covered Havilah. No need to debate where that is. The second parting of the river is Gihon. This tributary covers Ethiopia.

Forget any debate over Cush and does it mean Ethiopia. Since the passage plainly says Ethiopia, deal plainly with the read. We know Ethiopia is in East Africa. That being established, the text references two separate locales; the "garden" and "Eden." Given Ethiopia is in East Africa, and the garden was planted "eastward" in Eden," the entire continent of Africa has to be Eden. Subsequently, Genesis 2:8 could read, "And the LORD God planted a garden eastward in Africa."

Is that simple enough for you?

Supporting Eden being Africa is the fact that the river "went out of Eden." In order for this river to go out, it has to be in. Intelligently ask yourself where in Africa is there a river that meets the geophysical specifications the Bible presents.

Remember the Richard Pryor movie, *Which Way is Up* (1977)? Well, in order for this river to flow out of Eden and branch into four tributaries with the second tributary flowing through Ethiopia, and the fourth river being the Euphrates, this requires that river to be flowing in a northerly direction. The only river on the entire continent of Africa that flows north is the Nile.

Looking at a flat map of Africa with reference to those geophysical specifications, the only way for a river to flow out of Eden/Africa is for that river to flow out of an existing body of water. The Nile River's source is Lake Victoria. The countries bordering Lake Victoria are Kenya, Tanzania, and Uganda. Indisputably, the Garden of Eden was located in Uganda.

Now it's significant to note that Genesis 2:8 doesn't read east, it says "eastward." And, when looking at a relief map of the African continent, Uganda is not located in central Africa as in the Democratic Republic of the Congo. And it's not in east Africa like Kenya, Tanzania, or Somalia which border the India Ocean. Factually, Uganda is positioned exactly where the scripture geographically describes; it's "eastward" in Africa.

Additionally, Uganda has both the topography and climatic conditions that would be most conducive to what could be called a "garden spot." The equatorial average annual temperature of present day Uganda is 78° Fahrenheit; mostly sunny with the temp rarely rising above 84° Fahrenheit. So, if you are walking around buck naked all day, all night, and all year long, the weather ain't gonna be your biggest problem!

Further, Uganda is situated almost entirely within the Nile Basin. More than 98 percent of Uganda's total land area is in the basin. This means the outflow from other lakes fed by other water sources (tributaries) also pass through Uganda before flowing into neighboring Sudan. This makes Uganda both an upstream and downstream state. Subsequently, by Uganda being situated almost totally in a geographical water basin, it was the ideal locale for a garden to be planted!

There's no doubt about it. Indisputably, the Garden of Eden was deep in the heart of Africa. And, this fact undeniably makes Adam and Eve Africans.

But some, however, will argue that the Garden of Eden is in the Middle East – Iraq. This theory is based on the Biblical reference to Assyria and the Euphrates. But no matter how much that theory is pushed, it just doesn't fit the Biblical footprint.

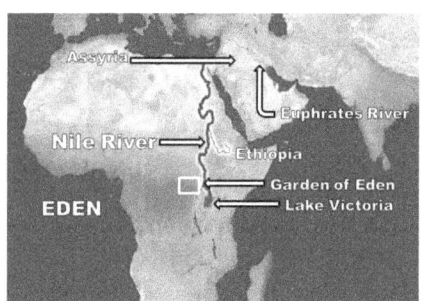

If the garden was planted eastward in Eden, and a river went out of Eden to water the garden, and then the river parted into four more rivers after watering the garden with the second parting covering Ethiopia, intelligently ask your own self just how on earth could the Garden be north of Ethiopia?

Genesis 2:14's third river references Assyria. Today, the indigenous Assyrian homeland areas are part of today's northern Iraq. Isn't Iraq north of Ethiopia? Since the fourth parting is the Euphrates, the Garden had to have been planted south of the Euphrates. The Euphrates flows through Iraq, not Ethiopia!

But some *"die hard with a vengeance archaeologist"* will still argue that even though the river went out of Eden, it didn't immediately water the garden. It had a ways to go before it got to the garden. Therefore, it was the Euphrates tributary, or the fourth head, that actually watered the garden.

Indulging that argument, once again, the "third" river goes east into Assyria? And isn't Assyria south of the fourth river which is the Euphrates that's located in Iraq?

So, here's the question and answer to that second argument. If it was either the third or fourth river that did the watering, why wasn't the home of Adam and Eve called the Garden of Assyria or Iraq? In order to be called the Garden of Eden, the garden spot had to have been in Eden. Since we all know by looking at a map where ancient Assyria, modern day Syria, and Iraq are all geographically, once the Bible references Assyria, we know we're not in Kansas anymore.

Along that line, literally, if the Garden of Eden were that far north it would be running parallel to Georgia, Alabama, Mississippi, North Louisiana, and North Texas. The geodetic coordinates for Atlanta, GA are 33°44'56.4" N 84°23'16.73" W, and for Baghdad, Iraq, they're 33°20'26.09" N 44°24'3.17" E. Bottom line, literally, you're not going to be walking around buck naked in any environment on the same parallel with Atlanta even if you could. The daily and seasonal weather fluctuations simply won't permit that kinda "let's stay nekkid" freedom.

Accept it or not, "out of Eden," is straight outta Africa. When Matthew 2:15 reads, "out of Egypt," it's also saying "out of Africa."

What the problem is, because of cultural bias, many Biblical scholars and theologians refuse to acknowledge Eden being Africa and Adam and Eve Africans. And many other scholars find it a politically inconvenient truth to think of Adam and Eve not looking anything like a German Renaissance artist's painting. Certain mindsets can deal with Adam and Eve being from Mesopotamia because most don't know where that is anyway; but Uganda, uh-uh.

The possibility of Adam looking anything like Saddam Hussein: "*Well?*"

The possibility of Adam looking anything like Idi Amin: "*Hell to the no!*"

Unfortunately, due to bigotry, few there are who realize that Uganda ain't the house that Idi Amin built; it's the one first built by God Almighty himself. Even though Forest Whitaker got an Oscar for his portrayal of Amin in *The Last King of Scotland* (2006), the film furthered the view that Uganda is not the place to be promoted as birthplace for the first king of the world.

Google Newsweek magazine: *The Search for Adam and Eve* (1988). You may be surprised at the admission you'll find. Even though there are those who want to run, hide, or historically try to dodge that out of Africa bullet, truth will still find a way. By disavowing one's African roots as established in the Bible, a phony, fake, and delusional sense of racial supremacy is pushed by white supremacist and nationalist groups that have neither Biblical nor genetic credibility. And even though Satan knows the fallacy of their push, he waters it anyway. These groups are grown in the devil's garden and their leaders and front persons are his wilted flowers.

Satan works overtime to keep the continent of Africa as a whole one of the most spiritually shadowed, politically exploited and socially impoverished lands on the face of the planet. Because Africa is the "cradle of civilization," not Mesopotamia as popularly and falsely believed. Satan has to keep his false light projection of Mesopotamia as Eden moving. It is consistent with the strategy used to keep Sunday as the Sabbath moving.

When history books, TV shows, and people refer to Africa as the "dark continent," it's imperative to understand that this type of demeaning statement doesn't stem exclusively from flesh and blood origins. Satan has an issue with Africa spiritually speaking directly due to its employment by the kingdom of God as the birthplace of human kind.

Example: intelligently ask yourself what's really up when you find terrorists and their sympathizers saying they hate America. What's the motivation behind the insults and demeaning rhetoric? Did America as in the North America continent do anything to cause the vitriol? The land mass itself is an inanimate object. Subsequently, it's automatically understood that the object of terroristic hatred is not land, but the people who occupy the land.

But, and this is a big butt, there are people in the land of America who are not ballers and shot callers. They get up every morning; kiss the wife, husband, girlfriend, boyfriend, pet the dog or cat and go to work. They *ain't bothering nobody* as the expression goes. Yet, some "butt" who has a problem with America hides a bomb in a public place and a bunch of folks who were just about life, liberty, and the pursuit of happiness become the dead embodiment of a song by *Jaheim* titled *Just in Case*. Hence, there's the term "collateral damage."

Because of what America as a geographical land mass represents, all Americans are targets. And, as such analogously applies to America, so goes it with Africa. So, what's really up when you find a "moron" needing to call countries in Africa "shitholes?" What's the real motivation behind the insults and demeaning rhetoric? Did Africa as in the African continent really do anything to cause the vitriol? But, borrowing from the Doobie Brothers, should anybody in their right mind really care "What a Fool Believes!"

Again, Satan is the *Original Terrorist*. Satan hates the kingdom of God because God kicked him out of the kingdom.

Be the devil's advocate for a hot second and honestly ask yourself how you'd feel. As a human being, human nature takes offense at being kicked out of any place; just cause or not.

If you are satanically pissed enough to declare war, you are going to target anything and everything that represents your enemy.

"Another parable put he forth unto them, saying, The kingdom of heaven is likened unto a man which sowed

good seed in his field: But while men slept, his enemy came and sowed tares among the wheat, and went his way. But when the blade was sprung up, and brought forth fruit, then appeared the tares also. So the servants of the householder came and said unto him, Sir, didst not thou sow good seed in thy field? from whence then hath it tares? He said unto them, An enemy hath done this."
— MATTHEW 13:24-28

There is duality in the above parable that points straight at the continent of Africa. Adam and Eve were planted in a field that wound up being called Africa. They were the "good seed." But, keeping it real, the continent can't blame it all on the devil. Africa opened its mouth to those who "sowed tares." These sowers came in the form of European slave traders. Without a doubt, the African slave trade was the consequential result of African men sleeping. While these "men slept" and are still sleeping, Africa keeps its mouth open to contemporary sowers of tares in the forms of Al-Qaeda, Al-Shabaab, Boko Haram, ISIS, and Tarzan.

With disease and famine added, reversing the negative is extremely difficult when positive images aren't proactively snapped and chatted. Given this reality; assuredly Satan has a hand in framing the shots if not altogether holding the camera. But if folks are gonna pose for those shots and say cheese, they're willing participants in their own victimization – oppressed and demeaned state.

All of the above contributes to Africa's negative image. It's this negative image that supports the power context of racism and white supremacist thinking that's part of a satanic agenda.

At the writing of this book, the world population averages 7.5 billion. Those who classify themselves as White and being of European descent total around 1.1 billion. Now, seriously consider how roughly 15% of the world's population is capable of controlling a predominating world image of 85% of the world's population.

With respect to the Black or African Diaspora, the population total is 1.28 billion or 17% of the world population.

Now seriously, if you believe this predominating control is due to some kinda predominating high IQ, then you might as well believe Santa Claus has a red-nosed reindeer that can fly. There is a supernatural factor in play that's first brought to view in Luke 4:5-7. And, when being mindful that presidential elections can be manipulated by the media, it's really "no marvel" that Satan is not constrained by time and technology to pull from the same stunt elsewhere.

Yes indeed, God selected Africa to be the birthplace of mankind. Minus Satanic intervention, there's no logical explanation for this continent being so challenged in reflecting such a divine blessing.

Consider Matthew 2:13:

> "And when they were departed, behold, the angel of the Lord appeareth to Joseph in a dream, saying, Arise, and take the young child and his mother, and flee into Egypt, and be thou there until I bring thee word: for Herod will seek the young child to destroy him."

Africa was even chosen as a "City of Refuge" for Jesus and family to run. Jesus hiding out in Africa is also a problem for Satan. Important is the realization that you can't hide out amongst people that you look nothing like. Joseph, Mary, and Jesus had to look like Africans in order to blend in. But looking like Africans doesn't mean all Africans look alike. Eighty percent of the African continent is between the Tropics of Cancer and Capricorn. That means Africa gets a whole lot of sun, which spells heat. That translates to there being an assortment of skin tones that are predominantly brown to black complexioned. Bottom line, if Jesus had looked like a Leonardo da Vinci depiction, Herod's posse, driven by the devil, would have caught up with the Christ child quick, fast, and in a hurry.

Maybe Jesus' out of Africa connection is a sidebar regarding another issue problematic with "making any graven image or any likeness of anything that is in heaven above" (Exodus 20:4). God knows some can't handle the truth when it comes to ethnicity and race. What would happen if all the pictures and paintings out there right now of Mary, Joseph, and Jesus as White accurately portrayed them as dark complexioned or Black?

Likewise, instead of all the movies and TV programs out there now with Mary, Joseph, and Jesus cast as Europeans with British accents, what if those film features were cast both racially and ethnically accurate – dark complexioned with Hebrew accents? If being "*Blackish*" is cool when it comes to a network sitcom, why not when it's series and features portraying Biblical figures in the context of historical accuracy?

Simply because of the spiritual role Africa has played with regards to "war in heaven," Satan does everything he can and he uses everybody he does to cause this continent and its people "woe" not unlike what's forewarned in Revelation 12:12.

Consider the fact that the African continent, a.k.a. Eden, is an 11,608,000 square mile piece of real estate. This means, relatively speaking, Africa is big enough to swallow the United States, China, India, Spain, France, Germany, Italy, and Japan, with room still left for Portugal, Belgium, the Netherlands, Switzerland, and the U.K., as well as all of Eastern Europe.

A firsthand eyewitness perspective of Africa's relative size from afar can be gleaned every time you raise your head to the sky and look at a full moon. Almost 80% of the entire moon could be covered by Africa's total land mass. The breadth of Africa from northwestern hump to northeastern horn will easily cover the moon's entire face.

Now, we don't know much about the physical features of Bible characters because physical features are not the critical issue. What matters most about the Bible folks we encounter is not their physical features but their hearts and their motivations. In the Bible, the heart is the center of physical, spiritual and mental life. And that's where the head of all should be. But the spirit of Satan has made looks all that and a bag of chips. And consequently, since the media has decided to go there with him, the gloves have to come off in order to make and keep it real; to tell it like it is rather than how some would falsely like it to be. So, instead of "Newsflash" it's Fact Check!

Consider Acts 21:37-38:

> "And as Paul was to be led into the castle, he said unto the chief captain, May I speak unto thee? Who said, Canst

thou speak Greek? Art not thou that Egyptian, which before these days madest an uproar, and leddest out into the wilderness four thousand men that were murderers? But Paul said, I am a man which am a Jew of Tarsus."

The implication of the above verse is the fact that the face of the Apostle didn't look Roman or Greek. Paul looked like an Egyptian. Egypt is in Africa.

The chief captain was a Roman soldier. If Paul looked Roman, he probably wouldn't have been profiled and arrested in the first place. If Paul looked like he was a Greek, the soldier wouldn't have asked if he could speak Greek. The soldier didn't even ask Paul if he was Jewish or a Hebrew-Israelite. Rather, the soldier ethnically prejudged him. *"Art not thou that Egyptian"* based on what, hairstyle? Some say the apostle Paul was bald.

More than a few theologians maintain that the Israeli Jews of today don't have the physical appearance of the Jews that lived in the land during the time of Jesus Christ and earlier. Whether or not that's true, for sure the physical appearance of ancient Israel and the Hebrews were dark-skinned. How is this factually proven beyond speculation? Again, all you have to do is read the Bible for what it says.

Moses was born a Hebrew-Israelite and was raised by Pharaoh's daughter as her son (Exodus 2:1-10). Once more, Pharaoh's Egypt encompassed a dark-skinned populous. Go online and see what you find. The ethnicity and racial composition of this people cannot be confused with that of European or Asian ancestry.

Pharaoh, as a dark-skinned Egyptian, raised Moses as his son for 40 years. How many times over the course of forty years do you think Pharaoh looked into Moses eyes as a loving grandfather? Not once do we read Pharaoh saying to his daughter, *"Who's this baby's daddy?"*

Consequently, Pharaoh, all Egyptians, and all Hebrew-Israelites alike thought Moses was an Egyptian. Not until Moses got some political awareness and embraced some nationalistic pride in his Hebrew-Israelite heritage by helping a brotha out did the truth come out (Exodus 2:11-15). Again, the help-out here wasn't racial identification, it was about ethnicity.

But let's back it up. Let's not forget how Moses as a Hebrew-Israelite got into Egypt in the first place. Let's remember the Hebrew-Israelite Joseph whose brothers orchestrated his unceremonious family departure into Egypt/Africa via the slave trade. According to Genesis 42:8 Joseph toasted it up so well while there in Egypt that none of his brothers recognized him thirtysomething years later. How was it that a pre-Moses Hebrew-Israelite blended so well in the company of dark-skinned Egyptians if Hebrew-Israelites prior to going into Egypt/Africa looked like the Jews in Israel look today? If Joseph, the Biblical patriarch, had the skin tone of his theatrical stage counterpart as played by Donny Osmond in *Joseph and the Amazing Technicolor Dreamcoat*, do you seriously think the brothers would have been clueless regarding the brotha's identity?

Even though it had been years since Joseph had last seen his family bloods, for him to be totally unrecognizable to them suggests there was a little more to it than age or Egyptian *Dark and Lovely*.

Then there's Genesis 50:1-11. Joseph's father Jacob dies. The body is carried to Canaan. The funeral procession out of Egypt/Africa included the "house" of Pharaoh's Egypt and "all the house of Joseph" as Hebrew-Israelites. The procession is described as a "very great company."

Verse 11 says something very interesting:

"And when the inhabitants of the land, the Canaanites, saw the mourning in the floor of Atad, they said, This is a grievous mourning to the Egyptians."

If you picked up on it, the Canaanites as impartial third-party observers didn't see two ethnic/racial groups; they saw only one group of people. The Egyptians and the Hebrew-Israelites were indistinguishable by physical appearance. If the Egyptians and the Hebrew-Israelites had appeared different in terms of complexion, the Canaanites would have said, "*This is a grievous mourning to the Egyptians and the Hebrews!*"

All of the above ranging from the physical location of the Garden of Eden to the physical appearance of Moses gives insight into the racial strife affecting this planet. Racism, bigotry, and discrimination based on skin color are rooted in the war between God and Satan; Michael and his angels versus the dragon and his. Just as Jesus refers to the devil as a liar, and the "father of it," the devil is also the father of all racists and bigots.

In colloquial terms, Satan is the OR – Original Racist. And, when it comes to the OR, as in "operating room," racism has to be operated on spiritually. It cannot be surgically dealt with effectively through social measures only. An individual cannot choose to be born black or white. But, an individual can choose to be good or evil. Racism is evil. Those choosing evil embrace the spirit of Satan. And, having the spirit of Satan makes you a physical manifestation of the devil.

We've all watched enough crime dramas on television to know once a pattern of behavior is detected, a psychological profile follows shedding light on possible motives. The need to discriminate based on skin color spiraling into practices of bigotry and racism is demonic. And when adding the compulsion to enslave other human beings as a systematic process and institution, it becomes supernaturally pathological.

Whether one accepts it or not, Satan puts the spin on race as a divisive tool for human beings to run with. The devil creates the wedge and then hands it to mankind to use for the purpose of racial separation and segregation. When Charlton Heston is cast as Moses and Elizabeth Taylor gets the role of Cleopatra take a tip of *Ice-T*; "*Don't hate the playa or playette, hate the game.*"

Sharpening the aim on the game means focusing on the power brokers who finance features that play mind games. If posting a fake picture is a problem on Facebook, posting a fake picture on television and in movies is just as problematic. Deception is neither innocent nor benign; it's calculated. In the case of race, deception serves the interests of those who have a need to appear more than they are to feel good about who they're not.

When Proverbs 6:6 says, "Go to the ant, thou sluggard; consider her ways, and be wise;" well, be wise enough to intelligently ask yourself if you should take the time or interest in separating or segregating ants into species classifications?

When grazin' in the grass, sun beaming down between the leaves, lunch spread out on a blanket, do you care how ants define themselves?

Even though there are big ants, small ants, red ants, yellow ants, brown ants, and black ants, if you see an ant, unless you're into "ant-ology," you see an ant. Ten times out of ten, you're going to refer to what you see simply as an ant. You don't say, "*Oh my God, there's a Pogonomyrmex barbatus from the genus Pogonomyrmex.*"

Don't you think it might be the same way with extraterrestrials as far as their viewpoint of human beings? Do you really think extraterrestrials see color with regards to race, or do you think they only see human? If there are Martians invading this planet bent on your destruction, would your favorite Martian be red or green? Chances are you'd see Martian; color would/should be irrelevant.

But because Satan is a racist, racism is Satanism. The devil wants humans to self-define in terms of races; that's integral to his war strategy. The devil knows that his spiritually corrupt purposes are best served by the indignities of hue-manity over the dignities of humanity. That means the princedom of Satan is about hue-man rights, not human rights. And those who follow the devil's lead go right down the alley to hell with him.

Consider the subtext of a societal mentality that applauds the first to do this or that based on skin color. The first black major league baseball player; the first black doctor to perform open heart surgery; the first black president; the first black journalist to solo anchor a national network's daily evening news. Inevitably, that road goes full circle and one day becomes the first White man or woman to do this or that in a hundred years.

Intelligently put those "black" firsts into the context of Luke 17:7-10:
> "But which of you, having a servant plowing or feeding cattle, will say unto him by and by, when he is come from the field, Go and sit down to meat? And will not rather say unto him, Make ready wherewith I may sup, and gird thyself, and serve me, till I have eaten and drunken; and afterward thou shalt eat and drink? Doth he thank that servant because he did the things that were commanded him? I think not. So likewise ye, when ye shall have done all those things which are commanded you, say, We are

unprofitable servants: we have done that which was our duty to do."

When a country and its people profess to be Christian, the kingdom of heaven doesn't give any brownie, blackie, or whitie points for doing what it should have been doing anyway. Particularly when the doing is in accordance with what it proclaims:

> "We hold these truths to be self-evident, that all men are created equal, that they are endowed by their Creator with certain unalienable Rights, that among these are Life, Liberty and the pursuit of Happiness." — The Declaration of Independence (July 4, 1776)

But when an achievement or accomplishment is color coded, it marginalizes it with a mental asterisk by making skin color as significant as skill. Because of a devilish derived obsession with racial categorization, being the "first" according to skin color embeds racism in the public psyche as opposed to eradicating it. While the subtext in acknowledging racial firsts is a societal pat on the back, it should be a kick a foot lower.

So, when does it stop if a God conscious as opposed to a color-conscious society doesn't stop it? Make no mistake, when it's the media pushing the first black this or that narrative, it's the media who's putting the spin on skin. And, by the media being the culprit, it also establishes how tight of a hold the devil has on many of the minds employed in the media industry as professional journalists. When a paycheck takes precedence over integrity, Luke 4:5-7 shows itself to still be in play. Where spiritual things aren't spiritually discerned, and when mind control is a satanic objective, journalists become unwitting participants in carrying out an extraterrestrial agenda. They are paid to question everything other than the company issuing their paycheck. They are bought with a price that one day they will have to pay (1 Corinthians 6:20).

The extraterrestrial forces at play are good and evil making good or evil both a personal and professional employment choice. Because the world is color conscious, by necessity we have to deal with it the best that we can. Of course, the best is based on the terms principled by Jesus Christ and not the principles established by Satan.

The utopian belief that the *Age of Aquarius* will usher in a colorblind global village when the last die-hard bigot or closet racist takes his or her last breath is wishful thinking. Not until the Second Advent of Jesus will the so-called fat lady sing "nada nada" regarding racist attitudes and behaviors.

God created human beings as a species called "man." Even though God created man uniquely with respect to appearances, the Bible makes it plain that one blood is the common denominator (Acts 17:26). However, because more than a few have hang-ups regarding God and his one blood perspective, thus preferring to be governed by Satan's hemoglobin analysis, the color of the skin will continue having precedence over the content of character.

12 JUNGLE FEVER

"But if they cannot contain, let them marry: for it is better to marry than to burn."— 1 CORINTHIANS 7:9

There is a cosmic media war just as conflagrant as the "war in heaven." The media war objective is mind control by either agencies of good or evil. When images are planted in your head that foster a twisted concept of self and others, the end game is destructive behavior regardless of fame, fortune, or station in life. This behavior is not only self-destructive; it impacts all who are in your immediate vicinity as well as all who intersect your orbit.

For some, the verdict is still out, but for many others it came in decades ago that movies and television shows have a psychological impact. Seeing positive cinematic male and female interactions produce positive real-world results. Likewise, seeing negative male and female interactions do the opposite.

Because of the media's pervasiveness, and societal ability to influence positively and negatively, what we think and believe can easily be molded by whoever is providing or sending the message. Of course, few want to even remotely consider "to be or not to be" on TV or in the movies as having a spiritual connection. But if Luke 4:6-7 has a media connection as contended, then the power wielded by Satan not only applies to media ownership, it has applicability to who's seen on camera, behind the camera, and the messages delivered.

The position is taken in the last chapter that Satan is a racist. In order to further clarify that point, it's important to understand that the devil's racial predilections are not the same as humanity's. How so?

When talking about Africa, Eden, and Adam and Eve being Africans there will be those who can only process the postulation in terms of black and white. In arguing Eden being in Africa thus making the Edenic couple Africans has nothing to do with the politics of race as most have become programmed and thereby conditioned to deal with racial subject matter. Likewise, in taking the position that Joseph, Moses, Jesus, and

Paul were incognito amongst dark-complexioned people doesn't make them "incognegro." Being dark-complexioned doesn't make you Black when Black is viewed as a racial categorization for Americans of African descent.

Consider Vijay Armitraj, the tennis player of James Bond *Octopussy* (1983) fame. Is Vijay Black? How about Charlize Theron, the Academy Award winning actress who was born in South Africa and has dual citizenship in America. Is Charlize African-American?

Then there's Tiger Woods, who once needed no introduction. Once upon a time, Tiger said he was "Cablinasian." Who's qualified to argue with any individual who is bi-or-multiracial when it comes to self-determination with regards to self-definition respecting self-identification? God is not the author of confusion. But you sure as hell know who is. Being dark-complexioned doesn't make you Black any more than being albino makes you white if both your parents are colored in the NAACP sense of the word.

Black is a racial categorization that is self-imposed by those who choose to identify as such. The same self-imposition applies to the term African-American. Like it or not, accept it or not, both terms are political. Calling yourself either Black or African-American is socio-political acknowledgement and acceptance of an ethnicity and heritage identified as being derived from a continent of Africa ancestry or experience. That means if an individual says they are Black, because Black is political, self-definition is more a matter of head and heart than it is blood type. The reason being is blood bleeds red, even when it comes to being a dog.

The issue raised when an individual "passes for black" is demonstrative more a head and heart problem with the individual having the issue not the individual doing the passing. Pundits and psychologists show their "true color" when maintaining a white woman passing for Black is delusional when an estimated 34,940 women in the U.S. in 2018 will be diagnosed with invasive melanoma with an estimated 3,350 of those dying.

The fact of the matter, a vast majority of melanomas are caused by the sun. In fact, a compilation of studies easily found by *Googling* show that on the average about 85 percent of melanomas can be attributed to exposure to ultraviolet (UV) radiation from sunbathing. Additionally, in the U.S. alone, more than 419,000 skin cancers are annually linked to indoor tanning. Factually, more people develop skin cancer because of tanning than develop lung cancer because of smoking. Needless but necessary to say, close to 99.9 percent of these sunbathing/tanning victims aren't black women attempting to either look Caucasian or "pass for white." Rather, they are white women (and white men) wanting a dark complexion. The expression "tall, dark, and handsome" didn't originate amongst a Black or African Diasporic population. It was straight outta Europe.

Subsequently, in the face of such facts, what's the real reason behind the media pushed brouhaha warranting national news coverage when a white woman says she doesn't identify with being labeled Caucasian? Is it her problem? Or is it the problem of those having a white fragility complex that can't deal with group rejection by group members? When a devil or the devil really has a hold on you, delusion is the *pot calling the kettle black*!

Since race is a socio-political construct, with emphasis on the political, any white person rejecting their "whiteness" for the "blackness" that a post 1860's U.S. president holds as originating from "shithole countries" should be given respect as opposed to disdain. But, when you've been hoodwinked and bamboozled by television and film images that habitually portray "blackness" with disdain, your mind can't help being led astray. You don't realize that chemically straightened hair, skin lighteners, pastel contact lenses, and vanilla wigs on dark chocolate skin are prima facie evidence of mind manipulation.

The doctor phil-goods don't feel-bad when a Black woman culturally rejects her African originated beauty to adopt a European standard. Only when the script is flipped does "Houston" have a problem.

The socio-political problem termed "cultural appropriation" is like finding "love on a two-way street." On a professional/personal note, as a once-upon-a-time college professor, I asked a class of media students, "Hypothetically, if getting an on-air gig as a news reporter or anchor meant changing your hair style from Afro-centric to Euro-centric would you do it?" A resounding nine out of ten said "hell to the yes" without hesitation. Bottom line, look at the local news in your city. If there are any Blacks on the street beat, or sitting behind the anchor desk, how many are au naturale as far as women? How many have facial hair as far as men?

Because of socio-politico-economic realities, the love of money takes priority over the love of pride in self. Back to the Garden, "Who told thee that thou wast ugly?"

The devilish insinuation (emphasis on sin) that a person who visibly looks Black or African-American has to have shoulder-length straight hair or a non-mustachioed face to come into your home via television as a reporter or anchor is cultural misappropriation. And, those buying that brand in spiritual analysis have unwittingly bought into a cultural paradigm called "white privilege" that's just as psycho-delusional, contradictory, confusing, and divisive as that white woman or man that's lambasted for fraudulently identifying as Black when they biologically aren't. In the inverse, it's a case of bio-sociocultural assimilation being cool as long as the wig is on another head.

Imagine a world wherein 90% of Caucasian women are wearing Afro-centric hairstyles alien to their "roots" by conditioning not 'volitioning. And, white men have to grow a mustache, beard, or shave their heads vintage Isaac Hayes because the vintage Robert Redford look is culturally unacceptable. Societally, it's a parallel universe where it's all about what's palatable for mainstream consumption and Main Street is the corner of 125th and Lenox Avenue.

That honest conversation about race takes a dishonest approach every time actions speak louder than words. When racial identity is compromised whenever the price is right or by social pressures, actions evidence the compromiser wants that "membership has its privileges" card at all costs.

When Bob Marley says "Stand Up," sitting down when selfishly convenient isn't the "rights" he had in mind. But, when your mind is media manipulated by spiritually satanic forces that have extraterrestrial embodiment, the reality of what's really going on isn't tangibly grasped.

And, this explains and gives added meaning to exactly why Ephesians 6:12 says what it does.

The wrestling in 6:12 is with an alien personification just like Genesis 32:24. The only difference in Ephesians, the entity is evil. But, if you don't buy the existence of angels; or angels having the appearance of men; or angels being extraterrestrials, the reality of the Bible takes a back seat to surreality.

Ephesians 6:12 reads "principalities." While principality is a kangaroo word carrying principal; principal and principle are homophones; they mean two entirely different things. By definition, principality is a state ruled by a prince. Connecting the dots; doesn't the Bible identify Satan as a prince?

Matters of principality are not to be confused with matters of principle. Standing up for your rights (principles) quite often gets pretzel'd into becoming what's right for others (principalities) at the expense of personal/professional dignity and ancestral/genetic endowments. Only when the principality is accurately identified can one be successful in standing up against it in an effort to maintain principles. That's why the real fight isn't against "flesh and blood."

Principles are spiritual; the princedom of Satan is a principality. Satan uses "weapons of mind destruction" to war against the principles established by the kingdom of God.

With all due respect, Sarah Breedlove, a/k/a/ Madam C. J. Walker, did her thing as a matter of compromised principles. Her entrepreneurship was rooted in a mindset that's just as principly "rooted" today; but in a novel other than Alex Haley's. Her business decisions were compromised by "principalities" past just as business decisions are present; both personally and professionally.

Again, the satanic princedom is the author of confusion. Stirring it up over a White person wanting to be Black bad enough to perpetrate a fraud involves principles. It is in the same bag with a Black person wanting to be White bad enough to lighten their skin, surgery their nose and lips, blue their eyes, and perm their hair when a wig won't do. Therefore, if a mind is a terrible thing to waste, a subconscious mind that's wasted on needing to be who you genetically aren't is far worse.

The mind games Satan plays as a principality are based on compromising spiritual principles. That means where you are in principle is way beyond 'doos and dashikis; creams and contacts; music and mimics. It's not about what you do as much as it is about why you do it. The "what" comes from the head; the "why" comes from the heart.

It's no hidden secret that chemical hair relaxers and dyes associated with perms are linked to carcinogens spelled cancer. And, if by chance you don't live long enough to get the big C, there's an increased instance of premature baldness. Take an Internet stroll; you'd be surprised at what you'll find. And, if one of your favorite television shows is NCIS; check out some of the real life studies involving autopsies on Black females who've been perming since age 20.

Then, there are Black men and the question why so many brothas roll with the shaved heads? Well, other than adopted style, there is an increased instance of male pattern baldness that has become congenital as the result of the generational use of chemicals in the form of hair relaxers and hair dyes by parents.

Now, if health hazards are a result of being contaminated by soil and water that's become polluted over time by continued chemical dumping, intelligently ask yourself what do you think happens over time when chemicals are continually dumped on top of your head? Premature baldness not only becomes congenital, susceptibility to certain ailments preconditioning a shortened lifespan comes into play. The crack-baby syndrome is conceptually just as applicable when pharmaceutical purchases aimed at artificially altering skin tone and hair are addictive.

Back to the Garden; isn't it obvious who told you that you were ugly! Paraphrasing Hebrews 12:1, isn't it time to cut the crap in principle and see the big picture in terms of principality?

With regards to "war in heaven" now waged on earth, Satan as an extraterrestrial entity is not taking hostages. And, God is not negotiating with the devil as terrorist. The only negotiating being done is through

Christ. And, as The Negotiator, Jesus is only willing to talk to you while there's still time to get the hell outta Dodge.

"Come now, and let us reason together" (Isaiah 1:18) is intended to wake anybody up who is willing to be woke from the madness of Satan's alien methods that are aimed at killing principles that result in killing victims eternally.

In the face of Acts 17:26, isn't it obvious that it was not the kingdom of God's design that people would or should be referred to by colors. The irony in doing so, especially when it comes to the term "people of color," such terminology as a racial identifier is a misnomer. White is not the absence of color, but the composition of all colors. And, as brought to view in a previous chapter, black is the absence of all colors. Consequently, in the absence of making a political statement, racially self-identifying as Black means you are identifying as a person who is "colorless." In turn, if you're "black" apolitically speaking, NAACP membership becomes a paradox. There is no such thing as the National Association for the Advancement of Colorless People. Ralph Ellison's *Invisible Man*, a novel about an African American whose color renders him invisible, becomes a science book. Black being the physical absorption of all light wave frequencies is synonymous with invisibility.

Human being categorizations based on race is straight outta hell. It's a division orchestrated by the princedom of Satan. When searching the Scriptures, individuals were identified by nationality, place of birth, place of current residence. When it came to Jesus Christ, it was Jesus of Nazareth.

Do a self-examination. How many times when engaged in a casual conversation do you ask the question, "Is he/she black or white? Now, honestly ask yourself why is racial identity important to you?

Of course, let's not be socially or politically naïve; we live in a society where race has been made important. You want to know if the guy who went postal was chocolate or vanilla. But, dispensing with the socio-political implications, in the final analysis hurt is hurt and dead is dead regardless of the perpetrator's flavor.

In accordance with John 10:10, since the thief comes only to steal and kill and destroy, and it's spiritually understood that the thief being referred to is driven by the spirit of Satan, doesn't spiritual common sense suggest that the stealing, killing, and destroying has more to do with the thief's spirit than the thief's race?

Only incredibly stupid ass individuals believe a society composed exclusively of individuals who look like them ends stealing, killing, and destroying. Newsflash; the *"Love Train"* doesn't have segregated cars. *"Love, Peace, and Soul"* is spiritual, not racial!

When searching the internet, the practice of individuals being identified by race came straight outta the head of Charles S. Coon. Yeah, Coon. It was Charles' "S" that invigorated the "coonery" of racial classifications such as Negroid, Mongoloid, Caucasoid, and Australoid. And of course, that evolved into what you find on most official documents that identify you as either American Indian or Alaska Native, Asian, Black or African-American, Native Hawaiian or Pacific Islander, or White.

By definition, a "Black" person born in Alaska can be either "Alaska Native" or Black. But since Alaska is a U.S. state that individual can technically be an *"Alaska Native African American."* Same applies to the "White" person born in Hawaii. That individual could be classified as a *"White Native Hawaiian,"* thereby giving rise to sub-categorizations such as White Hawaiian and Black Hawaiian. Maybe even Hawaiian Punch, as in being Red!

Again, God is not the author of "coonery."

Since the sordid colors of racism are not the drawings of God's hand, what is the satanic motivation compelling all of this racial chaos and social confusion world round that particularly goes down in these here United States? From the 17th Century plantation big house to a 21st Century White House, historically, there's always been this obsessive-compulsive preoccupation with skin color and race. The fact that the house at 1600 Pennsylvania Avenue is called "white" is a national paradox right along with the hometown football team; the Redskins.

Having that so-called honest talk about race ain't about having it at the kitchen table. The family kitchen is not the most segregated spot in the family circle. It's the family church. Once more, racism and its assortment of flavors are satanic. That makes the matter spiritual. The inability and refusal to spiritually address the cause and effect is what keeps evil keeping on.

From racist tweets, posts, and commentary to racist rants, raves, and chants, rather than reporting the sensational aspects of racist behavior, wouldn't society be better served by examining the pathologies?

This book, *WMD*, is about "war in heaven" that makes for hell on earth. Unfortunately, those on earth politically categorized as Black and have dark-complexions catch more hell than those who are politically categorized as White having light complexions. What's really up with all of that? What's the story behind the story? Why are African Americans appearing in 90% of all national network television commercials "light-skin" or complexioned? What's up with *colorism* or *shadeism*? Aren't there any voices crying in the wilderness to call it out for what it is?

What it ain't is "equal protection" under the *Fourteenth Amendment*. It's discrimination involving a suspect classification based on race. The classification: *Ethnic Ambiguity*.

Ethnic ambiguity is hiring actors who can metaphorically kill two birds with one stone. In other words, it's looking black enough to prevent passing for white and white enough to be asked, "*What you is?* It's film/TV industry code word for off-white skin. It stems from a profit-driven advertising age more desperate to avoid offending anyone than *including everyone.* As far as being offensive, the agencies, studios, casting directors, producers, directors, and executives who subscribe to this racist practice are the offense. This modern-day *Hollywood shuffle* demands a lawsuit filing by each and every actor individually and as a class finding themselves victim.

Here again, the media is employed to implement Satan's agenda. The refusal to cast talent on the basis of skill, but rather on skin-tone, is not only a "weapon of mass destruction" targeting the actor, it's a "weapon of mind destruction" dropped on viewer. The inability to see actors on television and in the movies as black as the ace of spades or brown as a UPS truck placates the racist outlooks and orientations that should have been "*gone with the wind.*"

But what's the story behind the story from a Biblical perspective? What's the "why" spiritually speaking?

First, consider Genesis 30:32-42. The account of the speckled, spotted, and brown cattle illustrates the concept of genetic manipulation. The "colored cattle" as it were represented a dominant gene pool. The cattle that were not colored embodied recessive genes. Being recessive meant they didn't have the genetic capability to produce any characteristics other than what they already possessed. In other words, cattle that weren't speckled, spotted, and brown could not reproduce cattle that were.

Now, with respect to Adam and Eve, even though both were geographically Africans, both could not be created to embody the identically same gene pool. In other words, both Adam and Eve could not have all dominant genes. One had to have been created with recessive genes. Because Adam was created first, it stands to reason that Adam's genes were dominant. This genetically necessitates Eve's genes being recessive. When you look at the makeup of the human race, physical traits or characteristics that stem from recessive genes are light to white skin, green-hazel-blue eyes, red-blonde-straight hair, narrow noses, and thin lips.

Bottom line, in order for the human race to be composed of all the races that we see, and for Eve to be the "mother of all living" as written in Genesis 3:20, Eve would have had to appear as a female creature having white skin, blue eyes, blonde hair, narrow nose, and thin lips.

Regardless of one's ability to receive it, that's a genetic fact. It is absolutely impossible for both Adam and Eve to have identical gene pools and subsequently realize all of the human races that exist upon the face of the earth. While it is possible for two individuals having dominant gene pools to mate and procreate an offspring having a recessive gene trait, the odds of such an occurrence are significantly diminished. It would be analogous to shuffling a standard deck of 52 cards with the expectation of the ace of spades appearing at the very top of the deck on a significantly regular, routine and patterned basis.

In the case of two individuals mating that have dominant and recessive gene pools, however, rather than expecting the ace of spades' patterned appearance on top as a particular card; it becomes a particular suit's patterned appearance.

The genetic fact of the matter, two people having dominant genes can produce a baby with recessive gene characteristics through a process called gene mutation. In racial terms, two human beings with very dark skin can produce a baby with very light skin. It's call albinism. But two human beings with very light skin cannot produce a baby with very dark skin. In the context of two human beings that have a totally recessive gene pool genealogy, there's no such thing as an albino counterpart.

That means if you put the real in it in terms that everybody can understand, Adam was Black and Eve was White. Now, don't get it twisted. That's not Black and White racially and/or politically; but genetically. And this is symbolically affirmed by Genesis 2:22.

How so symbolically? Well, isn't the color of bone white? According to the Bible, Eve was made from Adam's rib. Since bone is white, the symbolism is there for all who are willing to receive it. This is why it's absolutely ludicrous for mankind to have embraced and adopted a parochial view of the world that pigeonholes individuals by racial categorization spiraling into racism. This genetic fact explains why the kingdom of heaven takes the "one blood" position presented in Acts 17:26. The Bible rejects racism based on the genetic fact that all human beings are derived from a mixture or combination of dominant genes and recessive genes. That means if you are "White" and racist, your original daddy (Adam) was a Black African man. And if you are "Black" and racist, your original mama (Eve) was a White African woman.

From a cosmic spiritual perspective, when statements stem from White men such as, "*they want our women,*" how ignorant they are that it was a Black man who had their "woman" from jump. Counterpoint, when statements stem from Black men and Black women that slam Black men with White women and Black women with White men, how uninformed they are that the black and white couple thing has nothing to do with "*jungle fever.*" Eden was a garden not a jungle!

Isn't it therefore rather obvious why Satan continually manufactures issues involving race? It doesn't even have anything to do with sex. The devil as an extraterrestrial intelligence just plays a game he knows most human beings can best understand. If you don't know chess, the game is checkers. If you ain't feelin' bridge then it's bid or spades?

Believe it or not, it's all about genetics. Once again, Isaiah 14:12 identifies Satan's angelic name as Lucifer. Lucifer/Satan is referred to as "son of the morning." The morning or dawn is characterized by light. Revisit 2 Corinthians 11:14: Satan is referred to as an "angel of light." And because there is a duality to the Bible, light is not restricted to illumination; it can also bear reference to a shade of color.

Note where this goes when Revelation 22:16 is brought into the mix:
"I Jesus have sent mine angel to testify unto you these things in the churches. I am the root and the offspring of David, and the bright and morning star."

Significant in the above passage is the appearance of the word "offspring." It signals genetics being fundamental to any interpretation and understanding.

Juxtapose the above with the following written in Isaiah 14:14:
"I will ascend above the heights of the clouds; I will be like the most High."

Satan as Lucifer, according to Isaiah, is the "son of the morning." And, Jesus, as God, is the "bright and morning star." Satan, according to Isaiah, wants to be like God. So, here we have Satan being referenced with morning and we have Jesus being referenced with morning. With regards to these two morning references, which is greater? Of course, the word "bright" makes the morning reference to Jesus greater. And of course, even though morning is morning is morning, when the word "bright" is applied, the morning referenced Jesus makes him dominant.

With respect to Satan's physical appearance as "light," the devil is "recessive." Place this in a Garden of Eden context and take skin color completely out of the narrative. Intelligently ask yourself who you think Satan best identifies with.

Satan identifies with Eve. Eve was made from Adam's DNA making her recessive just like Lucifer was made from God's DNA making Satan recessive. Satan doesn't see black and white. He sees dominant and recessive. Isaiah 14:14 doesn't say, "*I will be 'recessive' to the most high.*" Satan wants to be dominant like the Most High. The X-factor added to the equation is raw jealousy and envy.

In the Garden, it was obvious that God identified with Adam. Adam genetically represented God as the symbolic creator of Eve. Therefore, Satan stepped to Eve because she genetically represented him symbolically. In addition to everything else, the devil used Eve because he could metaphysically relate to her recessively.

Think about that for a minute. Intelligently ask yourself why didn't the serpent step to Adam? Even though a sexual theory is offered, the serpent could have just as easily tried to sexually seduce the male member of the garden party. Homosexuality could have been introduced in the Garden as carnal knowledge no differently than heterosexuality. Conversely, Adam, having been turned on homosexually, could have stepped to Eve causing her fall. The Nephilim infestation of the human race could've been achieved just as well through a bisexual stratagem once carnal knowledge was in play. But, it didn't go down like that.

Was Adam beyond being deceived? Was he that much smarter or wiser than his wife? Obviously not since Eve was able to turn him. Given the fact that Eve spun Adam like a top, it's naïve to believe Satan couldn't have done so as well if a concerted effort had been made.

But that wasn't the case because Satan could just better relate to Eve. Consequently, this also suggests in addition to everything else, Satan is an effeminate creature psychologically. Whether you accept it or not, the stereotypical behavioral patterns attributed to women are overemotional, flighty, fickled, erratic, vindictive, irrational, etc. When you seriously think about it, the behavioral patterns exemplified by Satan are basically all of the above and more. From Revelation 12, to Genesis 3:15; from Pharaoh, to The Flood; Satan has gotten the shaft every time. And, when viewed from a psychologically pathological vantage point, how illogical was Calvary's cross? Did the devil really think he could crucify Jesus Christ as Michael the archangel, who is God incarnate and getaway untouched? Calvary is the straight up behavior of a stereotypical woman spurned. It's *I'm Gonna Git You Sucka* (1988) for kicking me out of heaven. It's an extraterrestrial cosmic reaction no different than the human reaction that finds a man making bomb threats as a get-back against a woman who has rejected him.

Unquestionably, when viewed in human terms, Satan's behavior patterns evidence this extraterrestrial predatory alien doesn't "*Think Like a Man*" even though it has a penis (Genesis 6:4; Job 2:1). And it juxtaposes the opinion that Satan was both psychologically and physically predisposed to choose Eve in the Garden of Eden for the simple fact that when it came to her there was a psychosomatic bond. In the devil's mind, Eve exemplified a genetically symbolic recessive gene pattern. It's the recessive gene pattern that drove the physical attraction. The psychology intertwined is just icing on the cake when the compulsion is physical.

Undeniably, when put in contemporaneous terms, this extraterrestrial entity or "masculine" angel was more in touch with its feminine side!

Genetics is physical given the fact it's physiology. When you see someone you like, it's initially a matter of your liking what you see first. But underneath all of that there, serious consideration has to be given the possibility that you're wired that way. The wiring could have been done by you over the process of time or it could be genetic.

In a universe where there's "war in heaven" it's utter naïveté to think anything and everything from sexual preference to sexual addiction, having a sweet tooth to being a sourpuss is off the table and out-of-play. Just as God will meet you where you are, don't think Satan won't be about the business of doing the same. But, instead of just a meet and greet, the devil will force an immediate and personal relationship by giving you what you want as opposed to what you need.

If you've been praying out loud for a soul mate, Satan heard that prayer too. He'll try to answer that prayer before God by giving you a sole mate. That's someone who will walk with you until the soles on either pairs of shoes wears thin. The devil knows penny loafer lovers are a dime a dozen. And, best believe he's got a pocket full of change to meet supply and demand.

Unfortunately, the recessivity of light-skin or whiteness and the dominance of dark-skin or blackness camouflages what's spiritually going on.

Acts 17:26 viewed genetically finds no place or space for division beyond the sub-atomic molecular level. This doesn't work for Satan. Since the devil's agenda is based on division, the only place and space for such that can be readily seen is skin deep. That's why ugly is to the bone.

Satan psychologically targets those he feels he can relate to physically based on his symbolic recessive gene pattern. Whiteness in terms of skin color is a recessive gene trait. If Satan's anti-God spirit can infiltrate the body of his primary target, division based on skin color is the end result.

Obviously, this is a two-way street. If the devil is successful in pitting those with recessive gene traits against those with dominant gene traits, a reactionary relationship develops that's cause and effect. In other words, you slap me you get slapped back.

Matthew 5:39: "But I say unto you, That ye resist not evil: but whosoever shall smite thee on thy right cheek, turn to him the other also."

That's a spiritually physical attempt to diffuse a genetically divisive situation Satan has genetically orchestrated. It's dispute resolution at the expense of the victim.

> "Woe unto the world because of offences! for it must needs be that offences come; but woe to that man by whom the offence cometh! –MATTHEW 18:7

If you're the perpetrator of offensiveness, Jesus is saying to the victim, "I got this." This means Jesus is telling Satan and all who do the devil's bidding that their time is coming. And when that time arrives it won't be pretty. It too, will be ugly to the bone!

The irony of the recessive versus dominant gene saga is only on a killing floor or field where blood is being shed does the superficialities of skin color become a distant thought. Typically, only then does the color red take physical and psychological priority over all other hues. Satan uses the pathology of racism to create conflict based on superficial differences where the shedding of blood reveals there's really no difference at all.

Satan is masculine with gender recessive traits. He deals prolifically with symbolism in his war with God. And, that symbolism is manifested in the amplification of both sex and race as the one thing that umbrellas his grievance with God.

Black versus White in general, and interracial relationships that find Black men and White women mated in particular symbolize the Garden of Eden prototype. Both represent a pattern designed by the kingdom of heaven wherein dominant genes and recessive genes unite to procreate. But, the Peaches and Herb classic, *Reunited*, is a song Satan doesn't want sung.

It is a failure to have spiritual insight regarding the root cause of racism that perpetuates and sustains the sickness of skin color obsession. Satan is both a physical and spiritual force. The physical reality of racism is driven by the spiritual reality that fallen angels are faced with the cosmic reality of genetic annihilation (Revelation 12:12). Accept it or not, just as the devil chose Eve because of her genetic recessivity, he chooses others who share Eve's recessive gene traits.

It's therefore important to understand that this satanic selection is based on an individual's gene pool first and foremost, not due to some inherent racist predilection to be evil. It's simply "spiritual profiling" by the princedom of Satan based on historical behavior and current observations. If you've shown and show yourself to be racially prejudiced, the forces of evil will camp at your door to make displays of bigotry, discrimination, and racism even more.

Division based on skin color is the most efficient and effective means for instigating worldwide strife and mayhem. Examined genetically, recessive gene traits versus dominant gene traits prototype all coalitions entrenched in color consciousness. Subsequently, white versus black is the "perfect storm" that archetypes Satan's disdain for the "image and likeness" of God. The fact that God is all powerful, again, makes God "dominant." Again, directly from Isaiah 14:14, it's this dominance that Lucifer can't "be like" that he resents. And it's this resentment of the gene pool dominant traits that people with dark skin have that spiritually explains the root cause of white racism worldwide both historical and contemporaneous.

Here, however, is where it gets deeper. Even though Eve embodied a recessive gene pattern, she did not have to fall prey to the spirit of Satan. Eve was merely a pawn in a universal game of chess between the kingdom of God and the princedom of Satan. Even though Revelation calls it a war, common sense continually maintains that a fight between an almighty power and one that isn't is a match of will not might. Eve could have had the will to prevail and said *"hell to the no."*

Applicable to this day and age, telling it like it is when and where such is "white racism," the name of the game is still recessive gene traits versus dominant gene traits. A contemporary devil's temptations can still be met with an emphatic *"hell to the no."*

Whether the impetus behind white racism's perpetuity is motivated by a fallen angel spirit of "genetic annihilation" or not, social psychologists, psychiatrists, and theologians can debate that argument. The spiritual fact of the matter is if you call yourself a Christian, racism in all of its archetypical forms is of Satan; not of God. Eve's deception was consequential her failure to accept the Will of God by making it her will.

Monroe Nathan Work (1866-1945) was an African American sociologist who founded the Department of Records and Research at Tuskegee Institute in 1908. His documentation figures significantly in estimating nearly 5,000 Black Americans were killed by lynchings at the hands of White Americans between 1835 and 1964.

CBS' *60 Minutes* did a 2018 segment on lynching wherein actual photos of victims were shown. Doubly horrendous about those photos isn't the faces of the corpses. Rather, the chill factor is the faces beneath the overhanging bodies. Wanna see Satan in the form of demonic possession? Google "lynching stock photos" and behold.

What kind of spirit propels this kind of atrocity coupled with wide scale judicial impunity on local, state, and national levels? Intelligently ask yourself under any circumstances is it the Will of God inspiring such evil? The carnival atmosphere surrounding these vicious murders accentuated by the smiling faces of men, women, and children is beyond comprehension by any civilized human being. And, when considering the perpetrators and peanut gallery spectators were professed God fearing Christians, undeniably the wickedness captured photographically is supernatural. There's more to this terrorism than, *"I hate you."* It's pathological with deep-seated spiritual implications.

Since evil is timeless in concurrency, are horrific pictures of a people being gassed to death in Syria under the blind-eye of their government any more or less horrific than pictures of a people being hung, castrated, burned alive, murdered under the blind-eye of theirs? And, how about "film at 11" documenting trigger-happy policing with the use of excessive force giving appearance that Black lives don't matter as much as non-Black?

Inherent, the term pathological is not used lightly. More often than not what separates the criminal mind from the civilized is space and opportunity. The obsession by some to continually embrace sports logos and mascots that are deemed racially and ethnically offensive is driven by the same satanic spirit. The faces of those pictured inside and outside sports stadiums defiantly taunting protesters who oppose emblems that promote racial stereotypes and ethnic slurs would have been the same faces in the crowd if quantum leaped to an 1835-1964 lynching.

Once you are made aware that a name, term, symbol, or expression is racially/ethnically derogatory, mean, inappropriate, and insensitive and you go there anyway; that's a sickness.

Timeout for apologies after getting caught with hand in the cookie jar and the true you is finally spotlighted. Crocodile tears are easily shed when what's said could cost a job or opportunity.

Likewise, when it's a matter of bigotry, discrimination, prejudice, and racial hatred perpetrated by Blacks and "Others" as a response to being victims of racism, Adam, being the embodiment of a dominant gene pattern didn't have to fall prey to the spirit of Satan either. Adam was also a chess pawn. He, too, could have said no – but with much stronger language than "hell" given his much stronger genetic package.

Adam's applicability to racism that's here and now is the fact that reverse racism is not a deception it's a reaction. Adam reacted to Eve's invitation. It was a calculated response to a satanically produced overture. Black reaction to White racism is in the same spiritual boat with Adam. It is a physical response other than left-cheek turning. While this neither excuses nor spiritually justifies the responsive reaction, it illustrates Satan as being an equal opportunity employer regarding "war in heaven."

The devil is about his business by any means necessary. He doesn't care if you're Black or White. If Satan can push your button he will do so because he knows it takes two to tango when it comes to getting down and dirty.

Whereas white racism is a deception not unlike the *slickery* and the *trickery* that hung up Eve, "black racism" is the acceptance of an invitation not unlike the emotional manipulation used by Eve to jack-up her husband.

Of course, there is and always will be the argument that Blacks collectively cannot be racist given their lack of socio-political empowerment as a collective. Subsequently, this suggests that Black people can be prejudice or bigoted, but not racist generally speaking wherein racism involves power or the ability to control another individual's livelihood and destiny systematically. But, to be or not to be a so-called Black racist is not the spiritual question when it comes to genetics. Having dominant genes as opposed to recessive genes "are what they are." If you are black as that proverbial spade, the baby you help make is not going to rival that proverbial snowflake.

When MLK took the position "turn-the-other-cheek" and MX said, uh-uh, "Send 'em to the cemetery," realized or not, it was the argument of Martin that was genetically superior in its philosophical approach to that of Malcolm. King gave Gandhi credit for his 60's nonviolent methodology, but when viewed in terms of victimization being the result of having dark skin; it was way deeper than skin tone.

Turning-the-other-cheek means being slapped in the face again. Being slapped in the face solely because you are Black is both spiritual and psychological affirmation of gene pool dominance. Inferiority complexes stem from feelings of inadequacy. Slapping someone causing them to "turn-the-other-cheek" is aggressive behavior in compensation of psychologically perceived inadequacy. You don't "F" (Fool) with someone just because they are a different skin color unless you feel inferior to them. You don't call names or make demeaning and derogatory jokes unless you feel you ain't "S" (Special) comparatively speaking.

Realized or not, when you are spiritually "dominant" in terms of mindset, you can deal with situations and circumstances those of lesser character can't handle. When the genetic correlation to Matthew 5:39 is accepted, it's spiritually understood more so because Christ even in human form was genetically superior to Satan. By spiritually embracing God in fullness, you are comfortable in your own skin. It is the dominance of God period that makes skin color inconsequential. This means, as hypothesized, if there is a genetic connection between having recessive gene traits and the propensity to exhibit hostility toward those with dominant gene traits, it's nurtured by ignorance that's both biological and spiritual.

Biological ignorance is the biological fact that white skin is a genetic recessive trait. Racist views that are based on white supremacist logic are biologically illogical. Arguing that the progeny is "superior" to the progenitor is tantamount to making a case that the art is more profound that the artist. It's not only ignorant, it's stupid with a prior.

"For if any be a hearer of the word, and not a doer, he is like unto a man beholding his natural face in a glass: For he beholdeth himself, and goeth his way, and straightway forgetteth what manner of man he was." —James 1:23-24

Those who call themselves Christian are without excuse when it comes to the practice of racism both individual and institutional. That's because indictment is issued not only by the expressed written word of God (Acts 17:26), but by the bathroom mirror. If you are a racist having genetic recessive features, the biology inherently establishing those features is a "natural face" reminder of what manner of man or woman you in fact are.

If you are a racist having genetic dominant features, the biology inherently establishing those features is a "natural face" reminder of what manner of man or woman you in fact are.

This means no amount of bleaching cream, pastel contact lenses, perm, wig, weave, or plastic surgery is going to transform you into who you spiritually aren't.

"For now we see through a glass, darkly; but then face to face: now I know in part; but then shall I know even as also I am known."
— 1 Corinthians 13:12

13 HIDDEN FIGURES

"Are not five sparrows sold for two farthings, and not one of them is forgotten before God? But even the very hairs of your head are all numbered."
— LUKE 12:6-7

Faced with the fact that what we are witnessing both in traditional media and new media is very calculated, the validity of the Bible's practicality in a technocratic society regularly comes into direct and implied questioning. Compounding that, some still can't deal with King James having had his hands in the Bible's translation.

In spite of what you might think about the king, all his horses and all his men could not write, rewrite, construct, or reconstruct the Bible to flow with the consistency it displays from Genesis to Revelation. It's impossible, not improbable. Any writer who approaches writing casually or professionally knows the challenge required to maintain continuity in a literary work; particularly one containing thousands of words. Cover to cover the Bible has over 800,000.

In order for KJ to do anything other than translate what was provided would require supernatural intervention, much less a modern-day computer and software programming.

Did King James and Company make some editorial decisions that kept some manuscripts out of the 66 books?

Yes.

Did the *Book of Enoch*, which didn't make the cut, have some compelling things to say?

Yes.

It can readily be drawn from the Gospel According to Enoch (105:1-7) that Noah was an albino leading many to the righteous conclusion that his roots could be traced forward to Alex Haley's. YouTube *"Biblical Noah an albino"* or get this Dead Sea Scroll from a Smartphone near you and read. You may be enlightened (no pun intended).

But, this ain't about the *Book of Enoch* being dissed because Noah wasn't "white enough for 'ya." Yes, if Noah was an albino, genetically, he was what

Eurocentrism has racially termed a Black man. Consequently, that means not just Ham, but all three of Noah's sons according to Eurocentrism's "one drop rule" were Black men. Now, since there were only four men alive in the entire world after the flood and they were all Black men – go figure!

But this isn't about Eurocentric hang-ups when it comes to black and white. The "one drop rule" when it comes to the Bible is red. If you don't bleed red, you're dead. Satan's agenda pushes "one drop." The kingdom of God advances "one blood." Subsequently, the question all intelligent people need to ponder is whose blood you're willing to take to the blood bank. The blood of the devil? Or the blood of the Christ?

Allegorically, remember, *Freddie*. He "shot-up" with an agenda pushed by Satan. So, in the words of the poet: "*If you wanna be a junkie, wow!*"

All who have a problem with what's missing from the Bible by negligent omission or purposeful commission are misled no different from the *Super Fly* (1972) saga of Freddie. Bump what's missing and righteously deal with what's there? Even if you're diligently searching for a Biblical inconsistency or contradiction, borrow in part from the *Gospel of Marvin* and "*let the Spirit move and groove you; good*" by opening your body, mind, and soul to revelations that are not written in stone by preset denominational interpretations and influences.

God did not give one man, one woman, or one church all knowledge in spite of what each individually or institutionally may preach and teach. If God had done that, John 5:39 would have been written, "*Search the Preacher.*"

A testament to the Bible's God-inspired authorship that many folks are not hip to is its integration of numbers into the prose and poetry as literary content. Yes, numbers. Believe it or not, when examined in its original Hebrew and subsequent Greek (Septuagint) translations, the Bible is written entirely in mathematics. And doing the math here is not a complicated procedure because the process doesn't involve unraveling some hidden code, or equidistant letter sequencing. It's simple adding, multiplying, and dividing. The fact that one of the books of the Bible is named Numbers speaks to the significance.

In the English language, we express numbers using the Arabic digits 1, 2, 3, 4, 5, 6, 7, 8, 9, 0. The Hebrew-Israelites and early Greeks, however, had no dedicated way of expressing numbers digitally in their language system. In turn, they used the letters of their alphabet as numbers. Thus, both languages are alphanumeric. For example, the number 1 in English would constitute the Greek letter α, which is called *alpha*. The number 2 is β or *beta*. The number 3 is γ or *gamma*. The number 4 is δ or *delta*. The number 5 is ε or *epsilon*.

Alpha	Beta	Gamma	Delta	Epsilon	Zeta	Eta	Theta
Αα	Ββ	Γγ	Δδ	Εε	Ζζ	Ηη	Θθ
1	2	3	4	5	7	8	9
Iota	**Kappa**	**Lamda**	**Mu**	**Nu**	**Xi**	**Omicron**	**Pi**
Ιι	Κκ	Λλ	Μμ	Νν	Ξξ	Οο	Ππ
10	20	30	40	50	60	70	80
Rho	**Sigma**	**Tau**	**Upsilon**	**Phi**	**Chi**	**Psi**	**Omega**
Ρρ	Σσζ	Ττ	Υυ	Φφ	Χχ	Ψψ	Ωω
100	200	300	400	500	600	700	800

Where is this going, and why is the destination important? Well, let's back into an answer. In Daniel 12:4, we read "knowledge shall be increased." But immediately prior in the same verse we find the prophet being told to "shut up the words…seal the book, even to the time of the end."

What is this book? Just what is the time of the end? Well, again, it ain't rocket science. The Bible is the book; the book is the Bible. And if you go to its end you'll discover Revelation. If you study Revelation chapters 5 and 6, you'll find talk about a sealed book. You'll also find Jesus Christ unsealing and opening that book. Understanding Revelation is the knowledge that shall be increased. It's the prophetic words of Revelation that's been literally "shut up." Increasing the knowledge of Biblical prophecy is the Daniel 12:4 gist.

How long has an increased knowledge of Revelation's prophetic words been shut up? Well, the "shut" is up as soon as the book is opened and serious prayerful study is begun. Once again, understanding the prophecies (Daniel and Revelation) with respect to increasing knowledge is provided by the Holy Spirit (John 14:26). Only through the involvement of "the Comforter" as teacher is Biblical knowledge and understanding achieved. In that regard, "the time of the end" began with the commencement of Jesus Christ's public ministry in A.D. 26.

Consider Luke 4:17-19:

> And there was delivered unto him the book of the prophet Esaias. And when he had opened the book, he found the place where it was written, The Spirit of the Lord is upon me, because he hath anointed me to preach the Gospel to the poor; he hath sent me to heal the brokenhearted, to preach deliverance to the captives, and recovering of sight to the blind, to set at liberty them that are bruised, To preach the acceptable year of the Lord."

There's the open book that symbolically represents the metaphysical one referenced in Revelation chapters 5 and 6. Also, there's the "bruise" of Genesis 3:15.

Consider Isaiah 61:1-2; the prophetic text Christ is quoting:

> "The Spirit of the Lord GOD is upon me; because the LORD hath anointed me to preach good tidings unto the meek; he hath sent me to bind up the brokenhearted, to proclaim liberty to the captives, and the opening of the prison to them that are bound; To proclaim the acceptable year of the LORD, and the day of vengeance of our God; to comfort all that mourn."

It's significant that Jesus stopped abruptly at *"the acceptable year of the Lord,"* which is connected with his First Advent. *"The day of vengeance of our God"* is associated with the Second Advent. Subsequently, *"the time of the end"* wherein "the book" was unsealed and opened has been ongoing for the last 1,992 years. Jesus fulfilled the prophecy of Isaiah as well as that of Daniel. And with respect to Revelation, Jesus is the prophecy.

Many who should always remember for some reason forget that the prophecy about John as prophesized by Isaiah in 40:1-3, and the message of John that the "kingdom of heaven is at hand" in Matthew 3:1-3 is about Jesus. The "kingdom of heaven" was "at hand" as soon as Jesus used his hand to open the book of Isaiah and read from it.

Do you think Jesus uses the same expression, "the kingdom of heaven is at hand" for lack of another way to say he's now on the scene? Or do you think he is literally handing the world a not so hidden message that a sealed prophecy has now been opened.

Lest we all forget John the Baptist is a prophet. He belongs to a club of prophets that includes Joel, Jonah, Amos, Hosea, Micah, Isaiah, Nahum, Zephaniah, Habakkuk, Jeremiah, Daniel, Ezekiel, Obadiah, Haggai, Zechariah, Malachi, Nathan, Samuel, Miriam, Deborah, Huldah, Noadiah, Anna, and John the Apostle. So, for those who call themselves prophets/prophetesses, and are called prophets/prophetesses, they are members of a very exclusive club. Bottom line, being a member of *Club 25* means God the Father, Jesus Christ, and the Holy Spirit sponsor your membership. And just like it is when it comes to being a member in any exclusive club, your sponsorship has to be ongoing for your membership to be both current and up-to-date.

Just contemplate the duality of the previously twice referenced Matthew 4:16 with verse 17 added:

"The people which sat in darkness saw great light; and to them which sat in the region and shadow of death light is sprung up. From that time Jesus began to preach, and to say, Repent: for the kingdom of heaven is at hand."

The "great light" talked about in this instance is enlightenment. Jesus Christ as "the way, the truth, and the life" (John 14:6) is the knowledge of salvation. And this too explains why Jesus said, "The kingdom of heaven is at hand." Again, it was his hand that broke the seal and opened the book to the knowledge that is both his "Spirit" (as teacher) and his "Testimony" (as prophecy).

"…worship God: for the testimony of Jesus is the spirit of prophecy."— REVELATION 19:10

It's therefore important to understand that the "time of the end" is not "the end." The Bible's numerical appliances represent an increase in knowledge that's a result of Revelation, as a *New Testament* writing, technically having always been an unsealed book patiently waiting for individual opening.

John 4:24 reads, "God is a spirit: and they that worship him must worship him in spirit and in truth." Many worship in spirit. Unfortunately, many fail to worship in truth. In order to get truth, you have to search for it (John 5:39). "Seek and ye shall find; knock, and it shall be opened unto you." Forget Hector, many have read these words since they were a pup, yet don't really catch the drift. Who doesn't know truth takes forever to find when you search for it by a process of osmosis.

My best childhood friend didn't ride to school on the short yellow bus, but he failed the third grade (almost twice). If you don't open a book there's a fifty-fifty shot just sniffing the air around those who do will get you over. But if you don't open "the Book," air sniffing according to the *"kingdom of God being at hand"* gets you nowhere.

The duality of the prophecy is the fact that "the hand" being referred to is not just the hand of Jesus opening the book; the hand that's also being pointed to is yours. The "kingdom of God" is at your hand! It's your hand that unseals knowledge that's kept shut up from your mind. And of course, that's knowledge beyond the pages of the Bible. There's an old saying that the best place to hide money from folks is in a book! Go figure.

Again, the consistency of the words employed in the Bible in order to present its message in making its case is amazing; grace. When connecting the dots, there is in fact "line upon line, precept upon precept, here a little and there a little" for all to see who are willing to search. God, through his Spirit, makes knowledge the reward for those that "diligently seek him" (Hebrews 11:6).

Revelation's inherent knowledge is best described as present truth. The concept of "present truth" is not new truth, future or past truth. It's now truth. It's what you know now, right here in the present. When you presently find something out, you can keep-on-keeping-on and ignore it. Or you can give it your full consideration and act accordingly.

The revelation that the Bible has an interwoven mathematical component is present truth. Again, it's not new truth. It's always been there waiting for individuals to be hipped to the fact. Wherein after discovery, the ball is in each individual's court to either pass or shoot.

Admittedly, God is probably not going to expect an overwhelming number of people to go out and get either a Hebrew or Greek translation of the Bible and start running numbers. But for all of those who are into

Greek as far as a fraternity, sorority, or professional organization that is popularized by Greek letters, wouldn't knowing the Biblical application of Greek letters as Greek numbers be thought provoking? Right up the street that you've chosen to live? If you live as a soror or a frat bro, why wouldn't it be wise to increase your knowledge?

If anything, realizing that the Bible is more than both a history and science book, but a mathematics one further establishes Roman 11:33: "O the depth of the riches both of the wisdom and knowledge of God! how unsearchable are his judgments, and his ways past finding out!"

Example: Jesus in Greek is spelled, Iησouξ; pronounced *ee-ay-sooce*.

Iota	(I)	=	10
Eta	(η)	=	8
Sigma	(σ or ξ)	=	200
Omicron	(o)	=	70
Upsilon	(u)	=	400
Sigma	(σ or ξ)	=	200
			888

Once again, because Greek is an alphanumeric language, every letter has a correspondent numerical value. When counting the name Jesus just as we are instructed to do in Revelation 13:18 with regards to the beast, what are the odds that the number of the beast, which the Bible says is the number of a man (not the devil) would be three sixes and the number of man's savior, Jesus Christ, would be three eights?

Let's next look at the Periodic Table of Elements.

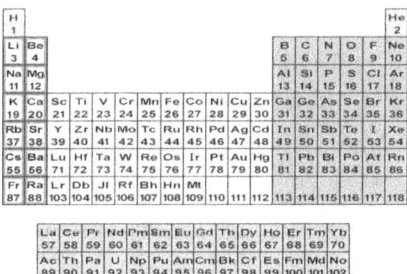

The letter-C on the chart with the number 6 underneath is the atomic number for carbon. That designation means that carbon in a stable state has 6 protons, 6 neutrons, and 6 electrons. And, of course, man is a carbon creature. Carbon forms the key component for all known life on earth. So, technically, even though the Bible says count the number of "a man," the triple 6 is actually representative of all life on earth. To be a man, you have to be an earthling first. When Revelation 12:12 says, "Woe to the inhabiters of the earth and sea," the warning is directed at all carbon creatures.

But putting a pin in that for a moment, it would be amiss not to address the term *Vicarius Filii Dei*, which means Vicar or "Representative of the Son of God." A previous chapter of this book submits the institution of the papacy as the subject of 2 Thessalonians 2:3-12 and Revelation 13:18. Whether one accepts that submission based on the papacy's admissions is the reader's choice. Roman Catholic publications say what they say; they read the way they read. All *WMD* has done is point it out.

Pivoting to *Vicarius Filii Dei*, many Protestants and theologians point it out that this one phrase, beyond all doubt, points to the Pope as being "the beast." Now, the term was purportedly first used in the Donation of Constantine, now dated between the eighth and the ninth centuries A.D. Whether it was or wasn't, it is used in an April 18, 1915 Catholic publication called Our Sunday Visitor. Google "Our Sunday Visitor, April 18, 1915" and read for yourself.

If you don't care to let your fingers do the Googling, the newspaper article reads:

> *"What are the letters supposed to be on the Pope's crown, and what do they signify, if anything? The letters inscribed in The Pope's miter are these: Vicarius Filii Dei, which is the Latin for Vicar of the Son of God."*

If you follow the yellow bricks and do what Revelation 13:18 instructs, the phrase *Vicarius Filii Dei*, reduced to its Roman numerals, where "U" interchangeably becomes "V" as seen on numerous buildings, the addition works as follows:

VICARIVS FILII DEI = 5+1+100+1+5+1+50+1+1+500+1 = 666.

Needless, but necessary to say, when somebody pulled the Vatican's coat to the fact that the phrase they were using added up the way it did, they backed up off that faster than the dude who brought a knife to a gun fight. The Donation of Constantine was proclaimed a forged document, the letters "supposed to be on the Popes crown/mitre" disappeared, and the Sunday Visitor article became a misinterpretation of what the publication's editors were really saying.

Be that as it may, the toothpaste had already been squeezed out of the tube. Just as 2 Thessalonians 2:11 affirms the capability of God to send "strong delusion" to believe a lie, he can also send enough rope to get tangled up in one!

"For the wisdom of this world is foolishness with God. For it is written, He taketh the wise in their own craftiness."
— 1 CORINTHIANS 3:19

Now, this is what makes a prophet a prophet and the Book of Revelation the revelation of Jesus Christ. Revelation 13:18 was written how many years prior to 1915? Why on earth anyone would use a term that makes them not a prime suspect, but the perpetrator of an offense is illogical when viewed with natural eyes. Having the term *Vicarius Filii Dei* inscribed on your head gear is tantamount to having "beast" written on your forehead with red lipstick. And, the trip part, it's your hand using your lipstick to do the writing. The "Our Sunday Visitor" publication wasn't written by Roman Catholic haters; it was written by Roman Catholics who love them some Roman Catholicism. Go figure.

Because spiritual things are spiritually discerned, if the Spirit of God is not leading, there's John 11:9-10 slapping you smack-dab in 'yo face.

Circling back to the Periodic Table, 666 has a scientific application because there is a big picture. The "war in heaven" is that bigger picture. Because life on earth in its molecular form involves and revolves around 6 protons, 6 neutrons, and 6 electrons, everything on this planet that breathes air is in a spiritually fallen state of existence. This particular man that 13:18 points out is no different from any other man with the exception being its presumptive arrogance in usurping authority that's vested exclusively in Jesus Christ as God.

The spiritual duality of 666 is the scientific fact that "war in heaven" puts all carbon creatures on earth in the same atom (Adam) smasher. When Adam and Eve fell, all life on earth trip-six'd. Like it or not, accept it or not, mankind immediately became a two-legged "beast of the field." This is why Isaiah 46:6 reads, "But we are all as an unclean thing, and all our righteousnesses are as filthy rags." And Jesus Christ says, "There is none good but one, that is God."

The fact that "the man of sin" and "the beast" are spiritually synonymous and numerically represented by three sixes is amplified by the fact that God, being spiritually synonymous with good, is numerically represented by three eights.

Consider the thoughts of Christ as expressed in John 2:23-25:

> "Now when he was in Jerusalem at the passover, in the feast day, many believed in his name, when they saw the miracles which he did. But Jesus did not commit himself unto them, because he knew all men, And needed not that any should testify of man: for he knew what was in man."

Of course, there is the obvious interpretation of the passage. That's the undisputed truth *"Smiling Faces"* factor. But, when you look at what Jesus is saying scientifically, it's a whole lot deeper. The scripture specifically says, "for he knew what was in man." Unquestionably, he knew what was in man at the subatomic level.

Example:

> "Then answered the Jews and said unto him, What sign shewest thou unto us, seeing that thou doest these things? Jesus answered and said unto them, Destroy this temple, and in three days I will raise it up. Then said the Jews, Forty and six years was this temple in building, and wilt thou rear it up in three days? But he spake of the temple of his body. When therefore he was risen from the dead, his disciples remembered that he had said this unto them; and they believed the scripture, and the word which Jesus had said." — JOHN 2:18-22

How many chromosomes are there in the human body?

What are the odds that the exact same number in years it took to build the Jerusalem temple (46), is the same number of chromosomes it takes to build a human body? There are 23 pairs, which total 46. In other words, "Destroy these 46 chromosomes, and in 72 hours I'll put them all back together again."

Naturally, the men Jesus was talking to had no way of knowing that there were 46 chromosomes in the human body. They thought Christ was talking about bricks and mortar. But the scripture plainly says, "he spake of the temple of his body." Chromosomes are the building blocks of life. One more time again, because there is a duality to the word of God, there's always going to be a deeper and more profound meaning to the tune. It was then, and it still is now.

Given the fact that the number 46 is directly associated with the Jerusalem temple, which is a place of worship, and the "body temple" where the spirit of God dwells, the Bible has placed a numerical design on that number. We'll call it a temple dispensation.

The first body that God created and made was Adam. The spirit of God dwelt in Adam's body. Adam was subsequently a temple. In Greek, Adam is spelled, Αδάμ. Let's count the number of the name Adam.

Alpha	(A)	=	1
Delta	(δ)	=	4
Alpha	(ά)	=	1
Mu	(μ)	=	40
			46

Just as was said before, there's no secret code, no hidden files, no club you have to pledge that has a secret handshake. This is all right there in your Bible. All you need is your Bible and an internet connection. You can go online and Google the Greek spelling of any name, word, or phrase.

But seriously, who's going to take the time to do the math? This kind of effort cuts into 101 things on the plate more preferable to eat. When it comes to TV-dinner 101, searching the scriptures just hasn't been programmed as an easy access or *On Demand* favorite. Consequently, the result is the "lack of knowledge" that separates the men from the boys, the women from *Being Mary Jane*, and of course, the elect from the "very elect."

If you're a member of "the elect" have you ever casually wondered wassup with all of the Genesis 5 pre-Flood begats? Since The Flood was an eraser, what's really purposed by the tombstone coverage running Adam through Noah?

Well, Biblical scholars maintain that the lifespan rundown demonstrates the effects of sin. That man lived longer before The Flood, and mankind has been in a deteriorating condition ever since. That's certainly true, but here we go again. For God to give the obituary of each of these antediluvian patriarchs, there's got to be a story behind the story of Noah and the Ark. Let's do the arithmetic.

Genesis 5:3	130 years
Genesis 5:6	105 years
Genesis 5:9	90 years
Genesis 5:12	70 years
Genesis 5:15	65 years
Genesis 5:18	162 years
Genesis 5:21	65 years
Genesis 5:25	187 years
Genesis 5:28	182 years
Genesis 7:6	600 years
	1,656 years

The total number of years between the creation of Adam and the Flood is evenly divisible by the number 46. In other words, the antediluvian age lasted 1,656 years, or the exact numerical representation of Adam's name. More about that will come in a later chapter. Until then, let's revisit Genesis 5:1:

> "This is the book of the generations of Adam. In the day that God created man, in the likeness of God made he him."

Essentially, the Flood closed the book on Adam; and God divinely sealed that book with the number of Adam's name. Is it all a coincidence? Or is the way these numbers do the things they do suggestive of way more than what meets the eye?

Well, just maybe it's God's way of telling us all in no uncertain terms that in spite of individual beliefs, church affiliations, political circumstances, social conditions, and against all odds whatever they might or may not be, "I AM" is bigger than you can ever even begin to imagine. Whether translated in Hebrew, Greek, English, or Swahili, absolutely no one can get it twisted unless a pretzel is really what they want to eat.

Returning to 888, the number of the name Jesus, let's delve deeper into the depths of its significance. Alpha and Omega are Greek numbers. Alpha is the name for the first number in the Greek numerical system. Alpha is comparable to the number one. Omega is the name for the last number in the Greek numerical system. Omega is comparable to the number 800.

Revelation 1:11:

"I am Alpha and Omega, the first and the last."

Revelation 22:13:

"I am Alpha and Omega, the beginning and the end, the first and the last."

Since Jesus makes this declaration in the first chapter of the book of Revelation and repeats it in the last, what do think the revelation happens to be? Oh yeah; Jesus Christ is a 1-800 number. Prayer to God is TOLL-FREE. Be you saint or sinner, there's no switchboard to go through in order to be connected. Jesus is the only priest you need to call!

Just as Jesus being Alpha and Omega, which designates prayer being "toll free," 888, the alphanumeric value of the name Jesus, is the number by which all numbers are digitally generated on an LED clock.

In order to convert a binary number between 0 and 9, there has to be a 7-segment display in the form of seven bars. Those seven bars when lit display the number 8. So, when it comes to "Redeeming the time" (Ephesians 5:16), every time we look at a LED digital clock, we are "figuratively" told that Jesus Christ is the Redeemer.

God controls man's knowledge of the divine and supernatural by either giving or withholding inspiration. We can know nothing about God Almighty unless he says it's cool and you're good to go. If God does not give a person the gift of faith, they will remain blind and this subject matter will hold no interest whatsoever beyond casual conversation.

Extensive and exhaustive research has been done on number patterns and clusters that appear consistently throughout the Bible by Del Washburn, and Jerry Lucas, of NBA basketball fame. You can Google Theomatics with reference to those co-authors and their work. The gematria research of Washburn and Lucas maintains that there is a statistical pattern throughout the Bible associated with numbers.

Example; while the name Jesus adds up (alphanumerically) to 888, according to the Washburn and Lucas research, the number 111 numerically represents that name. They maintain that there are numerous references to Jesus throughout the Bible that are multiples of 111. Here again there's the consistency; 888 is a multiple of 111.

Noting again, the Bible as being its own interpreter, Romans 12:5 reads: "So we, being many, are one (1) body in Christ, and every one (1) members one (1) of another." So, indisputably, the number 111 as the numerical representation of Jesus is also a multiple of one. And, the number one, which is the numerical representation of God's unity, stands in confirmation of Galatians 3:20: "God is one." God is "one" literally and God is "1" figuratively.

Just as people put the name Jesus on a license plate, theomatically 888 would be the alphanumeric representation. In other words, if you see 888, you are seeing the numerical spelling of the name JESUS. Instead of Greek letters, you're seeing the numbers or Greek alphanumeric equivalent.

Now, there are folks whose persuasion of faith will not permit them to acknowledge the name Jesus as God in the flesh. Subsequently, if you can't acknowledge the name, you're certainly not going to acknowledge the number. And there are those who acknowledge God in the flesh, but not under the name Jesus. Be both cases as they may be, there's an earth-load of human beings that embrace the name Jesus as God incarnate. Numbers doing that thing that they do speak to those who accept the name Jesus as being the manifestation of God in human form. These specific numerical expressions are a confirmation of faith and understanding for those who can receive it. Those who can't receive it, it ain't for you (Matthew 13:10-11). You aren't in the matrix – the numerical matrix of acceptance. Once more, not accepting truth doesn't make truth null and void.

If you have a so-called nickname, and there are those who call you by that nickname, does that nickname abolish the name on your driver's license? Reconsider Isaiah 9:6:

"For unto us a child is born, unto us a son is given: and the government shall be upon his shoulder: and his name shall be called Wonderful, Counsellor, The mighty God, The everlasting Father, The Prince of Peace."

If you accept the Bible as the "Word of God," then any one of the five names presented in that passage is representative, not only of the name Jesus, but with all other names of dignity identifying the incarnation of a *"Mighty God."* Even though doing the math doesn't add up when the name is *"Wonderful,"* it doesn't diminish the significance of the addition elsewhere when and where it does. When you "strain at a gnat and swallow a camel" you choke. When getting hung up on the name causes you to throw the baby out with the bathwater, "you've been had, took, hoodwinked, bamboozled, led astray, run amok" because this is what Satan does. He causes people to get choked over details he waves as most important. Is your name in particular more important than you are in general?

According to the research that's been done by Washburn and Lucas, when it comes to the Greek translation of the entire Bible, words, phrases, concepts, entire sentences that have anything to do with Jesus Christ, when you add up the letters in those individual word groupings, they each add up to whole numbers that are evenly divisible by the number 111. This means when you find that happening, that's what's called a mathematical design associated with that number as it relates to that particular subject matter.

Subsequently, the number 111 and Jesus are alphanumerically linked. Again, that's because the Greek letters spelling the name Jesus add up to 888 and 888 is evenly divisible by 111. Once more, 888 is the additive number of Jesus' name; and 111 is the mathematical design representing Jesus' attributes, characteristics, and properties. Putting it another way, 888 represents the name; 111 represents the image, logo, and trademark.

Recall the Newsweek article, *The Search for Adam and Eve*? Type "Newsweek 111" into your Google internet browser and behold. The Newsweek article referenced appears without any additional information.

Coincidence? Or is the fact that Adam and Eve as theorized in this book with respect to physical appearance is being divinely validated on two fronts – *WMD's* and *Newsweek's*?

The number 13 is also very special. According to Theomatics, the number 13 is found to be a representation of the names and attributes of God. That means, just as 111 is the logo for Jesus, the number 13 is the numeric logo representing God. But before getting into the number 13, it's needless but necessary to say that Theomatics has its critics and debunkers. Some say since it doesn't work that way with this word, this phrase, or this sentence it's a pseudoscience and the whole thing should be dismissed as fake. But for those who may be everyday people/casual observers, the numbers really do add up enough times to be convincing that there's possibly something mathematically there.

For example, just consider Jesus only selecting 12 disciples. Why only twelve? Well, Christ himself represented the 13th person in the group. When people saw Jesus and the men he called walk into the city, they saw 13 individuals. When you look at a portrait of the Last Supper, there are 13 people at the table.

Doesn't it all make sense? And, doesn't it explain why the world has a problem with the number 13?

Consider one of the world's most infamous logos – the swastika. This symbol was in play 5,000 years before Adolf Hitler stuck it on a Nazi flag giving it notoriety. The disdain most have for the swastika as a representation of Nazi Germany is the same contempt Satan has for the number 13 as a representation of the kingdom of God. Subsequently, the world has a problem with 13 because Satan has a problem with 13. Anything that represents God, the devil attacks. Hasn't the pattern time and time again already been established?

Clearly, by way of mass worldwide deception, Satan has removed the number 13 from most elevators and placed it in most minds as some kinda Creedence Clearwater Revival *"Bad Moon Rising."* Triskaidekaphobia is the clinical term for fear of the number 13. Legend has it that this mentality came about as the result of their being 13 people at the last Passover meal Jesus ate with his disciples. Those who suffer from superstition think Judas was the 13th person at the table. But, to the contrary, according to Mathew 10:2-4, Judas Iscariot is listed twelfth among the disciples. Judas has never been represented in the Bible as being the 13th anything. Jesus called 12 people to the "supper table." He was the 13th.

This disrespect for the number 13 comes from the same place where scorn for the 7th day Sabbath, the continent of Africa, and dark skin comes from. The source is Satan.

Consider the following movies: *Friday the 13th* (1980); *Friday the 13th Part 2* (1981); *Friday the 13th Part III* (1982); *Friday the 13th: The Final Chapter* (1984); *Friday the 13th: A New Beginning* (1985); *Friday the 13th Part VI: Jason Lives* (1986); *Friday the 13th Part VII: The New Blood* (1988); *Friday the 13th Part VIII: Jason Takes Manhattan* (1989); *Jason Goes to Hell: The Final Friday* (1993); *Jason X* (2002); *Freddy vs. Jason* (2003); *Freddy vs. Jason* (2009).

Why Friday the 13th and not any other day of the week? Well, Friday's selection reveals the spiritual implications of the number's heavenly meaning. It shows Satan's hand and criminal intent.

Once again, man is a carbon creature. Mankind's atomic number is six. Man was created on the sixth day. And, the sixth day is Friday. So, every time there is a Friday the 13th, there is divine significance with respect to man's nature (represented by the number 6), and God's nature (represented by the number 13). Friday the 13th is a meeting place and date. It's a "fist bump" every so often just to say in spite of situations, circumstances, and repercussions, "it's all good."

Whereas the Sabbath "was made for man" as a weekly day of rest and reflection, all Friday the 13's are like anniversary celebrations where man and God symbolically reach out and touch in commemoration of mankind's creation. But instead of a "birthday party," Satan has made it Halloween. Here again, a pattern. Halloween is on the 31st. And, just like dog is the etymological reverse of God, 31 is the digital reverse of 13. The number representative of God and his attributes is flipped. The positive is turned negative.

Viewed from another angle, "1" is representative of God himself, and "3" is representative of the Godhead in agreement as one. The kingdom of heaven has boxed these two numbers as 13 in order to reflect the oneness of God the Father, Son, and Holy Spirit, and the holiness their combined agreement in being "One" eternally shares. This is why 13 is not only the logo for the kingdom of God, it's the trademark for the Father, Son, and Holy Spirit.

But again, once you see a pattern that's repetitive in its attempt to undermine the works of God, it ceases to be sheer coincidence. Mankind operating unilaterally doesn't have the spiritual and physical capacity to mastermind and orchestrate a strategic plan that results in:

- the spiritual fall of mankind;
- the genetic manipulation of human DNA in order to spawn a hybrid race of giants;
- the change of the seventh day Sabbath to the first day of the week; and,
- the merger of Friday the 13th and Halloween the 31st.

If you believe you are created in the image of God, intelligently ask yourself why the images that represent God wouldn't be valued by him as much as you value the images that represent you? If there's a firestorm over failure to either stand or place hand over heart during the playing of the American national anthem, imagine the public response if Halloween's orange and black replaced America's red, white, and blue. Or to cover the American eagle's baldness, a jack-o-lantern was placed on its head.

The "war in heaven" is an extraterrestrial fight. The rules of engagement are no different celestially than the ones employed on earth. Removing an enemy's symbols of government is an "art of war" priority.

Exodus 20:7 reads:

> "Thou shalt not take the name of the LORD thy God in vain; for the LORD will not hold him guiltless that taketh his name in vain."

The text applies to Satan as well as human beings. Do you think it's possible that the dismissive use of numbers that represent God's name applies too?

From Genesis through Revelation there are 'hidden figures" that tell the story just as descriptively as the poetry and prose.

14 FRIDAY

"And that day was the preparation, and the sabbath drew on."
—LUKE 23:54

Because the electronic media functions within the realm of the electromagnetic spectrum, the war in heaven as waged by the devil uses wireless communications as a WMD. Cosmically speaking here, however, the W stands for wireless, the M for mind. Bottom line, as employed by the princedom of Satan, the acronym is Wireless Mind Destruction.

The heavens being the battlefield, the media is now navigating the airspace that was formerly only accessible to celestial beings. Wireless telegraphy was introduced as Morse code and transmitted by radio waves (electromagnetic waves), initially called Hertzian waves, discovered by Heinrich Hertz in 1886. Not until 87 years later (1973) was the first wireless cell phone call made. So, putting this in a technological perspective, from the Garden of Eden to 1886 (about 5,886 years), mankind's communications skills at-large were pretty much restricted to the *Pony Express* along with drums and smoke signals. When it came to a technological understanding of what was Biblically meant by the term, "prince of the power of the air," mankind at-large was clueless in connecting the dots.

All past things considered, look at where we are today? From 1973 until now, cell phones once the size of a brick can be carried concealed in a woman's hand purse or a man's vest pocket. Mobile phones with service once costing a thousand dollars are presently and practically being given away.

What happened between 1973 and the writing of this book? In 45 years, "knowledge increased" to the extent that those 2YKids on the block would see a phone with a rotary dial as a museum piece right beside something called an album that required something called a record player.

Some say this knowledge boom is attributable to a new day *Prometheus Effect*; i.e., mankind had extraterrestrial help. Whether you believe such or not, it's a fact that mankind is technologically functioning in the *Twilight Zone*. The *Outer Limits* of humanity's technological boundaries from Day 1 to Day 2,148,390 have been crossed with another 47,815 days added.

Within the cosmic realm, today's employment of radio, television, film, and the internet are in fact the cosmic "weapons of mass destruction." They give new meaning to having your mind blown.

Once the United States and Russia became competitors in a space race with rockets and moon shots, reports of UFO activity around military bases in both nations increased. When you get outside of your lane, you're going to attract someone's attention negatively. With the media it's no different. The ability to do what Satan did – that's showing "all the kingdoms of the world in a moment of time" – this time everyone with a handheld internet connection has got the hook up.

Do you really think that Satan, who Jesus refers to as "the prince of this world" and Paul calls "the prince of the power of the air," is just going to concede the use of his airspace for kingdom of heaven business? When it comes to taking care of God's business, the princedom of Satan has tried to establish a no-fly zone. There is going to be a serious fight for control of the airwaves when it comes to the transmission of any information Satan and both his extraterrestrial and terrestrial forces don't want transmitted.

This explains why some of the thoughts you're being exposed to in this book – as well as a lot of others you find compelling on the internet – haven't gotten any significant media attention or exposure. Google "alien structures dark side of moon." You might be surprised by what you find.

Intelligently ask yourself why the television and film media is so willing to exploit extraterrestrial interactions for science fiction entertainment, but refuses to deal with the subject matter as empirical scientific fact? Where are the major network exposés dealing with the conspiracy theories involving alleged governmental cover ups when it comes to what NASA knows regarding close encounters of each and every kind? Can't they give *15 Minutes*, *20/60*, or a *Datehyphen* ala *60 Minutes*, *20/20*, or *Dateline*?

The consolidation of major media outlets under the umbrella of a handful of major corporations is nothing less than a federally sanctioned *de facto* gag order. It allows these cover ups to conspire and continue. Only when you find five or six companies owning all of the major television networks, film studios, satellite and cable systems, theatrical distributor and exhibitor outlets, newspapers, magazines, and telecommunications service providers can this happen without serious question or definitive remedial challenge.

Without a doubt, there is a media war in heaven that's being fought just as ferociously as any war conventionally imagined. The media war, however, is for the wholesale-no-returns control of mankind minds. From movies like the *Manchurian Candidate*, to *Total Recall*, to *The Matrix*, human mind control is a reoccurring and predominating theme where, in the universal scheme of things, art is imitating extraterrestrial life in terms of agenda. And, because the war being waged involves spiritual beings, the issues being disputed are religious.

Why are the few with "all the money" (talkin' bout the real big ballers and shot callers) seemingly borderline atheists if not altogether full-blown?

Now, "all the money" should not be confused with those who have multimillion dollar homes with a three to five car garage. When the game came *Who Wants to Be a Millionaire*, the subtext is having a multimillion dollar home with a three to five car garage is no longer an improbable dream. Anybody can "scratch-off" or "Powerball" their way to a spot on M street.

"*All the money*" means you're kicking on the big "B" knocking on "T" as in the trillions. Billionaires to almost trillionaires are incognegro. They keep it on the DL. They've been schooled that it ain't about the Benjamins. On the real, it can be like that when you've got a bank of big Bens parked in a bank that you own. Seriously, those with "*all the money*" are about power. With them it's about control. It's being perceived not only by others, but by themselves as God whether willing to admit or not. Algebraically, a big EGO is simply GOD minus "d" plus "e" multiplied by "u." Infectiously, it's the fresh "Prince of Tyrone" equation Ezekiel 28 talks about.

Luke 4:5-6 made the Biblical cut for a reason. That one temptation of Christ is a red alert no different from the one given by Eddie Levert, Walter Williams, and William Powell (O'jays). Yes; for the love of that "almighty dollar." The Luke 4:5-6 temptation ties religion, the media, money, and politics all together in a tight little knot. When the devil said,

"All this power," even though there were and are wireless media applications, its multifaceted meaning was clearly understood by Jesus. Power is political given the fact that the word "power" is preceded by the word 'kingdoms." As far as money, a kingdom without any has no leverage to wield power. And, as far as religion; there's Luke 4:7: "worship me."

Again, it's been 1,992 years and counting since *The Last Temptation of Christ* (1988). Neither the game nor its name has changed to protect the innocent or the guilty. Given the fact that Satan has deceived so many of the financially rich into seeing the Bible as a story book or book of fables, they have not only been deceived by Satan, they have been sent "strong delusion" by the God that they have summarily rejected. They believe a lie and are clueless to the fact.

Consider Isaiah 29:9-12:

> "Stay yourselves, and wonder; cry ye out, and cry: they are drunken, but not with wine; they stagger, but not with strong drink. For the LORD hath poured out upon you the spirit of deep sleep, and hath closed your eyes: the prophets and your rulers, the seers hath he covered. And the vision of all is become unto you as the words of a book that is sealed, which men deliver to one that is learned, saying, Read this, I pray thee: and he saith, I cannot; for it is sealed: And the book is delivered to him that is not learned, saying, Read this, I pray thee: and he saith, I am not learned."

It's one thing to be ignorant. All are ignorant of something or another to a degree. The book titled "this and that" *For Dummies* took the edge off of being dumb. But stupid is the express elevator to the bottom.

Stupid without a cause can't be fixed. That's because in the event you've been blinded by your own light, the glare from the glory of yourself casts a shadow on everything else that surrounds. The spirit Isaiah is talking about is spelled with a little "s" (lower cased). That means the spirit of stupidity – "deep sleep" that's poured out upon you comes from the glass or cup you're holding in your own hand. You can't blame it on that bottle of *Mad Dog 20/20* "as majestic as the cascading waters of a drain pipe" might be. It ain't *Mogen David's* or *Hennessy's* fault. Just as profound as Forrest Gump's *"Stupid is as Stupid Does"* are the words of MLK: *"Nothing in the world is more dangerous than sincere ignorance and conscientious stupidity."*

Whenever a sincerely ignorant and conscientiously stupid individual is elected head of state, indeed stupid is as stupid does from top to below-basement bottom. A man or woman who has rejected God (but goes through the motions of a believer) is worse off than the individual who never heard the Word mentioned. Pharaoh was sincerely ignorant, but initially, he wasn't conscientiously stupid.

> "And Pharaoh said, Who is the LORD, that I should obey his voice to let Israel go? I know not the LORD, neither will I let Israel go." —EXODUS 5:2

Being sincerely ignorant means there's hope. Even ignorant with a prior means you've still got a chance. But when you're just a total "SAI" (Stupid Assumptive Individual), you're not only a danger to self, you're a clear and present danger to all around.

> "The Son of man goeth as it is written of him: but woe unto that man by whom the Son of man is betrayed! it had been good for that man if he had not been born." – MATTHEW 26:24

Judas was SAI. When you find a man is so stupid, assumptive, and ignorant that Jesus Christ floats that man's preemptive abortion; that's way beyond deep.

If you do the arithmetic, Ramses II is in fact the Pharaoh of Exodus. Contrary to *The Ten Commandments* (1956), *The Prince of Egypt* (1998), and *Exodus: Gods and Kings* (2014), however, Ramses II was around 18 years of age when he was put to the test. Because God is merciful, and in all likelihood given Ramses youth, God cut him some slack. Again, ten chapters (Exodus 5-14) clearly show God trying to slap some sense into homeboy's crown before his chariots carried him a bridge too far.

When an individual has totally grieved away the Spirit, it becomes *"talk to the hand."* Whenever and wherever it's *"Done with you"* time, that individual has become conscientiously stupid. It's only through the Spirit that a "living soul" can be reached. Breaking that God connection is what makes the actor or sin so unpardonable. It's comparable to setting up a block on the receipt of all calls, text messages, and emails from a particular party. And once it's that kind of party, both parties are technically done with each other.

When Ramses got real stupid with it (Exodus 14:23), enough was enough. That kinda stupid is no longer ignorance. It's not even deception. This is why there's nothing more dangerous than that kinda fool. When a "head of state" is shown to be that kinda fool, history shows God has to step in and deal with it.

Viewed in this context, one more time again, the Crucifixion of Jesus Christ was one of the stupidest moves ever made by a political leader operating under the spiritual influence of Satan. Jesus, even while hanging on the cross: "Father, forgive them; for they know not what they do" (Luke 23:34). And, of course, once again, here we find "they." Yes, "they" were doing the biddings of Satan and were sincerely ignorant of the facts to the point of being "conscientiously stupid."

Subsequently, this brings us to the significance of this chapter and the need to look at some facts that find a whole lot of theologians "sincerely ignorant." The facts are those surrounding the belief that the Crucifixion of Christ occurred on a Friday.

Look closely at Matthew 21:1, Mark 11:1, and Luke 19:29. These scriptures all say the same thing; Jesus was nearing the villages of Bethphage and Bethany.

Next, there's John 12:1:

> "Then Jesus six days before the passover came to Bethany, where Lazarus was which had been dead, whom he raised from the dead."

Now, consider John 19:14:

> "When Pilate therefore heard that saying, he brought Jesus forth, and sat down in the judgment seat in a place that is called the Pavement, but in the Hebrew, Gabbatha. And it was the preparation of the passover, and about the sixth hour: and he saith unto the Jews, Behold your King!"

The Bible makes it an undisputed truth that Jesus Christ was crucified on the day of the "preparation of the Passover." Even though the Jews measured a day from sunset to sunset, the Gospel of John is based on Roman time with the hours starting at 12 midnight and 12 noon like we do today. The "sixth hour" is therefore six-o'clock in the morning. Jesus stood before Pilate at 6:00am.

Hebrew time runs according to the sunset to sunset measurement – that's 6am to 6pm. According to Mark 15:25, Jesus was put on the cross at the "third hour," around 9:00am. And according to Matthew, Mark, and Luke all together, the time of Jesus Christ's actual death is established as being the ninth hour, or 3:00pm. The bottom line, Jesus was hung up for the whole world to see from 9:00 in the morning until 3:00 that afternoon. That's what this "war in heaven" is all about.

So, let's back into this and step on some toes. If Jesus came to Bethany "six days before the passover," and he was crucified on a so-called Good Friday, let's do the arithmetic. With Good Friday being ground zero, let's go backward six full days:

Day 1 = THURSDAY
Day 2 = WEDNESDAY
Day 3 = TUESDAY
Day 4 = MONDAY
Day 5 = SUNDAY
Day 6 = SATURDAY

Indicative of what you can clearly see for yourself, starting at the time of the Passover on a Friday evening, in accordance with how we reckon time, and traveling back six days puts Jesus and his entourage in Bethany on a Saturday.

Now, ask yourself intelligently, does it make any sense whatsoever to think in your wildest dreams that Jesus and his followers came to Bethany sometime on a Saturday?

How about considering what Jesus and his disciples were doing the day before – Friday?

Well, let's look at the facts. Where were Jesus and company the day before?

Luke 19:1:

"And Jesus entered and passed through Jericho."

What did Jesus do in Jericho?

Luke 19:5:

"Zacchaeus, make haste, and come down; for today I must abide at thy house."

How long did Jesus stay at Zacchaeus' place?

Luke 18:35:

"And it came to pass, that as he was coming nigh to Jericho, a certain blind man sat by the wayside begging."

Now, Mark and Matthew say something different than Luke.

"And they came to Jericho: and as he went out of Jericho with his disciples, and a great number of people, blind Bartimaeus, the son of Timaeus, sat by the highway side begging." — MARK 10:46

"And as they departed from Jericho, a great multitude followed him. And, behold, two blind men sitting by the way side, when they heard that Jesus passed by, cried out, saying, Have mercy on us, O Lord, thou Son of David. And the multitude rebuked them, because they should hold their peace: but they cried the more, saying, Have mercy on us, O Lord, thou Son of David. And Jesus stood still, and called them, and said, What will ye that I shall do unto you? They say unto him, Lord, that our eyes may be opened. So Jesus had compassion on them, and touched their eyes: and immediately their eyes received sight, and they followed him."
— MATTHEW 20:29-34

Luke says Jesus sees blind Bart on his way into Jericho, and both Mark and Matthew say Jesus saw the blind men on the way out of Jericho. Drawing from Mark, it's established that one of the men is still Bartimaeus. Luke says, "Jesus entered and passed through Jericho," and, both Matthew and Mark say the two blind men were seen by Jesus on his way out of Jericho. How do you think blind Bart, who's picked up a running buddy, managed to get to the other side of town so quick if Jesus didn't spend the night at Zacchaeus' house? But isn't it obvious Jesus spent the night in Jericho by the mere fact he asked Zach for accommodations?

Jesus was on his way to Jerusalem. Jerusalem is about 17 miles from Jericho. At an average foot speed of 3mph, it would have taken Jesus and his disciples another 5-6 hours to walk from Jericho to Jerusalem. Subsequently, the two blind men had all night to get to the other side of town. And, certainly, their persistence in begging for their sight paid off. Jesus didn't heal Bartimaeus at the first encounter on his way into Jericho; he healed the blind man and his friend on the way out. So, what does that fact tell all of us about "keeping the faith?"

But here's the deal, let's pause and consider. If six days before the Passover found Jesus coming to Bethany, and the day before coming to Bethany found Jesus in Jericho, Jesus would have come to Jericho on a Friday – the Preparation Day for the weekly Sabbath. If Jesus was crucified on a Friday, a week before Friday is another Friday.

Seven days before the Passover would have put Jesus, his disciples, the great number of people who were following, and blind Bart all in Jericho on the day before the weekly Sabbath – a Saturday.

Jesus was a Jew. Everybody around him at that particular geographic point in time was Jews. What do Jews do on the Preparation Day of the weekly Sabbath – hang out at Zacchaeus crib? There's absolutely no indication that the Jewish customs associated with Preparation Day activities were followed. Were centuries of Jewish tradition suddenly kicked to the curb? If Christ was crucified on "Good Friday," the Preparation Day, a week before that particular Friday neither Jesus nor the Jews following him were preparing for anything associated with the weekly Sabbath. Go figure.

Daniel 9:27 reads:

> "And he shall confirm the covenant with many for one week: and in the midst of the week he shall cause the sacrifice and the oblation to cease."

Daniel is prophesizing the death of the Messiah. Causing the "sacrifice and the oblation to cease" is referencing an abrupt end to the Jews priestly system requiring blood sacrifices in the form of a lamb. With the crucifixion and death of Christ, Jesus became the real life human "Lamb of God, which taketh away the sin of the world" in accordance with John 1:29. Actually, the crucifixion and death of Jesus Christ brought an end to not just Jewish, but all priestly systems. Jesus became the intercessor with God on behalf of mankind.

Consider 1 Timothy 2:5: "For there is one God, and one mediator between God and men, the man Christ Jesus."

Likewise, Hebrews 4:14:

"Seeing then that we have a great high priest, that is passed into the heavens, Jesus the Son of God, let us hold fast our profession."

And, finally in this regard, there's Hebrews 9:11-15:

"But Christ being come an high priest of good things to come, by a greater and more perfect tabernacle, not made with hands, that is to say, not of this building; Neither by the blood of goats and calves, but by his own blood he entered in once into the holy place, having obtained eternal redemption for us. For if the blood of bulls and of goats, and the ashes of an heifer sprinkling the unclean, sanctifieth to the purifying of the flesh: How much more shall the blood of Christ, who through the eternal Spirit offered himself without spot to God, purge your conscience from dead works to serve the living God? And for this cause he is the mediator of the new testament, that by means of death, for the redemption of the transgressions that were under the first testament, they which are called might receive the promise of eternal inheritance."

All of the above means when Christ died *Alpha and Omega* was activated. Power to the line that was disconnected by Satan in the Garden was restored.

"And it shall come to pass, that before they call, I will answer; and while they are yet speaking, I will hear."— ISAIAH 65:24

Back to Daniel 9:27, which day out of seven is the "midst of the week?" Wednesday is hump day. According to Matthew 27:51, as soon as Christ died on the cross, "the veil of the temple was rent in twain from top to bottom."

Jesus dying in the "midst" of a "prophetic week" had dual applicability to a literal seven-day week. So, let's apply the same "six days before the passover" rubric, this time starting with Wednesday as the day of the crucifixion of Jesus Christ and backtracking.

Day 1 = TUESDAY
Day 2 = MONDAY
Day 3 = SUNDAY
Day 4 = SATURDAY
Day 5 = FRIDAY
Day 6 = THURSDAY
Day 7 = WEDNESDAY

Referencing the exact same scriptures as before, let's go back an entire week before the Passover. Jesus and his disciples along with a great number of followers enter the city of Jericho on a Wednesday (Day 7) during the daylight hours. On his way into town Jesus sees Bartimaeus who begs for help. He doesn't heal Bart. But he does reach out to Zacchaeus. Jesus spends Wednesday night at Zacchaeus' house.

On Thursday (Day 6), during the daylight hours, Jesus and his entourage leave Jericho. On the way out of town, Jesus sees Bartimaeus again, and this time he heals him. The distance from Jericho to Bethany is around 13 miles. That's a four hour walk at least. Jesus arrives at Bethany sometime during the daylight portion of Thursday. And just like the Bible says, six days before the Passover, Jesus was in Bethany.

Now, what did Jesus and his disciples do the rest of Thursday as the day crossed over into Friday? Matthew 21:1-3, Mark 11:1-6 and Luke 19:29-34 tell us that two of Christ's disciples were sent to the village of Bethphage to get a donkey. Bethany is two miles from Jerusalem, and

Bethphage is only one mile. And, John 12:1-11 shares the rest of Thursday's "six days before the Passover" itinerary. Jesus spent the evening and night at the home of his friend Lazarus. Martha made supper. Mary anointed his feet.

John 12:12, by plainly saying, "On the next day," establishes the day to be Friday (Day 5). And, if you compare the notes of all four Gospel writers, it's crystal clear that Jesus is riding that donkey that was picked up the day before into Jerusalem. The *Triumphal Entry* of Jesus into Jerusalem occurred on a Friday. And, in accordance with Matthew 21:7-16, here is where Jesus heads straight for the temple and overturns the "tables of the moneychangers and the seats of them that sold doves."

Mark does not give an account of that day's temple tirade. Mark 11:11 only indicates that Jesus entered the temple and "looked around." What's significant about this Gospel observation, however, is the fact that Christ and his disciples went back to Bethany for that Friday evening to spend the night. Presumably to stay again with his friends Lazarus, Martha, and Mary.

So, clearly based on the actions of Jesus himself, the belief that Christ was murdered on a Friday exactly one week later just doesn't add up day-wise or numbers-wise when you backtrack allowing the Bible itself to be both roadmap and time marker.

Mark 11:12 then says, "On the morrow, when they were come from Bethany." Clearly, this establishes the day as Saturday (Day 4). Where are Jesus and his disciples going? According to Mark 11:15, it's back to Jerusalem. And, why are Jesus and his disciples going back to Jerusalem? According to the same chapter and verse, Jesus and his disciples are going to church.

Again, it's Saturday, the seventh day Sabbath. Mark 1:21, Mark 6:2, Luke 4:16, Luke 4:31, Luke 6:6, and Luke 13:10 make it plain that the custom of Jesus Christ was to be in the temple on the seventh day Sabbath teaching. And that's exactly where they are. But if the "six days before the passover" time marker is set by the so-called Good Friday scenario, neither Jesus, nor anyone in his company are anywhere near a temple. They're all in, and gathered around the house of Zacchaeus.

Unfortunately, Christendom tends to forget that Jesus was a Jew. Christianity is derived from Judaism. When it comes to the term Judeo-Christian, if you don't understand the Judeo part, you're going to miss something. Obviously, that something missed is what Jesus, family, and friends were doing seven days before the Passover if the Crucifixion was on a so-called Good Friday.

Now, there is the argument that Jesus was accused of not keeping the Sabbath. Matthew 12:1-14, Mark 3:1-6, and Luke 6:6-11 are pointed out in support of that argument. But if you read these texts intelligently, the issue isn't "keeping" it's "breaking." Jesus was accused of doing work that some Jews felt was a violation of what they thought keeping the Sabbath required. Jesus healed a man on the Sabbath and the religious leaders on the scene had a problem with that. And because they were high profile, their influence had an effect on their congregations and others. Whether motivated by jealousy or envy, if the scribes and Pharisees had a problem with this new dude on the block, the public at large was buying whatever the established clergy was selling without debate or consideration to the contrary.

Of course, the same is no different today. Most folks, if they see or hear something they haven't seen or heard before regarding the Bible, instead of running first to their Bible and praying to God for guidance, they'll run first to their pastor or someone considered a church leader. Either the Holy Spirit is the teacher Jesus says it is; or Jesus was just joking. But, if you don't give that "Comforter" a first shot, you'll never know, will you?

Finally, note Mathew 26:2 and Mark 14:1:

"After two days was the feast of the passover."

Given the fact that statement was made by Christ the very next day, Sunday (Day 3), indeed, after Monday (Day 2) and Tuesday (Day 1), the referenced feast occurred on Wednesday evening (The Passover). And, because Christ was crucified on a Wednesday during the day, the midst of the week was "ground zero" just as Daniel said.

So, if one really believes in the indisputable word of God, how does one continue to conscientiously hold on to Good Friday as the day Christ died?

The consistency of the Gospel writers in laying out the last week of Jesus is compelling.

But even more compelling is the revelation that if the crucifixion wasn't on a Friday, the resurrection couldn't have been on a Sunday.

Matthew 12:40 tells us that Jesus only gave one sign in proof that he is who he says he is; "the Christ, the Son of the living God" (Matthew 16:16-20).

> "For as Jonas was three days and three nights in the whale's belly; so shall the Son of man be three days and three nights in the heart of the earth."

Good Friday never has and never will pass a math test. Jesus plainly says "three days and three nights." He doesn't say a day and a half, and he doesn't say parts of days. If Jesus had been crucified on a Friday, then there would be a gigantic problem with Christ's statement. It wouldn't be true. And for Jesus to catch himself in a lie makes no kind of sense.

Consider the following:

> "And they shall kill him, and the third day he shall be raised again. And they were exceeding sorry." — MATTHEW 17:23

> "And he began to teach them, that the Son of man must suffer many things, and be rejected of the elders, and of the chief priests, and scribes, and be killed, and after three days rise again." — MARK 8:31

> "For he taught his disciples, and said unto them, The Son of man is delivered into the hands of men, and they shall kill him; and after that he is killed, he shall rise the third day." — MARK 9:31

> "And they shall scourge him, and put him to death: and the third day he shall rise again." — LUKE 18:33

> "And said unto them, Thus it is written, and thus it behoved Christ to suffer, and to rise from the dead the third day." — LUKE 24:46

Once more, Genesis 1:5-31 establishes the parameters distinguishing a day. The evening and the morning constitute a 24-hour period. That's 12 hours in the daylight portion and 12 hours in the night.

> "Jesus answered, Are there not twelve hours in the day? If any man walk in the day, he stumbleth not, because he seeth the light of this world. But if a man walk in the night, he stumbleth, because there is no light in him."
> — JOHN 11:9-10

Because Christ was crucified on a Wednesday, three days and three nights later is Saturday. Mark 15:42 indicates the body of Jesus was entombed on a Wednesday evening right before the setting sun. By necessity, this means Jesus came out of the tomb right before sunset on a Saturday.

An added certainty is 1 John 1:5: "God is light, and in him is no darkness at all." The "at all" both affirms and confirms that Jesus had to exit the sepulcher during the daylight portion of Saturday. Once the Saturday sun dropped below the horizon, evening would have started a new day. That being the case, a Saturday evening Resurrection would have made it the fourth day.

Matthew, Mark, Luke, and John report the women coming to the sepulcher right before dawn on the first day of the week. They found the tomb empty.

Matthew 28:6 reads: "He is not here: for he is risen, as he said." He said three days not four.

Just as Satan has kicked the seventh day Sabbath to the back of the bus, he has done the same with Saturday, the seventh day, as the actual day of Jesus Christ's resurrection. The devil has hijacked Sunday, and is using it to promote his ancient image as a "sun god" as well as his status as "the prince of this world."

The fact that most preachers, theologians, and teachers are confused by the "preparation day" being on a Friday and the Sabbath day being on a Saturday with regards to the week of Christ's crucifixion is no excuse. John 19:31 parenthetically establishes that the Sabbath being talked about "was a high day." Jewish "high days" are Biblical festivals. By the mere fact that John uses "that" as a demonstrative adjective to point out "Sabbath" should be sufficient to clue all that there were two Sabbaths occurring that week.

But in order to understand the fact that John is directing attention to a Sabbath other than the seventh day Sabbath, you have to "search the scriptures."

> "These are the feasts of the LORD, even holy convocations, which ye shall proclaim in their seasons. In the fourteenth day of the first month at even is the LORD'S passover. And on the fifteenth day of the same month is the feast of unleavened bread unto the LORD: seven days ye must eat unleavened bread. In the first day ye shall have an holy convocation: ye shall do no servile work therein." — LEVITICUS 23:5-7

The "preparation of the Passover," is the fourteenth day of the first month (Nisan) of the Jewish calendar. Regarding the Crucifixion and Resurrection; A.D. 30 is historically verified to be the year. In A.D. 30, Nisan 14 runs from Tuesday evening until Wednesday evening. This means the actual "feast of the Passover," was after sunset on Wednesday evening.

Christ and his disciples ate their feast of the Passover twenty-four hours earlier. *The Last Supper* was actually Tuesday evening. Christ was betrayed by Judas Tuesday night. The stage was set for a Wednesday execution.

			April A.D. 30			
Sun	Mon	Tue	Wed	Thu	Fri	Sat
						1 Nisan 10
2 Nisan 11	3 Nisan 12	4 Nisan 13	5 Nisan 14	6 Nisan 15	7 Nisan 16	8 Nisan 17
9 Nisan 18	10 Nisan 19	11 Nisan 20	12 Nisan 21	13 Nisan 22	14 Nisan 23	15 Nisan 24
16 Nisan 25	17 Nisan 26	18 Nisan 27	19 Nisan 28	20 Nisan 29	21 Nisan 30	22 Iyar 1
23 Iyar 2	24 Iyar 3	25 Iyar 4	26 Iyar 5	27 Iyar 6	28 Iyar 7	29 Iyar 8
30 Iyar 9						

Because the "preparation of the Passover" involved the killing of a sacrificial lamb, Jesus was the archetypal true sacrifice. Analytically note the chronology provided by Luke 23:54-56:

> "And that day was the preparation, and the Sabbath drew on. And the women also, which came with him from Galilee, followed after, and beheld the sepulcher, and how his body was laid. And they returned, and prepared spices and ointments; and rested the Sabbath day according to the commandment."

Now compare Mark 16:1:

> "And when the Sabbath was past, Mary Magdalene, and Mary the mother of James, and Salome, had bought sweet spices, that they might come and anoint him."

According to Mark's account, when the Sabbath had passed, the women bought the spices. But according to Luke, the women prepared the spices before the Sabbath arrived. Now, intelligently ask yourself how do you prepare something you haven't had the opportunity to get? The only way for these two accounts to harmonize is the fact that there was a "high day" Sabbath on Thursday, the day after the crucifixion as previously said. Mark is talking about the passing of Nisan 15, the "high day Sabbath." The day after the Crucifixion was the 15th day of Nisan. It's called the *Feast of Unleavened Bread*.

Once more, Leviticus 23 establishes the date as a ceremonial or festival Sabbath. This Sabbath, or "that" Sabbath as John refers to it in 19:31 has nothing to do with the weekly seventh day Sabbath. Remember, John 19:14 establishes the day that Jesus stood before Pilate as "the preparation of the passover." The scripture doesn't say anything about it being the preparation of the weekly Sabbath.

The Passover Sabbath (Nisan 15) started at sundown Wednesday evening and continued to sunset Thursday evening. Because this was a special Sabbath, the women who wanted to attend the body of Jesus were on ceremonial lockdown from Wednesday evening until Thursday evening. Given the absence of electricity and flashlights, the women were on technological lockdown as well. They couldn't visit the sepulcher and attend to the body of Christ in the dark. Since Friday was the preparation day of the weekly Sabbath, the women could have gone to the tomb during the daylight portion of Friday, but because they didn't have the burial spices and ointments needed, and had to "prepare" for the Saturday Sabbath, visiting the tomb on that Friday was also a no go.

The women referenced by Mark made their purchases on Friday, the preparation for the weekly Sabbath. Likewise, so did the women referenced in Luke's account. However, Luke is clearly speaking of the seventh day weekly Sabbath. The clue that this is true is found in his statement that the "Sabbath drew on." It therefore had to be Friday. Also, by saying "rested the Sabbath day according to the commandment," the only commandment commanding a day of rest is in reference to the *Fourth Commandment* weekly Sabbath.

Undeniably, God Almighty ordered events so that the body of Jesus Christ would remain undisturbed for 72 full hours. After the women went to the sepulcher and beheld how the body was laid Wednesday evening when it was first placed inside the tomb, the double Sabbaths prevented their return until dawn Sunday morning, the first day of the week which was also first light.

Now, here's something to seriously think about. Does your birthday fall on the same date every year or does it fluctuate? The answer is obvious. Easter is correlated with the Jewish Passover. And, since the Jewish holiday calendar is based on solar and lunar cycles, each Jewish feast day is movable with dates shifting from year to year.

Easter as an annual observance has nothing to do with the actual date of the Resurrection of Jesus Christ. If you aren't Jewish, the Passover basis upon which the Resurrection is calculated has no pertinence. Therefore, the commercial association of bunny rabbits and colored eggs with Easter that causes many to take offense and frown with righteous indignation is misplaced. It's as relevant as you being upset over a mockery being made of a date that's neither your birthday nor the anniversary of something personally significant.

Consider Galatians 3:26-29:

> "For ye are all the children of God by faith in Christ Jesus. For as many of you as have been baptized into Christ have put on Christ. There is neither Jew nor Greek, there is neither bond nor free, there is neither male nor female: for ye are all one in Christ Jesus. And if ye *be* Christ's, then are ye Abraham's seed, and heirs according to the promise."

If you are a baptized Christian, and being a Jew is not prerequisite for being Christian, intelligently ask yourself just why are Christians observing an event central to Christianity in a Jewish manner? The Passover is a Jewish thing. Easter is mentioned only once in the entire Bible (Acts 12:4) and it's connected with the "days of unleavened bread" (Acts 12:3) which is the Passover. Therefore, the Jewish Passover has more to do with the Crucifixion of Jesus Christ than it has to do with the Resurrection.

> "Therefore we are buried with him by baptism into death: that like as Christ was raised up from the dead by the glory of the Father, even so we also should walk in newness of life. For if we have been planted together in the likeness of his death, we shall be also *in the likeness* of *his* resurrection: Knowing this, that our old man is crucified with *him*, that the body of sin might be destroyed, that henceforth we should not serve sin. For he that is dead is freed from sin." – Romans 6:4-7

In light of the above, is Easter in the likeness of his death, or in the likeness of his resurrection? The original Passover as presented in Exodus 12:11-14 was about death. It had nothing to do with the "newness of life" as *Easter* being synonymous with the *Resurrection* is falsely believed.

The fact that you are probably clueless with regards to the date upon which next year's Easter will fall spells confusion. When a child asks why Easter is all over the calendar between March and April and you can't explain it in ten words or less, it's not complicated; it's confusion.

It's important to realize that it's the false belief that Jesus Christ was crucified on Friday and resurrected on Sunday that's used by Christendom at-large to justify the acceptance of Sunday as the Christian Sabbath. Therefore, in terms of a warring strategy, an attack on the true date of the Resurrection is consistent with the prime objective of establishing a day of worship that symbolically honors the name of the sun that has been co-opted as the image of Lucifer now Satan.

But again, whatever stunt the devil pulls there's going to be a detectable flaw that can be picked up if you really care to look. And the caring person doesn't have to look that hard.

Friday is that flaw. Three days and three nights consistent with the words of Jesus as written in Matthew 12:40 cannot be squeezed into a Friday evening tomb placement and a Sunday dawn resurrection. On the other hand, a historically correct Wednesday entombment and Saturday exit fits hand in glove.

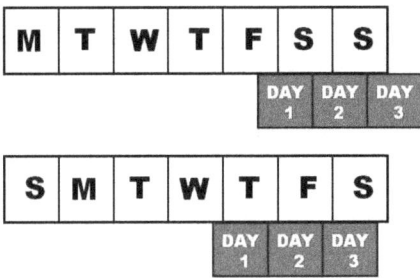

The crucifixion of Jesus Christ was on Wednesday, April 5, A.D. 30. The resurrection: three days later, Saturday, April 8.

God is not the author of confusion, particularly when it comes to his Crucifixion and Resurrection. Jesus kept it simple before Caiaphas and his kangaroo court, before Pilate in the judgment hall, and on Calvary's cross. And when it comes to the Resurrection, it don't get any simpler than an empty tomb.

15 BABYLON 5

"Babylon the great is fallen, is fallen, and is become the habitation of devils, and the hold of every foul spirit, and a cage of every unclean and hateful bird."
—REVELATION 18:2

Whenever there is a battle of Biblical proportions, even amongst so-called banana republics, one thing the victor immediately does is take control of the fallen land's communications systems. It doesn't matter if all they have communications-wise is just a newspaper, to the victor goes the spoils to spoil with their own message. And with regards to message sending, what better place is there to do so than from a tower?

Conventional interpretation says the Babel tower was all about the tongue, as in languages. Definitely, the mouth had a lot to do with the situation, but is that all it was?

What was Nimrod up to that drew the attention of God? For the Bible to give Nimrod a shout out as being "mighty" suggests more than meets the eye or ear. What made Nimrod all that?

When the scriptures say "he began to be mighty" and he "was mighty," these words have to be examined in a spiritual context as well as physical. Therefore, spiritually speaking, Nimrod wasn't being called mighty for hunting lions, tigers, and bears only. Everybody was doing that back in his day just to survive. In order for God to call him mighty, he had to be hunting something unconventional. Could it be that Nimrod's specialty was hunting fame and power, and achieving it in the process?

Now, some scholars say God's issue with the people of Babel was the fact that they didn't follow the Genesis 9:1 "prime directive." Don't think so. There's a little more to it than "replenishing the earth." In reading Genesis 10:8-10 and 11:1-9, it's apparent that Nimrod was attempting to set up a *New World Order* with himself as ruler. And what makes this readily apparent is Genesis 10:10: "And the beginning of his kingdom was Babel, and Erech, and Accad, and Calneh, in the land of Shinar."

The bad press the Tower of Babel gets so overshadows what was really going on; once again, the forest is hidden by the trees. Besides Babel, Nimrod had three more cities under his belt. That's why the Bible reads, "the beginning of his kingdom." Nimrod was about nation building. His kingdom began with four cities, not just one. God saw where homeboy was going, and that's why he had to be checked.

Nimrod had been groomed cradle-to-the-grave to restart the engine that had been literally and figuratively flooded during the time of Noah. Nimrod was a son of Cush. This fact genealogically means Nimrod's uncle was Mizraim whose roots are straight out of Africa as in Egypt. If the pyramids of Egypt are in fact older than theorized, that means their construction predates the creation of Adam. And, if that be the case, extraterrestrial technology was employed in the construction. Subsequently, Nimrod's Egyptian/African roots made him privy to extraterrestrial (satanic) influences from childhood.

When Genesis 10:8 says Nimrod "began to be a mighty one in the earth," read it for exactly what it says. The word "began" immediately follows the word "begat." Therefore, the point in time is Nimrod's birth. Nimrod "began to be mighty" the day he was born. He wasn't a "mighty hunter" until a whole verse later. That whole verse could span childhood to young adult at minimum.

More often than not, the word of God tells us up front what the deal happens to be, but because we have been programmed to think one dimensionally and linear, we don't step back and realize that the trees are, in fact, the forest. Take note from Luke 3:23:

"And Jesus himself began to be about thirty years of age,
being (as was supposed) the son of Joseph, which was the
son of Heli."

The word "began" is used here as well. Jesus "began" to be thirty on his birthday. Consequently, Nimrod "began" to be mighty on his birthday. Once more, simply because we find "begat" in the same sentence preceding began, the birthday being talked about was Nimrod's first.

Now, the only way for a baby to be mighty is to have some kind of "mighty" association. Genesis 6:4 talks about "mighty men." But we know these mighty men were destroyed by a flood. Nimrod's name comes up only two chapters removed from The Flood. So, where is all of Nimrod's mightiness coming from?

The fact that the word mighty first appears in Genesis 6:4, for the same word to be descriptively applied to Nimrod implies guilt by association. It's therefore reasonable to theorize Nimrod had extraterrestrial ties. He was doing Satan's bidding in front of God's face from jump. This illuminates why Genesis 10:9 says, "He was a mighty hunter before the LORD." Nimrod was acting out before God's eyes. He wasn't attempting to be slick or discreet.

When you are arrogant enough to erect a tower and slap it with your 5-letter name, the five letters used to spell it not only symbolize the five spelling *Babel*, but the five spelling Satan and devil as well. What's up with such "high five" symbolism? Is there more than meets the eye?

Nimrod had been handpicked by the devil to be leader of a New World empire. This means that the kingdom of heaven had Nimrod under surveillance as a person of interest from day one. In all actuality, Nimrod was attempting to make a post-Flood political counter move. The participants in this counter offensive weren't Nephilim, but again, use of the word mighty terms Nimrod as having the same criminal intent.

The extraterrestrial criminal minds working overtime in Genesis 6:4 were not only about the business of carnal knowledge, they were also involved in rocket science – aerospace engineering.

Consider Genesis 11:4 in the scope of here and now:
> "And they said, Go to, let us build us a city and a tower, whose top may reach unto heaven; and let us make us a name, lest we be scattered abroad upon the face of the whole earth."

Again, when connecting the "guilt-by-association" dots, Genesis 11:4 is just a follow-up to 6:4. Didn't Nimrod have an entire earth to subdue and conquer? Just where did this overreach "reach unto heaven" come from? Do you think these people thought this star trekking thing up all by themselves? Or do you think they had help?

The extraterrestrial connection is obvious. Remember, Satan and company had been kicked out of heaven, and by progeny proxy they are still trying to get back from whence they came.

For all we know, the devil and fallen angels may no longer have the ability to have hands-on which means the only thing these innumerable millions of predatory aliens bring to the table is technical knowledge. If that be the situation, human hands-on is a now a cosmic requirement for extraterrestrial missions beyond this solar system.

The question earlier posed: "Where did all of these devils/extraterrestrials go?"

Again, for all we know, they could be hiding in plain sight. Do we really know what's beneath the thick cloud covers of Venus or Jupiter? And what about those gas giants further out like Uranus and Neptune? Is it plausible, possible, or probable that there is a vast armada of extraterrestrial spacecraft docked on those planets? Whether you believe half-to-little of what appears on the internet, there are still reports of huge artificial structures on the far side of the moon. If men from earth weren't the builders, who are?

Consider Job 38 with particular focus on 7-9:

> "When the morning stars sang together, and all the sons of God shouted for joy? Or who shut up the sea with doors, when it brake forth, as if it had issued out of the womb? When I made the cloud the garment thereof, and thick darkness a swaddlingband for it."

Repeated, "stars" symbolize angels (Revelation 1:20). The "bright and morning star" (Revelation 22:16) symbolizes Jesus Christ. This means when the "morning stars" sang together, what's being referenced is "Michael and his angels." Since we know the "sons of God" are also angelic beings, if Michael and his angels and the sons of God shouted for joy, the reference here is prior to there being any "war in heaven."

But when revisiting the symbolism inherent in Jude 1:13:

> "Raging waves of the sea, foaming out their own shame; wandering stars, to whom is reserved the blackness of darkness forever."

Doesn't a comparison and contrast of the above verse with Job 38:7-9 clearly suggest something jumped off that disturbed heaven's sweet harmony?

Behold Jupiter again with Job and Jude providing perspective. Couldn't the thick clouds swirling around Jupiter be described as "swaddling bands?"

And if those cloud bands weren't making it plain enough, there's Jupiter's big red spot?

Is there any need to wonder why Revelation 12:3 reads the way it does:
> "And there appeared another wonder in heaven; and behold a great red dragon."

Doesn't Jupiter appear in heaven? And, hasn't Jupiter's red spot always been a scientific cosmic wonder?

So, could Jupiter be the camp for the "dragon and his angels?" Jupiter's certainly big enough. Jesus, Job, Jude, and Jupiter; that's a compelling number of J's to be pointing in the wrong direction.

In Acts 14:11-13, the people of Lystra behind the utterance, *"The gods are come down to us in the likeness of me*n," called Paul *Mercurius* and Barnabas *Jupiter*. Obviously, these people were impressed by the acts of the Holy Spirit, but why did they attribute those acts to fallen angels? Again, you're not going to hear it elementary school, but Mercury, Jupiter, and that blonde-haired boy Apollo were all devils. The Romans regarded Jupiter as the sky-god equivalent of the Greek god Zeus. Jupiter was the brother of Neptune and Pluto.

The fact that the supernatural gifts given Paul and Barnabas by the kingdom of God were immediately interpreted as powers derived from the princedom of Satan suggests awareness based on some kind of extraterrestrial close encounter. Calling the two apostles by two names that are extraterrestrial in origin requires introduction. A child doesn't use a 12-letter word unless he's been introduced to it before. Subsequently, the planet Jupiter being the "king planet" in the solar system to which Satan and Company are confined is just the kinda planet a narcissist like Lucifer would choose as hideout headquarters.

Returning to Nimrod, Genesis 11:4 is a very prophetic passage. "Let us make us a city and a tower" and "Let us make us a name" points directly to the United States of America. Yes, if you read between the lines, staring "us" right in the face is "US A." US A city and US A name has USA written literally all over it.

Who on earth can deny that a city with a tower that has a name is exactly what Washington, DC, USA, is when viewing its tower called the Washington Monument. And if you believe *We the People*, as in US Americans didn't pull a "*Capricorn One*" and we really did go to the moon and back, then we actually did take "one giant leap" literally and figuratively.

It was actualization of the same "giant" leap put in motion in the Garden of Eden, staged by the Nephilim giants of Genesis 6:4, and attempted by Nimrod. The irony inherent in astronaut Neil Armstrong's words as he set foot on the moon is compelling to say the least. That is, unless you think his use of the word "giant" was just a coincidence?

Just as human beings have code words that are sent as hidden messages, it's reasonable to presume extraterrestrial intelligences are capable of employing the same technique for both conscious and subliminal reception.

The Washington Monument is a tower. There are no buildings in DC taller. There's no law saying that a DC building can't be built taller. But the fact of the matter is, there just isn't.

Also, consider the fact that the Washington Monument is not only the tallest obelisk in the world; it's exactly 555 feet tall. Once again, we find a symbolic "high five."

Construction on the Washington Monument was completed in 1888. Knowing what we know about triple ones, triple eights, and triple sixes, do you really think triple fives as the total height of this structure is really just all coincidental?

Why exactly 555 feet?

If you've ever been to DC and took the opportunity to see the Washington Monument up close and personal, you'll note that there are four sides to the structure. Amazingly, each base side of the monument measures 55 feet and a half-inch on the average.

So what? Well, let's do the math. When those 55 feet and a half inch are decimally calculated in total inches, the product is a very interesting number. Take a calculator and multiply 55.5 x 12. You may be surprised at what you might find.

Coincidence?

The Washington Monument is an obelisk. Again, standing straight up in the midst of the word obelisk is the name "Bel." Again, Bel is the name of the Babylonian sun god.

Because there is "war in heaven" now being fought on earth, Satan and his angels are both indisputably and undeniably relentless. You may have thought construction ended with Nimrod's Tower of Babel, but the "secret of Nim" got picked up by the secrecy of freemasonry. George Washington, Benjamin Franklin, James Monroe, as well as a significant percentage of the signers of the Declaration of Independence and the U.S. Constitution were Free Masons. In essence, the United States was founded by Freemasons who have interwoven Masonic symbols into the fabric of American society, particularly in national seals, and streets in Washington, D.C., not to even mention architecture.

Intelligently ask yourself just what an Egyptian pyramid is doing on the back of a dollar bill adjacent "In God We Trust?" Did the Egyptian Pharaohs, who are credited with building that pyramid, trust in God? How does the emblem symbolizing a kingdom that fought God wind up on the currency of a nation that professes to love and respect God? That's makes just as much sense as Nazi Germany's Iron Cross being engraved on the back of a British Pound.

And while asking, ponder a pentagram's selection as the architectural design for the Pentagon? Since a pentagram is five-sided, here again the number five is symbolically connected with yet another D.C. landmark. But even more halting, isn't an inverted pentagram symbolically connected with Satan? There's more than enough movies and TV shows out there to answer that question.

Yes, Genesis 11:4 is prophetic. Indeed, "the beginning" of Nimrod's kingdom of influence had only just begun. Believe it or not, accept it or not, *"The Tower of Babel"* is standing 555 feet tall at 215th St NW, Washington, DC 20007.

This fact requires a very serious examination of what is really going on with the "kingdom of the United States" in the context of spirituality. Now, this may be a hard pill for many to swallow, but when you connect all of the dots, and the dollar bill is a very big dot, the USA was founded on the principles of a 5-letter word called deism. Deism is not the same thing as Christianity. The so-called Founding Fathers were deists, not Christians. And this is why they could draft and sign a document that says, "All men are created equal" and at the same time own African slaves, rape African and Native American women, and kill anyone who got in the way or hindered Manifest Destiny.

Research the histories of George Washington, Benjamin Franklin, and Thomas Jefferson beyond what's written in a typical fifth grade history book and you'll discover that many of the African and Native American women being raped by these three amigos were only 12-15 years old. Undeniably, they were sexual predators. Giving them a pass under the guise of being products of their time is like giving Cain a pass by reason of ancient history. The passage of time doesn't diminish the crime. Ask the next celebrity that gets busted for similar sex offenses.

When you know history (his story), you know there's nothing new under the sun or dwelling at 1600 Pennsylvania Avenue. *Sally Hemings: An American Scandal* (2000) didn't do Thomas justice. A young, gifted, and Black actress should have been pulled out of the ninth grade to play the title role. The so-called mistress of America's third president was 14 years young. Again, hiding behind being a "product of their times" doesn't fly in the face of "self-evident truths."

It's important to understand that being a deist enables you to exploit little girls and have it termed "scandal" as opposed to criminal. By definition, deism is:

> *"A belief in the existence of a supreme being, specifically of a creator who does not intervene in the universe. The term is used chiefly of an intellectual movement of the 17th and 18th centuries that accepted the existence of a creator on the basis of*

reason but rejected belief in a supernatural deity who interacts with humankind."

Breaking it down, it's the belief that God has created the universe but remains apart from it and permits his creation to administer itself through natural laws. Deism rejects the supernatural aspects of religion, such as belief in revelation in the Bible, and stresses the importance of ethical conduct only. And that's only if? It's the ambiguity of "if" that permitted and still allows all deists to live comfortably in their own skin.

In other words, you can stress without the stress of being held accountable by God for doing the wrong thing. That means you can stress on parchment (The Declaration of Independence) the equality of mankind; but you don't have to lose any sleep making it happen. Your belief system is comfortably content with the concept that what-will-be-will-be without any divine intervention. Basically, it's the *Star Trek* "Prime Directive" applied to your home planet.

Now, since we're not talking Captain Kirk, Spock, and the United Federation of Planets, what federation, or confederation, would have a vested interest in God taking a *laissez-faire* approach to human being civilizations?

It's no secret; Ben, George, Tom, and even Dolly's husband were all deists. And if you dare allow your fingers to do the Googling, you'd be surprised to find who else is a card-carrying member of that Outhouse crowd.

The so-called "founding fathers" fathered dozens of Black children. Seriously, how many Caucasians have you met or heard of with the last name Washington? Think about it.

Deism and its cohorts exemplify the sophistry of the devil. From Eden throughout, nowhere do you find Satan being presented as an atheist. Satan tried to quote the word of God to Eve, and he tried to do the same with Jesus Christ.

Satan knows there is a God. Satan doesn't accept the authority of God. What it is; folks get knowing and believing twisted. You know you have or had parents. Whether you believe or believed in what they say or said is another story. Borrowing from the Doobie Brothers, *What a*

Fool Believes is acceptance is synonymous with existence. The failure to accept a fact doesn't make the fact go away. It just makes turning a blind eye foolish. Those who say they don't believe in God don't have enough information to take that belief to the bank. They're trying to cash a check with insufficient funds. It would be better to just go up to the teller and say, *"Can you help a brotha (or sistah) out?"* Only a fool writes a check his or her proverbial ass is one day gonna have to cash. If you're betting your life that God does not exist and Jesus Christ isn't the way and only a myth, in the words from *Taken, "Good Luck."*

Deism is a sly and very slick way of joining the ranks of Christianity without being Christian. Deist say things like One Timothy, Two Peter, and Three John instead of using the appropriately ordinal approach; *First Timothy, Second Peter, Third John.*

Deism is a misperception of God the Father, God the Son, and God the Holy Spirit. Deism uses the name of God to justify whatever means and methods are required to achieve the goal or desired end result. Deism is do what you got to do and God will understand because *"he's an absentee landlord"* contrary to Luke 20:9-16.

Maybe it's historically inaccurate to say that Nimrod's is the founder of historical Babylon. But for sure, it can be said that Nimrod is the founder of Babylon spiritually:

> "And after these things I saw another angel come down from heaven, having great power; and the earth was lightened with his glory. And he cried mightily with a strong voice, saying, Babylon the great is fallen, is fallen, and is become the habitation of devils, and the hold of every foul spirit, and a cage of every unclean and hateful bird."
> —REVELATION 18:1-2

Of course, some make a very strong case that the Babylon figuratively referenced is literally the U.S.A. Because this book is focused on national media, it won't go national geographic as far as Babylon's new millennial physical location or political identity. The "war in heaven" is spiritual with physical ramifications. Satan's game plan in quest of establishing a *New*

World Order is media-centric. So, in a media context, how would Babylon be relevant to this discussion?

When looking at the Biblical characteristics of Babylon that are spiritual with physical ramifications, where in the world do we find "the habitation of devils, and the hold of every foul spirit, and a cage of every unclean and hateful bird" both figuratively and literally speaking?

Well, consider the following:

Devil (2010)
"A group of people are trapped in an elevator and the Devil is mysteriously amongst them."

The Devil Wears Prada (2006)
"A smart but sensible new graduate lands a job as an assistant to Miranda Priestly, the demanding editor-in-chief of a high fashion magazine."

The Devil's Advocate (1997)
"An exceptionally adept Florida lawyer is offered a job to work in New York City for a high-end law firm with a high-end boss – who is the devil."

Demons (1985)
"A group of people are trapped in a large movie theater in West Berlin that is infected by ravenous demons who proceed to kill and possess the humans one-by-one, thereby multiplying their numbers."

Devil in a Blue Dress (1995)
"An Afro-American man is hired to find a woman and gets mixed up in a murderous political scandal."

Devil Dog: The Hound from Hell (1978)
"Suburban homeowners and their family cannot escape from a demonic dog."

Bedazzled (2000)
"Desperate to gain the affection of a beautiful co-worker, a man strikes a deal with the Devil."

The Devil Rides Out (1968)
"Two men arrive at a fashionable party and discover that the party is in fact a gathering of a satanic cult."

The Devil and Daniel Webster (1941)
"A nineteenth-century New Hampshire farmer makes a compact with Satan to sell his soul for economic success."

Little Nicky (2000)
"After two of the devil's three sons escape Hell to wreak havoc on Earth, the devil must send his third son, the mild-mannered Nicky, to bring them back before it's too late."

The Birds (1963)
"A wealthy San Francisco socialite pursues a potential boyfriend to a small Northern California town that slowly takes a turn for the bizarre when birds of all kinds suddenly begin to attack people."

Birdemic: Shock and Terror (2010)
"A horde of mutated birds descends upon the quiet town of Half Moon Bay, California. With the death toll rising, two citizens manage to fight back, but will they survive Birdemic?"

Blood Freak (1972)
"Dracula on drugs."

Flu Bird Horror (2008)
"A group of teenagers go on an excursion to the mountains. There, they are attacked by birds infected with a lethal virus. When the teens reach a nearby village, the haunting birds start passing their virus on to all the dwellers."

Beaks: The Movie (1987)
"Vanessa, a television reporter covering a story of a farmer attacked by his chickens, discovers that this is not an isolated incident."

Kaw (2007)
"A small town is attacked by ravens and doesn't know why the ravens are working together."

Killing Birds (1987)
"A group of students goes into the woods to study birds, and soon the dead begin to rise to devour the living."

ThanksKilling (2009)
"A homicidal turkey axes off college kids during Thanksgiving break."

The Vulture (1966)
"A mad scientist turns himself into a half-man, half-bird monster to avenge the death of his ancestor."

Poultrygeist: Night of the Chicken Dead (2006)
"Zombified chickens attempt to kill the fast-food workers that cook them in a restaurant built on an ancient burial ground."

With a picture being worth a thousand words, and at least 16 letters, should Babylon's fallen spiritual identity be that great of a mystery?

Hollywood, as Babylon, is more than the capital of motion picture arts and sciences. The name in a word is a term symbolizing a culture, mindset, mentality. It's the glitz, glamor, and the bling. It's that magic wand that sprinkles pixie dust. And if you snort it just the wrong way, super nova, baby! You blow up before the ink dries on the contract you used a ballpoint pen to sign. It's probably the only place on earth where nobody can become somebody if enough any bodies are paying the kind of attention that can be translated into that "lean mean green."

When the reality of extraterrestrial spiritual forces is removed from the media equation, there is neither reasonable nor sensible explanation in defense of what most should agree is offensive. Forget profanity and gratuitous sex-capades, if you have a problem with evil when personally experienced, why embrace it spiritually as entertainment? Isn't that a contradiction if you call yourself a Christian? Isn't it hypocritical to talk what you're unwilling to walk?

When it comes to the real versus the play, the thin separating the two is a challenge for the spiritually challenged mind. When a society embraces moral turpitude for entertainment purposes under the profession of being guided by moral principles, the hypocrisy inherent finds "chickens coming home to roost" every time random acts of violence are witnessed. Spiritually playing with fire in the form of entertainment always results in getting burned.

The motion picture and TV programming term "suspending disbelief" is a two-edged sword when moral conscience is suspended in the process. Opening fire in a school, church, mall, or stadium evidences complete desensitization. Insensitivity to the point of total disregard for intelligent life requires a spiritual catalyst. Unfortunately, the 25-100 pound elephant in the room is a television set.

Fellowshipping with murderers, thieves, rapists, prostitutes, pimps, and drug dealers on television and in the movies isn't any different than kicking it with them on the street or in a club. Satan knows if there's where you find admiration, the only thing separating association is space and opportunity. Even when it comes to the spiritually unchallenged mind, "an eye for an eye" is not a great leap when you see your favorite movie/TV hero/shero do it enough times.

Can you honestly say James Bond's "license to kill" is a turn-off?

Perhaps cable and satellite music channels are the only true safe harbors when it comes to in-house TV dinners and a movie? Contemplate the fact that songs are embedded in your mind about love, but how many tunes bring back that loving feeling when it comes to killing somebody? And, that applies to *killing them softly*.

Just compare the message in most music contrasted with the message in an over-abundance of television shows and features that require mayhem to grab attention and sustain interest. For example, once upon a time in a land back in the day, those seeking musical entertainment were exposed to *temptations*. But even while being tempted, there were *miracles*. And seeing such *dramatics* caused *whispers* of a *Knight* named *Gladys* who wasn't *Gaye* because she had her *Pips*!

Seriously, how do you explain tunes that were heard 30, 40, 50 years ago and you can remember them word for word today, even if you might be flirting with Alzheimer's? The songs were called "sweet soul music" for a reason.

However, when it comes to what is seen, and not heard, a spell is put on your mind that ain't being sung by *Blue Magic*. Visual messages are digital photographs. Once captured by the lens of the eye, those images are printed in the brain to be accessed whenever and by whatever the right or wrong stimuli demands. This is why Psalms 101:3 reads: "I will set no wicked thing before mine eyes."

God, obviously, knows the susceptibility of the conscious and subconscious mind. And definitely, Satan knows human vulnerabilities too. Who can deny that the media has dumbed down artistic tastes to such an extent that analogously speaking, chitterlings (pronounced chitlins) is preferred over anything and everything the *American Heart Association* would recommend with *heart-check* certification.

When faced with "war in heaven," media at-large is managed by forces that are demonically driven to awaken and maintain an appetite for degradation and decadence. This is a fact exemplified by what's not only presented as entertainment, but news as well. When human beings are fed a diet of raw materials that are base in nature, those dining on such will by nature fly no higher than that to which they are continually exposed. You don't find lawyers talking like doctors just as you don't find kids talking like adults unless they've been influenced by a predominating adult environment. *"Birds of a feather flock together"* is a truism all should pick up on because we don't see eagles hanging with pigeons, robins with hawks, or buzzards kicking it with cardinals.

Do you see "the news" as entertainment, or entertainment as news? An honest answer is probably both. And of course, when that fine line is erased and the news becomes entertainment, all objectivity disappears with the line. Reporters of what's supposed to be news in the informative sense of the word become entertainers presenting news in the entertainment sense of the word. Consequently, the viewer or listener doesn't really know if the story being reported is factual in an effort to inform, or if it's being embellished in effort to better entertain.

It's the desire of Satan's princedom to smudge mankind's optics making evil entertaining as opposed to abhorrent. What's typically called television news is actually nothing more than an overview of Satan's daily accomplishments packaged to entertain under the allusion of being essential information. Rationalize the newsworthiness in a newscast routinely reserving its lead stories for crimes of murder, rape, and fatal automobile accidents. The newsroom mantra: If it bleeds, it leads. If it's sex, that comes next. The psychology is fear-based and sensually titillating programming.

What is the common sense and sensibility in asking someone who has just had their house blown away by a tornado, "*How do you feel?*" If your cat is entangled in tree limbs, and a news reporter asks your feelings, the appropriate comeback is answering with a question, "*If it were your cat, how would you feel?*" But these moronic queries from Maybelline maidens and typically non-mustachioed gents either standing or sitting in front of a camera are asked solely to exploit a situation. And the physically shaken and grief stricken are the ones being spiritually exploited just to satisfy a local or national news team's insatiable appetite for the dramatic, sensational, and bizarre. Putting a grieving mother, father, sister, brother, wife, and/or husband in front of a camera in the aftermath of a tragedy is insensitive. But "deism" masquerading as Christianity permits that Babylon 5, 4, 3, 2, 1…finger point approach.

Yes, when the countdown reaches zero and the red light signals "you're on" you're really off if your personal profession is Christianity. Because violence and sex have prurient appeal, and itching ears want to know who's zoomin' who, anything that feeds a spiritually morbid or deviant mindset is tantamount to "righteousness" professionally fellowshipping with "unrighteousness" on behalf of the almighty dollar. You cannot personally serve Jesus one day out of the week and professionally serve Satan the other six. 2 Corinthians 6:14-15 makes it crystal.

Just consider the contrived news significance in broadcasting distressed 911 callers; which has now been turned into a network television show. If you report a crime or horrific event, your voice becomes part of the news package and thereby something to be additionally thrown into the exploitation mix. The fright, horror, and exasperation in your voice become a news bite to munch.

The corporate media executives that direct their employees to participate in this spiritually reprehensible practice are just as disturbing as the incident being reported. Aiding and abetting the spiritual fantasies of the devil makes one a conduit, not a journalist.

Of course, the reporter's rationale is the public's right and need to know. But again, isn't that the very same argument Satan used as a rationale in the Garden of Eden? Didn't the devil take the position it was Eve's right and need to know evil?

Yes, evil – not good. When it came to The Tree, do you honestly think it was the "good" that Satan was pushing? Since God is good, the devil wasn't pushing Adam and Eve to "know" God any more than they already did. The serpent was pushing the "public right to know" all that's bad. And the fact that who got killed in your city is overwhelmingly considered more newsworthy than who helped an old lady across the street or rescued a cat from a tree is why what you see is what you get during the first fifteen minutes of a thirty minute news block.

When it comes to news in particular and the media in general, the public need to know "bad" is given preferential airtime/coverage over "good." The "right to know" rationale for intrusiveness when it comes to covering a story is no rational excuse. Rather than the power of the media being employed to expose and challenge, that power is used to support the agenda of the media company issuing the corporate paycheck. That makes news objectivity subjective.

The evil men do is far too overanalyzed by media in its purported effort to determine motive. Plastering the pictures and photos of people who raise hell throughout a newscast fulfills the desire and criminal intent of the perpetrator. Dramatizing bad boy and bad girl behavior as if it were a lifetime movie feature or PBS documentary rewards notoriety. It validates criminal minded and motivated claims to fame.

Be assured, it isn't coincidental that newscasts of bagged bodies, bloodstained sidewalks and mangled vehicles are put on air during the breakfast, lunch, dinnertime, and right before bedtime hours. Just as Jesus said, "Whoso eateth my flesh, and drinketh my blood, hath eternal life," Satan wants the same thing because, again, he wants to be like God. Eating the flesh and drinking the blood of Christ is symbolism for the mental consumption and digestion of the philosophy of Jesus. Consider the symbolism attached to the final Passover supper of Jesus Christ in the company of his disciples. Keep in mind that the Last Supper is called the "last supper" because at the supper table Jesus said, "Do in remembrance of me."

Now, the devil knows he's not going to get mankind to participate in a Holy Communion service to himself, but is it beyond the realm of conceivability that he might try to get man to participate in something symbolically similar? What could be more similar to eating the flesh and drinking the blood of Jesus symbolically, than eating the flesh and drinking the blood of Satan symbolically? Of course, the satanic symbolism is watching mayhem on the news while you eat?

Think about it. If you are watching "the news" and the majority of what you're seeing is crime where flesh is being torn and blood is being spilled, you are indeed literally and figuratively participating in an *"unholy communion service."* You are physically feasting on carnage and criminality, and both your conscious and subliminal mind is digesting it. This means biologically, if you are what you eat, Satan knows biology. You have made him your waiter. And the tip he expects you to leave is the one you leave with. It's a spiritual gratuity compliment of the server.

> "Do not ye yet understand, that whatsoever entereth in at the mouth goeth into the belly, and is cast out into the draught? But those things which proceed out of the mouth come forth from the heart; and they defile the man. For out of the heart proceed evil thoughts, murders, adulteries, fornications, thefts, false witness, blasphemies: These are the things which defile a man."
> – MATTHEW 15:17-20

The $144,000 question: *"How did all of that defiling stuff get into the heart in the first place?"* How about that elephant and its entire herd – television, film, radio, and the internet?

When stories of despair, death, and destruction are planted, immediately segueing to weather and sports doesn't bridge the psychosocial gap. Warning viewers the video they are about to see may be considered disturbing is like telling someone you're going to expose yourself before you unzip your pants. The mind is like a bell. Once dinged with a ding-a-ling, it can't be un-rung or *dung*.

But this is the "Hollywood shuffling" that generically includes the entire media landscape. And it's exactly what puts the babble in Babylon with regards to all that's said in Revelation 18:2. Undeniably, Hollywood as Babylon is the "habitation of devils" spiritually when its above-and-below-the-line talents are employed in the production and presentation of features that further a predatory alien agenda.

Mind control and manipulation is accomplished through osmosis. If you understand the chemical process involving osmosis, comparably speaking electronic media messages are spiritual molecules. The solvent is your soul. The messages are the solute. The membrane is your brain. When messages representative of the devil's spirit are filtered through your brain, those messages will inevitably dissolve into your soul molecularly making you who you are.

In genetics, the term junk DNA refers to regions of DNA that are noncoding. DNA contains instructions (coding) that are used to create proteins in the cell. However, the amount of DNA contained inside each cell is vast and not all of the genetic sequences present within a DNA molecule actually code for a protein. Consequently, more than 95% of the genetic sequence inside each of our cells is written off as "junk" because it is not well understood.

But when this so-called junk DNA is understood spiritually, the coding at a sub-atomic molecularly level could very well be spiritual. The proteins are what you digest spiritually.

Of course, that theory would be viewed as ridiculous by the scientific community in particular and probably a lot of other communities in general. But again, the fact that mankind is willing to call something "junk" just because it can't wrap its head around purpose, use, and relevance is not only the epitome of arrogance, it's an insult to God as a profession.

Rolling with that logic, if you are a scientist who considers him or herself a Christian, you're essentially maintaining God created man in his image and likeness with more than 95% of the DNA structure junk! Go figure.

Naw, to the contrary, bet your bottom dollar that the so-called junk DNA has something to do with man being a "living soul." And henceforth, Matthew 15:17-20 is chemically connecting the dots. This is the biological explanation and manner defiling matter spiritually gets into the heart; not figuratively but physically. In other words, more than 95% of who you are molecularly speaking is spiritual. That's why when the spirit leaves the body, it's the body that becomes junk.

What's encoded on your spiritual DNA is what you're working with when it comes to life eternal. The phrase *"Book of Life"* appears eight times in the Bible. Basically, that book's about who will receive God's gift of eternal life.

Imagine a book about your life that can only have 100 pages. How many of those pages will your personal resume cover? If the best you can do is a five-page resume (double spaced), you're left with 95 pages that have nothing to do with education, training, experience, extracurricular activities, honors, family and references.

Spiritually speaking, there's more to your story than what can be written on a resume, a social media profile page, or an obituary. There's 95 more pages to who you are that's not junk; unless junk is what you've made your lifetime. Metaphorically, this is the 95% that's scientifically termed "non-coded" DNA.

The Book of Life is the only codebook in the universe that can interpret what is on those 95 other pages that tell your story. That 95% appears "blank" because your story is still being written as long as you're alive. Who you are in terms of all you are ain't *"unsung,"* but rather untold. This is why Jesus says in Matthew 24:13:

> "But he that shall endure unto the end, the same shall be saved."

In other words, not until you get to "The End" will you or anybody else know your whole story.

16 THE WATCH

"While we look not at the things which are seen, but at the things which are not seen: for the things which are seen are temporal; but the things which are not seen are eternal." — 2 Corinthians 4:18

When it comes to word association, "watch" is hand-in-glove with television. Watching TV is a worldwide phenomenon that has no geographical boundaries. You can even get a hookup in Antarctica. So, given that kind of intercontinental connectivity, when it comes to what's typically watched it's usually all good being pitted against all bad. Since such is life, such is WMD; up to now.

While the undergirding theme threading this book is "war in heaven," the next few chapters are going to turn toward peace on earth. Not in a Leo Tolstoy *(War and Peace)* style, but in a manner called peace of mind.

Watching TV either for news or entertainment purposes only can make you wanna holler if you aren't reminded that there is a force in the universe all good called Almighty God. While Satan, as the "prince of the power of the air," may use the media to convey his message, God holds the remote control.

What does a television remote have in common with the Bible? It has numbers.

In Mark 13:37, Jesus gives the command: "And what I say unto you, I say unto all, Watch."

While in the Garden of Gethsemane, Jesus left His disciples with the expectation that they would patiently "watch" for His return. With the year 2000, the watch has lasted for more than 2,000 years. The fact that Jesus was disappointed that His main men could not watch with him for at least one hour has a spiritually profound implication. Just as tired eyes caused Peter and the other disciples to fall asleep in Gethsemane, the same weariness of the flesh causes sleepiness today. Should Jesus, "cometh unto the disciples" now, do you think he will "findeth" many sleeping, or in a state that's practically comatose?

Addressing the question of how long a watch, Jesus tells the world: "But of that day and hour knoweth no man, no, not the angels of heaven, but my Father only" (Matthew 24:36).

With the situation such, what Biblical data are we left concerning the approximate time of Christ's return? Believe it or not, the Bible is filled with clues. So many, God expects believers to be able to watch in accordance to Mathew 24:27 based on more than pie in the sky.

Facing the Biblical inflexibility of no man knowing the day or the hour of Jesus' return, it is possible to know the time of season. Ecclesiastes 3:1 says there is a season for everything. The parable of the fig tree as presented in Matthew 24 tells all: "When his branch is yet tender, and putteth forth leaves, ye know that summer is nigh: so likewise ye, when ye shall see all these things, know that it is near, even at the doors."

Speaking of His return to earth "with power and great glory," Jesus is prompting the hearer of His words to believe that temporal realities can provide a portent of both the invisibly and the celestially eternal. Christ, however, is not saying His Second Advent can be itinerated like some commuter bus, train, or plane. The Bible indicates we may know the "season," but we will never be able to pinpoint the hour.

Now, when people watch out for anything, it's important that they keep heads up and eyes open. But contemplate the customary concept of prayer. Just where in the Bible is the instruction given for the eyes to be closed and the head bowed for purposes of worshiping the God of Heaven?

Certainly, the Old Testament is filled with examples of God being worshiped with bowed heads. But Jesus didn't re-establish that model. And nowhere in the New Testament is there any instance of righteously performed, eyes closed, bowed head worship of God being conducted or continued.

When Christ prayed, John 17:1 indicates that Jesus: "Lifted up his eyes to heaven, and said Father, the hour is come; glorify thy Son, that thy Son also may glorify thee."

Is there more to be learned from martial artists than martial arts? Check out a Bruce Lee flick. When facing an opponent, the man would bow his head while keeping his eyes looking up and focused straight ahead. The opponent all face whether realized or not is the extraterrestrial Satan.

Amazing is the fact that the divine Model, whom 1 John 2:6 says we all should emulate, prayed to His Father with His head up and His eyes open. And the same example he set is the same example he preached in Matthew 26:41 and Mark 14:38 where it is written: "Watch and pray."

And, what is the prayer? Probably the one you first learned as a kid. Part of it goes: *"And lead us not into temptation."*

Now, think about that for a minute? Why would the Lord pray to the Father for him not to lead "us" into temptation? Matthew 4:3 calls Satan out as "the tempter." So, why would God lead anybody to Satan?

Isn't it obvious that the only way to be led anywhere is to go there blindly? The prayer is directed at those who are walking around with their eyes wide shut! When you "watch and pray" at least you've got a cane to tap in front of your path as you go your merry way.

Of course, the watching is metaphorical, but the praying isn't. That's where the other part of the sentence is finished: *"but deliver us from evil."* Watching and praying means you are working with God in your journey. You're not stumbling and bumbling around like a walking dead zombie. Unfortunately, a lot of "us" folks are willing participants in their own oppression. Being crazy as hell ain't the same thing as acting crazy as hell. When you're acting, your chain can be yanked. When it's your being, as in human nature, send the dog catcher. You off the chain!

The only example the New Testament gives pertaining to bowed head worship occurs when the Roman soldiers stripped Jesus and put a scarlet robe and a crown of thorns upon him (Matthew 27:29). The one other place giving mention to a bowed head is John 19:30. And there is where Christ "bowed his head, and gave up the ghost." The only thing the New Testament says with regard to closed eyes occurs in Matthew 13:15 and Acts 28:27. There is where Jesus and Paul are respectively quoting the prophecy of Isaiah, which references people closing their eyes to the truth.

So think about it. The only New Testament examples of bowed heads pertain to Jesus Christ being mocked and being dead. And the only examples of closed eyes are in reference to being blind to God's truth. Satan is the antichrist. It is therefore the nature and disposition of the devil to do the direct opposite of what Jesus, as Christ, requires. As demon-strated in the Garden of Eden, whatever God says, the devil is going to tempt human beings to do the opposite. Satan is a counterfeit artist when it comes to the currency of Christ.

With this in mind, consider the morbid practice of displaying the body of the deceased as part of a funeral service. What purpose does viewing a corpse serve theologically and psychologically? Does it show any respect for the deceased? How about therapy for the bereaved?

Honestly ask yourself would you like to see yourself dead? If you had a dream seeing yourself in a coffin, would you wake up feeling good or call it a nightmare? If it's the latter, why in the heaven or hell don't you think those you leave behind wouldn't feel the exact same way!

Borrowing from that movie, "seeing dead people" in a religious service not only expresses total disregard for the rights of the dead, it is a perversion of the religious significance of life and death. According to John 10:10, Jesus is about picturing life; not instagramming death. But, folks have been culturally programmed to think a view of lifelessness is an expression of life abundance. And, because of this satanic mind manipulation that's really "all about the benjamins," seeing a body lying-in-state has become one of the fundamental moneymakers of the funeral industry.

Realized or not, "viewings" provide Satan opportunity to make the work of his hands a departing snapshot and memory for family and friends. A service held to celebrate one's life that's fused with viewing one dead is straight outta Isaiah 5:20. It puts "bitter" with "sweet" and vice versa. Simply put, there's nothing celebratory when beholding the power of the devil. Writing in 1 Corinthians 15:56, Paul doesn't say, "the sweet sting."

Hebrews 2:14 reads: "Him that hath the power of death, that is, the devil." Unwittingly, funeral services that incorporate a body's display are paying public homage to an act of Satan. Death is not an Act of God; it is a consequence of sin that God permits. While cemetery tombstones are a socio-cultural necessity, they're also trophies in the glass showcase of the princedom. Therefore, is a taller, bigger, better, lavish, or more elaborate tombstone honoring the one in the grave? Or, is it more so paying tribute to the entity who put that one there!

In the seventh chapter of the book of Judges when God was choosing soldiers to fight against the Midianites, he told Gideon to bring his men down to the water. The ones who bowed down on their knees and lowered their heads to drink were rejected. And those who lapped as a dog, bringing their hands to their mouths were accepted. Knowing that God does not take pleasure in men either "being dogs" or imitating canine behavior, what was the real basis for selection? Could it be that those who brought their hands to their mouths kept their heads up and continued to watch even as they drank?

Since it is by virtue of the eyes that spiritual things are spiritually discerned, it is Satan who wants personal prayer mimicking behavior associated with sleep. The devil knows that a church filled with bowed heads and closed-eyes is ultimately symbolic of death, or a spiritually lethargic condition. Revelation 3:14-18 identifies the church of Laodicea as a primetime dateline new millennium example.

Now, given the fact that the name Laodicea appears nowhere in the top-100 as far as most popular names for local churches, it makes absolutely no sense to embrace the personal traits that make Laodiceans so unattractive. Yet, the same strategy used against the Midianites is applicable when dealing with modern day Laodicean media-knights. Clearly, the Bible foresaw the development of a Church age and its media connection with the divine mandate to watch.

Once more, Satan is intimately connected with the electronic media. It bears repeating, with specific regard to television, where a critical transfer of energy from one point to another takes place, a transducer, or transforming mechanism is required. A microphone transducer transforms sound patterns into electrical patterns. A television camera transforms light patterns into electrical patterns. And a transmitter transforms electrical frequency patterns into the higher-frequency domain of radio frequency energy, which is part of the electromagnetic spectrum earlier discussed. The principal Internet technologies associated with IP, HTTP, TCP (protocols), wireless DSL, etc. similarly applies. So given the appellation "prince of the power of the air," a more apropos conceptualization of the devil being "transformed into an angel of light" couldn't be offered.

Again, because television and Internet are used to foster and promote iniquity (however limited or expansive), the technological nature of both, along with electromagnetism's basic natural force, together provide a chemistry whereby the spirit of Satan is actually "transformed" into an electrical pattern that is radiant or "light" energy; not symbolically transformed, but literally transformed.

One more time again, if the airwaves are inundated with evil and wickedness, they are physically conveying the spirit of the devil no differently than the serpent in the Garden of Eden was used to physically convey the same. But in that regard, it's important to realize that it wasn't just the spirit of the devil that was being transmitted through the body of the snake, it was Satan's physical words and thoughts as well. The serpent was speaking. The serpent had been transformed into a biological transmitter. As a matter of fact, in Matthew 16:23 when Jesus turns to Peter with "Get thee behind me Satan," Peter had become a "transmitter" of a message that was anti the message the kingdom of God wanted to send.

Because both television and Internet protocols "transform" light patterns into electrical patterns which are reconverted into light patterns for reception by the human eye, Satan himself is technologically transformed into an "angel of light" just as the Scripture prophesizes (2 Corinthians 11:14). When the technological connection is missed, folks think "angel of light" connotes enlightenment as in wisdom. If that be the case, intelligently ask yourself if it's a wise move to be sly, slick, and wicked? How far does being "enlightened" to the arts and crafts of sex, lies, and videotape typically get the playa and the playette?

The marveling associated with 2 Corinthians 11:14 is Satan's technological transformation. It has little or nothing to do with pulpit pimps who are all about the "profit-in-my-pocket" i.e., P.I.M.P.

There is nothing marvelous about store front preachers where the emphasis is on "front." Angels are messengers. Being an "angel of light" is having the ability to send a message as an angel at the speed of light; 186,000 miles per second. NYC to LA roundtrip 75 times in the time it takes you to blink or wink a watchful eye. "Angel of light" is metaphorically referencing electronic communication via the electromagnetic spectrum!

There is a very real and literal aspect to the Holy Bible that transcends the figurative perceptions most are mentally locked into. When soberly reflecting on the "unholy communion" that is symbolized by "breaking bread" over the television display of Satan's body of work, give that reflection some added thought in view of the technology that enables television to work. Just as Jesus told Nicodemus to "marvel not" with respect to the spiritual reality of being born again, he tells us to "marvel not" with respect to the physical reality of Satan's ability to adapt to an electronic/computer age.

Again, because many, in spite of profession, embrace a one-dimensional view of spirituality, many do not see the duality of meaning inherent in Biblical allusions and metaphors. The Biblical reference to waves is not exclusively confined to water. The metaphorical expression "raging waves" also bears reference to light wave conversions of electrical energy that travel through airwaves.

As we bask in the non-ionizing radiation emanating from our TV screens, we do well to remember the words of Amos 6:1, 3-4:

> "Woe unto them that are at ease in Zion. Ye that put far away the evil day, and cause the seat of violence to come near; That lie upon beds of ivory, and stretch themselves upon their couches, and eat the lambs out of the flock, and the calves out of the midst of the stall."

Did the prophet glimpse the religion of television viewing? The word "television" is derived from the Greek word *tele*, which means "far off," and the Latin word *visio*, which means, "to see."

Etymologically, television in concept means, "to see far off." And whatever it is that can be seen far off is, by reverse application, made to "come near." A telescope, for example, brings distant objects near. Thus, by its very nature, television causes whatever happens to be shown to aurally and visually "come near." Subsequently, when Satan showed Jesus all those kingdoms in Matthew 4:8, those distant places, wherever in the world they happened to be, were actually caused to "come near" the view of Christ. Henceforth in techno-theory, Satan actually employed a "wireless television" concept. This necessarily means when we say the devil employed television in the temptation of Christ, we are not attempting to stretch your imagination. And consequently, if Satan used TV to tempt Jesus, it's still no stretch to "remotely" think he'd do the same against you.

Take note of the conservative estimate that the average U.S. citizen fortunate enough to reach age sixty-five would have watched the equivalent of nine years uninterrupted television programming, viewing more than 20,000 TV commercials per year. Bottom line: if your steps toward Christ can be paused, rewound, or stopped (anything other than fast forwarded), Satan has accomplished his goal for your eternal destiny. Whether realized or not, the devil has interjected an influence on time that is coldly calculated to preempt God's instructions as given in Matthew 26:41.

Additionally, consider how time is separated into the categories BC (BCE) and AD. But, when confronting the realities of these time markers, it is both a recognized theological and historical fact that Jesus was neither born in the year zero nor in the year AD 1. According to Dionysius Exiguus, a sixth century Roman Catholic monk who introduced the current calendric system of numbering years on the basis of Christ's birth, Jesus was born about 4 BC.

Now soberly consider. At the writing of this book it is 2018. But it has been at least 2,022 years since the approximate birth of Jesus Christ, which marked the beginning of the Fifth Millennium. Arrival of the year AD 1000 placed humankind four years inside the Sixth Millennium. So, right now, instead of 2018, this is actually the year 2022. We are presently twenty-two years inside the Seventh Millennium. So, with respect to the Seventh Millennium and it being 2022 at the reading of this book, perhaps it requires 20/20 spiritual vision to see what time it is on the kingdom of Heaven's shot clock.

Spiritually speaking, doesn't the number 7 signify perfection? What benefit would Satan have in a distorted calendar that's four years off? Unquestionably, as an evil prince, it is the devil's desire that people party like it's 1999 *ad infinitum*. In view of 1 Thessalonians 5:2, if Jesus will return as a "thief in the night," analogously speaking, what is it that a Holy God could be stealing? Is it possible that the stolen commodity is time? The time one individually has to get their act together, to get it right, repent?

All who procrastinate in their steps toward Christ may find that their time has done a Jimmy Hughes; it's "stolen away" once a decision to get serious about salvation is made. On the other hand, those who are spiritually in tune with the time will not find sickness, death, or the actual Second Coming of Christ catching them unaware and spiritually lost.

> "Watch, therefore; for ye know not what hour your Lord doth come. But know this, that if the good man of the house had known in what watch the thief would come, he would have watched, and would not have suffered his house to be broken into. Therefore be ye also ready; for in such an hour as ye think not, the Son of man cometh." — Matthew 24:42-44

Here again is the "watch" word. It's charged with Scriptural significance. Contemplate the fact that the Jewish day is divided into eight segments of time called watches. There are four watches in the day, and there are four at night. Starting at 6:00 a.m., each watch consists of three hours. The second watch begins at 9:00 a.m., the third at noon, and the fourth at 3:00 p.m.

Starting all over again, the evening's first watch begins at 6:00 p.m. It's followed by the 9:00 p.m., the midnight, and the 3:00 a.m. watches. Even the United States military refers to a guard duty shift as a watch. God, just like the Jews and the U.S. military, measures time with respect to these same three-hour intervals.

In furtherance of that fact, according to Psalms 90:4: "For a thousand years in thy sight are but as yesterday when it is past, and as a watch in the night."

God is eternal. He is not bound by time, but he has a perspective on time. The above verse states clearly that in terms of duration, one thousand of our years is like one day to him, as well as like a "watch in the night." Here again, the Word of God has to be either accepted at face value or rejected in totality. The Bible is not a smorgasbord of delectable delights wherein human beings have the privilege to pick and choose what is both spiritually and intellectually palatable. Accepting Psalms 90:4 for what it says, let's consider the minimal 2,000 years that have elapsed since Jesus Christ's First Advent. From God's point of view, as registered in Psalms 90:4, the time has been the equivalent of two days or two watches.

How so? Well, if a thousand years is as "yesterday" or a day gone by, we know that the year 2000 marked the two-thousandth year minimum since the birth of Christ. Presented with the fact that a thousand years to God is as one "watch" in the night, how many watches would 2,000 years be like? Of course, the answer is two. And in harmony with Psalms 90:4 is 2 Peter 3:8: "But, beloved, be not ignorant of this one thing, that one day is with the Lord as a thousand years, and a thousand years as one day."

We say it again; Jesus is what the Bible is all about. After Adam and Eve fell on hard times, the promise of mankind's redemption hinged on the advent of a Redeemer. Referenced again, when Paul speaks of "redeeming the time," he is pointing toward the redemption of humankind's grasp on eternity. Only through the advent of an Eternal Redeemer can an eternal life-time be recovered. So the First and Second Advents of Jesus are pivotal to the way God records human history and orders human events.

Nehemiah 9 commemorates the return of the Jews from captivity. Their return to Jerusalem is for the purpose of rebuilding the city wall and rededicating themselves to God. Verse 3 reads: "And they stood up in their place and read in the book of the law of the Lord their God one fourth part of the day, and another fourth part they confessed and worshipped the Lord their God."

A "fourth part of the day" equals six hours. That's twenty-four hours in a day divided by four equals six. Six hours equals two watches. And, in terms of God's time clock, how many years are two watches? Prophetically interpreted it's precisely 2,000 years.

The "old" legalistic covenant existed from Abraham to Christ. Since Jesus, the "new" covenant of faith has been in effect. As a matter of historical fact, there were 2,000 years between the time of Abraham and the

First Advent of Jesus Christ. It was this period of years that marked the so-called old covenant. Being under the law, it was during this period that Nehemiah says the Jews "read in the book of the law."

Bear in mind that even though Moses delivered the law, the old covenant was established with Abraham. This fact is made apparent by Nehemiah 9:7-8 and Genesis 15:18. Then, Nehemiah 9:3 speaks of "another fourth part of the day." This next six hours, they "confessed and worshiped the Lord, their God."

Now, if the first fourth of the day dealt with Moses and the Abrahamic Covenant, wouldn't the immediately following fourth part deal with Jesus Christ? Who do you think would be the object of confession and worship? Who is the Lord?

Roman 10:9-10 contends: "If thou shalt confess with thy mouth the Lord Jesus, and shalt believe in thine heart that God hath raised him from the dead, thou shalt be saved. For with the heart man believeth unto righteousness; and with the mouth confession is made unto salvation." Is there any doubt what's going on during the next "fourth part" of Nehemiah 9:3? This time frame symbolizes the "new covenant." And how many years does that "new covenant" period cover? That's right, 2,000 years. The same formula used to calculate the first "fourth part" measurement is applicable to the second. According to Nehemiah 9:5, after the people had made their confession, the scripture says they shall: "Stand up and bless the Lord for ever and ever." This means their redemption has been completed. And, according to Daniel 12:1, when Jesus, under the angelic name of Michael, "stands up" it's all over. The very next event is the Second Coming of Christ.

The Hebrew calendar, according to tradition, was supposed to have started with the Creation, an event believed to be some 5,778 years ago. But given the chronological discrepancies between Talmudic chronologists regarding the destruction of the First Temple and modern secular dating, there is a suspected 165 to 208 year differential. Neverthemore-or-less, giving both calculations full consideration, the general opinion held by more than a few theologians is that from Creation to Christ there has been the expiration of at least 3,943 years.

Employing the Hebrew calculation; that figures 5,778 plus the average of 165+208 or 187 minus the birth of Christ (4 BC) and 2018 or 2022 equaling 3,943.

But we can make our own rudimentary calculations of the time span between the creation of Adam and the birth of Abraham by simply adding all of the "begots" that are figured into Genesis 5:3-32 and 11:10-26. The sum is 1,946 years.

Given the fact that there's almost a 2,000 year separation between Adam and Abraham, and at least another 2,000 years between Abraham and Jesus, it does not stretch the imagination to think that there could possibly be 4,000 years between man's creation and Christ.

Now, continue to "watch" and consider very carefully. On God's time clock, how many days would 4,000 years symbolize?

That's right, four days.

And how many days did Lazarus lay dead? According to John 11:39:

> "Jesus said, take away the stone. Martha, the sister of him that was dead, saith unto him, Lord, by this time he stinketh; for he hath been dead four days."

Lazarus represented the symbolic length of time that man wallowed in sin without hope of salvation. From God's perspective, the four days that Jesus allowed Lazarus to lay dead represented the four thousand years mankind had to lay dead without Christ. When Jesus said Lazarus' sickness was "not unto death," he was also talking about the sin-sickness of humankind.

Those who are presently sick in the soul are not "sick unto death" either, if they allow Jesus to resurrect them as he did His friend Lazarus. But, as indicative of these passages and the numbers on God's watch, the time frame for "resurrection unto life" is very short. If we add on the two days for the 2,000 years since Jesus Christ's birth, we are looking at six days, or 6,000 years.

Note Matthew 17:1-3: "And, after six days, Jesus taketh Peter, James, and John his brother, and bringeth them up into a high mountain apart, and was transfigured before them; and his face did shine like the sun, and his raiment was as white as the light. And, behold, there appeared unto them Moses and Elijah talking with him."

This is a view of the raptured Church. Again, Moses represents the "translated dead" and Elijah, the "translated living." This vision symbolizes the "first resurrection" that Revelation 20:5-6 talks about.

Astoundingly, the entire Bible is a prophecy of the First and Second Advents of Jesus Christ. From the creation of Adam to Abraham to Christ to Lazarus to the transfiguration of Jesus, there is a numerical uniformity that simply cannot be dismissed as coincidental. In order for metaphorical allusions to gel with actual years and days in the manner as Biblically presented, everything that appears in the Scriptures must be there by divine appointment. It's an insult to the kingdom of God's *Central Intelligence Agency* to entertain the idea that these events and their numerical framing are merely chance occurrences.

Drawn from Ezekiel 9, there is no less a divinely appointed "proofreader" clothed in linen with a writer's inkhorn by his side that's looking directly over the shoulder of everyone blessed to present the truth of Jesus Christ in written form.

In truth, Jesus Christ instructed his church to "watch." Certainly, it is wise to believe that he is doing some watching also.

17 THIRD WATCH

"And he cometh, and findeth them sleeping, and saith unto Peter, Simon, sleepest thou? couldest not thou watch one hour?"
— Mark 14:37

Continuing "the watch," according to Revelation 20:4-6, there is a thousand-year period that immediately follows the first resurrection. Those who are to be transfigured with Christ, as symbolized by the appearance of Moses and Elijah, "shall be priests of God and of Christ, and shall reign with him a thousand years." Those who do not make the cut "lived not again until the thousand years were finished." Since Revelation 20:4-6 is indicative of the fact that humankind's seventh millennium involvement has already been divinely determined, just how far into the twenty-first century do you believe life as we now live it will stretch? Isn't 21 equally divisible by 7? Because the number 7 symbolizes perfection and mankind (as in the generations of Adam) has already crossed the threshold of the seventh millennium, are we all living on borrowed time? Doesn't 21 divided by 7 equal the "trinity?"

Pausing for a moment of clarification, "perfection" as used in the Bible is a semantic drift. The KJV was published in 1611. Over the course of 406 years, word meanings have shifted. Perfect to King James and his boys doesn't translate the same now. Instead of using the word "perfect," the word today might be "together."

Now, together is also a semantic drift. For example, take Matthew 5:48: "Be ye therefore perfect, even as your Father which is in heaven is perfect."

Can any human being be as perfect as God? Obviously, perfect as used is misapplied as we understand it today. But if we wrote that same verse today by saying, "Be ye therefore together, even as your Father which is in heaven is together" some folks would know exactly what is meant.

Now, changing perfect to "together" is not an attempt to be hip or cool or to make the Bible so-called "Living." It's just a matter of addressing the problem some have with the misapprehended concept of perfection as expressed in Scripture. While God knows no man or woman can be perfect, human imperfection is no excuse for not attempting to get your act together. Running the line "*Nobody's perfect*" in the aftermath of a screw-up is not a perfect defense.

Genesis 6:9 reads, "Noah was a just man and perfect in his generations." Well, Genesis 9:21 finds Noah drunk and buck naked laid up in his tent. Sound like perfection to you?

The number seven symbolizes "perfection" when perfection is interpreted as being "together" when viewed as synonymous with complete There are seven days in a week. When all seven are "together" what you have is a "complete" week.

There are seven primary colors in a rainbow. With respect to the basic principles of physics, that rainbow is complete.

When being "together" is understood as having "it" together, what is meant by "Be ye perfect" is better understood. Being a "just man" is what made Noah "together" or "perfect" in his generations. Having his head "spiritually together" made him "complete." It allowed God to employ the fullness of His grace to fill in any blanks and makeup any deficits.

Having knowledge of God coupled with faith in God makes one "perfect" in God even when one is burdened by imperfections.

The significance of Revelation 20:4-6 is the fact that there will be a millennial Sabbath of rest. The righteous will leave with Christ; the unrighteous will be dead; Satan and his demons will be imprisoned on earth alone. And since it was "after six days" that a vision of the first resurrection was witnessed, it is after the close of the sixth millennium that such a vision will come to pass.

Now, reflecting back on the previous chapter, it's significant to note that Matthew 17:1 doesn't read "on" the sixth day, it says "after." By pinpointing six as a time frame, this event did not reach a day eight in order for it to happen. After six days means the happening was on day seven.

In Matthew 25:1-13, Jesus spoke a parable about ten virgins who went out to meet the bridegroom. Verse 6 reads: "And at midnight there was a cry made, Behold, the bridegroom cometh; go ye out to meet him." Here, Jesus does a Wilson Pickett. He waits till the midnight hour to return for His Church, which begins the third watch of the night. Remember, the third watch symbolizes another 1,000-year installment of time after the birth of Christ. Because humankind has already been on earth 6,000 years, the third watch crosses the threshold of a brand-new millennium. Unequivocally, Jesus is telling His Church to look for him at the beginning of the Seventh Millennium.

Likewise, in Luke 12:35-40, Jesus told His disciples that he was like a man returning to His servants after having attended a wedding. Verse 38 reads: "And if he shall come in the second watch, or come in the third watch, and find them so, blessed are those servants."

Now, why doesn't Jesus refer to the first or fourth watch? Ponder the fact that it was not until 1611 (the middle of the Sixth Millennium) that the Bible was translated into the English language. Since there was not any widespread circulation of the Bible during the period AD 100 through AD 1000, what would have been the purpose of Jesus admonishing people to watch for His return during the Fifth Millennium? Remember, "faith cometh by hearing, and hearing by the word of God" (Romans 10:17).

How could human beings have faith in "hearing" if the printed Word could not be heard? Remember, even though there were preachers of God's Word as far back as Adam himself, not until the reading of God's Word did a comprehensive knowledge of God's Word begin to span the globe. The most casual student of history and the study of Western Civilization is aware of the fact that the Dark Ages were so-called mainly because the Church of Rome had restricted the Bible's public exposure. Only the religious hierarchy of the Roman Catholic Church was allowed to have copies of the Vulgate, which is a Latin version of the Bible.

The Dark Ages covered the period AD 476 to the end of the tenth century.

When the Apostle Paul wrote: "For the mystery of iniquity doth already work," his words were penned circa AD 51. It was iniquity working overtime that kept the written Word of God publicly obscure. Consequently, the testimony of Jesus, which is the "spirit of prophecy," did not draw attention to any "first watch" watching for the simple reason that very few people would have seen God's Word. Since Revelation 1:3 says: "Blessed is he that readeth," you simply can't be blessed in reading what isn't written.

With regard to Jesus not admonishing anybody to look for him during the "fourth watch" or Eighth Millennium is obvious. Jesus is not coming to save anybody's soul after the expiration of the Seventh Millennium. Again, Revelation 20:7 tells the world exactly what God's plans are after the "thousand years" of the seventh millennium have expired.

There are only two passages in the entire Bible that mention the "fourth watch of the night." They are Matthew 14:25 and Mark 6:48. Both of these verses indicate Jesus came to His disciples "walking upon the sea."

Consider this very carefully. What does the Bible metaphorically indicate the sea represents? Reflect back upon Jude 13's "raging waves of the sea, foaming out their own shame; wandering stars, to whom is reserved the blackness of darkness for ever." And then reconsider Job 38:8's sea waves being shut up with "bars and doors."

Do you think that it was just a chance occurrence that Jesus went to His disciples "in the fourth watch of the night" and the sea waves were tumultuous?

Note Revelation 20:7-10: "And when the thousand years are expired, Satan shall be loosed out of his prison. And shall go out to deceive the nations which are in the four quarters of the earth…to gather them together to battle; the number of whom is as the sand of the sea."

Notice the place from which Satan is "loosed." It's a prison. And where were Job's sea waves shut up? Behind bars. And when are Satan and his navy released from their incarceration? After the one thousand years of the Seventh Millennium.

This 1,000-year period is the Sabbath millennium symbolized by the third watch. It is after the thousand years of the third watch have ended that Jesus comes back to earth for the third time. The Third Advent of Christ is during the fourth watch. But again, this fourth watch Third Advent of Jesus is not to save souls; it is to destroy them. And Revelation 20:9-15 makes that point painfully clear.

Drawing from Revelation 20:8, Satan gathers the nations together in an effort to fight Christ. Here is where we find the battle of Armageddon. And who are these soldiers of Satan, "the number of whom is as the sand of the sea"? Unfortunately, they are participants in the second resurrection. They are people who won't even realize they have been dead for more than 1,000 years. These are the souls who will be resurrected by Jesus Christ at his Third Advent. These are those who have been a long, long, long time dead. So, the idea that there's consciousness in death or some kinda "limbo" just doesn't fly.

Revelation 1:7:

> "Behold, he cometh with clouds; and every eye shall see him, and they *also* which pierced him: and all kindreds of the earth shall wail because of him."

This is a prophecy of the Third Advent, not the Second. Revelation 20:6 reads, "Blessed and holy *is* he that hath part in the first resurrection: on such the second death hath no power, but they shall be priests of God and of Christ, and shall reign with him a thousand years."

Are the Roman soldiers who crucified Jesus Christ blessed and holy? They won't see him coming in the clouds during the Second Advent. Since they "pierced him" they have another thousand years to stay dead before they see anything. The bottom line, there's a second resurrection for those who didn't make it. And this is the "they" who belong to the "they said" club. They are the ones who will be gathered together for the battle of Armageddon. They will be gathered by Satan himself once they have been resurrected by Jesus himself.

However, their resurrection is not to fight against God, it's to stand in judgment. It's for them to see with their own eyes that they got it all wrong.

But by being a willing passenger on Satan's ride, they see for themselves that they've come to an eternal dead end. The thrill of the roller coaster has rolled to a dead stop.

Indicative of Revelation 20:11-15, it's all about standing in judgment for unrepentant sins. Members of the "*They Said Club*" will be so confused as to what's happening, they will probably think Satan is Jesus and Christ is the devil. Only through one final power play of deception will Lucifer, as Satan, as the devil stage a last-ditch effort against Michael, as Jesus, as God.

Who will prevail? The actions of Christ have always sent Satan a not so subtle message. Remember when Jesus went to His disciples during the fourth watch? Both Matthew and Mark say he went "walking upon the sea." What does it mean when you walk on somebody, or on something that's a representation of them?

Back in the day when Terrell Owens did his thing on the Dallas Star, what was the Dallas Cowboys' response? Despite T.O.'s explanation, they got the message.

The Bible cannot make it any more apparent that Jesus is going to walk all over Satan and stand on his "stars" once the Seventh Millennium has ended. And with that thought in mind, important is the realization that Peter "walked on the water" in the same manner as Christ. Unquestionably, Peter's walk was symbolic of the fact that all genuine saints of God will thrash the princedom of Satan too. In retribution for all the pain and suffering Satan has sponsored, the redeemed will join Jesus in a T.O. moment that will not be answered in any type of significant retaliatory manner.

The game will be over. The fact that the Bible refers to angels as stars and it was a "star" that Owens stood on is more than just a metaphysical coincidence. It's sends a message to all who are willing to receive it when applied to the thrill of victory and the agony of defeat in a cosmic sense.

By process of elimination, the second and third watches are the only ones that have practical applicability to the Second Coming of Christ. After the expiration of the Sixth Millennium, the Scriptures are remarkably consistent in directing attention toward the Second Advent. Consider Hosea 6:2: "After two days will he revive us; in the third day he will raise us up, and we shall live in his sight."

What does the "third day" represent? Flashback to that earlier reference made by Christ in Luke 12:35-40: "Let your loins be girded about, and your lights burning; And ye yourselves like unto men that wait for their Lord, when he will return from the wedding; that when he cometh and knocketh, they may open unto him immediately."

Note John 2:1: "And the third day there was a marriage in Cana, of Galilee; and the mother of Jesus was there. And both Jesus was called, and his disciples, to the marriage." Just as the "bridegroom cometh" at the midnight hour, Jesus Christ came to the "marriage in Cana" at a time that's prophetically synonymous.

Soberly ponder the fact that John 2:1 asserts that Jesus came to the wedding on the third day. And Luke 12:36 admonishes being ready to meet the Lord when he "returns from the wedding." That being the case, on what day do you think Jesus is telling folks to be prepared to meet him? Since weddings are not slumber parties, wouldn't it be reasonable to deduce that Christ would "return from the wedding" on the same day he attended the wedding?

Throughout the entire Bible, the prophetic consistency of day and watch, and the metaphorical analogies employing such are impeccable. Absolutely unbeatable is the fact that the third day symbolizes the Seventh Millennium and the Second Advent of Christ.

With such being the case, it is readily apparent why Jesus was adamant about His resurrection also being on the third day. The resurrection of Christ had to represent the resurrection of the righteous during the Seventh Millennium. If the Resurrection of Jesus had been on a Sunday, it would have been on the fourth day. The fourth day would have prophetically symbolized the fourth watch – the Eighth Millennium – after seven days instead of "after six days."

Consequently, obvious is the fact that the princedom of Satan wants the world watching a day late and a dollar short.

Therefore, when examining the prophetic import of the third day with reference to watch, the same has applicability to everything associated with the Seventh Millennium. And of course, when looking at the prophetic connection between third day and Seventh Millennium, what could be more associative than the divine command to "Remember the Sabbath?"

Unfortunate is the fact that few Christians realize when God says, remember the seventh day Sabbath, he is also saying: Watch for the

Second Advent of Jesus Christ. If one realized the prophetic link between the Biblical references to the third day and Seventh Millennium, one would realize that the actual seventh day Sabbath (Saturday) is also a weekly reminder of Christ's return during the Seventh/Sabbath Millennium. The Seventh Day Sabbath in name has dual applicability to "day" being a 1,000-year period.

Imbedded in Genesis 2:2-3, as well as in the middle of the *Ten Commandments* is a cloaked prophecy that points directly to the return of Christ. By following the Sabbath instructions on a weekly basis with respect to the actual seventh day, those who do so are reminded that their "redemption draweth nigh" from week to week; not month-to-month, year-to-year, or millennium-to-millennium.

Subsequently, remembering the seventh day Saturday Sabbath keeps the return of Jesus real. It prevents the Christian belief of a Savior's Advent from being conceptually pushed to some futuristic point that would invariably give the mind subliminal license to be lax in pursuit of personal salvation. Indeed, the "Sabbath was made for man" because from the very beginning it has always been about mankind's seventh millennial rescue and subsequent rest. And this is the dual implication of Hebrews 4:9: "There remaineth therefore a rest to the people of God." In addition to the weekly Sabbath, the ultimate Sabbath rest remaining is seventh millennial (Revelation 20:4).

When understood from a prophetic perspective, it is logical why the princedom of Satan wants spiritual attention focused on Sunday. When looked at prophetically, Sunday physically follows Saturday, the seventh day of the week, just as the Eighth Millennium follows the Seventh. Therefore prophetically, Sunday symbolically represents the Eighth Millennium!

Next, consider the powerful imagery provided by Esther 5:1: "Now it came to pass on the third day, that Esther put on her royal apparel, and stood in the inner court of the king's house, over against the king's house; and the king sat upon his royal throne in the royal house, over against the gate of the house."

When viewed within the context of Daniel 7:9-14 and Revelation 19:11-21, doesn't Esther's behavior parallel the actions of Jesus as he stands before God, who is called the *Ancient of Days*? From Esther's royal apparel to the royal attire worn by Christ, the symbolism is also irrefutable. And critical to this irrefutability is the fact that Esther, just like Jesus, does her thing on that prophetic third day.

But let's return to the story of Gideon. To say the least, the weaponry of Gideon was totally unconventional. In one hand there was a trumpet. In the other, there was a pitcher containing only a lamp. Judges 7:16 reads: "And he divided the three hundred men into three companies, and he put a trumpet in every man's hand, with empty pitchers, and lamps within the pitchers." Based on the inferences which may be drawn from Matthew 5:14-16, 25:1-9 and Philippians 2:15, a "lamp" represents the "light" which is reflected by God's Holy Spirit. Since a pitcher is a vessel and a vessel is connotative of the human body (as derived from 2 Timothy 2:21), Gideon's lamps and pitchers symbolized the physical bodies of all true believers. Such symbolism is a representation of Christ's true Church. And the trumpet in the hand of each soldier is significant because trumpets will herald Jesus' arrival back on earth (1 Thessalonians 4:16).

Most significant, however, is the timeframe established by Judges 7:19: "So Gideon, and the hundred men who were with him, came unto the outside of the camp in the beginning of the middle watch; and they had but newly set the watch; and they blew the trumpets, and broke the pitchers that were in their hands." Again, the scripture indicates Gideon and his men positioned themselves outside the enemy camp in the beginning of the middle watch. Once more, according to the Jewish day there are four night watches, so there is no precise "middle watch." What, then, is meant by this term?

Reexamining the passage, we find that the first watch was in Judges 7:13 when Gideon arrived to survey the Midianites. Verse 15 says after Gideon's reconnaissance mission was completed he returned to the "host of Israel." This means that during his absence from the enemy camp another sentry was posted. Hence, we find the second watch instituted. Verse 16 indicates Gideon then divided the Israelite army into the three companies and went back to the outskirts of the enemy camp, relieving those who had kept the second watch. Subsequently, this relief force was now the third watch, or what Judges 7:19 refers to as the "middle watch."

Now, watch what happens. The Bible says at the beginning of the watch, which they had newly set, they blew the trumpets and broke the pitchers exposing the lamps inside. Based on 1 Corinthians 15:35-54, at the time of Christ's Second Advent the resurrected dead and the translated living are "changed" at the sound of the trumpet. This change, according to the Scriptures, involves the physical body. Those who are raised and changed in the "twinkling of an eye" will have a spiritual body that is celestial.

The Apostle Paul, writing in 1 Corinthians 15:41, compares a celestial body with the glory of the sun, the moon, and the stars. In other words, the resurrected righteous will appear as "lamps of light." Is there any doubt that the blowing of Gideon's trumpets, and the breaking of the pitchers, and the exposing of the lamps inside are symbolic of the "corruptible putting on incorruption, and the mortal putting on immortality"?

Irrefutably, here we have a symbolic representation of the Second Advent of Jesus Christ. And again, the time to watch for His coming is at the "beginning of the third watch." More telling than any other scriptures cited, the story of Gideon establishes the fact that the trumpet shall sound when that third watch is "newly set."

But, pausing there for a minute or two, the question to be pondered, physically speaking, is why did the blowing of the trumpets break the pitchers? Well, here again is a scientific application. In addition to the obvious being obvious, the obvious being that the hand of God is involved, so also were those Dizzy Gillespie lips!

Back it up to Joshua 6:1-27. Hadn't Gideon and company been there before? Didn't they know by virtue of oral history what time it was? When reading how Joshua *fit the battle of Jericho* it's imperative to note that the instructions of God are to put the trumpet players "before the ark." This placement is pointed out at least three times. These trumpet players were Levites.

And just why was it important for the Ark of the Covenant to be behind the trumpets? Well, next time you go to a concert, why are the amplifiers placed behind the musicians? Have you ever seen musicians on stage with their amplifiers placed in front of them!

The ark had "juice." The ark was a power source. Scientifically speaking, some kinda way, the trumpets were "hooked" into the ark as amplifier.

If you've ever been to a concert where musical instruments are connected to amplifiers, you know perfectly well what time it is. Subsequently, given a situation that requires the employment of God's hands and Dizzy's lips, the trumpets were blown to the degree and extent that the decibel meter registered off the scale. This is why Joshua 6:9 reads: "and the rereward came after the ark." The rereward are the rest of the troops. The "rereward" were "buckled" (Jeremiah 46:3). They just weren't "buckled up" to ride in front of the ark.

The intensity of the sound waves emanating from the trumpets amplified by the ark was able to find the Jericho wall's natural resonance or "sweet spot." Everybody knows when you find that sweet spot, things will buckle and fall to the floor.

Resonance is the natural frequency at which an object readily vibrates. Hitting the same tone as the natural frequency of the wall stones induced vibration in the stones. However, the trumpet notes alone, scientifically, were not the only factor. Volume is important. The louder the sound, the more violent the vibrations will be. When the sound waves were focused on the wall by the ark like a laser and reached an intensified level that the stones could not withstand, "*the walls come tumbling down.*"

Obviously, the priests who blew the trumpets and the "armed men" or bodyguards who "went before" the priests were divinely protected from the sound waves. Again, the priests were Levites. Exodus 32:28-29 establishes that it was "the children of Levi" who had been consecrated to do a special work for the kingdom of God. For all we know, the "armed men" may also have been "children of Levi" who were not active members of the priesthood but were deployed as active members of the military. Joshua was a Levite as well as a soldier who could say a prayer and then administer some serious hurt (Joshua 1:1-9).

In the case of Gideon, even though the priests and the ark aren't mentioned, the trumpets are. Given the fact that the people of Gideon's time could reflect on how it went down during Joshua's time, they had a foundation of faith. When Gideon gave his men a trumpet to blow, not one of them blew him off. They went to do battle by faith and not by sight because they had already seen what those trumpets can do through the eyes and ears of those who "went before."

Likewise, today when there is a firm foundation of faith, we don't have to see either Jesus or Peter "walk on water" to know for a fact that we can do so as well metaphorically.

> "For verily I say unto you, That whosoever shall say unto this mountain, Be thou removed, and be thou cast into the sea; and shall not doubt in his heart, but shall believe that those things which he saith shall come to pass; he shall have whatsoever he saith. Therefore I say unto you, What things soever ye desire, when ye pray, believe that ye receive them, and ye shall have them."
> — Mark 11:23-24

So, when considering a scientific application in terms of sound wave amplification and resonant frequency displacement, don't get it twisted. The physics involved neither diminishes the power of an Almighty God nor does it explain it away. Again, the laws of physics are just as much the laws of God as the *Ten Commandments*. The kingdom of God has no reason outside the extraordinary to circumnavigate laws already created by God to govern the universe. Where rules of law are established, even when it comes to the kingdom Heaven, if they are broken at random, on a whim, for convenience sake, and unnecessarily, the end result is confusion. That's why the *Adventures of Superman* cannot venture off a television or movie theater screen.

Let's consider the Second Advent of Christ from a monetary perspective. Did Jesus ever use something as practical as money to symbolize the time of His earthly return?

In the parable of the Good Samaritan as presented in Luke 10:30-37, Jesus tells the story of a man who is accosted by thieves. The Good Samaritan, who symbolizes Christ, helps the man who is left for dead on the side of the road. The victim is representative of all humankind. The thieves are Satan and his posse of demons. Luke 10:35 states: "And on the morrow, when he departed, he took out two pence, and gave them to the host, and said unto him, Take care of him; and whatever thou spendest more, when I come again, I will repay thee."

A "pence," as described in the above verse, was one of several measures of money equivalent to one day's wage. Two pence, therefore, equals two days' wages. That means the value of the money that the Good Samaritan gave the innkeeper was just enough to take care of a two day stay at the inn. Obviously, this means the parable's "inn" has to symbolize planet earth. And the Good Samaritan, as Christ, simply provides enough currency to cover a period that symbolizes no more than 2,000 years!

Using the same monetary symbolism, the sixth chapter of Revelation describes a heavenly creature that announces a black horse whose rider holds a pair of balances. When examining verse 6, we read: "And I heard a voice in the midst of the four living creatures say, A measure of wheat for a penny, and three measures of barley for a penny; and see thou hurt not the oil and the wine."

What did the Samaritan pour into the wounds of the man he aided? Wasn't it oil and wine?

What did the five wise virgins of Matthew 25 carry in their vessels with their lamps? And, at the wedding in Cana, what was the water turned into?

Is there any question that the "oil and the wine" represent the respective indwelling Holy Spirit and the grace of God? As long as an individual's body or vessel is host to God's Spirit and grace, that individual can never be hurt with everlasting death. And, in light of that thought, just ponder the meaning of Matthew 10:28 and Luke 12:4.

The focus of the Revelation 6:6 pronouncements are on the "oil and wine" because it is God's Spirit and grace which together provide a formula that fuels the lamps of the righteous. Symbolically speaking, all who desire to inherit eternal life must carry lamps that are lit by the Holy Spirit. Any individual carrying a lamp that has no light, by implication, does not reflect God's Spirit. If that individual does not reflect the light of God's Spirit, that individual has rejected God's grace. Since it is Death that rides the "pale horse" of Revelation 6:8, it is the rider of the pale horse who is instructed not to "hurt the oil and the wine."

Recall Job 2:6. Doesn't the Lord tell Satan not to kill him?

Death is ultimately a spiritual reality that "is in thine hand" just as God told Satan. Death was introduced into the world through the Garden of Eden at the hand of Satan. It is connotative of spiritual darkness. If an individual does not reflect a spiritual light that can only be fueled by the grace of God's Holy Spirit, Death will inevitably consume that individual alive. In the middle of the word death is the word "eat." Therefore, implicit is the reasoning that what death does not see it devours. Etymologically, physically, and spiritually d-eat-h chews and swallows its victims. It literally "eats" them up alive. Just as darkness in terms of the absence of light engulfs everything covered by it, the same physical reality applies. Only by carrying a turned-on flashlight or striking a match does darkness step back, get out of the way, and leave you alone.

When the command is given to "hurt not the oil and the wine," spiritually speaking, the oil burning in the lamp is the only substance that can be seen in spiritual darkness. This explains why five of the virgins of Matthew 25 were labeled foolish. They could not leave with Jesus because they were void of God's Spirit. It was impossible for them to be seen in the darkness where spiritual death is lurking and so pervasive.

By the time these particular virgins of the eternal realm returned with a rushed knowledge of Spiritual truth that was probably purchased as books, DVDs and CDs, Jesus had already come and gone. And as a direct consequence of their previous procrastination and utter indifference the result of rejecting God's grace regarding eternal matters, they were left in the darkness to be devoured by the rider of that pale horse.

The two pennies of verse 6 are thereby symbolic of the fact that those who are embodied with the Spirit (oil) and grace (wine) of God will not be hurt by the "second death" because Jesus will receive them at the time of His Second Advent. Given the fact that the two pennies are referenced two verses before Death, the resurrected righteous and the translated living are evacuated from this planet prior to the pale horse's arrival.

Finally, relative Revelation 6:6, let's consider Matthew 3:12 and Luke 3:17. What will be gathered into the granary of God? Isn't it the wheat? And isn't barley also a grain to be stored?

Symbolically, the "wheat" and the "barley" represent those who will be saved at the Second Coming of Christ. Quite appropriately, the word "measure," by dictionary definition, is "anything determined by a standard." Since two pennies are equivalent to two days' wages (which are the equivalence of 2,000 years), Revelation 6:6 conclusively points to the Seventh Millennium reality of Jesus Christ's return.

But an even more compelling example of the Bible's use of currency to exemplify the Second Advent of Christ is found in the final verses of Matthew 17. There is where a royal tax collector who required the payment of tribute approaches Jesus and Peter. In the first century, the most common coin for the payment of "tribute" was the Roman denarius. In appearance, it was a silver coin about two-thirds the size of an American quarter. It was worth about sixteen cents and represented an ordinary day's wage for a common laborer. Since Jesus instructed Peter to make a payment that covered the two of them, it may be reasonably inferred that a day's wage each was the required assessment, i.e. two days.

In the Words of Christ: "Notwithstanding, lest we should offend them, go thou to the sea, and cast an hook, and take up the fish that first cometh up. And when thou hast opened its mouth, thou shalt find a piece of money; that take, and give unto them for me and thee."

Given the fact that Peter was to find a "piece of money" that would be sufficient to cover two grown men, rather than the Roman denarius, the coin that came out of the fish was probably the Greek didrachma, which is a double drachma. Coined locally, the didrachma was typically used as tribute money for payment of Temple tax. Keeping the above information in mind, consider the profound spiritual symbolism inherent in this fish story.

First, there is the fish that "first cometh up." According to Habakkuk 1:14-15 and Mark 1:17, fish represent all people who are redeemed by Jesus Christ. By being presented with that fact, whom do you think the "fish that first cometh up" would symbolize?

Of course, those redeemed righteous who will take part in the first resurrection (1 Thessalonians 4:16-17).

Second, the fish that comes up "first" has a coin in its mouth that's worth two days' wages. This creature could have had the coin lodged in its intestines. Rather, the coin was found in the mouth of the fish. Symbolically, anything coming out of a mouth is essentially speaking. Since the coin represented two days' wages, or 2,000 years, what was that fish saying with regard to the first resurrection? Well, consider the fact that Jesus instructed Peter to take the money "and give unto them for me and thee." Here, the Lord God of heaven is symbolically identifying with His Church.

But a fish story that's just as phenomenal comes from the 21st chapter of John's Gospel. That's the one about the all-night fishing expedition that resulted in empty nets. And the aspect of this story which grasps the interest with respect to a message that points to the time of Christ's Second Advent is illustrated by the eighth verse: "And the other disciples came in a little ship (for they were not far from land, but as it were two hundred cubits), dragging the net with fish."

Keeping in mind that the redeemed righteous who participate in the first resurrection are symbolized as being fish, just how far were those real fish away from actually reaching Christ? The scripture says the net was dragged 200 cubits.

How does the measurement of 200 cubits fit into this picture? Look at 1 Kings 7. Here we have an account of Solomon building his palace. Verse 24 reads: "And under the brim of it round about there were knops compassing it ten in a cubit, compassing the sea round about; the knops were cast in two rows, when it was cast." A "knop" is a knob, as in a door or drawer knob. When Solomon designed his home, under the guidance of the Holy Spirit, he placed ten of those ornaments in a space of one cubit. Subsequently, in one cubit we have a multiple of ten.

So, do the math. With both 1 Kings 7:24 and John 21:1-8 both using "the sea" and "the cubit" as parallel points of reference, how many cubits away from Jesus Christ was that net full of fish? Applying Solomon's design to John's fishing expedition and viewing both in relationship to Peter's tribute money, two hundred cubits also represent 2,000 years.

Coincidence, or is somebody trying to tell us something? Do you really think any one of the Gospel writers had the skills to manipulate all of these events, phrases, parables, and numbers in order to achieve such literary and arithmetic consistency with respect to prophesying the Second Advent of Jesus Christ? Or do you seriously believe that King James and his boyz 'n the woods of Europe got together one evening over a barrel of Crown Royal and dilly-dillied all these numbers to do what they do?

As 2 Peter 3:4 states, it is under the influence of Satan that men ask the question: "Where is the promise of his coming? For since the fathers fell asleep, all things continue as they were from the beginning of creation." In that regard, John 14:3-4 finds Jesus telling His disciples not to stress, that they already know the answer to such a question.

If you can't do the arithmetic with respect to 200 x 10 cubits, Joshua 3:4 does it for you: "Yet there shall be a space between you and it, about two thousand cubits by measure; come not near unto it, that ye may know the way by which ye must go."

But lastly, the prophetic backstory involving Lazarus' demands a one more time again look.

John 11:6-7, speaking of Jesus, says: "When he had heard, therefore, that he was sick, he abode two days still in the same place where he was. Then, after that, saith he to his disciples, Let us go into Judaea again." Now, consider the fact that the Bible makes it a point to mention that Jesus stayed where he was for "two days." Again, this is the symbolic representation of the 2,000 years that have transpired since Jesus was born into the world. After those two days or 2,000 years, the scripture says he went into Judaea "again."

Lazarus lived in a town called Bethany? Why doesn't Jesus simply say: *"Let us go to Bethany?"* But instead of saying that or something similar, the point is plainly made that Christ is not going to a town, but to a region.

Of course, Jesus said what he said because the business trip to Judaea was bigger than Bethany. Specifying a region as opposed to a town is a symbolic reference to earth. And the going again implies you've been before. It's a symbolic reference to the Second Advent.

Added to the previous chapter, just ponder the consistency of the numbers and how they are incorporated in support of God's perspective on time from Creation to Transfiguration. Jesus not only allowed Lazarus to lay dead four days, the Bible makes it a point to point out that two of those four found Jesus waiting in place. Therein, 4+2 or 6, the number associated with mankind's salvation (John 11:6 and 39) is the same number associated with mankind's resurrection (Matthew 17:1), is the same number associated with mankind's creation (Genesis 1:26-31).

Do you think it all coincidental? Or, do you think somebody is telling you something!

Also, consider if Jesus stayed where he was "two days," he didn't set out for Bethany until the third day. According to John 11:18, Bethany wasn't that far. It was only "fifteen furlongs off," which is exactly 1.8 miles. Consequently, when Christ left where he "abode," it didn't take him long to get where he was going.

Again, a person normally walks at a leisurely pace of about three miles per hour on the average. And since John 11:9 asks the question, "Are there not twelve hours in a day?" with reference to walking, it is a Biblical calculation that a person could walk thirty-six miles from sunup to sundown. In view of the fact that both the walking distance and walking hours are specified as factors in direct respect to something Jesus said (John 11:9) and did (John 11:18), a 1.8-mile walk is five percent of a 36 mile walking day. And since 1,000 years is prophetically equivalent to one day, what is five percent of 1,000?

How far into the Seventh Millennium before the return of Jesus Christ? Go figure.

18 THE TEMPLE OF DOOM

"And the temple of God was opened in heaven, and there was seen in his temple the ark of his testament: and there were lightnings, and voices, and thunderings, and an earthquake, and great hail"
— *REVELATION 11:19*

Say it one more time; the Bible is a book that explains itself. You don't need a PhD in Sunday school to understand all that's written from Genesis to Revelation. Psalms 111:10 reads: "The fear of the Lord is the beginning of wisdom: a good understanding have all they that do his commandments."

Psalms 119:33-34 echoes: "Teach me, O Lord, the way of thy statutes; and I shall keep it unto the end. Give me understanding, and I shall keep thy law; yea, I shall observe it with my whole heart." Keeping is in this context at least trying. Matthew 21:46 tells all that Jesus knows the "spirit indeed *is* willing, but the flesh *is* weak." The problemo is when you stop thinking about doing the right thing. It's when you throw your hands in the air and you really don't care.

Implicit in these two passages is the proposition that when there's a commitment to at least trying to do the Will of God, persistence will sooner or later pay off. It's that if at first you don't succeed, try again is what you do. It's axiomatic; *"Nothing beats failure but a try."*

A heartfelt commitment to God's moral law (The Ten Commandments) is fundamental to grasping and sustaining a knowledge-based understanding of soul-saving present truth. Having the heart takes you farther than having the head. If your heart isn't in it, no matter how hard you try to wrap your head around it (whatever it is), it's not going to work. Since there is a correlation between wisdom, understanding, and doing God's commandments, many prevent the Holy Spirit from taking them to the next level in their Christian experience as a result of having personally made tradition a controlling force.

Consider for a moment an airline employer/employee relationship. If you were a jet pilot, would you hire a copilot to sit next to you who is challenged by a fear of heights and speed? Mark 7:9 holds: "ye reject the commandment of God, that ye may keep your own tradition." And with applicability to God as jet pilot and us as copilot, can we seriously expect to be transported to heavenly heights if we can't perform at the plane we're currently on?

A copilot who is comfortable in a "traditional" seat to the extent that further preparation and study will be neither explored nor even entertained is going to stay either in or below the clouds. If a man or woman professing to know Christ is willing to reject God's game plan in preference of their own, they will never be all that God has desired them to be. This is why Jeremiah 12:5 maintains: "If thou hast run with the footmen, and they have wearied thee, then how canst thou contend with horses?"

Jesus is not a God of stagnant customs and traditions. He is a force that's always on the cutting edge of every moment. "I Am That I Am" is always in the present tense. This means "Jesus Christ the same yesterday, and today, and forever" will always be current and forever in the present. How is it that humankind can be on the cutting edge of science, technology, and medicine, but lag so far behind when it comes to matters of the heart? Spirituality is a matter of the heart.

When you tell homeboy or girl, *"I'm feelin' you,"* it can be said a thousand miles away. Feeling a person spiritually requires ESP – *Extra Soul Perception.* It has nothing to do with sight, smell, hearing, taste, and touch.

While the accounts of Daniel in the lion's den, along with a host of other Biblical stories provide ageless inspirational messages, they are simply not sources of "present truth" when preached in a context that does not keep pace with God's here and now. Church congregations that aren't "feelin'" their pastor or a visiting preacher probably have nothing to do with intellect, but everything to do with matters of the heart. If you can't speak to the heart, the head ain't hearing whatever you have to say.

If Jesus came to town today, would He be riding on a donkey or in a motor driven vehicle? If car, plane, and/or train are most plausible, should we expect anything less as such applies to God's revelations? Seminaries that are lost in the sixties (that's A.D. 60s) fail to realize that when

Hebrews 13:8 says, "Jesus Christ the same yesterday, and today, and forever," truth is a constant; present truth isn't.

Human beings are mortal. Strapped with mortality as opposed to having immortality requires living in the moment. The person you were at the beginning read of this page is not the same person you are now. You have aged by a number of seconds. Those seconds become minutes, hours, days, weeks, and years. God is immortal. Therefore, the truths of God will always be the same. The truths of human beings won't because they can be debunked through a process called learning.

Did you think Santa Claus was the truth? How about Columbus discovering America, or George Washington and that cherry tree? But maybe that's not the best analogy if that's still your truth!

Looking back over the years, honestly ask yourself has your learning been education or indoctrination? Regardless, the point is the so-called truths you knew K-12 maybe aren't the same now if you no longer accept them as true. And what you didn't know when you were in elementary school that you now accept as true isn't new truth; it was around then just as it's around now. As a kid you just had to catch up. Catching up with truth as a youngster is no different than catching up with it as an adult. Again, it's called "present truth" because it's what you discover to presently be true.

Let's revisit the case of the cheating spouse or significant other as an example. What's up with all the hostility and tears once you find out? You're mad and in tears because you were clueless. You finally caught up with present truth. Present truth didn't catch up with you. Hadn't they always been the drop drawers ho you didn't know?

Applied to Biblical knowledge, some people are comfortable with the knowledge that they don't have. They are comfortable with cluelessness. Folks who don't get it because they don't want to get it are ever ready to tell another soul what they woulda, shoulda, coulda. What the problem is, they wanna keep it real with everyone but themselves.

Reapplied to carnal knowledge, who hasn't heard of someone saying, *"Well, as long as they don't bring anything home to me?"*

Well, what can be said of such a compromising, degrading, and self-deprecating approach other than, "*Humph?*"

Living in the past denies the Holy Spirit opportunity to "*bring it on home*" in the present for purposes of guiding the future. While tomorrow in a mortal sense isn't promised, yesterday is gone forever. What's present is the only place to literally and figuratively find yourself. And if you don't find yourself dealing in "present truth," you are doomed to losing yourself futuristically.

Because the Bible as a whole is a book of prophecy, the numbers thus far spotlighted reveal a prophetic purpose. When research finds a design on a particular number and the Bible itself reveals the same design where the same discovery can be made by use of pencil and paper, or calculator, then essentially the Kingdom of God has made it plain for all to see. The Bible's divine authorship is established beyond both reasonable and unreasonable doubt.

Previously, the significance of the number 46 was brought to view. Recalling its significance is the purpose of this chapter. The indisputable facts that the Jerusalem temple took 46 years to build and the human body temple has 46 chromosomes genetically assigned is compelling.

DNA (deoxyribonucleic acid) is the blueprint of life, and the codes for the structural and enzymatic proteins that make up every cell in the human body are packaged into those 46 units. Definitely, the number 46 is an impeccably suitable genetic/numerical descriptor of humankind. And it's one God conceptually placed in the Bible some 1,815 years prior scientific realization. It wasn't until 1842 that Karl Wilhelm von Nägeli discovered subcellular structures that would later become known as chromosomes. This served as a classical antithesis to Edouard van Beneden's 1883 discovery that chromosomes are individual entities.

But with respect to 46 having Biblically prophetic relevance, it doesn't begin in AD 27 with a Godly double entendre and it doesn't end in the 1800's with a double discovery. The 46 connection inclusive the number of Adam's name are only swatches in a much bigger tapestry of Biblical revelation. Again, the antediluvian age lasted 1,656 years. This period began with Adam and ran concurrently through Noah. Given the fact that the number 46 is directly associated with the Jerusalem temple, which is a place of worship, and the "body temple" where the spirit of God dwells, the Bible has placed a numerical design on that number. We'll call it a TEMPLE DISPENSATION.

The first body that God created and made was, of course, Adam. The spirit of God dwelt in Adam's body. Adam was subsequently a living temple. Adam's name and the number of years running from Adam to Noah (1,656) being evenly divisible by 46 are a collective physical representation of the temple concept.

Again, ponder the odds that historically it would take 46 years to build the Jewish temple; genetically, it would take 46 chromosomes to build the human body; alphanumerically, the name Adam would have a Greek value of an even 46; and arithmetically, the number of years running Adam through Noah would total a number evenly divisible by 46? And if you go so far as to add all of the "begots" that are figured into Genesis 5:3-32 and 11:10-26, the time span between the creation of Adam and the birth of Abraham is 1,946 years?

The Flood that came upon the earth exactly 1,656 years after the creation of Adam brought about the destruction of a vast number of human beings that can be conceptually termed "defiled temples." This destruction or interruption of what may be considered the status quo is a temple dispensation. The antediluvian age is considered a temple dispensation. A temple dispensation is therefore defined as any period evenly divisible by 46, after which an established order is interrupted. Definitely, an extinction event is a temple dispensation.

In order to further illustrate, an examination of Israel's first Biblically documented census is made. Historically, some 1,060 years after the Flood, or the end of the antediluvian age, God commissioned a census of Israelite males from twenty years old upward. This act is referenced by Numbers 26:2.

Conducting the census were Moses and Eleazar, the priest, both of the tribe of Levi. According to the Biblical account, the last tribe to be counted was the Levites. Numbers 26:62 gives the tally of the Levites:

"And those that were numbered of them were twenty and three thousand, all males from a month old and upward."

God commanded Moses to appoint the Levites over everything pertaining to the tabernacle or temple (Numbers 1:50-53, Numbers 18:2-6, 1 Chronicles 23:28-32). The number of the Levites in the census, 23,000, is a multiple of 46; i.e., 46 x 500. Thus, the temple concept is reflected in the number of persons from the tribe whose duty it was to attend to the temple. No other tribe except Dan had a head count evenly divisible by 46.

So, here we find the Bible itself referencing another number that just happens to be divisible by the exact number of years it physically took to construct the Jewish temple and the exact number of chromosomes it physically takes to genetically construct a human body.

These numerical computations are right there in the Bible. There's no direct or implied request that you accept some second hand-me-down information from any third party. Individually, you can research and provide the verification independent all others. The numbers do what they do without any help or guidance from any other than the Spirit of God. The Bible itself provides un-coded Biblical substantiation that can either be viewed coincidental or providential.

Now, it was mentioned that no other tribe except Dan had a headcount evenly divisible by 46. According to Numbers 26:43, the Schuhamites numbered 64,400. Mathematically, that computes 46 x 1400. What do Levi and Dan have in common that would warrant linking them numerically?

In Revelation 7:4-8, the Apostle John lists by tribes the remnant of Israel that is redeemed when Jesus Christ returns. Curiously, the tribe of Dan is excluded from Revelation's salvation scenario. The historical reason for this exclusion is suggested in Judges 18 and 1 Kings 12, which states that the area in Israel inhabited by the people of Dan was the center of idolatry.

Consider the prophecy of Jacob in Genesis 49:17 concerning his son Dan, for whom the tribe is named: "Dan shall be a serpent by the way, an adder in the path, that biteth the horse heels, so that his rider shall fall backward."

Jacob's reference to a "serpent" undoubtedly alludes to Satan in the Garden of Eden, while biting "at the horse's heels" recalls God's curse upon the serpent: "thou shalt bruise his heel" (Genesis 3:15).

In addition, the role of the tribe of Dan in Bible prophecy is indicated numerically by its population as given in the census of the book of Numbers, chapter 26. Recall that God specified the census criteria (Numbers 26:1-2), in effect choosing the persons to be numbered among His holy ones. Yet, these same persons had sinned and continued to sin against their particular "present truth" (Numbers 14:27-30, 26:63-65). This fact affirms that having your name on the church roll doesn't usher you into the Kingdom. The tribe of Dan is confirmation that there is no salvation simply in being "numbered" among God's chosen.

In John 6:70 Jesus said to His disciples, "Have I not chosen you twelve, and one of you is a devil?" The inclusion of the Danites in God's census and their tally reflecting the temple concept show that being chosen by God is a necessary, but insufficient condition for whomever would live as God's temple.

The rebellious Danites may also be understood as types of temples; i.e. defiled ones. Subsequently, the concept of the temple finds expression in the tribe of Dan as well as the tribe of Levi despite their different prophetic roles. In the case of the Levites, the judgment of their generation in the wilderness foreshadowed a temple dispensation in connection with Solomon's temple that was to come.

It is scholarly surmised that Solomon began construction of the first Jewish temple circa 966 BC. It stood until Nebuchadnezzar destroyed it during an assault on Jerusalem in 586 BC.

There are academics who assert that the construction on the temple Solomon built started much earlier – 1000 BC. That would mean its 586 BC destruction results in a 414-year stand. The number 414 is a multiple of 46. But since there are competing dates relative the 10th Century temple's groundbreaking, if someone is going to state a date for any event in the history of anything, then they can't provide that date in isolation. This is to say that if someone uses the Bible to demonstrate that their date for something is correct, then you have to check to see if that date is supported by all of the surrounding Bible chronology beyond reasonable doubt.

Reconstruction of the Jerusalem temple began in 538 BC and was completed circa 515 BC. At this time, it was renamed the temple of Zerubbabel after the Jewish governor of the period.

In 20 BC, Herod tore the temple down and commenced a rebuilding initiative. It was this structure of renowned beauty whose completion forty-six years later in AD 26 coincided with the beginning of Jesus of Nazareth's earthly ministry. Thus, the reconstruction of the temple of Zerubbabel was a temple dispensation that concluded with the dedication and manifestation of the "living temple," i.e. Jesus Christ.

Definitely, the antediluvian age is a temple dispensation in which a multiple of 46 years was followed by the interruption of an established order. The interruption in the case of the temple of Zerubbabel is the First Advent of Jesus Christ.

Pausing briefly on that note, it is a historical fact that construction of Herod's Temple began in 20 BC, and at the time of Jesus Christ's first Passover visit to Jerusalem this Temple had been "in building" 46 years. This establishes AD 27 (spring) as a dateline.

With respect to the year 27, the concept of temple dispensations may also be applied to our day and age. Commonly called the last days, the generations of Adam are no less numerically consistent in Biblical appearance. Chapter five of the book of Genesis details the antediluvian patriarchs of the early generations born in Adam's image and likeness. Each person symbolizes an important aspect of divinely inspired truth no matter how brief his biological sketch.

Enoch was Adam's seventh descendant. Perhaps the most noted number in Bible numerics, seven (7), once again, symbolizes spiritual perfection/completion. According to Genesis 5:24: "Enoch walked with God; and he was not for God took him." Given this portrayal of Enoch and the symbolism of his numerical order in Adam's generations, it is obvious that Enoch prefigured Jesus Christ.

Extending the analogy throughout the generations of Adam, we identify Enoch's son Methuselah as the prefiguration of Jesus' "son." Jesus, of course, had no son according to the flesh. He did, however, generate a new spiritual order of man. The Bible's portrayal of Enoch's son Methuselah is vital to understanding the spiritual order of man after the coming of Jesus Christ. Herein, the *Methuselah Syndrome* is not a genetic disorder which causes people to succumb to aging too quickly as portrayed in the *Blade Runner* (1982), but rather the birth of an *Old World Order* renewed (Romans 12:2).

Renewal of the "Old World Order" is all about the Second Advent of Jesus Christ. The return of Christ, of course, will bring forth an interruption of this world's currently established order. By definition, it will be a temple dispensation.

For all in denial of and opposition to Jesus Christ as Lord, however, it will be the title of an *Indiana Jones* movie (1984).

19 OUT OF TIME

"And that, knowing the time, that now it is high time to awake out of sleep: for now is our salvation nearer than when we believed."
— ROMANS 13:11

Staying with the numbers, Genesis 5:27 says that the number of all Methuselah's years was 969. That's a long time until you get to your 968th year. Then, it's just not long enough.

Methuselah's lifespan is very important alphanumerically, and here's the reason why. In the days of Jesus' earthly journey, John the Baptist was a preacher of righteousness, or right standing with God. But before considering the Greek spelling of the name John, it has to be noted that there are many Greek spellings of the name John. However, when it comes to Greek and alphanumeric languages, one has to look at the overall context of the phrase or sentence wherein the word appears.

The Greek spelling of John employed herein is taken from Matthew 3:13. The reason that John is called John the Baptist is for one primary and principal reason – he baptized Jesus Christ. Matthew 3:13 reads: "Then cometh Jesus from Galilee to Jordan unto John, to be baptized of him."

If you Google search "Greek spelling of John," there are multiple sites to reference. BibleHub.com/Greek/2491.htm is the reference in this writing. The Greek spelling of the name John in this setting is Ἰωάννην.

Iota	=	10
omega	=	800
alpha	=	1
nu	=	50
nu	=	50
eta	=	8
nu	=	50
		969

Interestingly, the numeric value of John's name is the same as all the years of Methuselah's life. This is why it's just a must that we keep "playing the numbers." Again, is it coincidental or providential?

Important is the realization that God, himself, chose the preacher's name (Luke 1:11-13), thereby pre-determining its numeric value. According to Luke 1:59, the family wanted to call the boy "junior." This provides additional clarity with regard to precisely why Gabriel was demanding that Zacharias and Elisabeth name their son John.

Say it one more time, to those who think there is no God, or Supreme Being, or Master Intelligence, and Jesus is a joke invented to keep the masses on a drug called Christianity, and you're basing that belief on something "they" said (whoeva' they are) – newsflash! You're betting your life that "they" are right. So, if you are willing to take that bet, you'll either "*get rich or die cryin'*."

When considering either the merits or demerits of the Christian Bible, if full consideration is not given the fact that it's a book that's heavy off into prophecy and metaphoric symbolism, one will always have more questions than they're able to find answers.

Why the seventh day? Why only 12 disciples? Why four days when it came to the resurrection of Lazarus and only three with Jesus? What *WMD* endeavors to do is show a prophetic pattern. There is a consistent and repetitive design to the works of God, just as there's a method to Satan's madness. As continually stressed and offered, there is a purpose to such selection of an original 12, dry land and grass appearing on the third day, God commanding remembrance of the seventh day sabbath, and Jesus being adamant about his resurrection on day three. These are not random numbers popping out of some kinda cosmic lottery machine. Their meanings are symbolically tied to and communicative of a deeper message than what superficially appears. Once again, to think mortal men spanning centuries and diverse places could play such a numbers game is tantamount to you being able to pick the final score for all 16 regular season games played by your favorite NFL team.

But the $144,000 question here is, "Wassup with 969?" Was John the Baptist given the number because Methuselah lived 969 years? Or did

Methuselah live 969 years because that was to be the number of John's name?

Well, believe it or not, what makes 969 special has nothing to do with sex. It's the fact that the prime factors of 969 are the prime numbers which divide 969 exactly, without remainder, as defined by the Euclidean division. Breaking it down, the number 969 has seven (7) factors: 323, 57, 51, 19, 17, 3, 1. All seven of these numbers can divide 969 evenly.

Herein again, we find the number 7 signifying "perfection" or completion. This means the terms 'factors' and 'divisors' of 969 can be used interchangeably.

In order to illustrate, if you select the rightmost and leftmost integer in the list 969, 323, 57, 51, 19, 17, 3, 1 and multiply these integers, you'll get 969. For example, 1 x 969 = 969; 3 x 323 = 969; 17 x 57 = 969; 19 x 51 = 969.

Additionally, 969 is a composite number. In contrast to prime numbers, which only have one factorization, composite numbers like 969 have at least two factorizations. The prime factorization of 969 is 3 x 17 x 19. This is a unique list of the prime factors, along with their multiplicities. In other words: 3 x 17 x 19 = 969.

And what makes prime numbers so special, Biblically speaking? They cannot be divided by any number other than one (1). And what or who does the number one (1) represent?

Galatians 3:20: "God is one."

The kingdom of God employs prime numbers for the factual reason that with respect to mathematics being the universal language beyond the confines of planet earth, the universe knows that prime numbers cannot be divided by any number other than that which represents the creator of the universe. Since Mark 3:24 maintains that "a kingdom divided against itself cannot stand," intelligently ask yourself why God would employ numbers in key situations and circumstances that are a numerical contradiction.

If you are a Christian and know a little something about Christianity, would you sport a license plate having the number 666? Conceding that

God is deeper than us when it comes to digits, do you really think the numbers selected to represent him wouldn't be a factor? Pun intended.

The consistency of the kingdom of Heaven's employment of prime numbers and their individual factors is compelling when you consider one (1) being representative of God, three (3) representing the trinity (Father, Son, Holy Spirit), seven (7) spiritual perfection and definitiveness indicative days of the week and colors in a rainbow, and the number (13) indicative of God only calling 12 men as disciples, making him the thirteenth "one" at the table.

In looking at the list of 969 multiplicative factors, 19 x 51 stands out. Not only because many reading this writing might be "baby boomers" born in the 1950s, but because given the fact that John the Baptist was preaching repentance, 1951 is plus or minus a generation or two from being within the next "temple dispensation." Also, 1951 is in the middle of a century that has "last days" prophetic significance.

Normally, a generation is considered to encompass a 30-year period. A generation on the back side of 1951 would place someone still around in their late 90s. Two generations on the front side would find that individual in their 60s. And of course, anyone reading this writing who is 25 or older, then a generation added this point forward would place them beyond the year 2055, God willing. Prophetically, the "season" of 2050-something could be significant.

It was previously said that Enoch prefigures Jesus Christ. Such being the case, Enoch's son, Methuselah, prefigures humankind subject to Christ's Gospel. Representing the crucial decision either to accept or reject Jesus' offer of salvation, Methuselah is God's numeric ultimatum personified.

Historically, when Methuselah was 187 years of age, he bore a son named Lamech (Genesis 5:25) who, at age 182, had a son named Noah (Genesis 5:28-29). The flood, which ended the antediluvian age, came when Noah was 600 years old (Genesis 7:6). By adding the numbers 187, 182, and 600, it is determined that the flood came 969 years after Methuselah was born. Given that this interval was also the length of Methuselah's life (Genesis 5:27), it is reasonably deduced that he died the year of the flood. And since the Bible gives no further information about the death of Methuselah, the question arises as to whether the flood merely coincided with his death or brought it about. In any event, that Methuselah did not survive the flood is certain. Methuselah was not on the ship with his grandson Noah. He ran out of time.

For some reason, Methuselah literally missed the boat. Subsequently, this is why Methuselah represents humans subject to the Gospel of Jesus Christ, whether they accept it or not.

With Lamech being Methuselah's son, as in the case of Methuselah, Lamech's lifespan furnishes important clues about his symbolic meaning. Genesis 5:31 says, "And all the days of Lamech were 777 years: and he died." The fact that we find triple 7s associated with Lamech is attention getting.

Again, the number 7, which represents spiritual perfection/completion, is significant regarding the Christian church in the "last days." In Revelation 1:11-20, Jesus holding 7 stars in the midst of 7 golden candlesticks symbolizes a revelation of the "end times" church.

Methuselah's father, Enoch, is the only patriarch listed in the antediluvian lineage that was raptured by God prior to death. Again, this is why Enoch symbolizes a "type of Christ," not a type of Church, and Lamech a "type of church" and not a type of Christ.

What is important is the sequence of symbolic events leading up to the flood. Lamech died before his father Methuselah. After Lamech's departure, Methuselah's remaining on earth connotes that after the prophetic rapture, a residue of mankind will be left to face the end time wrath of God. And because of Revelation 1:7, those left behind will be devastated but not completely clueless.

Matthew 7:13-14 summarily indicates many enter the gate leading to destruction, and few find the one leading to life. This certainly accords with the numbers surroundings Adam's generations in that God used Methuselah's lifespan, the longest of all the antediluvians, to represent the many who perish and Lamech's, the shortest, to represent the few who are saved through faith in Jesus Christ.

Interestingly, in Greek, the name Methuselah has a numeric value of 752:
Μαθουσαλά

Mu	=	40
alpha	=	1
theta	=	9
omicron	=	70
upsilon	=	400
sigma	=	200
alpha	=	1
lambda	=	30
alpha	=	1
		752

And, the name Lamech has a value of 676. Λάμεχ

Lambda	=	30
alpha	=	1
mu	=	40
epsilon	=	5
chi	=	600
		676

The bottom line literally – hearing the Gospel of Jesus Christ without receiving it is Biblically the concept of Methuselah devoid the concept of Lamech. That concept may be mathematically expressed as the value of Methuselah's name (752) minus the value of Lamech's name (676).

The difference of these two numbers: 752–676=76. Thus, the number 76 is the product of 19 x 4. The number 19 is a prime number; 4 is a composite number. The product 76 is an evenly divisible factor and multiple of both. The mathematical representation for rejecting the Gospel of Jesus Christ results in a multiple of the number 19, which numerically symbolizes the number (19) that's associated with John the Baptist's name.

In other words, when it comes to multiplying 19 x 51 to get 969, if you refuse to repent, heed the call, or reject the knock, you are on the figurative short end of the stick. You are positioning yourself to receive God's wrath. You get caught up in the Flood, not the Rapture.

Conversely, hearing the Gospel and receiving it may be expressed mathematically by adding together the value of the names Methuselah (752) and Lamech (676).

Their sum: 752+676=1,428. The number 1,428 is the product of 51 x 28. With 51 being the higher number, when it comes to the kingdom of Heaven, the "higher" road is figuratively taken. Represented mathematically, receiving the Gospel works out to be a multiple of the number 51. Subsequently, 51 numerically signifies repentance towards God and belief in Jesus Christ.

The year 1951 is theorized to be a "temple dispensation" time marker that makes the "voice" of John the Baptist just as "crying" today as it was 1,992 years ago.

With the stage now set by all of the above, follow very carefully. If Lamech and the flood symbolize the Church and the conclusion of the "last days," respectively, then the period from Lamech's birth to the flood represents the last days. Since Lamech's father, Methuselah, lived until the year of the flood, this period may be expressed in years as the length of Methuselah's life after he fathered Lamech, i.e. 782 years (Genesis 5:26). This interval spans the 777 years of Lamech's life plus five years before the flood. The "last days," then, are represented in the generations of Adam by a symbolic 782-year span.

Back to the future. Remember the number 46 and the definition of a "temple dispensation" being any period evenly divisible by 46, after which an established order is interrupted? Well, the number 782 equals 46 x 17. Again, this means the period symbolizing the "last days" is a temple dispensation. And quite consistently, this is the one forecast by the 414-year period from the birth of Enoch (who symbolizes Jesus Christ) to the birth of Lamech (symbolizing the Church).

Therefore, Biblical and other historical evidence thus far discussed suggests that temple dispensations are not merely symbolic, but historical as well. This would mean that the "last days" will not only conclude a multiple of forty-six years from their onset, but do in fact find their conclusion in actual historical events. Indisputably, the Bible indicates that the "last days" commenced at Pentecost, the religious festival where devout persons from all nations gathered in Jerusalem.

The first chapter of Acts shows that Jesus fellowshipped with His disciples for "forty days" after His resurrection. In reference Leviticus 23:15-22 and 1 Corinthians 15:23, the Day of Pentecost took place "fifty days" after the offering of "first fruits." Based on the assertion that the crucifixion of Jesus Christ was on Wednesday, April 5, AD 30, the Day of Pentecost brought to view in Acts 2, occurred on Sunday, May 28, AD 30.

Undoubtedly, Pentecost was the occasion signaling: (a) the birth of the Christian Church and (b) a new temple dispensation. By establishing the dawn of Pentecost in AD 30, one may simply identify the subsequent years which are divisible by the number 46 as the temple dispensation pattern heretofore predicts.

Now, if you have bought into the Easter application identifying the crucifixion and resurrection of Jesus, the prophetic revelations in the Bible that are numeric concerning the return of Christ are impossible to discern. Consequently, isn't it logical and consistent with Satan being a deceiver to have Christians focused on the Jewish Passover that's established by Jewish tradition instead of the Spirit of Prophecy that's the testimony of Jesus?

But, keeping it real, a whole lot of folks, including many professed Christians, aren't interested in the return of Jesus Christ. That would be too much of an "interruption to their established order."

Say it one more time, the Creation, the Fall, the Flood, the Seventh Day Sabbath, the time of the Crucifixion, the time of the Resurrection, and even the Day of Pentecost are all inextricably connected when it comes to salvation. JESUS SAVES when the Scriptures are searched and the deeper meanings inherent are prayerfully understood.

At the time of this writing, the year is AD 2018, or 1,988 years after Pentecost. The next multiple of 46 years after Pentecost will be 2,024 years, or 46 x 44 years after Pentecost. The addition of 2,024 years to AD 30 spotlights the year AD 2054 as the next candidate for the end of the present temple dispensation.

There is a preponderance of Biblical prophecy *WMD* has presented that suggests the Second Advent of Jesus Christ will occur near the beginning of the Seventh Millennium.

How near is near? Again, Matthew 24:36 and 42 are adamant. The purpose of this chapter, therefore, is not about prediction. It's only intended to show that the Bible is remarkably consistent when it comes to showing all who want to see that where a complex design exists a complex designer exists to design it.

Recall this book's Chapter 17 Biblically based calculation that a person could walk thirty-six miles from sunup to sundown? And the distance between Jerusalem and Bethany being referenced at 1.8-miles is five percent of a 36 mile day? Well, five percent of a 1,000 year prophetic day is 50 years. Fifty years inside the Seventh Millennium is plus or minus five when it comes to an AD 2054 temple dispensation.

Certainly, just as the Word says, no one will know the exact time of Jesus' return; only the season. When considering Lamech and the flood symbolize the Church and the conclusion of the "last days" – well, the period between Lamech's death and the flood being exactly five years is certainly "seasonal."

Again, the numbers are what they are and do what they do. Biblical prophecy accentuated not only by historical events, but by numbers, is mind-boggling. It just so happens that when it comes to historical events, numbers, and prophecies, a byproduct of knowing the reason is understanding the season really is closer than you think. Not at the door, but one foot inside.

This suggests in order to *"get on the good foot"* with respect to the kingdom of God, half-steppin' is not an option.

20 THE MATRIX RELOADED

"There is a difference between knowing the path and walking the path."
— *Morpheus*

The above quote is taken from The Matrix (1999). It was spoken by Laurence Fishburne. I professionally became interested in this movie about a decade after its release when my cousin introduced me to a lady that says her manuscript, The Third Eye (1981), is the work upon which the feature is based. Whether it was or wasn't, this writing isn't about copyright infringement. It's about the dual meaning of the above quote and its similarity in principle to James 1:22-24.

Back-in-the-day it was very well understood, "If you gonna talk the talk, you better walk the walk." Subsequently, what Morpheus is cinematically saying is philosophically the same. It's one thing to know the path. It's another thing to actually walk it.

How many people know it ain't cool to be a liar and a cheat? Yet, how many people are liars and cheats? Why do they choose not to walk the path they know to be righteous? Borrowing from that Earth, Wind, and Fire tune Reasons; there are many why we're here; or there sometime in our life.

For some, sometime it's about not getting caught. For others, sometime it's a matter of moral or ethical code summed up in another song, "If loving you is wrong, I don't want to be right."

Whether it's sometimes one or the other, integrity is important. And, even though easier said than done, strict adherence to a moral code is the moral compass that keeps all who want to be kept on the straight and narrow. That's a path with a road sign reading ETHICAL STRAIGHT AHEAD.

Ethics are a personal thing that intrudes the professional. If you are plagued by a bad case of hand-to-mouth disease when it comes to eating, drinking, smoking, snorting, slapping, or shooting in all that such implies, you know what's bad ain't good for your health or others. You already know if where you find yourself is not the right path to be on. And, quick fixes spelled rationalizations are not going to put you where you righteously need to be. No one other than yourself needs tell what you already know.

Because being human is not a rationalization but a fact of spiritual physics, we are all "naughty by nature." No one stays on the right path all the time. We all wander off from time to time. But, the real deal is to notice when you're off and get back on before reaching that smoky fork in the road that leads to a dead end if taken.

The duality to the Morpheus quote, however, makes it deeper than discussions of morals, codes, righteousness, and ethics. The statement is also about walking a path and at the same time not knowing the path you're walking.

In The Matrix, the Oracle is a God figure because the Oracle knows everything. But, the Oracle does not tell Neo he is the One. Why did the Oracle allow Neo to believe he is not the One when he is? Did the Oracle lie by silence?

Therein lies the quote's depth of duality. Neo said, "I'm not the One." The Oracle didn't say that. Consequently, since the statement came out of Neo's mouth. He was not the One until he believed he was the One. The Oracle does not tell Neo he is the One because Neo is not ready to be the One. The Oracle only tells Neo what he needs to know in order for him to be on the path he wants to be on by choice and not by Morpheus' belief, suggestion, or instruction.

Doubly deep, the Oracle tells Neo: "Being the One is just like being in love. No one can tell you you're in love you just know it. Through and through; balls to bones." The implication of the Oracle's statement: no one can tell you to be on a specific path; sometimes it's a matter of knowing the path only when you are on it. Your moral compass thereby comes into play with respect to keeping you true to that path once you're walking it. The right path often has side roads that wind up leading in either a wrong or circuitous direction.

Bottom line, it's not enough to tell others what the right path is to walk. Rather, it's telling what needs to be known to walk the right path.

Instead of preaching what the right thing is to do, the Oracle approach is simply telling only what needs to be known to do the right thing.

Drawing from The Matrix, paths can be unknown until you're on them in a reality that extends beyond textbook, classroom, boardroom theory. If you are the One who's called to do great things, you have to know it before it can be known by anyone else. And, that's even before an all knowing Oracle is even willing to admit.

Neo means new; it's a new day. Many are called to be in the radio, television and film business that includes the internet; new media. Know it or not, a media calling puts all on that path in a position of power.

"The media's the most powerful entity on earth. They have the power to make the innocent guilty and to make the guilty innocent, and that's power. Because they control the minds of the masses," something Malcolm said.

The statement isn't an exaggeration. It's not hyperbolic. It ain't giving credit where credit ain't due. It just is what it is because the media is about the business of mediating.

Just look at that word itself – mediate. There are a couple things going on there. There's "media" and there's "ate." Etymologically speaking, it would have been more palatable (symbolically) to find the spelling medieat. At least when you eat something, there's the opportunity to spit it out. But when you "ate," it's too damn late. It's past tense. It's already in your system well on the way to being fully digested.

A dictionary defines mediate as: (1) occupying a middle position; (2) acting through an intervening agency; (3) exhibiting indirect causation, connection, or relation.

If you buy that definition and apply it to the words of Malcolm, it's easy to see how the media as an entity has the power to do what it does. The "middle position" is right between your ears. The "intervening agency" is either good or bad. The "indirect causation, connection, relation" is the end result; the truth or consequences.

The notion that the "med" in media denotes "middle ground" objectivity as the word mediate implies is a misapprehension of human nature. People are influenced either by their good angels or their bad. Whether one believes in the physical existence of angels and devils is irrelevant.

The fact that people are motivated and driven by the spirit that's in them establishes the presence of forces that do exist whether verbally defined or not. Subsequently, it's the ability of spiritual forces (verbally defined or not) to employ radio, television, film, and the internet to send messages that either cause or effect an animated response.

Juries are sequestered in acknowledgement to the power of the press. But how do you sequester a juror whose biases are a preexisting condition?

Time and time again, the *Voir dire* jury selection process screams its limitations. Oh yeah, OJ got off, but he still did time. Barring serious mental health issues, when it comes to having affection for spiritually defiling things, the lean in that direction is not congenital; it's spiritually introduced after you've arrived on the scene. You don't pull a wing off a butterfly strictly out of curiosity. You do so as a soul whose senses have been desensitized. The media as a conveyor belt for all messages electronic or as simple as a message in a bottle is the method to a whole lot of folks' *crazy-as-hellness*.

It's significant to note that back in the day, the movies starring Richard Roundtree as *Shaft*, Ron O'Neal as *Superfly*, Jim Brown as *Slaughter*, Fred Williamson as *Hammer*, Melvin Van Peebles as *Sweetback*, and even Isaac Hayes as *Truck Turner* were bastardized by the term "Blaxploitation." Slapping a negative label on these features spiritually branded them anathema. The Black audience these movies were produced to appeal to gradually started rejecting them because they were termed exploitative, and a rainbow coalition followed out of so-called political correctness. Today, rarely will you find these movies as a collective getting frequent mainstream exposure outside a Black programming channel or network.

Even though a generation of folks found the TV antics of *Amos 'n Andy* (1951-1955) "LMBAO" funny, were those serious Black actors (Alvin Childress, Spencer Williams, Tim Moore, Johnny Lee, and Ernestine Wade) any less award-winning performing artists than the ones getting paid to clown in a new millennial era of shows specializing in coonery and buffoonery? Or is so-called coonery and buffoonery strictly in the head of the beholder?

On the real, however, the only thing that was "exploitative" about the "kick ass" features of the 70's was the fact that they exploited black male masculinity in a manner that was threatening to the racist ideal of black men as solely/souly Amos n' Andy.

Think what you will, in the final analysis these movies offered a diverse portrait of Black masculinity that could be both vicariously and cathartically experienced. Seriously, if mainstream media could have *Larry*, *Moe*, and *Curly*, weren't there any adults in the room to keep it as real about George "Kingfish" Stevens then as they do about Mabel "Madea" Simmons now? Boo to booya; certainly, we'd like to think so? But due to the media's pervasiveness and societal ability to influence positively and negatively, what we think and believe can easily be molded by whoever is providing or sending the message.

Comparably, *Cleopatra Jones* (1973), *Coffy* (1973), *Christy Love* (1974), and *Friday Foster* (1975), along with a must-mention *Bushrod*'s other half, *Thomasine* (1974) collectively balanced the screen image of a 50's *Sapphire* as well as a 60's *Julia*. And even though Tamara Dobson, Pam Grier, Teresa Graves, and Vonetta McGee didn't take any hostages, no one got their roles as ladies twisted.

But back to the future, depending on your vantage point is the bar set to high jump or limbo rock? This question, however, is not about the color of skin that's seen on screen, it's about the content of characterizations. The significance of the past is its ability to guide in charting the future. If you see the seventies as a golden age with respect to diversity, the moral of the story is control. When you control the bottom line, you control what's "above-the-line." Controlling the A-T-L takes care of B-T-L.

The issues involving "Hollywood" as well as "the newsroom" as well as most mainstream media "corporate boardrooms" are spiritual. Sprinkling an Oscar here and an Emmy there peppered by a face-in-the-place every now and then somewhere only treats the symptom; it doesn't cure the disease. Ephesians 6:12 can't break it and make it any clearer:

> "For we wrestle not against flesh and blood, but against principalities, against powers, against the rulers of the

darkness of this world, against spiritual wickedness in high places."

Again, the thesis statement of *WMD* is the media's employment as a weapon of mass destruction wherein mass communications is the bomb and your brain is the target. The topic sentence throughout is Luke 4:6: "All this power…for that is delivered unto me."

If you believe there is a God somewhere out there who is somewhere in there (there being inside your heart), you have to believe there is also a devil somewhere out there too. When the Word of God is applied, we should fully understand that non-flesh and blood arms can't be twisted into "doing the right thing." When it comes to extraterrestrials, grabbing hold of their arms requires grabbing hold of the arm of Jesus Christ first. Leaning on those "everlasting arms" are the only arms long enough to box with principalities, supernatural powers, rulers of darkness, and spiritual wickedness.

Unapologetically, Satan, an extraterrestrial and predatory alien entity, has used and continues using the media to camouflage his existence. If you are one of the many who don't believe what you can't see, and ain't feelin' what you can't touch, *WMD* summarily rests its case. Circumstantial evidence framed by having faith in an "invisible God" (Colossians 1:15) will never be enough to convict a devil beyond reasonable doubt. Satan knows that. And that's why the princedom of Satan puts the burden of proof on all earthlings who choose to prosecute his case.

But the fact that Luke 4:6 says what it says gives it a spiritual reality just as genuine as John 3:16. That means in order for human beings to deal with evil manifested through the social diseases termed hatred, bigotry, discrimination, racism, sexism, sectarianism, *whatevaism* that radio, television, film, and the internet have a propensity to push, the Holy Bible is as close to a spiritual *Gray's Anatomy* (the text book) as mankind is going to get. Just as "The Great Physician" without a fight is not going to concede earth's health to Satan as "the prince of this world," Satan is not going to concede to human beings, without a fight, his title "prince of the power of the air."

When Janet Jackson sang, "It's all about control," she got it right. This is why there's "war in heaven" that finds this planet ground zero.

But once again, finally said, this war isn't war as we've been conditioned to conventionally see it. Everybody and everything in this battle has free will. No entity as an intelligent life form is forced to line up on the side of Michael and his angels or Satan and his. As human beings, we have a voice in the choice. That's why planet earth as a war zone is a spiritual mind-field.

The extraterrestrial entity called the devil may give you a gun; he may even put bullets in that gun for you, but the operative word here ain't gun, it's give. You have to put that weapon to your own head and pull the trigger before using it on anyone else.

The weapon of mass or mind destruction is always in your hand. You have "remote control" when it comes to what bullets you're willing to fire into your head. You can blow your brains out with the bullets Satan gives you. Or you can use the ammunition provided by Jesus Christ as God. The IED's in this war are *Individual Electronic Devices*. Rather than being roadside bombs, these IED's are hidden in plain sight. There's probably one in your reaching distance right now.

A grabbing thing about Ephesians 6:12 is the phrasing, "the rulers of the darkness of this world." Just who are the rulers of the darkness of this world? Since Satan is the "prince of this world," the logical presumption/assumption is it's a reference to the devil and all inspired by his spirit exclusively. But when you look carefully at that passage and know a lil' sumpin-sumpin about fifth grade science, you readily realize there's more to it than initially meets the eye.

The "rulers of the darkness of this world" is you just as much as it is a devil and/or anything else. Every time we walk into a room and flick a light switch, we've just "ruled" the darkness. We've ruled it out. Darkness, whatever the degree, is canceled, neutralized, and erased by the smallest amount of light. Light that's even as small as a "mustard seed!"

Darkness cannot exist where there is light. Don't believe it? Go into a dark room and turn on the lights. There's no coexistence. You just became a ruler over "the darkness."

God has equipped all of us with the power to do some serious battlin.' It may not be ownership of a radio station, a television channel/network, a film studio, or an internet enterprise that defines your rulership. It may only be your ability to rule yourself by saying "no" to radio and television programs, along with motion picture and internet features that are shrewdly and subliminally designed to darken your mind, body, and soul – socially, politically, and spiritually.

Your ability to flick a switch, change a channel, not buy a movie ticket, and avoid websites not only makes you a ruler of the darkness in your world, it makes you a ruler of the "rulers of the darkness in this world" that Ephesians is customarily understood to be talking about.

With regards to Luke 4:6-7, there's Luke 4:8. Jesus said, "No." The power to say "no" expressed either in word or by action is more powerful than a speeding bullet or even a train that appears *Unstoppable* (2010). Those who know the power of *"not today"* know that a vision seen from a towering vantage point is bigger than any image that can be captured by a camera and framed on a screen.

When you don't see the big picture from a height that allows you to understand the power context, you won't understand the behavior. The word of God gives all who are willing to see and hear a tower. The narrative that encompasses social ills typically ignores and rejects the metaphysical. While most will see that Cheerios commercial with the interracial family depicting the husband/father as an overweight lazy Black man subliminally racist, how many will see Satan as the subliminal messenger?

If you're either fan or foe of the television series *Scandal*, does the "Scandal Watch" house party you regularly attend or the "Critic's Blog" you occasionally write see *"for entertainment purposes only"* or respectively *Just Another Girl on the I.R.T.* (1992) – this one, a high priced White House hoochie. While *Shots Fired* (2017) grabbed an audience, was it really necessary for an actress with the props of the lead to be *"Me So Horny?"* Yes, even though the rationale might be the character's personal challenges required "sexual healing," the saga of the sexually loose professional Black woman remains *"Just Another Girl on the I.R.T."*

And, as far as the present day imbalanced presentation of Black male actors (with the exception of one or two) that would cinematically rival the likes of a yesteryear Sean Connery, Tom Selleck, Paul Newman, or Robert Redford – well, borrowing from the Dramatics since it is drama: "*Whatcha See is Whatcha Get.*"

Consider *The Last O.G.* (2018) compared to the first. The first being the Ice-T 1991 release in album form. Herein, the release wasn't from a 15-year prison stint. There was nothing comedic about that script in the form of lyrics.

And, then came the second to the *"Last."* There was certainly nothing funny when it came to the 1996 O.G. portrayals of Fred Williamson, Pam Grier, Jim Brown, Richard Roundtree, and Ron O'Neal joined by Paul Winfield, Isabel Sanford, Christopher B. Duncan, Shyheim, Eddie Bo Smith Jr., and Oscar Brown.

The bastardization of O.G. by playing the term for laughs cleverly whitewashes black stereotypes. It makes them palatable for digestion by a mainstream market. When it's really all about the money, cooning and buffooning has no shame for the comatose. Actor-comedians willing to be the socio-political asses of their own jokes are cheaper by the dozen. And, unfortunately, it's the preponderance of images showcasing Black actor/actress as clown that gets more play than Black actor/actress as hero/heroine.

On the real, the Black actor as either stud or hunk is an intimidating image that undermines the satanic agenda mainstream media at-large has adopted. The same applies to the Black actress in a role other than a loud, potty-mouth, trash talking sistah with either attitude or man that's causing personal issues. Actresses "of color" are principally stripped as a principle from "Streep" type roles in preference of those commonly seen routine. And, the brotha who ain't playin' some kinda red-nosed *Whizzo*, red-eyed pimp, or red-handed drug-thug is typically quiet, soft-spoken, and passive to the extent that growing a pair wouldn't be much help beyond moonlighting in a Viagra commercial.

Borrowing from *Bucktown* (1975), the thinly veiled racism and corruption that ran rampant is no different than that in any town when it comes to the operative word being "buck." The buck stops in respect to economic empowerment. When Deuteronomy 28:13 says, "And the LORD shall make thee the head, and not the tail; and thou shalt be above only, and thou shalt not be beneath," that's a vision of empowerment.

Hollywood is a town where bucks are passed to those who make images. Don't like the images? The buck only stops when whatcha see ain't whatcha wanna hear and you're willing to do something about it economically. Understanding that the stakes are spiritual more so than political refreshes the meaning of John 8:32: "And ye shall know the truth, and the truth shall make you free." Truth when accepted provides freedom from the mental chains that make slavery acceptable. A twenty-first century plantation mentality is just as debilitating as any yester-century.

Weapons of Mind Destruction don't liberate users from self-destruction. Just as "a mind is a terrible thing to waste," so is the time spent during the wasting when the detriment is at your own expense.

Again, there is a physical science application to the Word of God. When it comes to mind, body, and soul, your mind is the engine that drives everything else. If your mind ain't right, just like that Benz, Lex, or Honda Civic, it might look good and be all that on the outside, but if the engine is screwed up, you're going nowhere fast.

Isaiah 65:24 is such a powerful "engine" that it demands repeating:

"And it shall come to pass, that before they call, I will answer; and while they are yet speaking, I will hear."

The "Bluetooth" being referred to here is prayer. Prayer is the only technology that's capable of going the distance faster than the speed of light. Best believe, in order for a call to be answered before it's made, that's space travel at the speed of thought.

The human brain is full of electrical activity. Electroencephalography (EEG) measures voltage fluctuations resulting from ionic current within the neurons of the brain. When the electrical activity of the brain can no longer be detected or monitored, that individual is clinically brain dead.

Once again, electrical activity creates radiation. Technologically, a very sensitive radio receiver can pick-up the transmission of radiant energy. So, from a physical science perspective in a wireless technological sense, given the fact that your brain is transmitting electrical current in the form of radiant energy, what do you think is really going on when you pray to God?

Theoretical physicists maintain that the universe is a sea of invisible quantum energy waves. Since prayer is a physical act, when a person prays to God in the name of Jesus, the only way for that heaven-forwarded information to be propagated or physically sent through space is through these quantum waves no differently than your voice is physically propagated through the same waves via your cell phone. Both depend on the same equations. This means, when it comes to quantum physics, given the fact that every electron in your brain is both a transmitter and a receiver, information can physically traverse to any part of the universe instantaneously through electromagnetic/quantum wave propagation.

Now, this is not speculation, pseudo-science, superstition, or hocus-pocus. This is a basic law of physics making quantum wave propagation as a communications vehicle fact not fiction. There is an imperceptible reality to the cosmos that can only be detected scientifically. Because prayer is physical, and according to the Bible God hears prayer, in a universe governed by physical laws, prayer has to be governed by those same laws. If not, prayer as a phenomenon is interpreted as magic. The kingdom of God does not deal in magic.

Because most folks only get caught up in the entertainment value of television shows like *Quantum Leap* (1989-1993), there is a failure to understand the physics behind the programming content. When recalling all those *Frankenstein* movies, the concept of the monster's brain being jumpstarted by a bolt of lightning was not thrown in for entertainment purposes only. There is a scientific real world/cosmic method to the madness.

If you are a praying person, have you ever asked your Pastor or Sunday/Sabbath School teacher to explain exactly how prayer works? That's technically speaking not spiritually.

But, if you have direct-deposit, and if you're like most, you technically don't care how the money shows up in your account on the day it's supposed to be there as long as it's there. Only when it's not there do you WTF (What's The Foul-up) and 1-800 customer service.

If you've been praying about something and that prayer hasn't been answered to your personal satisfaction, then "What the problem is" just might be "no answer" is the answer. Or, your cosmic consciousness is not technically on the same cosmic frequency with God. Matthew 15:22-26 is indicative of the fact that there are some calls that Jesus won't take; at least not during the caller's first attempt.

So, "on earth as it is in heaven," if you're not physically on the same electromagnetic frequency with respect to the party that you're trying to reach, your voice cannot be heard. Likewise, if you don't have the "right" number of the party you're trying to reach, there is no intended connection. You've dialed a "wrong" number.

God as Jesus Christ is the "very sensitive radio receiver." This is exactly why Jesus Christ says he is Alpha and Omega; a 1-800 number. And, when it comes to "war in heaven" involving the media as a *WMD*, being a "prayer warrior" is way more than a phrase. With earth being both our sole and soul vantage point, prayer is the only advantage we've been given to be cosmically competitive.

WMD: Angels, Devils & the Media (The Extraterrestrial Control of Radio, Television, Film, and the Internet) has endeavored to floodlight the lowlight conditions that prevent many from reading the Bible in full light. While conjecture and theory are offered in many instances, 1 Thessalonians 5:21 reads, "Prove all things, hold fast that which is good."

When "it is what it is" or it ain't, the responsibility to "go figure" is not on the author, but the reader. Be it you as reader, only by knowing the real public enemy as spotlighted, can you as victor *"fight the powers that be"* knowing both the battle and the war are won/One.

ADDENDUM

A.D. 30 CRUCIFIXION AND RESURRECTION OF JESUS CHRIST

The fact that Jesus Christ was 33 years old at the time of his death is fundamentally established by Luke 3:23, which indicates Christ as "being about thirty years of age" at the commencement of his public ministry. By referencing John 2:23, 5:1, 6:4-7:14, and 11:55, it is Biblically documented that Jesus attended four annual Passover feasts. The first feast during the spring of his 30th year (John 2:23), the second (John 5:1) during the spring of his 31st year, the third (John 6:4-7:14) during the spring of his 32nd year, and the fourth (John 11:55) marking his crucifixion, during the spring of his 33rd year.

Since the ancient Jewish calendar was primarily lunar and based on astronomical observations as opposed to calculations during the first centuries, the New Moon marked the date for the commencement of the Jewish first month called Nisan. With reference to the publication: **Handy Book of Rules And Tables Verifying Dates With The Christian Era, Concerning the Year Thirty-three**, (John J. Bond, New York/ Russell & Russell, 1966), the first day of Nisan fell on the same day as the vernal equinox. This means that during the thirty-third year of Jesus Christ, the New Moon and the first day of spring fell on the same day.

By accessing the U.S. Naval Oceanography Portal by keying **Spring Phenomena 25 BCE to 38 CE - U.S. Naval Observatory**, we are able to verify Wednesday, March 22, A.D. 30 as being both the first day of spring and the first day of Nisan during the thirty-third year in the life of Jesus Christ.

Provided with the Biblically established fact that the fourteenth day of Nisan marked the beginning of the Jewish Passover (Leviticus 23:5), two full weeks from Wednesday, March 22, A.D. 30, establishes Wednesday, April 5, A.D. 30 as the day upon which Jesus Christ was crucified, keeping in mind that Nisan 14 begins at sunset on April 4th and concludes at sunset on April 5th. Jesus and his disciples ate their Passover meal Tuesday evening, April 4th, 24 hours before the actual Passover feast that was Wednesday evening, April 5th. This was done because Jesus was crucified during the daylight hours of April 5th.

In accordance with Leviticus 23:6, Nisan 15th (April 6) is a "high day" or ceremonial Sabbath. In turn, this makes Nisan 16th (April 7) the Preparation Day for the weekly Sabbath according to the Fourth Commandment. This means the seventh day Saturday Sabbath during the week of the crucifixion occurred on Nisan 17th (April 8). Three days and three nights from the time of Jesus Christ's death on Wednesday, April 5th terminate on Saturday, April 8th. The resurrection of Jesus Christ was on Saturday, April 8, A.D. 30.

NUMBER OF YEARS "BEFORE CHRIST" (BC/BCE)

The guesstimate is 4,000. However, since the term "Before Christ" or BC is still the most popular categorization, the Bible should provide the standard in making the calculation if guesswork is going to be practically employed. By adding the Genesis 5:3-5:32 and 11:10-11:26 genealogical "begats" there are 1,946 years between the creation of Adam and the birth of Abram or Abraham.

Abraham was 100 years old when he begat Isaac (Genesis 21:5). Isaac was 60 years old when he begat Jacob (Genesis 25:26). Jacob is guesstimated to be around 86 years old when his son Joseph is born. But because Jacob's age is a speculation and the genealogical records as presented in the Bible do not reveal birth ages from that point forward, Biblical sources other than those previously employed have to be examined. One such source is Genesis 12:1-4. Therein, at 75, Abraham is directed by God to leave his country. Genesis 12:10 indicates Abraham and his family "went down into Egypt to sojourn."

The significance of Genesis 12 in calculating the number of years totaling BC is Genesis 15:13 and Acts 7:6, wherein the Genesis text prophesizes the nation of Israel's 400-year bondage in Egypt and the Acts text confirms the prophecy's fulfillment. It's important to note that there is no discrepancy between Genesis 15:13 establishing Israel's Egyptian captivity being 400 years and Exodus 12:40 maintaining 430 years.

The reason being the fact that Genesis 12:10 employs the word "sojourn" as does Exodus 12:40. This means the "captivity clock" started ticking with Abraham and his family going into Egypt at age 75, and not with Jacob and his family entering Egypt 215 years later with Jacob being 130 years old (Genesis 47:9).

The 400 years encompasses sojourning and bondage in Egypt. The 430 years encompasses time spent in Egypt that is pre-Exodus 1:8. Both timeframes run concurrently. In this regard, it is imperative to understand that the promise or covenant regarding the "nation of Israel" was first made with Abraham (Genesis 12:2), even though the name of that nation originates with Jacob by virtue of the change in name to Israel. Subsequently, in calculating the number of years between Adam and the birth of Jesus Christ, Genesis 12:4 becomes a reference point. Since the 430-year period is established with Abraham being 75 years old, the two numbers are combined and added to the genealogical list of patriarchs bringing the 1,946 number to a sum total 2,451. From Adam to the Exodus (Exodus 12:40-41), 2,451 years can therefore be Biblically established as having transpired.

But in order to calculate the number of years from the Exodus to the birth of Jesus Christ, such can only be reasonably speculated based on Matthew 1:17. Matthew 1:1-16 traces the genealogy of Jesus Christ from Abraham forward. Genesis 25:7 establishes the lifespan of Abraham to be 175 years. Isaac, Abraham's son, is 75 years old at the time of Abraham's death. According to Genesis 25:26, Isaac was 60 years old when his son Jacob was born. This necessitates Jacob being 15 years old at Abraham's death. In accordance with Genesis 35:28, Isaac died at age 180. This means Isaac lived 105 years after Abraham's departure.

Given the fact that Isaac is 60 years older than his son Jacob at the time of Isaac's death, Jacob was 120 years old. Drawn from Genesis 47:28, Jacob survived Isaac by 27 years passing on at age 147. And Jacob survived Abraham by 132 years. Genesis 37:1 establishes Joseph at 17 when his brothers caused him to be sold and brought into Egypt. Genesis 41:46 establishes Joseph as being 30 when he "stood before Pharaoh." Drawing from Genesis 41:47 with reference to "seven plenteous years" and Genesis

41:54 referencing "seven years of dearth" an additional 14 years are added to Joseph making him at minimum 44 years of age at the time Jacob is established as being 130. This factually suggests at minimum, Jacob was at least 86 years old when he fathered Joseph. Subsequently, when Jacob died, Joseph was at least 61 years old. And when Joseph passed on at age 110 (Genesis 50:26), his great- grandfather had been dead at minimum 181 years.

With reference to Matthew 1:17 and the "fourteen generations from Abraham to David," four of those generations account for 181 years. Given the absence of any further Biblically sequential genealogical listings accompanied by years lived, Matthew 1:17 still offers a rubric by which a best guesstimate regarding BC year totals can be made without sheer speculation.

The genealogies beginning with Genesis 11:12 (Arphaxad) and running through Genesis 11:26 (Terah) provide a post-Flood baseline. These eight lifelines establish a mathematical mean of 36, a mathematical mode of 30, a mathematical median of 31, and a range of 41.

Subsequently, the two sets of fourteen generations encompassing "David to Babylon" and "Babylon to Christ" have a mathematical mean of 504. "Abraham to David" is calculated based on ten generations since the generations of Abraham, Isaac, Jacob, and Joseph far exceed the parameters of the baseline averages Biblically established after the death of Joseph. Therefore, the number of years between Joseph's death and Abraham's death (181) are used as a composite baseline thereby excluding four generations from the fourteen encompassing the Abraham to Babylon category.

MEAN
Abraham to David = 541
David to Babylon = 504
Babylon to Christ = 504
Total = 1,549

Between Adam and the birth of Abraham the Bible chronicles 1,946 years. When adding Abraham's age 75 to the 430 years relative the Exodus, a total of 2,451 years can be calculated Adam to Exodus. Based on a mathematical mean derived from Matthew 1:17, the number of years between Abraham and the birth of Jesus Christ are 1,549.

Adam to Exodus = 2,451 years
Exodus to Christ = 1,549 years
Total Years BC = 4,000 years

ABOUT THE AUTHOR

Gary Flanigan is a University of Kansas graduate with a BA in African Studies and Psychology, and a MS in Radio/Television-Film. Additionally, the author holds a PhD in journalism.

Previously, Gary was chair, Department of Media Studies at Paine College, as well as chair, Department of Mass Communications at Edward Waters College. Prior to those positions, he was director of Supportive Educational Services/assistant director for Minority Affairs at the University of Kansas; adjunct professor/program director for CAU-TV and WCLK-FM at Clark Atlanta University; assistant dean for academic support/adjunct professor at John Marshall Law School in Atlanta; and he was formerly associated with North Carolina A&T State University, Grambling State University, and the University of Maryland Eastern Shore as both assistant professor and general manager for their respective radio-TV broadcast facilities.

Aside from these administrative and academic standings, Gary is author of *111: The Media War Between Jesus Christ and Satan*. He also co-authored with Richard Street *Ball of Confusion: My Life as a Temptin' Temptation*.

www.ingramcontent.com/pod-product-compliance
Lightning Source LLC
Chambersburg PA
CBHW071150300426
44113CB00009B/1146